Tolley's Tax Planning for Farm and Land Diversifi_____

Julie Butler (Butler & Co)

with contributions by
Suzy Ashworth, Robert Brodrick, Jane Dearle and
   Michael Gouriet (Withers[LLP])
Allison Broadey (The VAT Consultancy)
James Cleary (Pro Vision Planning and Design)
Andrew Miles (Thomson's Wealth Management Limited)

Tolley
LexisNexis™

Members of the LexisNexis Group worldwide

United Kingdom	Butterworths Tolley, a Division of Reed Elsevier (UK) Ltd, Halsbury House, 35 Chancery Lane, London, WC2A 1EL, and 4 Hill Street, Edinburgh EH2 3JZ
Argentina	Abeledo Perrot, Jurisprudencia Argentina and Depalma, Buenos Aires
Australia	Butterworths, a Division of Reed International Books Australia Pty Ltd, Chatswood, New South Wales
Austria	ARD Betriebsdienst and Verlag Orac, Vienna
Canada	Butterworths Canada Ltd, Markham, Ontario
Chile	Publitecsa and Conosur Ltda, Santiago de Chile
Czech	Republic Orac sro, Prague
France	Editions du Juris-Classeur SA, Paris
Hong Kong	Butterworths Asia (Hong Kong), Hong Kong
Hungary	Hvg Orac, Budapest
India	Butterworths India, New Delhi
Ireland	Butterworths (Ireland) Ltd, Dublin
Italy	Giuffré, Milan
Malaysia	Malayan Law Journal Sdn Bhd, Kuala Lumpur
New Zealand	Butterworths of New Zealand, Wellington
Poland	Wydawnictwa Prawnicze PWN, Warsaw
Singapore	Butterworths Asia, Singapore
South Africa	Butterworths Publishers (Pty) Ltd, Durban
Switzerland	Stämpfli Verlag AG, Berne
USA	LexisNexis, Dayton, Ohio

© Reed Elsevier (UK) Ltd 2002

A CIP Catalogue record for this book is available from the British Library.

ISBN 0 7545 1769 1

Typeset by Phoenix Photosetting, Chatham, Kent
Printed and bound in Great Britain by The Cromwell Press Limited, Trowbridge, Wiltshire

Visit Butterworths LexisNexis direct at www.butterworths.com

Preface

This book has evolved from the current UK farming crisis and the need for farmers and landowners to look at alternative land uses. Sometimes the survival of a farming unit can completely depend upon the ability to diversify successfully. This book accepts the fact that tax planning cannot be looked at in aspect. The farming unit, business and structure must be looked at in the 'round'. Diversification combined with tax planning can be the key to survival for the diversifying farm unit. Proactive practical tax planning has to be embraced by all farming activities.

The author has joined forces with Withers[LLP], the solicitors, to present the need for tax planning with the joint resources of the legal and accountancy professions. Throughout the book there are references to the need for well-drawn legal agreements in all areas, eg wayleaves, options, share farming, contract farming, all letting arrangements etc. The need to consider well-drafted Wills and the interaction of Trusts deserve their own chapter. Protecting the asset on divorce is also considered. All changes will have a potential VAT impact and Allison Broadey of The VAT Consultancy devotes a chapter to this subject. In addition, this book embraces the consideration that tax planning can be enhanced through the financial services sector. The author has, therefore, invited Thomson's Wealth Management Limited to explain the benefits of tax planning using the tools of their industry. One of the clear developments of client service for the practitioner is the need to look at all angles of added value. The advantages of tax planning through financial services are a good manifestation of this.

Obvious examples of diversification and profitable land usage are the planning permission opportunities available to the landowner. This is not just the opportunity to sell off land for development, but all angles of diversification. One of the most apparent directions is the use of redundant farm buildings for other purposes, such as commercial or residential lets. James Cleary of Pro Vision Planning and Design explains the current planning policies, how the process works and the need to seek the help of a professional.

Julie Butler
Butler & Co
October 2002

Author Biography

Julie Butler qualified as a Chartered Accountant in 1980 and in 1990 she became a Fellow of the Institute of Chartered Accountants. She formed her own practice, Butler & Co, in 1986 which was initially based at her farmhouse in Hampshire with offices then opening in Alresford, Bishops Waltham and Fareham.

Julie lives on a farm and her family is very integrated into the farming way of life. She acts for a large number of farming and equestrian clients and has strong roots with the countryside as she is an MFH. Julie has started various newsletters and periodicals and has written for a large number of the tax and farming journals. Her views on the countryside and the surrounding tax planning issues have been featured in newspapers such as *The Daily Telegraph*.

Julie's involvement with diversification has arisen from the need for farmers to survive and look at alternative land uses. She is involved in this process in her day-to-day working life, both as a wife of a farmer and as an adviser to a large number of farming clients.

Julie is a trustee of a local gypsy church on Bramdean Common known as The Church in the Wood and has been Chairman of the Alresford Chamber of Commerce. These roles have involved her very heavily in the local community and have helped her understand the needs of the rural community.

Introduction to the Contributors

Withers^{LLP}

One of the aims of this book is to highlight to farmers, landowners and their professional advisers the need to get comprehensive advice and help on what are very valuable assets and essential tax reliefs.

We are very lucky to have the benefit of Withers^{LLP} writing on the chapters covering Divorce and Farming, Trusts and Wills as it would be impossible to embrace tax planning under diversification without giving consideration to all of these matters. However, the use of good legal advice is not just restricted to the chapters that they have written as the importance of such advice is raised in chapters throughout the book. Examples of this are seen in the chapter on Share Farming, Contract Farming, Farm Business Tenancies and Other Farming Agreements – the need to have well-drafted legal agreements is vital in respect of these arrangements. This goes further to embrace all areas of tenancy and rental agreements from licences to casual arrangements between landowners and users. One of the most obvious examples of that is the occupation of land by horses as an extra source of income under diversification.

Traditionally, in the countryside transactions are conducted verbally and it is very difficult as the law is complex and the only record of the agreement is recollection. The need for well-drafted contracts and ensuring their tax efficiency goes without saying.

Diversification in itself is going to present the farming community with a multitude of legal consideration, not least the need for consideration of the right business structure, the correct partnership agreement, the tax implications of partners owning assets outside the business and only achieving 50% IHT reliefs, the possibility of the tax advantages of passing down to the next generation now and with a move from pure agriculture to diversification the need to ensure correct terms of business, protection via insurance, considerations as to employment contracts, cottage lets – the list is endless.

Another area of large legal involvement is that surrounding land disposals with particular reference to the option agreement and provisions for clawback of future development profits etc.

Pro Vision Planning and Design

Most diversification projects require some form of planning permission. It is helpful to understand the planning process before undertaking diversification projects. Optimising planning consent can increase the value of the landholding and should not be overlooked in the current farming crisis.

The VAT Consultancy

We have worked closely with The VAT Consultancy for many years and are delighted to include their contributions with regard to the complex VAT issues faced by the diversifying business. The Planning for VAT chapter offers the reader a comprehensive picture of the VAT issues that must be considered as part of the overall review of business activities and diversification. Many of the planning points and issues cross refer to the other chapters so that the reader is able to build a well planned and tax efficient model for their desired diversification. VAT advice should always be sought before the start of a new venture and the commentary provided by The VAT Consultancy should ensure that the reader is aware of the nature of any likely VAT exposure that may threaten.

Thomson's Wealth Management Limited

When approaching diversification and survival in the farming crisis, it is relevant to look at projects and problems 'in the round'. Financial services can be incorporated into diversification projects to provide practical, and sometimes innovative, solutions. It is hoped that useful opportunities will be presented to help in the overall aim of mitigating potential tax liabilities. The suggestions and ideas link closely with the other chapters in the book.

Contents

Appendices

Abbreviations

ABA	=	Agricultural Building Allowance
ABI	=	Association of British Insurers
AIM	=	Alternative Investments Market
APR	=	Agricultural Property Relief
AONB	=	Areas of Outstanding Natural Beauty
ASLI	=	Areas of Special Landscape Importance
BATR	=	Business Asset Taper Relief
BEN	=	Business Economic Note
BPR	=	Business Property Relief
CAP	=	Common Agricultural Policy
CGAS	=	Capital Goods Adjustment Scheme
CGT	=	Capital Gains Tax
CLA	=	Country Land and Business Association (previously the Country Landowners Association)
CPRE	=	Council for the Protection of Rural England
CTO	=	Capital Taxes Office
DEFRA	=	Department of the Environment, Food and Rural Affairs
EIS	=	Enterprise Investment Scheme
EPA	=	Enduring Power of Attorney
ERDP	=	England Rural Development Programme
ESA	=	Environmentally Sensitive Areas
EZT	=	Enterprise Zone Trust
FBT	=	Farm Business Tenancy
FHL	=	Furnished Holiday Let
FMD	=	Foot and Mouth Disease
FURBS	=	Funded Unapproved Retirement Benefit Scheme
GTP	=	Green Transport Plan
GWR	=	Gifts with Reservation of Benefit
HDC	=	Horticulture Development Council
IAS	=	International Accounting Standard
IBA	=	Industrial Building Allowance
IFA	=	Independent Financial Adviser
IHT	=	Inheritance Tax
LFA	=	Less Favoured Areas
LLP	=	Limited Liability Partnership
LPA	=	Local Planning Authority
NFU	=	National Farmers' Union
OEIC	=	Open Ended Investment Company
PET	=	Potentially Exempt Transfer
PMG	=	Processing and Marketing Grant
PPG	=	Planning Policy Guidance Notes
PPP	–	Personal Pension Plan

PPR	=	Principal Private Residence
RES	=	Rural Enterprise Scheme
RIBA	=	Royal Institute of British Architects
RICS	=	Royal Institute of Chartered Surveyors
RTPI	=	Royal Town Planning Institute
SIPP	=	Self-Invested Personal Pension
SSAP	=	Statement of Standard Accounting Practice
SSAS	=	Small Self-Administered Scheme
SSSI	=	Sites of Special Scientific Interest
TOGC	=	Transfer of a Going Concern
VCT	=	Venture Capital Trust
VOA	=	Valuation Office Agency
VTS	=	Vocational Training Scheme
WGS	=	Woodland Grant Scheme

Table of Statutes

Table of Cases

H

I

J

L

Farming and Diversification   **1**

Julie Butler

- **Farming and diversification**
  This chapter explains the need for the tax planner to be aware of the difference between farming and diversification. Farming attracts unique tax reliefs and rules, eg agricultural property relief (APR), farming as one trade, averaging and the five-year rule for losses. It is currently essential to understand what is *farming* and what is *diversification*.

- **Protecting against the loss of valuable reliefs**
  With the move to alternative use of land (diversification), it is essential that all the tax reliefs currently available to the farming industry remain intact. It is imperative that the reliefs are used effectively.

- **Tax planning through change**
  The move to diversification might trigger tax planning opportunities that can create advantages as well as problems, and this book attempts to identify these.

The farming crisis

1.1 As the crisis in the farming industry deepens, more and more farmers are choosing to 'diversify' their activities. The principal aim of this book is to aid the tax planner in ensuring that, with such diversification, the tax reliefs of land ownership are retained.

How much is the farming industry in decline?

1.2 Let's look at quotes from the Policy Director at the National Farmers' Union (NFU), Martin Haworth:

> 'Effectively, the farming sector has been in recession since 1996. The problems that the sector is facing now can't simply be attributed to recent crises such as BSE or FMD. Each year since 1996, both income and profitability have fallen.'

Sean Rickard, Professor of Economics at Cranfield School of Management, says:

> 'We're shedding farmers and the industry is hollowing out. The pace of development is being arrested by the operation of agricultural support policies, which are essentially only there to slow down the decline in the number of farmers ... Other industries provide 96% of employment in rural areas. If we want a more vibrant rural economy ... we have to provide jobs. And what I can say categorically is that farming will never create additional jobs in rural areas. It will shed jobs. The direction is clear and it will not change. So I think we should support other industries in rural areas. For example, if we removed agricultural support, the price of lamb will fall – some estimates say by as much as 60%. I would guess that that would create a lot of opportunities for land use for other activities that would create more jobs and be better for rural Britain.'

If we take these quotes as being an immensely gloomy forecast for farming in the UK, but nevertheless accurate, it shows the need for landowners to openly embrace potential opportunities for alternative land use.

For the purposes of income tax where there is no longer any 'investment income surcharge', the definition distinguishing farming income and non-farming income could appear to be of little relevance. However, the impact of the definition on other taxes such as inheritance tax (IHT) and capital gains tax (CGT) means that the interpretation assumes considerable importance, and it is these borderline situations which create the most problems.

Is the farming unit itself generating a 'true commercial profit'? The question of a true commercial profit is dealt with in CHAPTER **12**.

The main tax advantage open to a landowner is that they can obtain income tax, CGT, IHT and VAT reliefs from running their land as a genuine business. This will be explained in greater detail throughout this book and the underlying principal is the need to obtain/maintain business/commercial status.

With the increase in land value and some potential for development profits the landowner has a very valuable capital asset, which must be protected. In order to preserve business status it is essential to understand the definitions of farming, diversification, agriculture and business.

Definition of farming

1.3 The definition of farming can be found in Income and Corporation Taxes Act 1988 (ICTA 1988) s 832(1): 'the occupation of land wholly or mainly for the purposes of husbandry'. It must be noted that 'land' is actually a reference to 'farmland'. Farming is further defined in the case of *Lean and Dickson v Ball (1925) 10 TC 341* where it is stated that for a business activity to be classed as farming it must depend on the produce of land occupied by the person carrying on the activity.

It is very interesting to note that in an intensive activity where, for example, livestock is kept indoors and fish are kept in tanks and they are fed on purchased feed then this is not considered to be farming. The Inland Revenue, however, state that the occupation of land for the purposes of breeding thoroughbred horses is to be treated as farming but this does not extend to any activities involved in racing horses (Inspector's Manual at IM2350B).

The sale of land is generally not subject to income tax and is instead subject to CGT. The benefits that can arise from this are discussed in CHAPTER **14**. However, there may be some instances where the Inland Revenue might try to classify land sales as a trading activity.

The difficulty may be in deciding whether the new activity falls within the definition of farming [ICTA 1988 s 833]. For example, some letting activities may qualify as farming such as:

- letting land for grazing or 'grass keep' under an agreement for less than 365 days and with no right of renewal (Inspector's Manual at IM2256); unless
- the animals grazing the land are racehorses, hunters or children's ponies in which case the Inland Revenue may argue that the letting was not farming.

The reasoning in respect of the above is that although the landowner is still occupying the land he is not occupying it for the purposes of husbandry. In the Inland Revenue's view the grazing of horses, unless it forms part of a commercial stud operation, is not 'agriculture' and therefore not husbandry. Exceptions are made if the grazing forms only an occasional or small part of a larger farming operation (CTO Advanced Manual L.246.2).

So what activities are considered to be farming?

- the production and sale of cereals (arable);
- the production and sale of milk and associated products (dairy);
- the production and sale of animals (livestock);
- stud farms (see **20.3**);
- share farming and contract farming (see **Chapter 11**);
- fruit farming (see **20.5**);
- 'set aside' (see **20.29**);
- income from grazing (see **11.3, 11.31–11.35, 14.29–14.30**);
- short rotation coppice (see **6.2** and **6.7**);
- farm shops selling farm produce (see **20.30**); and
- certain minor receipts from granting licences over farmland may be treated as farming income (see **20.31**).

See the article published in *TAXline* 'Farming and the Enterprise Scheme' (April 2002) (see **A.3**) which questions the definition of farming, particularly in relation to Enterprise Investment Scheme (EIS) relief.

There are strong arguments to support the claim that the definition of farming should be expanded to incorporate diversified activities (see **2.15** and **20.21**).

Activities not considered to be farming

1.4 It is very important to also look at what activities are not considered to be farming. These would include the following:

- parking, mooring and storage of vehicles and vessels (see **9.36**);
- share farming agreements with minimum return (see **Chapter 11**);
- quota leasing (see **15.24**);
- farm shops selling bought-in items (see **20.30**);
- crops that grow naturally;
- gaming and fishing rights (see **9.33**);
- grazing by horses (see **9.38**);
- letting of sports facilities (see **9.34**);
- income from industrial and office units (see **14.23**); and
- land let for 365 days or more (see **Chapter 11, 14.16–14.17** and **15.9**).

Alternative land use — non-farming activities

1.5 If the alternative land use is for a new business activity that falls outside farming, it will be advantageous if the new venture qualifies for the previous tax reliefs achieved. The tax reliefs are set out at **1.13**.

Definition of agriculture

1.6   In trying to understand what is and what is not farming it is vital to look at the definition of agriculture. Again it is important to go to the definition of agricultural land, which is found in IHTA 1984 s 115(2):

> 'Agricultural property means agricultural land or pasture and includes woodland and any building used in connection with the intensive rearing of livestock or fish if the woodland or building is occupied with agricultural land or pasture and the occupation is ancillary to that of the agricultural land or pasture; and also includes such cottages, farm buildings and farm houses, together with the land occupied with them, as are of a character appropriate to the property.'

Agricultural land is further statutorily defined in Capital Allowances Act 2001 (CAA 2001) s 361(1) and it means land, houses or other buildings in the UK occupied wholly or mainly for the purposes of husbandry.

There are many who promote the argument that the definition of agriculture should be widened so as to incorporate non-agricultural diversification.

Farming income by concession

1.7   There are certain types of income which are treated as farming income by concession, ie the receipt is included in the farming profits especially when the amounts have been small compared with the total income from farming. However, should that farming income be greatly diminished this concession would no longer be available and this type of income would then be considered as a non-farming receipt. Examples of non-farming receipts are:

* contracting income (see **11.10**);
* licences given to treasure seekers (see **20.31**);
* rental income of farm buildings (see **12.6**); and
* wayleaves (see **15.20**).

Definition of diversification

1.8   So what is 'diversification'? It has been defined as putting land to a different use. It is generally considered that in the UK economy, agriculture is no longer of strategic importance and the farmer has to look for alternative types of farming or alternative uses for his land and buildings.

Alternative land use

1.9 Diversification may involve the use of land for other farming uses, or non-farming uses.

The main assets of a farm business are the land and buildings it occupies for the purposes of farming. An inability to generate profits from farming the land, or some other circumstance, may dictate that:

- a different type of farming should be carried on using the same land and buildings;
- the land and buildings should be used for a non-farming purpose; or
- the land and buildings should be sold and the farmer may then try to make a living outside of farming (see CHAPTER **14** on property disposals).

All of these changes could be described as diversification of one form or another.

Examples of alternative enterprises or diversification are as follows:

- turf (see **20.16**);
- Christmas trees (see **6.2**);
- war games;
- trading in land property developments (see CHAPTER **14**);
- bed and breakfast (see **9.31**, **13.48** and **15.14**);
- caravan and camping sites (see **15.15–15.18**);
- clay pigeon shooting including conventional land lasers;
- furnished holiday lettings (see **9.31**, **12.7** and **15.10**);
- horse liveries, riding schools and horse trekking (see **9.38** and **15.19**);
- golf;
- motor sports;
- farmland disposals (see CHAPTER **14**);
- car boot sales (see **9.35**);
- mobile phone masts;
- commercial shoots (see **9.34** and **13.2**);
- sites for the music industry (see **9.35**);
- commercially exploiting aggregates (see **20.14**);
- mineral royalties (see **20.7–20.12**);
- landfill (see **20.17**); and
- farm buildings and cottages, previously used in the farm, let out to residential and commercial tenants (see **13.26–13.46** and CHAPTER **15**).

It should be noted that none of these can be entered into without legal advice and that planning permission may be required.

The VAT position on the renovation of dwellings and the VAT position on residential conversions are dealt with respectively at **9.20** and **9.21**.

It is important to look at:

- the effect that such changes may have on the landowner's entitlement to all forms of tax reliefs;
- how the landowner might use these CGT reliefs to implement the changes forced on him, without incurring a tax liability because of the change; and
- how the impact of VAT will affect such changes (see **Chapter 9**).

Farming as one trade

Alternative land use — new farming activity

1.10 All farming carried on in the UK by any particular person or partnership or body of persons is treated for Schedule D purposes as one trade [ICTA 1988 s 53(2)]. Accordingly a change from one farming use to another should present an opportunity to make use of the reliefs set out in this book.

Farming has always been considered as one trade: thus, an estate in Scotland, a farm in Yorkshire and a farm in the Home Counties owned by the same legal structure are all treated as one trade. This provision is found in ICTA 1988 s 53. It is a rule that does not apply to market gardening and its provisions can have a major effect on the computation of farming profits and losses. Its application results in the aggregation of profits and losses (including capital allowances) from more than one farm into a single taxable source of income when more than one farm is operating at the same point of time but in different parts of the country. It is not relevant that perhaps two farms are managed as separate economic units, nor that separate sets of financial accounts are prepared. Likewise, there is no cessation of trade nor any new trade commenced where a farmer ceases trading at one farm, sells up, buys a new farm and starts afresh there.

The rules for commencement and cessation, which would include different basis periods, do not normally come into operation. However, if there has been a significant amount of time between the giving up of one farm and starting of another the Inland Revenue might take the view that a trade has ceased and a new one commenced. This can be an important factor when looking at tax planning principles surrounding hobby farming and IHT reliefs.

A study of the tax reliefs that need to be preserved is set out in CHAPTER **12,** which explains the need to have business status.

The need for diversification

1.11 Diversification could include a whole range of possible activities, some of which will bring in new tax regimes and therefore potential problems: see the article on diversification published in *TAXline* 'The need for diversification' (March 2002). (See **A.6**.)

The problems that the difference between 'farming' and 'non-farming' income and expenditure creates in the preparation of the tax computation cannot be overlooked. Most farmers look at their diversified business as 'one unit', one business entity, but the tax rules dictate that there should be division. This is complex, time consuming and invites error. In **20.21** the views of the Countryside Agency and their suggestion for Rural Taxation are set out. It is proposed that all income from farming and farm diversification (including lettings) should be assessed under Schedule D.

The tax statutes

1.12 To understand the nature of these problems we must recognise the nature of the tax statutes.

The Income Tax Acts place income into a particular Schedule and Case, according to the nature of the source from which the income is received. Each category has its own detailed treatment as regards scope of charge, basis of assessment, person chargeable and relief given. In order to determine the tax rules appropriate to, and the category of income, the source of the income needs to be identified and allocated to the correct Schedule and Case.

It follows that when a farmer changes the nature of his land use, say, from owner-occupier to landlord, he moves from one tax Schedule to another, and from one set of rules to another, which may introduce a new tax treatment.

What is true of income tax may also be true of other taxes, including CGT.

The main reliefs

Capital gains tax

1.13 It is essential that with the move to alternative use of land or diversification that all the tax reliefs available to the farming business are preserved.

The CGT reliefs that might be affected by diversification, or that might be used to assist diversification, are:

- replacement of business assets (rollover relief) [TCGA 1992 ss 152–159] (see **14.19–14.27**);
- disposal of a family business (retirement relief) [TCGA 1992 ss 163–164 and Sch 6 (to be phased out on 5 April 2003)] (see **14.35–14.39**);
- gifts of business assets and gifts on which IHT is chargeable (holdover relief) [TCGA 1992 ss 165, 260, Sch 7] (see **14.29–14.33**);
- rollover relief on reinvestment (reinvestment relief) [TCGA 1992 s 164A–N] and Enterprise Investment Scheme (deferral relief) [TCGA 1992 Sch 5B] (see **14.61–14.65, 19.60** and **20.28**); and/or
- taper relief [TCGA 1992 s 2A, Sch A1] (see **2.11–2.12** and **14.3–14.18**).

Expenditure incurred in the diversification process will be disallowed if it is not deductible in arriving at the true commercial profit on business or accounting principles. Share farming and contract farming are actually considered to be farming and are taxed under Schedule D Case 1, provided they meet all the conditions (see CHAPTER 11).

Emphasis on tax reliefs

Inheritance tax

1.14 It might be considered that this book places too much emphasis on the importance of inheritance tax relief with a lot of dedication to business property relief (BPR) and agricultural property relief (APR). However, the author feels justified in this direction (which does include some blatant duplication) in an attempt to communicate the value of these tax reliefs. Increasing property prices only serve to augment the need to protect against the loss of the tax relief.

How to Approach Diversification   **2**

Julie Butler

- **Need for awareness**
  The need for awareness of government direction, grants available, the administration processes and planning permission considerations.

- **Tax planning through obtaining planning permission**
  Various diversification projects, once formally authorised, will not only result in an increased income stream but also possibly add capital value to assets and involve considerable set-up costs. These can present tax planning opportunities. When the asset is sold it should be classified as capital (see **Chapter 14**). The favourable capital gains tax (CGT) reliefs can then be claimed and overall tax kept to a minimum.

- **Tax planning through the choice of business structure**
  The changes brought about by the farming crisis and the need to diversify should make the tax planner review the business structures to ensure that tax reliefs are preserved and tax planning opportunities are maximised.

Introduction

2.1 This book does not dismiss the benefits of farming. To quote Mid-Wales Country Land and Business Association (CLA) regional director, Julian Salmon:

'Farming remains at the core of a vibrant rural economy. It acts as a repository for our national traditions and cultural heritage. It provides us with a sense of identity and a means of delivering the stewardship of our countryside.'

Farmers have to survive and an objective approach to diversification is the only way forward. In order to be allowed to diversify, planning permission will normally have to be obtained. This is a matter that is dealt with by James Cleary in CHAPTER 3.

Government financing — rural development v direct farm subsidy

2.2 At European level there is a move away from direct subsidy for production towards financing rural development. All farmers and landowners should therefore be ready to try to understand what this will mean to them in the future.

The Common Agricultural Policy (CAP) is undergoing reform. However, it would be useful if there was more knowledge about what is going to happen to farmers and landowners in the future. Key factors are the Government's long-term strategy for farming – *A New Direction in Agriculture* – which was published in December 1999: in October 2000 there was the launch of the England Rural Development Programme (ERDP); and in November 2000 there was publication of the Rural White Paper *Our Countryside: The Future – A Fair Deal for Rural England.*

The National Farmers' Union (NFU) carried out a member survey in 1999. It showed that there were over 150 different types of diversification activities entered into by farmers. It also revealed that two-thirds of all farm businesses got some form of income outside of farming.

The front page of *The Times* on 28 June 2002 referred to the draft strategy paper for the reform of CAP. Proposed reforms include promoting rural economies and the environment, and capping EU subsidies to the largest farms.

With the reform of CAP, reduced farm subsidies and the relevant collapse of farm incomes the only direction has to be diversification for economic survival. For most farmers and landowners diversification is an economic reality. The traditional farmer's heart may be in agriculture but survival means looking beyond the traditional. This chapter will explain some of the funding available but it must be noted that diversification plans should not be led by grant availability. All projects must be well researched, commercial and sustainable.

The England Rural Development Programme (ERDP)

2.3 This is the main European funding source for diversification. It was launched in October 2000 and combines rural development with measures for environmental improvement. £1.6 billion has been allocated for funding between 2000 and 2006. The allocation is as follows:

Activity funded	Percentage of total allocation
Training	1
Energy crops	2
Processing and marketing	3
Organic conversion	8
Rural Enterprise Scheme (RES)	9
Less favoured areas (LFAs)	11
Woodland planting	13
Environmentally sensitive areas (ESAs)	20
Country stewardship	33
	_100%_

The ERDP is scheduled for a review in 2003 with a further review of the various schemes' literature and application processes before that date.

The Rural Enterprise Scheme (RES)

2.4 Over the period of the programme of the RES there is £152 million of European funding for the UK. Grant rates of 30–50% are offered for diversification activities. These activities include the conversion of farm buildings, but they must be able to prove economic viability.

The RES applications must be supported by the appropriate planning permission. This is dealt with in more detail by James Cleary in CHAPTER 3.

Funding is also available for improving and developing infrastructure that develops agriculture, including access roads, bridges etc. Projects such as marketing quality agricultural products, as well as the construction of water storage facilities, are included for funding availability.

The ERDP has specific plans for each region to set out rural development in environmental, economic and social terms. A good RES application submitted by the farmer or landowner should show that it deals with all these priorities. It has been said by the Department of the

Environment, Food and Rural Affairs (DEFRA) that RES applications have not had sound business plans and research. It is important to seek professional advice. The RES bids are assessed on a regional basis by a quarterly Regional Appraisal Panel. How prepared is the agricultural industry for this? It has been argued that the system benefits the well-equipped entrepreneur and not the genuine diversifying farmer trained in pure agriculture.

Clearly, in order for a RES to succeed it must be planned well in advance and there must be a realistic allowance for the town planning process. There must be sufficient resources to cover the costs of developing the project and obtaining professional advice.

The free planning advice service for RES applicants was launched in September 2001. Each applicant whose project proposal is approved by DEFRA in summary is eligible for one day's free planning consulting advice (up to a value of £800). The advice includes a site visit and appraisal report. Initial sketches are included but not detailed drawings etc. The consultant must be a member of the Royal Institute of Chartered Surveyors (RICS), the Royal town Planning Institute (RTPI) or the Royal Institute of British Architects (RIBA) and have five years' planning experience, particularly in rural planning.

The Farm Business Advisory Service was first introduced in October 2000 to provide three days of one-to-one on-farm advice free of charge. The aim is an initial health check of the farm business culminating in an action plan to take the business forward. This can include diversification as well as restructuring of traditional farming activities.

Processing and Marketing Grant (PMG)

2.5 This is another part of the ERDP scheme that provides funding to diversify. There are grants available for 30% of eligible capital costs for the larger processing and marketing ventures. The minimum project size is £70,000 and the maximum grant that is available is £1.2 million. There is a requirement for planning permission to be obtained. This is again competitive.

Vocational Training Scheme (VTS)

2.6 This is a service that helps diversification with the provision of training in areas such as business and processing skills. There has been a lack of applications in some areas. Again, DEFRA have criticised the quality of application.

The planning system

2.7   The whole issue of obtaining planning permission is dealt with by James Cleary (**Chapter 3**). Guidance on a range of planning matters is found within the Planning Policy Guidance notes (PPGs).

The Government publication *The Countryside – Environmental Quality and Economic and Social Development* (PPG7) includes the latest (town planning) policies on farm diversification and other rural planning issues. Local planning authorities (LPAs) must take account of PPG7 when preparing their own development plans.

A review of PPG7 must be understood to consider the future direction of PPGs.

Guidance in the PPG most directly relevant to farm-based diversification is as follows:

- When preparing their development plans and deciding planning applications, LPAs should take account of any statutory designation and then weigh the need to:
  - encourage rural enterprise, including the diversification of farm businesses;
  - strengthen rural communities by encouraging new employment.

Farming continues to make a significant contribution to the economy of rural areas but increasingly diversification into non-agricultural activities is vital to the continuing viability of many farm businesses. Ideally, LPAs should set out in their development plans the criteria to be applied to planning applications for farm diversification projects.

The range of industries that can be successfully located in rural areas is expanding. Many commercial and light manufacturing activities can be carried out in rural areas without causing unacceptable disturbance. There are attractions to the firms and their staff in a countryside environment, and there are benefits to the local economy and employment. These firms also help to bring new life and activity to rural communities and are generally welcomed and quickly assimilated. LPAs should bear in mind the vital role of enterprise, especially small-scale enterprises, in promoting healthy economic activity in rural areas, which can contribute to both local and national competitiveness.

The re-use and adaptation of existing rural buildings has an important role in meeting the needs of rural areas for commercial and industrial development, as well as for tourism, sport and recreation. It can also reduce demands for new buildings in the countryside, avoid leaving an existing building vacant and prone to vandalism or dereliction, and provide jobs. There should be no reason for preventing the conversion of rural buildings (including modern buildings) for business re-use provided that:

- they are of permanent and substantial construction;
- conversion does not lead to dispersal of activity on such a scale as to prejudice town and village vitality;
- their form, bulk and general design are in keeping with their surroundings;
- imposing reasonable conditions on a planning permission overcomes any legitimate planning objections (for example, on environmental or traffic grounds), which would otherwise outweigh the advantages of re-use; and
- if the buildings are in open countryside, they are capable of conversion without major or complete reconstruction.

Planning permission for diversification — the reality

2.8 Having set out the detail of PPG7 it is important to look at the reality of applications.

It would appear that many LPAs, even in rural areas, are not effectively committed to the diversification agenda. General policies relating to commercial and employment development in the rural economy are traditionally restrictive in character. There is always a natural conflict between protecting the countryside and the promotion of diversification.

The resolution of this conflict is left to the development control process on a case-by-case basis. This can result in great inconsistency. It is often found that local planning authorities fall behind declared policy for a number of reasons.

There seems to be a small-scale craft type approach to rural diversification without a realisation of exactly what is the evolving rural economy and the nature of modern rural business needs. There is seen to be excessive delay, unnecessary restriction and high development costs including professional time.

Application to the LPA for diversification must be well presented with full supporting information. Ideally, competent professional advice is obtained at an early stage.

Planning Green Paper — *Planning: Delivering a Fundamental Change*

2.9 The Green Paper sets out the Government's proposals for the reform of the land use planning system. The Secretary of State has described the existing system as 'inflexible, legalistic and bureaucratic'.

The whole tone of the Green Paper is deregulatory, aimed at simplifying the system, reducing the delay and uncertainty for users of the system. It is hoped to engage the local community in the process. It is unlikely to come into effect before 2004.

The driving force behind the Green Paper was thought to be Lord Falconer (the previous Planning Minister). Now that he is no longer involved a question exists as to whether his successor shares his enthusiasm. This is especially so as that official and his teams will have to deal with all the negative feedback from the conservation groups who are opposed to any changes to the current rigid system.

Tax planning surrounding successful planning permission applications

2.10   The previous sections have made clear the problems of currently obtaining planning permission. This highlights the value that could be added to land when an application is successful. By definition the application should be for business use, and under the current advantages of business asset taper relief (and rollover relief) the new activity has to be trading for at least two years. It might be that a subsequent disposal will need to take advantage of business asset taper relief (BATR).

It is essential therefore to ensure that the asset going into the application is 'clean', ie of correct business status, and does not get caught in the trap of 'tainted' business asset taper relief. It is important to review the business structure of ownership prior to the application and upon commencement of the new project.

There are concerns that the traditional farming unit will be bought by entrepreneurs experienced in business planning applications etc, who will exploit the opportunity to buy failed genuine agricultural farms and restructure them and make quick tax efficient profits through the threefold combination of failed farms through the farming crisis, the proposed more lenient planning policies through rural development together with the more advantageous tax regimes.

Business asset taper relief (BATR) — the serial entrepreneur

2.11   When business asset taper relief was introduced in the Finance Act 2000 as capital gains tax relief with a four-year business ownership requirement, it was heralded as the tax relief that encouraged the 'serial entrepreneur'. The business ownership period has now been reduced to two years. How will this affect the diversifying farmer and landowner? As the capital taxes are so favourable it will encourage the opportunist landowner to try and develop projects that will add value to their assets and to possibly dispose of this after the two-year ownership period with a view to obtaining a tax efficient gain with BATR of

75% and the effective capital gains tax rate being 10% or less. There is still scope to rollover into other projects.

In a worse case scenario the farming crisis could cause traditional farmers who only understand farming and pure agriculture to dispose of all or part of their farms to the profit-seeking entrepreneur. The latter would be able to cope with all the skills needed to organise a diversification project and the relevant planning permission and could look to take advantage of the favourable tax advantages. The chapter on land disposals (CHAPTER 14) clearly sets out the tax anti-avoidance provisions.

The development of failed farms under the rural development scheme could represent great opportunity for tax planners to create tax efficient gains as opposed to harshly taxed business profits.

There is not the scope to review BATR in depth in this book. The suggested reading is F Michael Cochrane's *Taper Relief* (LexisNexis Butterworths Tolley).

Business asset taper relief (BATR) — tainted taper

2.12 It will be essential to ensure that all diversified projects qualify for BATR before and after the project, as mentioned previously. One of the major problems of the BATR legislation is tainted taper relief.

In simple terms this is where an asset qualifies as a business now (or will qualify) but has not done so at some earlier time (or now). The previous non-qualifying period will prejudice the eventual taper relief and the proactive tax planner must do something about it. The solution is to eliminate the non-qualifying history of ownership. This should mean transferring ownership into a new entity to cause a new taper relief clock to restart. Thus, if the land or building that is to be used in the diversification project currently does not have business asset qualification then it should be given new ownership, eg *transfer* to a trust.

Again, the full detail of the rules should be fully researched. The important points are that if some form of subsequent disposal is envisaged then it is essential to review the BATR provisions and the structure of the ownership. The latter is never easy as there are so many considerations such as history, family politics and the full range of tax issues from capital gains tax to inheritance tax incorporating VAT, income tax and corporation tax. Sometimes farming family politics greatly overrule the tax planner.

What business structure?

2.13 Again, this book does not have the depth to fully review the complete choice of business structure but it does attempt to highlight some clear planning points.

The sole trader is the simplest trading operation for the farmer. Although there is the risk of unlimited liability there are all the benefits of tax flexibility.

The partnership is the traditional trading vehicle for the farming family having the advantages of combining resources whilst not risking some of the tax disadvantages of asset ownership and the limited company. One of the risks of partnership is the problem of joint and several liability. In family farming arrangements this was considered not such a risk. However, the experienced farmland agent, lawyer and tax adviser will be very aware of many other problems of the farming partnership. Many farm partnerships involve the husband and wife, and the protection of assets in a divorce cannot be overlooked (see **16.25**). Likewise, the need to have the Will drafted to match the farming partnership is set out in **18.16**. The problems surrounding partnerships and gratuitous licenses are dealt with at **11.4**.

The advantages and disadvantages of a limited liability partnership (LLP) are set out below. However, before this angle is researched it is important to look at the limited company. The latter has become a very attractive trading vehicle for non-farming and non-landowning businesses. Examples of the reasons are:

- no audit required if turnover is over £1 million;
- low corporation tax rates for retained profits;
- NIC efficient distribution via dividends;
- the introduction of a new nil-rate band.

Many of these advantages do not apply to the farming and landowning businesses. The problems of agricultural property relief (APR) and business property relief (BPR) for limited companies are set out in CHAPTER **13**. When BATR is considered in CHAPTER **14** it must be emphasised that this does not apply to the limited company. Under the current farming trading position the limited company has other disadvantages:

- trading tax losses are locked in the company and not available to be offset against other income; and
- dividends do not apply if there are no profits.

The position on incorporation and EIS is dealt with in **20.29** and **20.33–20.35**. This then leads to the detailed review of the LLP.

Limited liability partnerships (LLPs)

2.14 The Limited Liability Partnerships Act 2000 received Royal Assent on 20 July 2000 and, as a result, LLPs became available from

6 April 2001. As the name suggests, members of such a partnership have their liability 'capped' in the event of dissolution, but there is a price to pay: the LLP will have to publish and file corporate style accounts which will have to follow UK General Accounting Practice and be true and fair. There are different requirements for small and medium-sized LLPs and there is provision for an audit.

The Inland Revenue *Tax Bulletin* No 50 (December 2000) confirms that while an LLP trades it is 'tax transparent' just like a conventional partnership. However, the new structure comes into its own when the trade ceases, when it is no longer regarded as a partnership for tax purposes but is regarded instead as a corporate body.

There will be anti-avoidance legislation targeted at LLPs established for investment purposes, including denial of tax relief for those investing in an LLP.

It is suggested that there may be some uses for an LLP in the context of agriculture. A farmer diversifying might be seeking to let surplus buildings to a small non-agricultural business. He could consider forming an LLP with the other party, instead of granting a tenancy, in order to secure future capital gains tax business asset taper and rollover relief, together with 50% BPR, without exposing his estate to unlimited liability.

The structure could be of help in the context of a 'retired' partner in a small family business. *Beckman v IRC [2000] STC (SCD) 59* has demonstrated that the conversion of a partner's capital account to loan account upon retirement results in a loss of BPR, as the 'debt' is not an interest in a partnership. There are, of course, personal reasons for such a course of action, not least of which is to avoid the burden of 'joint and several' liability. The LLP would allow him to remain a partner (thus benefiting from BPR) whilst not having his estate exposed over and above the capital that he has left in the partnership.

Broadly, a conventional partnership can be converted to an LLP without any tax implications since the tax regimes are the same. This is intentional to encourage certain partnerships to convert. There is a restriction of sideways loss relief [Income and Corporation Taxes Act 1988 (ICTA 1988) s 380] against other income, which is limited to the capital that the partner has introduced into the business.

It would be possible to list the comprehensive advantages and disadvantages of all the trading alternatives but this book does not have the scope to go into that amount of detail.

Conclusion

2.15 This book hopes to set out not only the positive tax planning points but also the extreme tax complexities of farming and alternative land usage. The choice of trading vehicle and ownership structure is not easy and should be totally tailor-made to the business activity and the tax requirements.

In the recent CLA report 'Reform to Perform', which has been sent to the Chancellor, there are requests to introduce changes to boost the rural economy. Whilst changes in the tax legislation have helped limited companies the problems of sole traders and partnerships that predominate the farming industry have been overlooked.

Suggested changes by the CLA are the widening of the definition of agriculture to have property income from areas such as let office space in farm buildings redefined as trading income. Likewise, the suggestion that the cost of repairs/improvements to put diversification in place such as upgrading redundant farm buildings for office lets should be reclassified as repairs allowable against future income.

Obtaining Planning Permission   **3**

James Cleary MA, DipUD, MRTPI
(Managing Director, Pro Vision Planning and Design)

- **The need for planning permission**
  Review of the situation where planning permission may not be required. Feasibility considerations and categories of diversification that normally require planning permission.

- **How to obtain planning permission**
  Review of the current planning system, the application process together with consideration for change of use of land or buildings and erection of new structures.

- **Optimising planning consent**
  The planning and development appraisal together with processes of consultation, negotiation and lobbying. The importance of design is considered together with relevant highway or transport issues and the negotiation of planning obligations.

Note from the Editor

3.1 The British planning system emerged in a consolidated form shortly after the Second World War. It is now complex and often difficult to understand with national, regional and local policies that can be of vital importance to the owners and developers of land and property.

Attend a planning committee in any part of the country and you will usually see ranks of specialist planners waiting to address the meeting or to hear the debate on a particular proposal. Planning is no longer a subject for amateurs to handle. It is a profession with a range of specialisms.

In this chapter, James Cleary explains how the application process works in relation to the principal forms of diversification. Policy guidelines are summarised and ways in which planning consents can be optimised are discussed.

Feasibility and the need for planning permission

3.2 Generally speaking, diversification is 'development', which is defined as engineering operations, building works or change of use of land or buildings. Development rights within the British Isles were effectively nationalised over 50 years ago and hence planning permission must be acquired before you can proceed with most forms of new development.

The main thrust of this book is the financial and tax-related implications of diversification – its viability or profitability. However, these are matters that should normally only be considered if the project is feasible or permissible. You can't count your chickens before they have hatched. Unfortunately, there are many examples of well-intentioned and viable projects on which legal and accountancy fees have been incurred that have not been realised because of planning-related problems.

Financial viability is, nonetheless, a matter that should be considered but within a wider feasibility assessment. The overall feasibility assessment may include a range of non-financial matters and a planning appraisal is essential at an early stage. Some careful consideration of the full range of effects on land use is advisable at the start of any diversification project. The trade name for this task is the 'planning and development appraisal'.

Many diversification projects give rise to factors which farmers may not at first be fully aware. For example, there can be a considerable management burden of taking on a planning battle or responsibility for a new enterprise. Time and resources may be diverted away from necessary and continuing farming work. Also, the new enterprise may adversely impact on the amenities previously enjoyed by the landowner, farmer or his neighbours. Relations can become soured.

Within this chapter we seek to outline the planning factors relevant to diversification projects. There is a need to understand what does and does not require planning permission and to appreciate current national planning priorities. These topics are worthy of a book each and hence the coverage here is necessarily brief. The chapter concludes with specific reference to the planning process and techniques for optimising planning consents.

Where planning permission may not be required

3.3 There are some diversification projects for which planning permission may not be needed, and hence this chapter may not be of
interest to all readers. If you think you don't need planning permission
for an enterprise either in its initial form or in terms of what it is likely
to become it is best to check as it is better to be safe rather than sorry.
Be warned, the position is not always clear and is sometimes open to
interpretation. Advice from an experienced planning consultant may
be worth acquiring.

Categories of diversification projects that may not require planning
permission include the following:

- Use of farmland or buildings either directly for agricultural purposes or for certain purposes ancillary to agriculture – this includes
horticulture and most forms of 'pick your own', shooting, fishing,
turf stripping (on a limited scale), agricultural storage, farm shops
(selling homegrown produce), food packing and some forms of
dairy product processing.
- Activities that constitute development but do not need planning
permission by virtue of permitted development rights, such as:
  — temporary buildings and uses – including most moveable
    structures for animals such as pigs and hens and the use of
    land for any purpose such as war games, clay pigeon shooting
    and gymkhanas for not more than 28 days in any calendar
    year (or 14 days in the case of markets or motorcar and motor-
    cycle racing);
  — caravan sites – for up to three caravans on a site without a
    licence for up to 28 days each year (on holdings of not less
    than five acres in size); and
  — agricultural or forestry buildings and operations – including
    the erection of agricultural buildings up to 465 sq m in size,
    reasonable extensions to existing buildings, replacement plant
    or machinery, hard surfacing and mineral working for agricul-
    tural purposes.
- Activities that are exempt from enforcement action by virtue of the
ten-year rule (established uses) – that is the use of buildings that
can be shown to have been continually used for a period of ten
years or more for some purpose other than agriculture. The established use may continue without the need for planning permission
whether it is for the existing business or another business.

The reader requiring a robust assessment of the need or otherwise for
planning permission should refer to the Town and Country Planning
Act 1990, the General Permitted Development Order 1995
(SI 1995/418) and the Town and Country Planning (General

Development Procedure) Order 1995 (SI 1995/419). Legislation is complex; therefore, advice from a qualified, experienced and recommended planning consultant may be the best route to an accurate assessment.

Categories of diversification that normally require planning permission

3.4 Diversification is by definition a diversion. In the current economic climate, it may be the means through which the embattled farmer can survive financially or develop activities that complement his core business. Diversification activities may also enable the farmer to retain ownership or control over property assets.

The degree of agricultural diversification or extent of diversion may vary considerably. It may be a small-scale diversification proposal or a progression from an existing operation, such as the farm shop on the roadside or the cheese-making facility on the dairy farm. Alternatively, it may involve a complete change in direction or a transformation of the farm. It may involve the re-use of cattle buildings for commercial purposes or the change of use of land to a golf course. With these types of development the buildings or land are most unlikely to be available for re-use for agriculture in the foreseeable future. In other words, there's no going back.

Reference to a range of diversification projects was made in CHAPTER 1 of this book. Within this section we refer briefly to the main categories of diversification projects that require planning permission. One doesn't need to look far for live examples of each. The full range of options is worth considering before any existing farming operations are discontinued or buildings demolished.

Change of use of land

3.5 Planning permission may be needed whether the change of use of land is permanent or temporary. In some cases, temporary or short-term changes of use may be 'permitted development', but in the cases referred to below, planning permission *will* normally be needed:

- golf courses and driving ranges – in vogue ten years ago following the reports from the Royal and Ancient Society and others on demand outstripping supply. Still deemed to be a worthwhile alternative to farming on accessible sites close to centres of population;
- formal outdoor recreation/sports pitches – land may be leased to local sports clubs or district or parish councils for purposes such as football, rugby, hockey or bowls;

- equestrian use – can include a wide range of grazing, training, trekking and other uses associated with liveries, riding centres, training schools and stud farms;
- fishing lakes – either for commercial fishery purposes or for recreational fishing. If the venue is not for commercial fishing or day visitors alone it is likely that accommodation in the form of lodges or similar will be needed;
- outdoor educational facilities, interpretation centres or tourist facilities – for local schools or colleges or in areas with large numbers of visitors or holiday makers;
- animal/wildlife centres – for rare breeds or birds of prey, for kennels or catteries, or for animal sanctuaries, animals for scientific testing etc;
- activity centres or recreational events – to meet the continuing demand for corporate hospitality/team building days and venues for children's parties (war games, aerial runways, quad biking, clay pigeon shooting, archery, barbeques etc). Events that need planning permission can also include car boot sales, open air markets, motorcycle or motor car racing and riding events except where these uses are temporary and fall within the 'permitted development' tolerances referred to earlier.

New structures or change of use of buildings

3.6 New buildings or structures may sometimes be needed to enable a diversification proposal to proceed. More often than not, these will be small scale or ancillary to other existing buildings or land uses. They normally require planning permission and can include:

- golf club buildings and covered driving ranges;
- ticket kiosks and changing rooms or a café/restaurant ancillary to formal recreational facilities;
- stables, hay stores or tack rooms;
- fishing or shooting lodges;
- interpretation centres or lecture facilities;
- animal cages, kennels, aviaries etc;
- toilet blocks or shower rooms on camping or caravan sites; and
- telecommunication masts or aerials.

Diversification proposals involving the change of use of existing or redundant agricultural buildings can include most of the above and:

- visitor accommodation – either general tourist/holiday accommodation or overnight accommodation for fishermen, shooting parties, golfers etc;

- arenas or grooms' accommodation for equestrian development;
- storage or distribution purposes – ranging from boxed archive stores, facilities for local market traders, craftsmen or other tradesmen to bulk goods storage or winter storage of caravans, boats and vintage cars;
- workshops or industrial uses – including agricultural engineering, motor repairs, general engineering, craft workshops or other forms of light engineering either with or without related stores and offices; and
- offices or research facilities – ranging in specification from the *'rough and ready'* to highly prestigious and suitable for a wider range of small to medium-sized local businesses or large corporate concerns if the accommodation is strategically located, accessible and well fitted out.

Current planning policies

3.7 Planning policies and legislation are complex and wide-ranging in their effect. There are now over 20 subject-related Planning Policy Guidance notes (PPGs), many of which contain guidance that can impact on diversification proposals. (See www.planning.odpm.gov.uk for details of all the current planning policies of the Government, including copies of all the PPG statements.) The relevant guidance or statutory instrument depends on the nature of the proposal, the location of the site and factors such as environmental designations, landscape protection policies, the presence of listed buildings, ancient monuments or other protected sites.

The Government recognises that the system has become inflexible, legalistic and bureaucratic and is committed to a review to achieve 'a better, simpler, faster, more accessible system that serves both businesses and the community' (Planning Green Paper: *Delivering a Fundamental Change* (December 2001)). Priorities for reform include national planning guidance for the countryside, industrial and commercial development including premises for small firms, and also the development plan system that impacts directly upon most types of diversification project.

It is, however, relevant to note certain current policy priorities relevant to diversification together with the main areas of guidance that are likely to last through reform processes.

Probably the overriding priority at the present time is the use of policy to secure forms of development that are 'sustainable'. It is recognised that the environment should be managed in a way that protects it for future generations. This means support for proposals that re-use existing, redundant or underused property. It also means controls to achieve a reduction or minimal increase in private vehicle trips. Re-use proposals may sometimes conflict with traffic minimisation priorities and this is where the planning system seeks to impose various forms of checks and balances.

In November 2000, the Government published the Rural White Paper *Our Countryside: The Future – A Fair Deal for Rural England.* This included statements of support for diversification opportunities including re-use of redundant farm buildings, support for rural businesses and opportunities for new recreational facilities. The general response from the farming community was not positive because it appeared to say very little that had not already been said before. The White Paper places increased emphasis on the need for control systems to restrict development pressures in the countryside, to prioritise landscape protection, promote tranquillity and steer development toward brownfield sites and urban areas.

National planning guidance for housing (PPG3: March 2000) now includes a definition of brownfield sites or 'previously developed land'. It expressly excludes land that is or was occupied by agricultural or forestry buildings. It also introduces a sequential test to the consideration of housing development proposals. This seeks to steer new housing to central urban or edge of urban areas and away from rural areas.

A similar test already exists for retail development (PPG6: June 1996), but there is no such test for industrial and commercial development. The latter is subject to guidance that emphasises the need for locational factors to be taken into account and for small firms to be treated positively by local planning authorities (PPG4: November 1992).

Similar guidance for transport generally aims to promote more sustainable transport choices for people and freight, as well as promoting accessibility to jobs and services and opportunities for travel by modes other than the private car (PPG13: March 2001). The good news is that national planning guidance on transport recognises the need for adequate employment opportunities in rural areas and also the increasing trend in diversification of agricultural businesses. Conversion and re-use proposals are referred to specifically. Local authorities are advised not to reject proposals in rural areas where small-scale business development or expansion is likely to give rise to 'modest, additional daily vehicle movements' and where the impact on minor roads would not be significant.

Further good news is contained within national planning guidance for the countryside *The Countryside – Environmental Quality and Economic and Social Development* (PPG7: February 1997 and the 2001 additions). Sustainable development priorities are set out as the cornerstone of rural planning policy; but the guidance goes on to recognise the need to accommodate change in the countryside to encourage further economic diversity and to allow for a variety of employment opportunities; particularly in areas still heavily reliant on agriculture. Diversification proposals should, however, seek to maintain the character and qualities of the countryside and any new building should, according to the guidance, be of good quality.

National planning guidance for the countryside also indicates clearly that planning authorities should generally discriminate in favour of re-use proposals for business rather than for residential purposes. Local Authorities are advised not to prevent the conversion of traditional or modern rural buildings for business use provided that:

'(a) they are of permanent and substantial construction;
(b) conversion does not lead to dispersal of activity on such a scale as to prejudice town and village vitality (see paragraph 2.10);
(c) their form, bulk and general design are in keeping with their surroundings;
(d) imposing reasonable conditions on a planning permission overcomes any legitimate planning objections (for example, on environmental or traffic grounds) which would otherwise outweigh the advantages of re-uses; and
(e) if the buildings are in open countryside, they are capable of conversion without major or complete reconstruction.' (paragraph 3.14).

PPG7 is the guiding national policy document for farm diversification proposals. It also contains guidance and support for a range of other diversification options such as farm shops, food processing, food packing, farm sports, energy crops, workshops, horticulture and the re-use and adaptation of rural buildings generally.

Following the publication of the Government's long-term strategy for farming (*A New Direction in Agriculture* (December 1999)) and the England Rural Development Programme (ERDP) in October 2000, PPG7 was altered to contain quite clear and unequivocal support for agricultural diversification. Local planning authorities are now told that they 'should be supportive of well-conceived farm diversification schemes for business purposes that are consistent in their scale with their rural location' (new paragraph 3.4a). This alteration has helped tip the balance back in favour of diversification proposals after a period where limits on traffic generation were ruling out many forms of diversification in the more remote rural areas.

A wide range of other national planning policies may also impact upon diversification proposals. These include policies for Areas of Special Landscape Value, Green Belts, Environmentally Sensitive Areas, Conservation Areas, aquifers, SSSI's (Sites of Special Scientific Interest) and National Parks. There is also a raft of guidance specific to proposals affecting coastal areas and listed buildings and proposals for tourism-related development and sports and recreation.

The identification of relevant policies is a key part of the normal planning appraisal exercise familiar to most experienced planning consultants.

The application process

3.8   The process by which planning applications and listed building consent applications are determined is known as the 'development control process'. District councils are generally responsible for the preparation of Local Plans and for deciding planning applications. The system is plan-led and hence applications must be considered against Local Plan policy, which in turn should accord with national policy.

Local Plans are usually reviewed on a five-year cycle and everyone has the right to object or to support local policy initiatives or designations. The right extends to a right to be heard in front of an Inspector when the objections to the plan are considered at a public inquiry.

Planning applications submitted to district councils can be decided either by elected councillors (the Planning Committee) or under delegated powers by trained planning officers. The planning officers are accountable to the elected councillors.

Pre-application discussions with a planning adviser and subsequently an officer of the relevant planning authority can sometimes be useful, particularly with proposals that are complex or are likely to give rise to objections. In some cases the pre-application discussions can continue over a longer period of time than the time it takes for the application to be processed.

After an application has been submitted it is usually checked and registered by administrative staff within the local planning authority. Applications are often returned if they include insufficient information (such as inadequate plans, inadequate details of the proposal or insufficient ownership information) or the application fee that has been paid is insufficient.

Once registered, the application is allocated to a planning officer, the applicant is informed and the consultation process begins. Consultees can include statutory parties (the Highway Authority, the Environment Agency, English Nature, English Heritage etc), parish councils, residents groups, neighbours and other organisations such as the local civic society and the Ramblers' Association.

After a period of several weeks, although in some cases much longer, the planning officer reviews consultation responses, relevant policies and other case specific or site specific factors and comes to a view on the proposals. With all applications, officers normally make a recommendation for either refusal, approval or deferral.

Straightforward proposals are usually determined by senior officers under delegated powers and are only taken to a planning committee if the council's standing orders allow elected members to request that this should happen. Proposals to be considered by elected members are usually subject of a written report on the planning committee agenda and often there will be a site visit by councillors before the application is determined.

In the past, it was normal for there to be discussions between the planning officer and the applicant or his agent if there was a need for amendments to the proposals to make them acceptable. This often delayed the application processing period and the period of time between submission and determination could often extend to several months. Planning authorities are now given relatively strict performance standards and with the advent of 'Best Value' criteria most officers seek to minimise application stage discussions. Applications can be refused even though difficulties could have been resolved by negotiation. In this way, pressure is placed on the applicant to ensure at the outset that the proposal is carefully conceived and takes account of relevant policies.

Applications that are approved are always subject to conditions. These range from straightforward requirements for agreement on the use of certain building materials or planting species to complex requirements that impose pre-commencement obligations on the applicant. They may also impose restrictions on the construction process or limitations on either hours of use or the scope for further changes under normal permitted development rights.

If an application is refused or subject to a condition that is not acceptable to the applicant, then there is a right of appeal. Clear reasons for refusal of an application or reasons for the imposition of conditions should always be stated on the decision notice. The likelihood of success of an appeal depends on the ability of the appellant to argue that the reasons are without justification.

The appeal process is quasi judicial. It is regularly used for all types of development proposal. Whilst it can be expensive and time consuming it is often the only means of achieving consent and can be cost effective in terms of the overall value of the development proposal. If the actions of the planning authority can be shown to have been unreasonable a claim for an award of costs can be made. Likewise, if the actions of the appellant are shown to have been unreasonable a claim for an award of costs may be made by the planning authority.

As an alternative to the appeal process, the applicant may resubmit and seek to overcome reasons for refusal or unacceptable conditions. The nature or form of the proposals may need to be varied. Officers representing the planning authority will often seek to persuade applicants to take this route. Sometimes it may be appropriate.

Planning policies, the planning system and reasons why the system operates in the way that it does are becoming ever more complex and difficult for the layman to understand. Clear and appropriate planning strategies should be developed at an early stage. Planning consultancy is a burgeoning profession and good consultants exist in most districts. Chartered town planners have taken over from general practice lawyers and surveyors who used to advise on planning matters before the complexity of law and requirement for sophisticated strategies gave rise to the need for a specialist approach. They are usually known to land agents, solicitors, accountants and bank managers who may all be able to make appropriate recommendations.

Ways of optimising planning consents

3.9   As outlined at the start of this chapter, there is a need to ensure that diversification proposals are viable and capable of achieving planning consent. At an early stage in any project there is a need to undertake a feasibility study or planning and development appraisal. There may be a need to re-assess costs and values throughout the application stage as development schemes often change or can be subject to unexpected planning conditions or necessary legal agreements.

The value of a development proposal can often fall during the application stage if the planning authority rules out some element as unacceptable, be it a driving range on a golf course, a café with tourist facilities or an office element of a commercial re-use proposal. Similarly, values may fall if conditions imposed by the planning authority restrict opening hours or the nature of proposed activities.

On other occasions the cost of development can increase significantly as a result of the imposition of conditions requiring driveway diversions, extensive landscaping or the use of only local materials and building techniques. The objective should therefore be to achieve the optimum planning consent. That is a consent that accords with relevant policy without incurring excessive delays during periods over which borrowing may be needed, excessive building costs or unnecessary operational or other restrictions.

The planning and development appraisal

3.10   At the time of writing the Department of the Environment, Food and Rural Affairs (DEFRA) provides finance for farm business advice (via Business Links) and for initial planning consultancy advice. The latter may cover only the first stage of a thorough feasibility exercise but could be sufficient to provide advice on likely levels of development potential or on some new ideas for diversification.

A full planning and development appraisal for a diversification proposal would normally contain:

- information on the site or buildings that demonstrates an understanding of key locational factors and the aspirations of the landowner or developer;
- a summary of relevant planning history (or the outcome of earlier planning applications) for the site and its surrounds;
- a summary of relevant national, strategic and Local Plan policies insofar as they are likely to impact upon the development opportunities under consideration;
- a review of key issues and in some cases a discussion of key constraints and principal opportunities;
- some consideration of development costs and values; and
- recommendations on the course of action that should be followed.

A first appraisal of this type may be prepared by a planning consultant, an architect, a specialist surveyor or another property professional. It is more likely that the appraisal will be value for money if it is prepared by someone who regularly deals with agricultural diversification proposals, who understands national and local planning policy and who can easily access key sources of relevant information.

Consultation, negotiation and lobbying

3.11   Beyond the appraisal stage the scheme must be drawn up and should be subject of a reasonable level of consultation with relevant parties both prior to and during the planning application stage. The consultation process may have begun already at the appraisal stage and it should continue right through to the conclusion of the application stage.

Gauging the appropriate level of consultation can be difficult and it can be costly and time consuming. There is a need to understand when consultation is necessary and when consultation may be inappropriate. In some situations, early consultation may be essential to help determine the course of action to be followed. Parties such as the Highway Authority, the Environment Agency, the council's tree officer, conservation, landscape, archaeological or ecological experts or the parish council may need to be approached. Their responses may give rise to the need for additional advice from specialist consultants.

By its very nature, the planning process is a process that often requires subjective assessments. Frequently, a proposal may be deemed to be in the balance or not clear-cut. Should the authority place the emphasis on the need for employment opportunities in the countryside or restrictions on vehicle trip generation? Should the emphasis be on the need to make best use of redundant land or the need to protect valuable landscapes or certain types of vulnerable wildlife? These are matters that can often be handled in favour of the applicant by engaging appropriate specialist consultancy advice. Negotiations may need to be with the application case officer or with the specialist officer advising the planning officer on the matter in question.

Sometimes consultees are not experts. They may be parish councillors or representatives of neighbourhood committees or residents groups. It may therefore be appropriate to lobby these parties either before or during the application period.

Likewise, it may be appropriate to make contact with district councillors within the ward or parish or with district councillors on the appropriate planning committee. In instances such as this, there is a need to understand the make-up of the relevant committee, party politics and the views held previously by elected members. Some councillors can be reluctant to meet or to express a view on a particular proposal. Sometimes information provided may be used against the applicant. If party politics are not taken into account the applicant may be successful in winning over an elected member only to find that he or she is a member of the minority group whose views are likely to be opposed by those holding the balance of power.

Fortunately, we live in a democracy and elected members are effectively performing a public role and should therefore always be contactable. Their addresses and telephone numbers should be disclosed by the district council. Sometimes an approach may be best in writing only, although at other times it may be appropriate to call, speak to or meet with certain councillors.

The lobbying activity can be carried out by either the applicant or his agent. It is often better if the approach can be direct from the applicant who is more likely to be a constituent with voting rights. However, he must be very clear on the purpose of the approach and the nature of the argument to be pursued and, where the case is complex, there may be no alternative but to bring in specialist advisers. In the most complex and political of cases it may even be appropriate to hire a lobbyist.

The importance of design

3.12 Over recent years we have seen an ever-increasing emphasis on good design. Design is now a key issue in the determination of planning applications. Some applications for development that are acceptable 'in principle' fail because of poor design. On the other hand, good design can help make a scheme more attractive, more viable and significantly increase prospects for success at the planning stage.

Design can be particularly important in areas with special designations such as National Parks, Areas of Outstanding Natural Beauty (AONB) and Areas of Special Landscape Importance (ASLI). It goes without saying that good design is also important for buildings to be located within very open or exposed sites. Even buildings that can be erected under permitted development rights must respect guidance on good design. At the national level, there is extensive advice on the need for new agricultural and forestry buildings to be carefully considered in terms of their setting, size, shape, colour, texture and overall appearance (PPG7, Appendix E, paras 24–35).

The importance of good design generally is set out in PPG1 (Annex A) *General Policy and Principles.* Applicants for planning permission are advised to provide a short written statement setting out their design principles with reference to the wider context and related photographs, perspectives, plans and elevations.

Planning policy guidance for the countryside sets good design as a clear objective in order to help achieve local distinctiveness and make new development more acceptable to local people (PPG7, para 2.11). Where it exists, consideration should be given to relevant supplementary planning guidance such as Countryside Design Summaries or Village Design Statements.

Generally speaking, there is a need to consider design aspects at an early stage and to take forward design issues in parallel with the initial stages of the planning case. There is a need to avoid the trap of getting an architect or experienced designer who is competent on the design side but overlooks planning policy matters. Likewise, applicants should not be misled by a planning consultant who focuses on planning policy matters but overlooks design issues. Applicants should either appoint an individual or company who can handle both matters or appoint two people who can work well together.

When handling building conversion matters it is particularly important that the designer understands the need to convert and re-use rather than demolish and rebuild. Current Government guidance is quite clear that buildings in the open countryside can generally be converted providing it is without the need for 'major or complete reconstruction'. A scheme to demolish and rebuild either in part or in whole may be preferred by the owner or proposed occupier as it may be more cost effective, but it is more likely to be a non-starter when it comes to planning.

Proposals for development within particularly sensitive areas such as Areas of Outstanding Natural Beauty or Environmentally Sensitive Areas may require a special approach to design. To achieve a development that is respectful there may be a need to design with nature that requires the appointment of a landscape architect or an ecologist to work alongside the planning consultant and designer.

Dealing with highway or transport issues

3.13 Many diversification schemes fail for highway or transport-related issues. For many years a wide range of schemes have failed because of inadequate visibility splays at the junction of the site entrance with the adopted highway. More recently, there have been a significant number of planning refusals because of traffic generation concerns, particularly in areas that are relatively remote where compliance with sustainable planning policies is brought into question.

It is important that applicants should not give up on a scheme just because of negative comments at an early stage from a local authority highway engineer or a planning officer. There are frequently ways of presenting a scheme or of altering it to address Highway Authority objections. Further, it is important to note that the Highway Authority can only advise the planning officer and no longer have powers to direct refusal of a planning application.

If the new development gives rise to the need for substantial visibility splays, existing hedges or banks may need to be cut back or kerbs realigned. Visibility splay distances along the main road depend on traffic speeds. It may be possible to show that speeds are actually relatively low (or agree traffic orders to force them to be lower) and hence reduce requirements for splay lengths. Alternatively, traffic calming or traffic management measures may be suggested to bring traffic speeds down.

When the Highway Authority considers development proposals it is mindful of the level and type of traffic that is likely to be generated. It is therefore important that information is obtained on earlier levels of trip generation. Did cattle lorries regularly enter or leave the site, or were there daily milk tanker collections? It may be possible to argue that a scheme with a substandard access should be allowed because of the highway engineer's fallback principle. This requires that development should not be resisted if levels of traffic generation for a new use would not exceed the levels associated with an earlier use that may be recommenced.

In some cases the Highway Authority or the local planning authority may seek to resist commercial development on the grounds that it should not be located in remote or relatively inaccessible rural areas. Clearly, some forms of commercial development may be inappropriate where they give rise to a substantial level of private vehicle trips along small rural roads. However, by devising green transport measures and Green Transport Plans it may be possible to show that private vehicle trip generation will be reduced to more acceptable levels, hence removing the reason for refusal.

Green Transport Plans can be highly complex and expensive. They can include measures such as company owned minibuses, public transport subsidies or restrictions on parking to limit associated levels of car use. However, there are other elements that may be relatively easy to achieve such as the operation of flexible working hours, display on site of bus timetables and notice boards for car sharing opportunities. Other measures that are frequently put forward include provision for secure undercover cycle storage and the incorporation of showers and changing rooms within offices or workshops to encourage cycling to work.

Measures such as these may be the key to a successful planning application. Without them, a building may only be re-used for low-key, low-value purposes or for tenants that are difficult to manage and frequently default on payment rather than the more respectable professional or business user.

Negotiating planning obligations

3.14   The Planning Acts make provision for planning obligations to be attached to planning consent. These obligations are normally formalised within Section 106 Agreements, so called because the main provision is contained within s 106 of the Town and Country Planning Act 1990. Planning obligations take various forms. They may be needed to restrict occupancy of buildings or prevent the sale of a building or buildings separate from a wider estate. In other cases, obligation may require the removal of buildings if they are no longer needed in connection with a specific diversification proposal. In some cases, a planning obligation may require traffic routing or may be used to embrace Green Transport Plans.

The planning obligation may be necessary to persuade the local planning authority or the Highway Authority that the development can go ahead. To be reasonable the obligation should be deemed to be necessary and clearly related to the development proposed, and it must cover a matter that cannot be dealt with in a standard planning condition. These tests should be applied in each case.

Planning obligations can sometimes take many months to resolve. They can also be onerous and as they run with the land they are likely to bind successors in title. In some cases, an applicant may be required to pay for off-site highway improvements because of forecast traffic generation associated with a diversification scheme. If the measures that have to be underwritten are extensive, the diversification scheme may not be viable.

Once agreed, a planning obligation is difficult to remove. However, in some instances, after a period of five years following the grant of planning permission they can be renegotiated or even removed altogether.

It may be best to take legal advice either at the stage of negotiation or just prior to signing the obligation. Clauses can sometimes be added that may be of considerable benefit to the applicant. For example, if required to contribute to a road improvement scheme it is unreasonable for the Highway Authority to retain the money if the scheme is never implemented. By applying a clause requiring that funds be returned if not used within, say, five years an applicant's interests are more likely to be protected. Other similar clauses will be well known to consultants and lawyers who regularly deal with planning obligations.

These are just a few of the ways in which the value of a planning consent can be optimised. There are others and clearly the relevance of each depends on the nature of the diversification proposal. Planning policy guidance, statutes and local plan policies regularly change and hence the purpose of this chapter has been to give a broad outline of the most relevant matters at the time of writing.

Don't fall into the trap of letting planning matters become the tail that wags the dog. The diversification proposal should be well-conceived commercially and should be a workable business venture. At the same time, make sure that planning matters are taken account of and handled professionally to ensure that they do not become an obstacle to success.

James Cleary

James Cleary is a Chartered Town Planner and qualified Urban Designer who has practised for over 20 years. He has experience with the public and private sectors, has lectured at Oxford Brookes and Portsmouth Universities and was a member of the RTPI Development Control Panel for five years. He is the Managing Director of Pro Vision Planning and Design – a company that he helped to establish in 1996. Pro Vision is the trading name of P V Projects Ltd. The company now has two offices and handles planning consultancy and architectural projects throughout the country. Large country estates are one of the company's key client sectors. Over recent years, the company has advised on proposals for over one hundred different diversification projects.

Protecting the Farmhouse 4

Julie Butler

- **Protecting the farmhouse against loss of tax reliefs**
  Traditionally the farmhouse has always attracted favourable inheritance tax (IHT), capital gains tax (CGT) and income tax reliefs as a farming business asset used in the business of farming. However, as land is put to a different use the tax reliefs could be at risk and the tax planner must take action to prevent this.

- **The tax benefits of a principal private residence (PPR)**
  The tax benefits of PPR for CGT relief must not be overlooked, and the tax planner needs to be aware of at the fine balance between business usage and PPR.

- **The tax benefits of a large garden**
  Farmhouses have traditionally enjoyed large gardens with an extensive curtilage and with this comes the opportunity for development opportunities. Buildings in the curtilage can qualify as part of the garden. Again, the tax planner must look at maximising both PPR for the garden and business reliefs where appropriate.

- **The danger areas for the farmhouse**
  The structure of the farming unit could affect the agricultural property relief (APR) on the farmhouse. Examples of risk areas are farm business tenancies (FBTs), land let out, grazing arrangements, ownership in the limited company, reduced land ownership, hobby farming and no history of commerciality.

The farmhouse — introduction

4.1 The assets comprised in the farming activity can principally be divided between farmhouse, farm cottage, farm building, farmland and investment in the farming business. The need to preserve inheritance tax (IHT) reliefs, both agricultural and business, are featured throughout the book. Likewise, the importance of the business status for capital gains tax (CGT) is emphasised.

Protecting the farmhouse

4.2 With the move from traditional farming activities and structures, as a result of the recent farming crisis, a lot of the previously assured reliefs could be lost without careful tax planning.

The self-sufficient family farm unit could once exist happily with as little as 100 acres. The farmhouse was part of this 'business' unit and had many advantages such as input VAT claims, business expense claims and, above all, agricultural property relief (APR) for IHT. A very happy scenario then, but where does that leave the farmhouse now? Do these small family farms still exist on a commercial basis? The farmhouse is likely to have a very high value but less likely to achieve all the reliefs it previously enjoyed.

The most valuable tax relief at stake is therefore the APR for IHT purposes. The first point to consider is the 'character appropriate' test. This is dealt with in **4.23**. If land is put to a non-agricultural use, or is gifted or sold, then the farmhouse and any land associated with it may no longer be 'of a character appropriate' to the farmland and APR may be restricted. The Capital Taxes Office (CTO) Manual says that the CTO will be interested in cases where the value of the farmhouse is in excess of £250,000 but no more than 100 acres is farmed. Likewise, if the value of the farmhouse is less than £250,000 but no more than 20 acres is farmed.

The instant reaction is clearly that the CTO Manual is not geared for the recent increases in property prices. However, what is the impact for today's farming clients? Is the land still used for agricultural purposes? Has the move to diversification meant that the relief has been lost? With so many advisers seeking the benefits of business property relief (BPR) as opposed to APR, has the farmhouse been overlooked? What chance would it have with a BPR claim? The same problem arises where the owner lets the land but retains the farmhouse. Reference should be made as to what qualifies as agricultural property and the Inheritance Tax Act 1984 (IHTA 1984) ss 115–117 should be looked at. The adviser must be mindful of the occupational or ownership tests of two and seven years respectively.

The definition of farming is found in Income and Corporation Taxes Act 1988 (ICTA 1988) s 832(1): 'the occupation of land wholly or mainly for the purpose of husbandry'. See **Chapter 1** for more detail. So what does not qualify? Grazing by horses (*Wheatley's Executors v IRC [1998] STC (SCD) 60*), fishing rights, industrial units, farm shop selling only bought in produce, farm as a tourist attraction are but a few examples. The case of *Farmer (Farmer's Executors) v IRC [1999] STC (SCD) 321* provides great assistance to the farmer who diversifies. Several of the properties at the farm were surplus to the requirements of the farm and had been let to tenants on short leases. The letting activities were held to be ancillary to the farm business and the business as a whole was not one of mainly holding investments. This is dealt with in detail in **Chapter 13**.

So where does that leave the farmhouse and the professional adviser? One of the first points of concern must be the income tax computation. Is there a clear division of farming and non-farming profits despite the fact they might be all taxed under Schedule D Case 1? Is the adviser mindful of ICTA 1988 s 397, the hobby farming rules, despite the extension under ESC B55? (See **Chapter 12**.)

Under the strict allocation of farming and non-farming income would some enterprises be able to demonstrate recent farming profits? This is not an assumption that the clients are 'bad' farmers, but that for a number of years it has been difficult to show a profit from a small traditional farming unit.

So what planning points are there for consideration by the tax adviser? In addition to looking at the tax computation, all angles of the diversification must be looked at. Farmers are considering (or have been considering) farm business tenancies (FBTs) and various areas of diversification. The angle of FBT, contract farming and share farming arrangements are dealt with in **Chapter 11**.

Perhaps it could be argued that as farming now provides such a relatively small amount of the total UK income such issues are not so relevant, but the land and high asset values still surround us. The land should be put to some commercial use and traditional assumptions will have to be re-thought.

Historically, there have been claims of 70% input VAT on farmhouse repairs and one-third claim for business expenses, but the viability of such claims in relation to the newly-structured farming enterprise have to be questioned by both the farmer and their adviser.

Consideration is given to the protection of the matrimonial home at **16.27–16.28**.

Capital allowances

4.3   The general rule is that on each farm there is only a single farmhouse which is the central controlling point of the farm, ie its use is restricted to the person running the farm. Other houses occupied by individuals working on the farm may be 'cottages'. As the agricultural building allowance is only 4% it is not capital allowances queries that are likely to drive the need for clarification of exactly what is a 'farmhouse'.

In *Lindsay v IRC (1953) 34 TC 289* the taxpayer lived abroad and farmed through agents. The head shepherd occupied the only house. Despite the fact that he was an employee his dwelling was found to be the farmhouse and expenditure on it was restricted to one-third.

In *IRC v John M Whiteford & Son (1962) 40 TC 379* a house was built for a farmer's son who was a partner in the business. This was held to be an agricultural cottage so there was no restriction.

Where any expenditure is incurred on a farmhouse, not more than one-third can qualify [Capital Allowances Act 2001 (CAA 2001) s 369(3)]. This proportion may be reduced if the accommodation and amenities of the farmhouse are out of relation to the nature and extent of the farm. Likewise, if the farmhouse has been used partly for husbandry and partly for some other purpose, the expenditure is apportioned for the purpose of the allowance.

Capital gains tax

Principal private residence (PPR)

4.4   The most important relief available to the farmhouse is that for a 'principal private residence' (PPR) [Taxation and Chargeable Gains Act 1992 (TCGA 1992) s 222]. The exemption applies to a gain arising on the disposal of the dwelling house and its garden and grounds. The latter are restricted to half a hectare or such larger areas as the Commissioners concerned may determine on being satisfied that, regard being had to the size and character of the dwelling house, a larger area is required for the reasonable enjoyment of it as a residence [TCGA s 222(3)]. The garden and grounds have to be for the owner's own occupation and enjoyment.

The practical tax planning point is that the business usage and PPR relief must be finely balanced. Strictly, any element of the farmhouse that is used exclusively for business will not be eligible for private residence relief. Some tax practitioners advocate not dedicating 100% business usage to specific rooms so that the PPR relief is preserved.

The ordinary meaning of dwelling house can be found in *Batey v Wakefield [1980] STC 572* (see **4.5** below).

It must be noted that in *Makins v Elson [1977] STC 46* the dwelling house was held to include a caravan jacked up and resting on bricks. Contributing facts were that the wheels were not touching the ground and that electricity, water and telephone were connected.

Adjoining houses

4.5 It was held in *Batey v Wakefield [1980] STC 572* that a chalet bungalow, which had been built to house staff employed for the purpose of providing gardening, housekeeping and caretaking services for the benefit of the main house, was part of the main dwelling. In order to qualify for PPR, it's adjoining house (or part of it) must not be acquired for the purpose of realising a gain on the disposal nor must any expenditure be incurred on the property wholly or partly for the purpose of realising a gain from the disposal. This is set out in TCGA 1992 s 224(3).

The Inland Revenue do recognise that anyone who buys adjoining houses will hope that the property will appreciate in value. A realisation of this is not caught by the anti-avoidance legislation in TCGA 1992 s 224(3) if the property had been genuinely acquired for the use of a residence. The case that sets this out is *Jones v Wilcock [1996] STC (SCD) 389*. The Inland Revenue only use it where the primary purpose of the purchase was for early sale at a profit. However, it is likely that the treatment will constitute 'an adventure in the nature of trade' and if this is so the gain will be taxed under Schedule D Case 1 as an income tax charge which must take priority over a CGT charge. This is dealt with in more detail in Chapter **14**.

Artificial transactions in land

4.6 Section 224(3) of the TCGA 1992 most commonly applies where expenditure is incurred on the property to enhance its value prior to a sale. The effect is to deny exemption to part of the gain which is attributable to the particular expenditure. This can most aptly apply in the case of barn conversions. It could be that ICTA 1988 s 776 could be applied to the disposal of a main residence which is exempt from CGT – or it would be were it not for the provisions of TCGA 1992 s 224(3). The provision concerning artificial transactions in land is dealt with in more detail in Chapter **14**.

The scope of ICTA 1988 s 776 is broad and catches transactions which have little or no element of artificiality. Therefore the avoidance can be accidental or unwitting. This is of particular relevance to any farmer who is currently considering selling his farmhouse so as to make as much profit as possible, and attempting to obtain planning permission for another property on the same site, or to move to a smaller dwelling connected to the land. It is essential that taxpayers carefully review the implications of TCGA 1992 s 224(3) and ICTA 1988 s 776 when looking at any possible restructuring, including the disposal of possibly the most valuable asset, the farmhouse, ideally completely tax-free with the benefit of PPR.

Curtilage

4.7 The argument of whether separate outbuildings could be part of the main dwelling house was advanced in the apparently conflicting decisions of *Markey v Sanders [1987] STC 256* and *Williams v Merrylees [1987] STC 445*. However, the conflict was resolved in the Court of Appeal case *Lewis v Rook [1992] STC 171*, which established the more restrictive curtilage test. A cottage occupied by the gardener was not within the curtilage of the main dwelling house and therefore could not form part of it. Whilst *Lewis v Rook [1992] STC 171* appears to offer assistance where out dwellings are within the curtilage of the main house, this is not so because the Crown in that case reserved the right to argue in the future that a 'dwelling house' can never consist of more than one building.

To assist with the interpretation the Inland Revenue have published *Tax Bulletin* No 12 (August 1994) which gives the interpretation of the meaning of curtilage. The Inland Revenue have adopted the dictionary definition as being 'a small courtyard or piece of ground attached to a dwelling house and forming one enclosure with it', which emphasises the smallness of the area involved. Contrast this to *Markey v Sanders [1987] STC 256* (bungalow 130 metres from the house) and *Williams v Merrylees [1987] STC 445* (bungalow 200 metres from the main house).

The Inland Revenue will not normally regard another building as being within the curtilage of the main house (and hence not part of the dwelling house) in the following circumstances:

- where the buildings are dispersed, having no geographical relationship between them;
- where a wall or fence separates the two buildings;
- where a public road or stretch of tidal water separates the two buildings; or
- where the buildings pass under separate conveyances or are separately mentioned.

It is considered that a house and outbuildings around a courtyard will comprise a curtilage.

With the very beneficial tax relief of PPR combined with the ability to include in this relief gardens and grounds under TCGA 1992 s 222(1)(b) and the current ability to sometimes take advantage of planning opportunities for another dwelling house in the gardens and grounds, it is essential to clearly understand exactly what is meant by their definition for CGT PPR relief.

The meaning of garden

4.8 For PPR the garden takes its everyday meaning, ie an enclosed piece of ground devoted to the cultivation of flowers, vegetables or fruit. Grounds merely extends this definition to 'enclosed land surrounding or attached to a dwelling house or other building serving chiefly for ornament or recreation'.

The Inland Revenue are very aware of the development value of gardens and grounds and in the same way that the taxpayer is very keen to try and maximise the tax reliefs so too are the Inland Revenue to disallow it. This is clearly shown in the case of *Varty v Lynes (1976) STC 508*. In this case exemption was denied as the land was sold nearly a year after the house because it was no longer occupied and enjoyed with the residence. In practice, the Inland Revenue no longer apply this rule unless the land concerned has development value. This shows that it is a concession with virtually no practical value.

It is essential that the gardens and grounds must be occupied and enjoyed with the residence at the time they are sold. TCGA 1992 s 222(1)(b) is concerned with the present time, which should be contrasted with s 221(1)(a), which concerns itself with the past tense. It is not sufficient that the garden and grounds have been occupied and enjoyed with the residence at some time during the period of ownership. Land will be excluded from garden and grounds if used for an agricultural or other business purpose, since they would not be chiefly recreational or not occupied and enjoyed with the residence. Land fenced off from the residence to be sold for development is also excluded.

It is, however, not a requirement that the land is used exclusively for recreational purposes. For example, the owner-occupier of a guesthouse may allow guests to use the garden.

Within the provisions of this section, land includes buildings situated on it [TCGA 1992 s 288]. Buildings usually qualify if they are part of the garden or grounds within the permitted area and are not used for business purposes or let out.

Development opportunities

4.9 When a landowner does have development opportunities on land which is situated very close to the PPR it is clear that part of the planning advice can be to make sure that maximum use is made of the PPR relief as far as it does relate to the garden and grounds. Some tax practitioners would take this as far as to see development opportunities a long way in advance and to ensure that maximum use is made of the garden and grounds. It has been known for hedges to be planted (usually of the fast growing fir tree type) and for greater opportunity of recreational garden space over paddock land to be made.

Permitted area

4.10 This leads neatly to the question of what is the permitted area. It is generally accepted that this is probably the most contentious area. If the garden and grounds do not exceed 1/2 an hectare, which does include the site of the dwelling house, relief for the whole of the garden or grounds is given automatically. This will include the buildings situated on the relevant land provided that they are not used for business purposes or let out. If the garden and grounds exceed 1/2 an hectare relief will only be available for a larger area if that area is required for the reasonable enjoyment of the dwelling house having regard to the size and character of the dwelling house.

If the area of garden and grounds is greater than the permitted area, the part which is chosen is the part most suitable for occupation and enjoyment with the residence. This is found in TCGA 1992 s 222(4). Any buildings situated on that part will qualify provided that they are not used for business purposes or let out. Other buildings on the garden and grounds that are not quite as suitable will not qualify.

As set out in **4.5**, it is important to recognise that the dwelling house can comprise more than one building, as seen in *Batey v Wakefield [1980] STC 572*, and when determining whether additional garden and grounds in excess of 1/2 an hectare is required for reasonable enjoyment it is important to note that larger houses tend to require larger grounds. This might seem obvious but it is an important tax planning point.

'Required' incorporating Longson v Baker

4.11 How is the word 'required' defined? It is an objective test. One clear tax case is *Re Newhill Compulsory Purchase Order 1937, Paynes Application [1938] 2 All ER 163* in which du Parcq J stated:

> 'I call attention to the word "required". The use of it raises a question of fact which is necessarily a difficult one. Again, I do not wish to repeat myself, but one has to remember that it is pleasant, and, one must say, both an amenity and a convenience, to have a good deal of open space round one's house, but it does not follow that open space is required for the amenity or the convenience of the house. "Required", I think, in this section does not mean merely that the occupiers of the house would like to have it, or that they would miss it if they lost it, or that anyone proposing to buy the house would think less of the house without it than he would if it was preserved to it. "Required" means, I suppose, that without it there will be such a substantial deprivation of amenities or convenience that a real injury will be

done to the property owner and a question like that is obviously a question of fact.'

In the case of *Sharkey v Secretary of State for the Environment and South Buckinghamshire District Council (1990) 62 P&CR 126* it was held that 'required' meant something more than desirable. One of the most important cases in this respect is set out in *Longson v Baker [2000] STC (SCD) 244*. This relatively recent case gave a ruling that will be of great importance for landowners looking to dispose of the PPR and the surrounding ground.

In this case the taxpayer claimed that the permitted area (which included a farmhouse, stables and an outhouse all facing a central courtyard) amounted to 7.56 hectares. The claim failed despite the parties agreeing that the stables accommodating 12 horses were part of the dwelling. The Inspector contended that 'required' meant close to necessary. The permitted area was reduced to 1.054 hectares – exactly the same area that the previous owner secured. This appears to set a precedent in that, where the issue has cropped up in the past, the Inland Revenue may review earlier disposals of the property since 1965.

It is an interesting tax planning point that, when advising clients on their ability to claim PPR relief for the grounds, they should look at conveyance documents which may have set some form of precedence. Another source of reference for looking at PPR relief is found in the Valuation Office Manual in Section 8 *Principal Private Residence Relief* Part 4, 8.43. This gives an indication on how the district valuer will approach the objective test.

'In considering the area "required", the most obvious evidence to consider is the extent of the gardens/grounds enjoyed with houses of similar size and character in the locality. Evidence of sale prices is immaterial and should not be used.

The extent of the locality will for this purpose depend upon the proximity of sufficient comparables to obtain a fair impression. It may be necessary to bear in mind:

(i)   that there is a general tendency towards smaller gardens because of cost, convenience, lack of gardeners etc, and

(ii) that houses in urban localities are generally found to have smaller gardens/grounds than in rural districts.

It follows that houses which were built many years ago and/or are in districts which were once rural, but now urban, may no longer strictly require the area of garden/grounds which they retain. The lower end of the range of areas of garden/grounds occupied with comparable dwellings is evidence of requirement. Larger areas are often accounted for by historic reasons, or the owner's caprice. It should be sufficient to show that there are some closely comparable houses with 0.5 of a hectare or less. No value based test should be used.'

Electing for the principal private residence

4.12 When looking at PPR relief for landowners and farmers it is easy to forget some of the basic principles of this relief and ensure that they do apply to the farmer. No taxpayer can claim exemption on more than one house. If a farmer owns more than one, for example, a farm and a town house, he can elect within two years of the date of purchase of the second house which of them is to be his PPR for CGT purposes. If he fails to elect the issue becomes one of fact for the self-assessment return. No election is required where one of the properties is not owned but merely occupied under licence as, for example, job-related accommodation occupied under a service occupancy.

Job-related accommodation

4.13 Special privileges are accorded to a representative occupier. An individual who lives in job-related accommodation may find on leaving his job that another residence which he has owned has lost the CGT exemption for PPR. This would be because he had failed to occupy it continuously.

To meet this situation of the occupation of the job-related accommodation, for example, the farmhouse (after 30 July 1978) is treated as if it were occupation of the employee's own house providing he intends in due course to go and occupy it. This is set out in s 222 of TCGA 1992. Whether he does so intend is a question of fact. If he has occupied it before the relevant sale that would clearly represent persuasive evidence. If the sale occurs before occupation intention can still be demonstrated, particularly if the proceeds are applied to buy another home.

For the purposes of CGT the definition of job-related accommodation is set out below and there is a similar denial of relief where the accommodation is provided by a company for a director unless he has no material interest and works full-time, unless the company is non-profit making or a charity. The clear tax planning point here is that farmhouses owned within farming companies and lived in by directors must be given a careful review.

The conditions for the job-related accommodation are:

1   Where it is necessary for the proper performance of an employee's duties that he should reside in the accommodation [ICTA 1988 s 145(4)(a)].

2   Where the accommodation is provided for the better performance of the duties of his employment and he is in one of the kinds of employment in the case of which it is customary for employers to provide living accommodation to employees [ICTA 1988 s 145(4)(b)].

3   Where there is a special threat to an employee's security, special security arrangements are in force and the employee resides in the accommodation as part of these arrangements.

The most relevant, therefore, is the second item. This is the exemption most likely to be sought where employees are provided with accommodation on a rural estate or farm. One of the requirements is that the accommodation has been provided for the better performance of the duties of the employment: this requirement is clearly aimed at questioning the employer's reason for providing the accommodation.

The kinds of employment and the identification thereof do need review. Oliver Stanley, in his book *Taxation of Farmers and Landowners* (LexisNexis Butterworths Tolley), states that it is important to see whether a head gardener on a rural estate is likely to have duties very different from a gardener employed to tend a municipal park. Here, the question arises whether rural estate head gardeners are in a kind of employment distinct from gardeners in general. Stanley suggests that a careful examination is made of the duties of the employment contrasted with both those of similar employees on other rural estates and the duties common to the generic class to determine whether those of the rural estate employee are neither rare nor indistinguishable from the duties of the generic class.

Stanley also looks at this question of the provision of accommodation and whether or not it is customary. He quotes the *Vertigan [1988] STC 91* case, where the court determined there were three constituent factors to be examined: the statistical evidence on how common the practice was; evidence on how long the practice had gone on; and whether the practice had achieved general acceptance. Stanley advises examination of the CLA published survey in 1991 of 313 rural estates which obtained evidence in respect of 4,790 rural estate employees, of whom 3,704 were provided with accommodation. This table can be found in Oliver Stanley's book (*Taxation of Farmers and Landowners* (LexisNexis Butterworths Tolley)) at section 5.51.

Tenant farmers

4.14   The CGT relief for PPR can be of interest when looking at tenant farmers who have to live in the farmhouse of the tenant farm, but have their own house that qualifies as a PPR. It is vital to consider the whole position concerning occupancy of farm cottages by workers and retired workers, especially with fewer and fewer farms employing farm workers and providing them with their own cottage and the move towards contract farming. This is compounded by a falling workforce due to the reductions in farming income.

Partnerships, trusts and beneficiaries

4.15   As part of any tax planning exercise, it is imperative to see who owns what and who lives where within the farming unit . There are a large number of farms throughout the UK where farmhouses are owned jointly by a partnership, where one partner owns one house and lives in another, where the farm is owned by the limited company that farms the land and also where the house is owned in a trust or settlement.

Exemption is available to trustees if during their ownership of a property a beneficiary under the trust has been occupying it as his only or main residence [TCGA 1992 s 225]. This applies whether he is entitled to occupy or is occupying by permission of the trustee. A similar concession is available to personal representatives who sell a property used immediately before or after the death as a main or only residence by beneficiaries under the Will or intestacy who are entitled to the whole or substantially the whole of the proceeds of the sale, whether absolutely or for life. This is set out in the Inland Revenue *Tax Bulletin* No 12 (August 1994). For more details on Trusts see Chapter **17**.

It must also be noted that where there are lodgers or paying guests, for example, where a paying guest lives with the owner and family sharing accommodation and meals, that the exemption is not lost. However, where the whole or part of any PPR has been let by the owner as residential accommodation some relief could be lost. The case of *Pod v Mud (1987)* helped to give direction for joint, but unrelated, owner-occupier. In the case where the owner-occupiers are not husband and wife they will each be entitled to relief. Each one of them is treated as having an undivided share in all the property. This is on the assumption that each has unrestricted access to the whole property even though some parts may in practice not be used by both the joint owners.

Preserving principal private residence

4.16   In summary, it is important that when carrying out the full exercise of asset ownership the whole question of PPR is not only reviewed but action is taken to make sure that it is preserved and the correct conditions are in place. This is not just with regard to ownership but period of occupancy, the size of the garden and all the points mentioned previously. The question of trying to create artificial PPR relief must be looked at. An example is found in *Goodwin v Curtis [1998] STC 475* in which case the taxpayer purchased a farmhouse on 1 April 1985 and personally moved into it. On 11 April the farmhouse was advertised for sale and it was sold on 3 May. The Commissioners found that the taxpayer's occupation lacked permanence and continuity and that the farmhouse had been purchased with a view to realising a gain on its disposal. It was not his PPR and relief was not due. In this case the finding was upheld both in the High Court and the Court of Appeal.

Capital loss on principal private residence

4.17   In the current climate of rising prices it is always assumed that PPR relief will be claimed. However, there have been cases where capital losses have been made on property and the taxpayer has tried to deny relief saying that the property was purchased for the intention of realising a gain.

This is set out in *Jones v Wilcock [1996] STC (SCD) 398*. In this case the taxpayer purchased a property in need of modernisation and spent £20,000 on improving it. The property was sold five years later and a substantial capital loss was made, as the taxpayer wanted to set the loss against other gains. In this case the Inland Revenue held that the expectation of a gain on the sale had been hope but not a purpose. The Inland Revenue stated that there was no sign of commerciality in the improvement expenditure to suggest an adventure or concern in the nature of trade. Nor was there clear evidence that realising a gain or disposal had been even in part a purpose. The taxpayer had bought the house with a view to providing himself and his family with a home. With the increase in value in property at the present time it is hoped that this case will be beneficial to the taxpayer.

Separate garden

4.18   Another factor that farmers and landowners must consider is the question of a separate garden. The case of *Wakeling v Pearce [1995] STC (SCD) 96,* in which relief was contested by the Inland Revenue over the issue of the land, should not be overlooked. Here, the taxpayer had a separate piece of land 30 feet away from the bungalow where she lived. She did not use the land disposed of with the land on which her bungalow was situated. However, it was held that the distance between the two pieces of land did not disqualify relief. The taxpayer had not ceased to use the land disposed of at the time of sale. The Inland Revenue sought to clarify this in *Tax Bulletin* No 18 (August 1995) and they set out the following conditions which must be in place for a separate garden to qualify:

- It must be land of which the owner has occupation and enjoyment with the residence.
- It must be garden or grounds of the residence.
- The area of land must not exceed the permitted area.

Where land is physically separated from a house the Inland Revenue take the view that the fact that it is in common ownership and used for a garden does not automatically secure relief. It must be shown objectively to be naturally and traditionally a garden of the house so as to be normally offered as such to a prospective purchaser. This again is important to many farmers who historically have built additional farmhouses with a separate garden.

House and garden sold separately

4.19 As set out at **4.8** it is also useful to consider the scenario where the house and the garden are sold separately. In the case of *Varty v Lynes [1976] STC 508* the house was sold first and the garden separately afterwards. Grounds covered by the house and garden together constituted less than one acre, but the exemption was lost because once the house had been sold the garden ceased to be occupied and enjoyed with the house. The Inland Revenue will not normally take this point unless the garden has development value; but it is clearly this development potential which makes not only a valuable asset for the farmer, but also a tax headache.

Barn conversion and redundant buildings

4.20 Another area that must be closely looked at is barn conversions, which are obviously very prevalent amongst the current farming community. There is a risk that the sale of such conversions could be caught under the anti-avoidance rules of TCGA 1992 s 224(3). This section denies the relief on a residence wholly or partly for the purpose of realising a gain on its disposal.

As mentioned above, the Inland Revenue interpretation RI75 specifically draws attention to barn conversions and other development of outbuildings or land attached to the dwelling house, which in their view are caught by this sub-section. The Inland Revenue might try to withdraw relief on that part of the gain, which is attributable to particular expenditure.

It must be noted that where the relevant expenditure is incurred on obtaining planning permission of a moving restricted covenant the restriction is not applied. Thus, generally a garden with planning permission can be sold and relief under the PPR obtained. However, where the owner of the residence decides to develop the garden themselves this will fall into tax.

These matters are discussed in more detail in CHAPTER **14** but it must be noted that land where a farmer decides to develop a redundant building himself in order to maximise development potential will be taxed under Schedule D Case 1 and not as a gain. The property would be treated as having been appropriated to the trade under TCGA 1992 s 161(1). The effect of this is that the farmer is seen to have disposed of the asset at market value at the time of apportionment and a CGT computation fails to be made. There is, however, a form of holdover relief contained in TCGA 1992 s 161(3) which has an effect of taxing the gain up to the date of apportionment as part of the trading result rather than as a capital gain. Obviously only the capital gain element of the transaction is eligible for rollover relief.

Period of occupation

4.21 In relation to the period of occupation, the extent of exemption is proportionate to the extent to which the house has been occupied by an owner during his period of ownership. If he has lived in the house throughout all capital gains are exempt.

In addition to this, as long as he has lived in the house as his PPR at any time then the last 36 months of ownership are exempt. If, for half the period of ownership, he lived elsewhere and let his house then only half the gain would be exempt. Again, the last 36 months will be exempt.

There are a series of exceptions to the general rule designed to meet special circumstances. These include overlapping ownership, breaks in occupation, absences abroad, employer's requirements, occupation deferred use, alterations to use and representative occupation. This is again set out in some detail in Oliver Stanley's *Taxation of Farmers and Landowners* (LexisNexis Butterworths Tolley) at section 7.44.

Inheritance tax

Agricultural property relief (APR) at 100%

4.22 Essentially farmhouses are eligible for 100% APR with additionally the ability to claim BPR where appropriate. In practice, few difficulties have arisen over claiming APR on a farmhouse which is fairly modest in size and which has for generations been occupied by farming families, together with any adjoining land.

In the light of current prices being achieved for the sale of farms and farmhouses, it could be stated that every claim for APR on a farmhouse will be looked at in some detail by the CTO.

Character appropriate

4.23 In order to maximise the APR claim, every farmhouse should be reviewed with regard to ensuring that it would be deemed to be of a character appropriate to the property. The summary criteria are:

- *The primary character test* – is the farm essentially a house with some land or an agricultural business incorporating a suitably-sized farmhouse?
- *The local practice test* – is it quite normal for a house of this type and size to be matched with land of this quality of use and size?
- *The commercial viability or financial support test* – is the size and character of the farmhouse in line with the scale of the agricultural operation? To take this further, can the agricultural operation support the owners of the farmhouse?

It must be stated here that the occupation rules apply to a farmhouse as well as to any other land. To reiterate the position, the owner must occupy the property for agricultural purposes for at least two years before the date of the transfer or must have owned it for at least seven years prior to the transfer with some person occupying it for agricultural purposes throughout that time.

Financial viability and the economic test

4.24 The question of financial viability is one of great interest in the current climate of very low farming income. APR is at risk where there are changes to the business. Examples of this would be as follows.

- When agricultural land is sold, gifted or put to non-agricultural use and the transferor retains the farmhouse to live in.
- Where the owner of the farmhouse lets the land but retains the farmhouse.

It will be necessary to look at economic tests here to determine whether the farm can support the respective farming families. This will be very interesting in view of the fall in farming income. Other situations are where there is a large estate where the transferor has an interest in farms in-hand, ie known as home farming, as well as let farms. In this case the farmhouse occupied by the transferor will have to be shown to have a character appropriate to the in-hand farms and not the let farms.

When looking at the primary character appropriate to the farm-house, use can be made of the Valuation Agency's Practice Notes (Chapter 1B Practice Note 10) which states 'is the unit primarily a dwelling with some land or is it an agricultural unit incorporating such a dwelling as is appropriate? Is the property as a whole an agricultural unit, ie land albeit amounting to a small hectarage and a few buildings which is not suitable primarily for agricultural use?' This would be important in the recent case of *Dixon v IRC [2002] STC (SCD) 53* (see **4.25** below).

Other areas that the district valuer might look at are how the agri-cultural unit would be described to the outside world. For example, if it were to be marketed by an independent agent. It is also important to consider other comparable farming activities in the local area. It is known that the district valuer will look to see whether the farming operation is commercially viable, ie does it produce sufficient profits to support the occupant of the farmhouse?

In looking at this they will also look at what income could have been produced on the farm if it had been carried out by a reasonably competent farmer. The district valuer does take into account the fact that farming profitability can decline due to old age or infirmity, which would often be appropriate to an estate on death.

Dixon v IRC

4.25 The recent case of *Dixon v IRC [2002] STC (SCD) 53* gives an interesting ruling.

In this case APR was denied on the basis that the cottage was not of a type and character appropriate to agricultural land. In actual fact the opposite was the case. The orchard and garden were of a character appropriate to the cottage, which in truth was a private residence in a rural area and could be regarded by a lay person as being a residential cottage with land.

Although there had been some agricultural activity on the land it was not enough to encourage the Inland Revenue to allow APR in respect of the cottage, garden and orchard on the grounds. Sheep had been allowed to graze on the land and from time-to-time fruit from the orchard was sold for money. The owner of a neighbouring property grew vegetables and fruit commercially and would pick fruit in the orchard and sell it with his own fruit. The sale proceeds were about £70 per year. A farmer had at times been allowed to graze sheep on the land and in return his wife carried out general household duties for the deceased. The price received for the fruit had not been included in income tax returns and this is an important point.

The principle appears to be that the purpose of APR was not to provide relief for private residence and gardens but to relieve land and pasture use for agriculture. This decision indicates that it is not simply enough for a person to buy an attractive cottage in the country, keep some form of livestock there and try to avoid IHT on the value of the property. It is essential that the property is first of all truly used for agricultural purposes and then relief should also apply to any cottages and farm buildings occupied with the land, as long as they are of a character appropriate to the property.

The whole question of the validity of APR is something that is causing a large number of agricultural practitioners some sleepless nights. At one end of the scale there are some genuine farming activities which, if looked at in the cold light of day by a harsh tax inspector, might result in some loss of APR on certain parts of the asset. At the other end of the scale there are tax practitioners who are actively encouraging anybody who lives in anything like a rural or semi-rural location, with some degree of land, to try and establish some form of business, often of an agricultural nature on this land, so as to become eligible for not only APR for IHT but also business asset taper relief (BATR) for CGT.

It is a pity that the case was at such an extreme level of the scale, ie hardly any agricultural activity at all, without accounts being prepared, without income being declared on the tax return etc. The sadness is that the facts of the case cannot be used to help give practitioners and clients guidelines as to what is and what is not allowable in the eyes of the Inland Revenue under the current trading conditions.

Nevertheless, the case does give practitioners some practical tax planning points. Firstly, if there is income it should be recorded on the tax return; and, secondly, if such a valuable claim as APR is to be made it is essential to ensure that the case is more valid and the conditions are adhered to to a far greater extent. Many practitioners are aware of clients who are virtually inventing agricultural activities around some small plot of land in the hope of obtaining APR. In the Home Counties and in areas close to them a small cottage with a small parcel of land can easily be valued at a figure in excess of £1 million and the APR is therefore very substantial and the benefits of establishing a trading activity for the required period of time is of the utmost importance.

Farm business tenancies (FBTs)

4.26　The tax position of FBTs is looked at in more detail in Chapter **11**. It is worthwhile to note that the period of business activity necessary to obtain the APR is two years. It must also be noted that in order to claim APR for a farm business tenancy (FBT) the period of ownership is seven years. Therefore, anybody moving to the country with a view to obtaining IHT relief on a large amount of their assets must look carefully at the structure on which they trade.

Not only does *Dixon v IRC [2002] STC (SCD) 53* show the need to have the correct conditions in place if a landowner wants to take farming activity further and actually have a neighbour farm the land with the use of a FBT, but he must also be aware of the fact that the FBT is a much slower route to obtaining APR, ie seven years instead of two. A serious planning point with regard to this relief is to always look at the farming activity with a view to the landowner themselves farming or using contract or share farming agreements for the first two years, and *then* taking the route of (the sometimes easier) FBT once the conditions for APR have been established.

It must also be noted that whilst a FBT will allow the farmer APR on the land generally the asset does not qualify for the business reliefs available in respect of CGT, eg rollover relief and BATR, and likewise where there has been no trading activity as such, just a FBT, the APR will only apply to the land and not to the farmhouse in the majority of cases.

Structure of farming

4.27   In a changing farming climate it is essential that practitioners review the structure of the farming activity, the tax computation, the commerciality and viability of the operation and assess how potential reliefs for IHT and CGT could be reduced by the current lack of commerciality and farming activities. Many landowning clients automatically assume that the asset of their farmhouse will escape IHT and it is essential for the practitioner not only to make sure that the necessary conditions are in place, where possible, but also to warn the client of the potential loss of relief.

Other areas of concern include a restriction to the provision concerning BPR where relief is restricted to 50% (as opposed to 100%) where the assets are held by an individual and used in the company or partnership of which he is a member. This is explained in some detail in **Chapter 13**. In some partnerships farmhouses are kept out of the main partnership accounts as the partners feel happier with the ownership of this asset. Likewise, BPR is limited on property used by a limited company but held outside the limited company.

With the move towards diversification and more emphasis being placed on BPR as opposed to APR, this could become a very important factor and it is essential for every farming enterprise to review in exactly what business structure the farmhouse should be held.

Starke v IRC

4.28   Another case that is interesting to look at in regard to the claiming of IHT relief on the farmhouse is that of *Starke v IRC [1995] STC 689*. In this instance the claim was for a six-bedroom farmhouse and an assortment of outbuildings standing in a 2.5 acre site – essentially a medium-sized farm which carried on mixed farming. It had several small areas of enclosed land. In this case, the appellant tried to use the Interpretation Act 1978 to argue that the farmhouse was included in the interpretation of land, as this would include buildings and other structures unless there was a challenge. The rest of the land was mainly owned by a farming company, and it is this land and farmhouse in different ownership that must be given careful consideration. This case turned on the character appropriate position of the farm buildings. The Court of Appeal dismissed the appeal by the executors and refused APR on the house. Currently, therefore, it should be noted that it cannot immediately be assumed that a farmhouse will automatically qualify for IHT relief.

It is not only where the land is owned by a company that *Starke v IRC [1995] STC 689* could apply. It is also important to look at trusts. It can be argued that for as long as there is substantial unity of ownership between the farmhouse and the land which is farmed, APR can still be claimed on the farmhouse. However, if the farmhouse does go into a trust it may, once it is within the trust, cease to be of a character appropriate in the context of the ownership. It is mainly with the position concerning a discretionary trust where the most risk lies. If there is an interest in possession trust the deeming provisions of IHTA 1984 s 49 might protect the position.

In Toby Harris' book *Business and Agricultural Property Relief* (LexisNexis Butterworths Tolley) he states two instances where he thinks that a difference of ownership between the agricultural land and other types of estates might not be, as he calls it, 'fatal' to a claim for APR. Firstly, where land is owned by a company controlled by the transferor that land is treated as part of his estate. Secondly, land which is occupied by the transferor under an agricultural tenancy is treated as part of his estate regardless of the value of the tenancy as part of that estate which might be negligible.

In *Taxation of Farmers and Landowners* (LexisNexis Butterworths Tolley) by Oliver Stanley, the author states that 'there is no restriction of APR in respect of that part of the farmhouse which is used for non-farming purposes as there is for CGT. This seems to be so even if there is another building used as a farm office separate from the farmhouse itself'. Stanley goes on to say that the CTO have sought to narrow the scope of what constitutes a farmhouse of a character appropriate to the property.

When looking at the claim for APR consider situations where there are very large and valuable farmhouses that are not actually being fully occupied. There are cases where parts of farmhouses are being left to moulder and it is difficult to argue that parts of these buildings are occupied for any purpose, whether it be agricultural or otherwise. In these instances, it could be argued that APR should be restricted to that part of the building actually being occupied.

Land occupied under a grazing licence

Right to vacant possession

4.29   In this instance provided the landowner has the right to obtain vacant possession within 24 months he may qualify for APR at 100%. If the landowner grants a FBT then in relation to the farmhouse he is no longer a farmer but merely a landlord. The landowner is not occupying the farmhouse for the purposes of agriculture. The right to APR on the farmhouse could then be lost. The alternative is to grant a right of herbage to a grazier. The landowner must be very careful when trying to ensure that this scheme succeeds. There is the case of *IRC v Forsythe Grant (1943) 25 TC 369* where the owner was considered to be occupying the land for the purposes of husbandry and it is accepted for both purposes of income tax and IHT that there was 100% relief due on both farm and farmhouse. In this instance the income will be taxed as farming income under Schedule D Case 1 and the tax payable will preserve any entitlement that had already been achieved for CGT.

Grant to right of herbage

4.30   It is essential when looking at a grant to right of herbage that the responsibility for any manureing, seeding or fertilising the land are retained by the landowner. The CLA have prepared a form of deed to grant a right of herbage and this has obtained approval from the Inland Revenue. There are essentially seven points which must be achieved. The points concerning this whole area are discussed in some detail in Chapter 11 and it is worth noting an observation of the Financial Secretary to the Treasury when looking at agreements in the context of Schedule D that 'owners wishing to enjoy the generous tax reliefs that trading status brings should take care to ensure that they comply with the statutory definition of farming'.

The principal seven points of the CLA recommended deed are as follows:

1   The owner must harrow and roll the grass as necessary.

2   The owner must cut or spray all weeds to prevent seeding.
3   The grazier must covenant not to mow or cut the grass.
4   The owner must cultivate, sow and establish the grass crop.
5   The owner must fertilise the grass crop in the spring and through the season as necessary.
6   The owner must do all mowing that may be required for whatever reason or purpose on the ground to be grazed.
7   The owner must do any hedging, fencing and ditching needed and any other work of a proprietorial nature.

This is dealt with in detail in CHAPTER 11.

It should be noted that not all owners of the farmhouse will have the required machinery to deal with the art of fertilising, hedging and ditching and they might wish to employ a contractor to deal with this. It would be unwise for the contractor to be the same person who has the grazing arrangement.

There is a fundamental principle that for grazing income to be accepted as farming under Schedule D the landowner must be able to show that the is the 'paramount occupier'. Thus, the owner must be able to show that he is in paramount occupation and that he will be regarded as the trading farmer.

It must always be remembered that the Inland Revenue will look behind the wording of a legal deed to see what are the actual facts of the case.

Agricultural value

4.31   Other points to note are that the inheritance tax relief is given only on the agricultural value of a farmhouse, ie on the assumption that the property is not capable of use other than as a farmhouse. The agricultural value is the value of the farmhouse, the asset, if subject to a perpetual covenant prohibiting its use otherwise than as an agricultural property. This is set out in IHTA 1984 s 115(3). (See **13.2**.)

It has been suggested that a perpetual agricultural covenant on a farmhouse might reduce its value considerably. Oliver Stanley uses the figure of one-third. However, it should be possible to claim BPR on the difference between the agricultural value and the full market value. The difference between full market value and agricultural value will be of particular relevance in areas such as the Home Counties. It is also important to look at the position where there is more than one farmhouse, ie where separate farmhouses are occupied by different members of the farming family in partnership.

Working farmer provisions

4.32 When trying to look at farmhouses and their eligibility for APR it could be useful to consider the concept of the working farmer provisions. It used to have much greater importance and is therefore not discussed in great detail in this book. However, it does give a guide to whether the farmhouse is seen to be of a character appropriate to the working farmer test. This related to working farmer relief. Before 10 March 1981 working farmers had the benefit of gaining two advantages where they let their land before 10 March 1981. Firstly, that the value on which it could be applied was less; and, secondly, because the land was let and the relief was partly available on agricultural property.

It is essential that the practitioner has a working knowledge of working farmer relief in looking at how the district valuer could apply this in such matters as APR under today's rules. Some help was gained from the Finance Act 1975 (FA 1975) Sch 8 para 3(3), which defined the main, but not exclusive, test of 'wholly or mainly engaged' by providing that where at least three-quarters of the relevant income of the transferor was derived directly from his engagement in agriculture in the UK then the condition is taken as being satisfied.

The relevant income is the aggregate of income in any five of the last seven years of assessment immediately preceding the transfer, including unearned income but excluding income from a pension, superannuation, other allowances, deferred pay or compensation for loss of office. For this purpose, the rules as to aggregation of a wife's income, which were enforced in 1991, are to be disregarded.

Where a transferor fails the 75% test he might still show by other means, such as time spent on other sources of income, that he was a working farmer. In certain situations a farming widow or widower enjoys the benefit of transferred years to help satisfy the seven-year test.

There are those that argue that a farming family who have farmed for a large number of years and meet the type of conditions required in the working farmer relief are far more likely to succeed in a claim for APR on a farmhouse than someone who has other income outside of the farm and has acquired the property relatively recently.

Farmhouse held in a limited company

4.33 No relief is available for shares in a company if the business of that company consists wholly or mainly of dealing in shares or securities, land or buildings or making a holding investment. The question of whether a qualifying business was carried on or whether the assets concerned were merely being exploited as investments has been given a lot of attention by the Inland Revenue. Where the farmhouse is held in a limited company it must be given special attention, as indeed all farming companies (see **13.14–13.16**) must be mindful of these provisions and the possibility of jeopardising APR and BPR.

Agricultural property including the farmhouse may be the underlying asset of the company. This then qualifies as a relevant business property. APR will be applied automatically through the operation of IHTA 1984 s 114(1) and BPR will be available on the value of the underlying assets reduced by APR. APR will not be available in respect of minority holdings of shares in a farming company but 100% BPR will apply where, as will often be the case, the holding is in unquoted shares.

A significant limitation on BPR is that where a company owns a tenanted farm, BPR may not be available because the company may not be trading. The company could be wholly or mainly holding investments within IHTA 1984 s 105(3). Thus, if a farmhouse were in this company there would be problems with a claim for APR and BPR.

With the move to diversification and more land failing in its claim for APR but succeeding in its claim for BPR it will of course make the claims for the farmhouse more vulnerable.

In summary of the danger areas another problem can arise under the hobby farming rules (see **CHAPTER 12**) whereby a farm fails in its commerciality and therefore has losses restricted under ICTA 1988 s 397 and this can result in a loss of claim for APR. However, there are differing schools of thought, as set out in that chapter, as to how ruthless the inspector can be in disallowing the claim if there has been a previous period of strong profitability, a big history of farming etc.

Death in a hospital or nursing home

4.34 The inheritance tax reliefs in respect of the farmhouse could be at risk where the farmer dies away from home. A farmer may not be in physical occupation of the farmhouse at his death, if he dies in a hospital or a nursing home. However, the CTO are known to grant relief in cases where the farmer had every expectation of returning to the farmhouse were it not for his intervening death, and have been known to give relief in cases of absence of up to two years.

Farmhouse — the danger areas

4.35 It is important, therefore, to summarise for tax planners the points which could give rise to problems on the claim for APR on a farmhouse. They are as follows:

- Land not of a character appropriate to the house, eg very large house, small unit.
- No history of commerciality – see *Dixon v IRC [2002] STC (SCD) 53* (see CHAPTER 12).
- Land used for diversification purposes jeopardising APR/BPR claim on farmhouse.
- Farmhouse held outside of farming partnership or limited company.
- Farmhouse held within limited company with question as to qualification in total for BPR.
- More than one farmhouse on farming unit – character appropriate review required.
- Hobby farming (see CHAPTER 12).

Protecting the Farm's Assets   5

Julie Butler

- **The risk of only 50% IHT relief**
  Where farm assets are used in the business but held outside the business, the inheritance tax (IHT) relief can be restricted to 50% and not 100%.

- **Farm cottage not occupied by farm workers**
  These valuable assets can be at risk from the loss of capital gains tax (CGT) and IHT relief, and the tax position must be protected.

- **The bold step of gifting assets now**
  In order to maximise the current favourable tax reliefs there are strong arguments for making gifts now. This must not be undertaken lightly and consideration to gifts with reservation of benefit together with 'failed PETs' must not be overlooked.

- **Protecting and managing assets**
  There are a multitude of pitfalls and opportunities for the tax planner and landowner, such as where the cash deposits and liabilities are allocated and how to best use related property. With a move from agricultural property relief (APR) eligibility to business property relief (BPR), great emphasis must be placed on understanding the interaction.

Introduction

5.1 Having looked at the protection of the farmhouse at length, let us now look at the protection of other farm assets to ensure maximum tax relief under the inheritance tax (IHT) rules. Many of the points are contained in Chapter **13** in more detail, but this chapter is meant to be an aide-memoir for IHT problems that can befall farmers, especially those looking towards diversification. The basic inheritance tax rates, exemptions and reliefs are dealt with in Chapter **18** on Wills and in Chapter **19** on tax planning through financial services.

The theme of this chapter was featured in *Farmer's Weekly* in March 2002 by Andrew Shirley under the heading 'Farm assets at risk'. Two very useful 'tools' to protect farm assets are the well drafted Will and Trust deeds. These are dealt with in Chapter **18** and Chapter **17** respectively. Farm assets must also be protected from problems such as divorce, and this subject receives serious review in Chapter **16**. It is relevant in the current climate to look at how assets can be protected through financial services and this is dealt with in Chapter **19**.

Business property relief (BPR) — 50% relief is not enough

5.2   When deciding who should own what and where, it is necessary to see how 100% relief can be reduced to 50% relief. This is dealt with in more detail in Chapter **13** on the interaction of agricultural property relief (APR) and business property relief (BPR), but a simple summary is set out below.

100% relief is available in respect of a business carried on by a sole trader, a partnership interest and any unquoted shares in a company. 50% relief is available in respect of land, buildings, machinery or plant owned by an individual and used by a company which he controls or by a partnership of which he is a partner or by a quoted company of which he controls shares.

The property must have been owned by the transferor throughout the two-year period prior to transfer, or it must have replaced other relevant business property and the combined period of ownership must amount to two out of the five years prior to the transfer. In respect of replacement business property, BPR is given only on the lower of the value of the original property or replacement property (see **5.17**, **13.13** and **13.17–13.25** where this is discussed in more detail).

EXAMPLES OF 100% RELIEF

1   Sole trader business.
2   Partnership interest.
3   Shares in an unquoted company.
4   Business assets held in trust (transferred with the company).

> **EXAMPLES OF 50% RELIEF**
>
> 5 Land, buildings, machinery or plant owned by an individual used by a company he controls or by a partnership in which he is a member.
> 6 Business assets held in trust (not transferred with business).
> 7 Controlling holding of shares in a quoted company.
>
> Is the landowner aware that by holding assets outside of the partnership or company he is jeopardising 100% relief? It could be that there are strong personal, family or control factors that dictate the ownership status. Has the client been warned of the problem? The inheritance tax position on divorcing couples is set out at **16.32**.

Excepted assets for BPR — how can this be avoided?

5.3 For practical planning purposes it is essential that a claim for IHT relief does not fail due to certain assets being excepted [Inheritance Tax Act 1984 (IHTA 1984) s 112].

For the purposes of calculating BPR, the value of the relevant business property should exclude excepted assets, which are those:

- that have not been used wholly or mainly for business purposes throughout the two years preceding the transfer (or since acquisition if acquired within the two-year period); and
- not required for future use by the business.

The purpose of the rules is to prevent abuses by denying relief to what are essentially non-business assets. This is achieved by isolating those assets which, at the time of the transfer, either were not used in the business or had been inadequately or too briefly used, and those not actually required for future use in the business, eg surplus cash balances (*Barclays Bank Trust Co v IRC [1998] STC (SCD) 125*). With the farming crisis assets can become 'too briefly' used. The tax planner must focus on the words 'inadequately' or 'too briefly used': it is important not to leave assets redundant whilst alternatives are looked at.

It is permissible for a business asset to replace another business asset provided that both were used for periods comprising at least two years within the five immediately before the transfer.

Where only part of any land or building is used exclusively for business purposes, that part will be treated as a separate asset qualifying for relief with the other non-qualifying part treated as an excepted asset [IHTA 1984 s 112(4)]. This can provide assistance where a room in the farmhouse is used exclusively for office purposes, as it would not qualify for APR. It may be possible to argue for BPR for other rooms where there is substantial and genuine business use (eg the kitchen) (see CHAPTER **4**). However, excepted assets include assets used wholly or mainly for personal benefit [IHTA 1984 s 112(6)].

Farm cottages — maximising the rate of IHT relief

5.4 The tax planner must try to maximise the IHT relief for cottages occupied by farm workers.

100% relief will be available (provided the two-year occupation/ seven-year ownership conditions have been satisfied) if:

1   the occupation began on or after 1 September 1995; or
2   the tenancy began before 10 March 1981 and the 'working farmer' tests are satisfied.

Relief may therefore be available in the case of an occupier with no protected service tenancy, perhaps a partner or an occupier with the benefit of an assured agricultural tenancy; so, for example, a farm worker or an occupier who has an assured shorthold tenancy will normally be regarded as occupying the cottage for agricultural purposes.

It is therefore imperative that every farmer and landowner reviews all cottages in their ownership to ensure that they qualify in the first instance for 100% APR and that this is not restricted to a 50% claim. 50% APR applies where the landowner does not have the right to vacant possession of a farm cottage occupied by an employee with protection under the Rent (Agriculture) Act 1976 or the Housing Act 1988 because the landowner cannot grant 'unimpeded physical enjoyment' of a cottage so occupied. Where farm cottages have protected rights that have existed since before 1 September 1995 then the 50% restriction hits (see **5.21** for vacant possession). Where a claim for APR fails a claim for BPR may be eligible under the provisions of the case *Farmer (Farmer's Executors) v IRC [1999] STC (SCD) 321*. This is looked at in detail in CHAPTER **13**. The conditions are complex and to fully protect farming clients the maximum relief under APR must be sought. Until more cases such as '*Farmer*' have been tested it would be risk-taking in the extreme to place too heavy reliance on BPR because of the complications. The farmer and landowner must be forewarned and a serious review of all assets should be undertaken.

The difficulty arises in relation to cottages first occupied after 10 March 1981, ie without the protection of the old Working Farmer Relief and before 1 September 1995 (when the new rules began to operate).

In these cases the nature of the occupation determined the rate of relief. Where there is an unprotected service tenancy or an assured shorthold tenancy 100% relief is available. Where there is an assured agricultural occupation, whether by a farm worker or by a retired farm worker or by a surviving spouse of a farm worker, the rate is 50% only.

The provision in IHTA 1984 s 115(2) relating to farm cottages is extended by ESC F16. That concession provides that, on a transfer of agricultural property which includes a cottage occupied by a retired farm employee, or by the widow or widower of such an employee, the condition as to the occupation for agricultural purposes is regarded as satisfied with respect to the cottage if one of two conditions is satisfied, namely:

1 the occupier is a statutorily-protected tenant (for example, under Housing Act 1988, Rent (Agriculture) Act 1976 or similar legislation in Northern Ireland or Scotland); or
2 the occupation is under a lease granted to the farm employee for his or her life and the life of any surviving spouse as part of the contract of employment of the employee. That contract of employment must be by the landlord for agricultural purposes.

The first of these situations arises when someone employed in agriculture for the previous two years has occupied a dwelling house provided by the employer. Depending on the date when the tenancy licence or occupancy began, that employee's right of occupation is normally protected under the 1976 Act or is protected as an assured agricultural occupancy under the 1988 Act or, in Scotland or Northern Ireland, under other legislation giving similar results. That protection can be extend to any living surviving spouse following the death of the employee. The second situation will arise where there is a similar result from any other lease granted to an employee as part of his or her terms of employment for the purpose of agriculture.

Interaction with the income tax position cannot be overlooked. It is interesting to turn here to the Inspector's Manual on farm cottages at IM2278:

> 'Where a cottage is provided rent-free for a farm employee, related expenditure of a revenue nature which is incurred wholly and exclusively for the purposes of the trade and does not otherwise offend the provisions of ICTA 1988 s 74 is an admissible deduction in computing farm profits.'

Tenanted farm owned in a limited company

5.5 It might be that agricultural property is the main asset in a limited company. This should qualify as relevant business property with APR being applied automatically in the first instance. BPR may apply to the assets which did not qualify under APR.

APR is not available on minority holdings in the shares of a farming company. However, 100% BPR will be available against the minority holding providing the requirements are met. The rules relating to replacement property set out at **5.17** will apply.

This does lead to the big problem of a tenanted farm being owned in a limited company as IHTA 1984 s 105(3) provisions of 'wholly or mainly holding investments' means that the minority holding fails in its claim for APR and BPR. Clients must be made aware of this potential failure.

A majority holding may seek the benefit of 50% APR if it can be shown that the company has owned the farm for seven years and the majority holding has been held for a minimum of seven years.

Deed of variation — surviving spouse exemption

5.6 There are some very basic IHT planning techniques that are often overlooked by the farmer and landowner. These include the nil-rate band (increased to £250,000 by Finance Act 2002), the deed of variation and surviving spouse exemption. The need for a Will, the tax planning associated therewith and the problems of intestacy are set out in CHAPTER **18**.

The farmer and landowner will generally own assets that do not qualify for APR and BPR and the tax planner will have to look to the nil-rate band and the surviving spouse exemption for tax relief. This can be incorporated in Will planning but if this is not achieved then the Will can be 'varied' by the beneficiaries within two years of the date of death. For variations on or after 1 August 2002 there will be no need to send in a formal election for exemption from CGT and IHT provided the deed specifies the exemption will apply.

The surviving spouse exemption can be used for tax planning. If the surviving spouse is fit and healthy there can be scope for further potentially exempt transfers (PETs). If on the first death there are non-business assets, which should be subject to inheritance tax but escape under the surviving spouse exemption, then the surviving spouse can make potentially exempt transfers in the hope that he/she survives the required seven years.

It is frequently the case that a Will creates a trust for the benefit of the surviving spouse, who has the right to income as it arises but no right to the capital, which is passed under the terms of the Will to the children at the death of the surviving spouse. Under the IHT regime, no tax charges arises on the property that passes to such a trust, as a consequence of the inter-spouse exemption. On the death of the surviving spouse, the property in trust in which the surviving spouse has an interest in possession is treated as if it were property beneficially owned by the surviving spouse and, thereby, attracts a charge to IHT. The use of Trusts is dealt with in more detail in **CHAPTER 17**. The tax planner must review the future possible claims for APR and BPR.

Binding contract for sale

5.7   No BPR is given if the property is subject to a binding contract for sale. This will be a particular consideration if buy-out arrangements are in place. See Statement of Practice SP 12/80 *Business Relief from IHT: 'Buy and Sell' agreement for circumstances in which s 113 IHTA 1984 might apply*: the Inland Revenue view is that mere options to buy and sell (distinguish obligations) will not trigger s 113 of IHTA 1984. However, there have been recent signs that the issue may not be completely clear-cut for CGT (as distinct from IHT) purposes: it may be prudent to have successive (and different) exercise periods for the put and call options respectively.

The other area of concern is partnerships and shareholder agreements. The Inland Revenue consider that there is a binding contract for sale where partners or shareholder directors enter into an agreement under which, in the event of the death or retirement of one of them, the personal representative of the partner/directors is obliged to sell and the survivors are obliged to purchase the interest of the deceased in the company or business.

The tax planner should review partnership agreements and structure shareholder agreements in the light of this rule. Note the need to structure life assurance arrangements tax-efficiently within the context of shareholder agreements.

The bold step of gifting the assets now

5.8   Where the assets are of significant value and families can be trusted to look after family assets there could be merits in making gifts now. Subsequent sections look at the angles of gifts with reservation and possible clawback within seven years. This is looked at further in **CHAPTER 13** and **CHAPTER 14**.

Any transfers must be looked at in 'the round', for example:

- Can the transferee maintain trading status for future reliefs?
- What is the CGT position? Is this a good time to use some business asset taper relief? With the generous indexation rules to 5 April 1998 and the relatively low increases in agricultural values, would there be relatively no CGT due whilst preserving a high base cost for CGT for future disposals?

- Has the holdover position of gifts to family members been considered (see **14.29**)?
- Does the loss of this agricultural asset affect the trading status of the transferor or the assets he retains, eg farmhouse when land is transferred?

Any transfer must not be undertaken lightly or with one tax relief (namely IHT) in sole focus. The gift could take the form of a transfer into a Trust (see CHAPTER **17**).

Land — single unit of property on death

5.9   When carrying out a review of all farming assets, their ownership and their tax efficiency, the ruling which values agricultural land as one unit cannot be overlooked.

In *IRC v Gray [1994] STC 360* the deceased owned a freehold interest in land that was farmed with two partners and was subject to certain tenancies granted to the partnership. The CTO attempted to aggregate the freehold interest with the share in the partnership business as a 'single unit of property' for the purposes of IHTA 1984 s 160. The executors appealed to the Lands Tribunal which allowed their appeal and the Crown appealed further.

The Court of Appeal held that the two interests must be aggregated for valuation purposes. This follows the House of Lords' decision in *Buccleuch v IRC [1967] 1 AC 506*, which established the principle that the vendor must be supposed to have 'taken the course which would get the largest price for the combined holding' subject to that not entailing 'undue expenditure of time and effort'. The Lands Tribunal had been wrong to have held that the freehold reversion and the partnership share did not form a single unit of property for purposes of IHTA 1984 s 160.

Note that concession F17 published on 13 February 1995 has reduced the harsh effect of this decision. 100% APR will be given where (in particular) the interest in property subject to tenancy is valued at an amount broadly equivalent to the vacant possession value. See **5.21** on vacant possession and **13.7** on lotting.

Gifts with reservation of benefit

5.10   Where farm assets or land have been gifted it is important to ensure that they do not fail to obtain subsequent relief due to being deemed to be a gift with reservation of benefit. As mentioned earlier, many tax advisers worry that the current level of favourable IHT reliefs may disappear and gifts are often considered. From a planning point a gift of a non-business asset which qualifies as a PET could be considered first so as, hopefully, to maximise reliefs.

A gift falls foul of the gifts with reservation of benefit rules where:

1 possession and enjoyment is not at or before the beginning of the relevant period bona fide assumed by the donee; or
2 throughout the relevant period the property is not enjoyed to the entire exclusion or virtually the entire exclusion of the donor and any benefit to him by contract or otherwise [FA 1986 s 102(1)].

The 'relevant period' is that beginning on the date of the gift or the date beginning seven years before the donor's death, whichever is the later.

If the benefit remains until death, the donor is treated as then entitled to the property [IHTA 1986 s 102(4)], with no pro-rata rule. Hence, it is important to identify the subject matter of the gift. If the benefit ends inter vivos, there is a notional PET at that time [IHTA 1984 s 102(4)].

From a farming perspective the key issues are the possible payment of a full market rent and negligible benefit. The former is not popular; the latter is set out in *Tax Bulletin* No 9 (November 1993). This includes negligible use such as dog walking and horse riding.

It can be possible to gift the land but exclude the shooting rights so shooting can continue by the donor. The rules apply only to gifts made on or after Budget Day, 18 March 1986.

Related property

5.11 Related property rules are of wide application and generally serve to increase the valuation. The rules apply to shares and land, and links them to be valued as part of an imaginary larger holding of the individual holding and the related property. The tax adviser and landowner should always be mindful of these provisions.

The normal rules of valuation

5.12 In general terms, the IHT value is the price that the property might reasonably be expected to fetch if sold on the open market at the date of death, ignoring the costs of sale and without reduction on the ground that the whole property is placed on the market at the same time (IHTA 1984 s 160). Relief is available when sales are made of shares within one year or land within four years after death at a value lower than probate.

Open market value applies even if the property can only be sold to certain people or at a certain price or otherwise subject to restrictions (*IRC v Crossman [1936] 1 All ER 762, HL*). However, if those restrictions will necessarily bind the purchaser the market price will be lower than it would have been in the absence of restrictions at all. Under IHTA 1984 s 163 where there is a restriction or exclusion on the right to dispose, that restriction or exclusion is to be taken into account only to the extent that consideration in money or money's worth was given for it.

On death, the property is to be valued as it was immediately before the death. However, changes that occur by reason of the death are generally taken into account [IHTA 1984 s 171]. Any goodwill in a business that depends directly upon the deceased personally will have less value and as BPR would apply it means that this could reduce the value for CGT base cost on subsequent disposal.

How does related property work?

5.13   IHTA 1984 s 161 states 'Where the value of any property comprised in a person's estate would be less than the appropriate portion of the value of the aggregate of that and any related property, it shall be the appropriate portion of the value of that aggregate'. This means that where property is 'related' it will need to be added to the overall value for valuation purposes.

Property is related if it forms part of the estate of the deceased's spouse (including land), or if it is property that has within the preceding five years been property of a charity or other exempt body under an exempt transfer made by the transferor or his spouse after 15 April 1976. If the trust or body disposes of the property it remains related property for five years.

So far as land and shares qualifying for 100% BPR or APR, the rules are now of less concern. However, they could still bite with, say, a property development company (as one example of an investment company) where BPR does not apply. As the probate value will be the subsequent base cost for capital gains tax there could be advantages of pushing towards a higher value where 100% relief is available.

Managing liabilities and money deposits

5.14   The rescheduling of debt can be used as IHT planning. The focus here for farmers is due to an advantage of APR over BPR. There is not the scope in this book to go into the full detail but to highlight this under-utilised useful tax-planning tool. The basic BPR and APR rules must be understood. Rescheduling liabilities is not a PET and therefore it does not need to be held for seven years to benefit.

For BPR where a liability is charged on an asset used in the business the value of the asset is reduced by the amount of the debt, even if the debt was *not* incurred for the business. Under IHTA 1984 s 162(4) for BPR a 'liability which is an encumbrance on any property shall, so far as possible, be taken to reduce the value of that property.' IHT relief will therefore only be available on the net amount. There is scope to repay debts that reduce tax reliefs with liquid assets that would be subject to IHT. The philosophy of taxpayers towards borrowings and cash reserves varies considerably and some might not like debt management to be tax driven. However, this is one of the few tax planning points that can be 'death bed' tax planning. Farming is different. Section 110 of IHTA 1984 is restricted to BPR, and for APR s 162 applies. APR is reduced *only* by liabilities charged on the land, and not by debt which was incurred to buy that land but secured on other property.

We looked earlier (see **5.3**) at ways of avoiding 'excepted' assets failing in their claim for BPR. Money (cash surpluses) was a specific quote of the excepted assets, and questions that are often asked include:

- Are the assets used at all in the business?
- Were they used throughout the whole of the two years prior to the claim?
- Was the asset required at the time of transfer for future use in the business?

The proactive tax planner would try and take this planning further by actively leaving money or minor investments in the business and argue that it is needed in the business. Short-term deposits are more likely to qualify for BPR than long-term fixed deposits. Obviously, the favourable tax environment of the business is tempting but it must have a palpable business purpose. There must be no risk of causing problems under IHTA 1984 s 105 'wholly or mainly holding investment'. The case of *Brown v IRC [1996] STC (SCD) 277* showed that tax relief for the 'money box' can be achieved but it must be supported by records.

The allocation of liabilities and debt are an excellent tax planning tool for APR as opposed to BPR. A review of debts and liabilities should be undertaken.

Reducing the trading activity or ceasing to trade with gifted assets

5.15   One practical problem for the tax planner is that genuine farming activities are having to be ended or reduced. If they were the result of a gift (a PET) there could be adverse tax consequences. These are known as 'failed PETS'. The combination of better farming results in, say, 1996 together with the fear of a change of government in 1997 meant that some farming businesses were gifted at their highest value (1996–97) and at the time of writing the seven-year period has not yet been achieved. These businesses are currently worth less. This is dealt with in more detail in **13.17–13.25**.

Lifetime transfers — clawback rules

5.16 The transferor may have gifted agricultural property to family members within the last seven years. This will be a PET and the transferor will need to survive seven years for it to be exempt (assuming that there are no retained benefits). If he dies before the seven-year period is up, the emphasis will be on APR.

APR will be lost where the transferee ceases to use the property for agricultural purposes at any time from the date he received it to the date of the transferor's death. A similar consequence will arise if the property is subject to a binding contract of sale at date of death, as IHTA 1984 ss 114 and 124 effectively convert the property into the proceeds of sale.

On the death of donor (or donee) within seven years, to avoid a clawback:

- the transferee must have held property until the transferor's death or the earlier death of transferee – this allows transfer by the transferee to life interest settlement on himself but not to his spouse; and
- the property should be agricultural/business property at the date of the relevant death and, in the case of agricultural property, should have been occupied continuously for agricultural purposes since the date of the gift (with relieving provision for companies) [IHTA 1984 ss 113A and 124A].

Relief is given for replacement agricultural/business property (three years' time limit or such longer period as the Board may allow), provided it was an arm's length deal and the whole consideration received on sale is applied in the purchase of new assets. The Inland Revenue have confirmed that this can be net of professional fees and incidental costs and of any CGT. This is dealt with in more detail in CHAPTER 13.

Replacement of agricultural property by business property

5.17 With the move to diversification, problems are envisaged where agricultural property qualifying for relief has been replaced by business property that does not qualify for relief at the time the transferor dies.

Such a problem is described in the Inland Revenue *Tax Bulletin* No 14 (December 1994). This is dealt with in more depth in CHAPTER **13**.

Where agricultural property, which is a farm business, is replaced by non-agricultural business property, the period of ownership of the former property can count towards the period of ownership for BPR purposes.

Where the transferee of a PET of a farming business sells the business and replaces it with a non-agricultural business, relief will be preserved if the conditions for BPR are satisfied.

Retiring partners — should a farmer ever retire?

5.18   It has been said that 'farmers never retire, they just die'. The tax consequences of the retirement of any partner should be very seriously considered as ceasing to be a partner is the ceasing of his trading status and various tax reliefs that go with it, including the relief on the farmhouse (see CHAPTER **4**). The position of retirement before death (no matter how unlikely that seems) must be reviewed.

Following the BPR case of *Beckman v IRC [2000] STC (SCD) 59*, it would appear that a retiring partner ceases to have a direct, proprietary interest in any particular partnership asset, including agricultural land. It was decided that the interest in the partnership, qualifying for BPR, had been converted into a debt owed by the partnership that was no longer relevant business property.

So what are the alternatives?

Where the partnership is to continue to farm the land, it would seem sensible for the land to be taken off the balance sheet and to not regard it as a partnership asset (there are various ways in which this could be done) with suitable adjustments being made in the accounts. The debt owing to the retiring partner would therefore be reduced accordingly and he would be left with an interest in agricultural property used for agricultural purposes by someone else.

The above strategy would not work in relation to the farmhouse or cottage in which the retiring partner lives, as the house would no longer be used for the purposes of agriculture. ESC F16 would not be of any help either, since this relates to retired employees, not partners. Again, this is not entirely satisfactory and highlights the need for careful retirement planning.

Protecting business property against disallowance

5.19   BPR is not due if a business deals in specific activities such as land or buildings, and stocks or shares. This applies to the shares of a company where the company itself is involved with such activities.

There is a more wide-ranging exclusion, which is particularly relevant when considering diversification. This is IHTA 1984 s 105(3), which precludes business consisting wholly or mainly of the 'making or holding of investments' from qualifying for relief. Landowners are particularly vulnerable where land is let for non-agricultural purposes since APR will be lost and BPR may not be due. Another example is where a tenanted farm is owned by a limited company. This was set out at **5.5**.

It is particularly important for tax practitioners to be aware of what clients might consider to be a business and what will actually qualify for BPR. It must be realised that historically claims for BPR have not been based on how much work is put in by the taxpayer over the years to generate the wealth which is now to be taxed.

There are arguments to say that recent cases have changed this. Examples of these positive cases are *Furness v IRC [1999] STC (SCD) 232* which is considered a victory for the taxpayer and the case of *The mixed use estate Farmer (Farmer's Executors) v IRC [1999] STC (SCD) 321*. (See **CHAPTER 13**.)

It should be emphasised just how significant IHTA 1984 s 105(3) is with regard to the fact that relevant business property could be deemed to be wholly or mainly holding investments. The actual wording of the Act says 'consists wholly or mainly of one or more of the following, that is to say dealing with securities, stocks or shares, land or buildings or making a holding investment'. Case history has seemed to focus almost exclusively on the last element of this phrase, ie the making or holding of investments. There is great concern that the diversified farmer could be deemed to be just holding land as an investment or even dealing in land. This is of particular concern for the limited company featured in **13.14–13.16**. The problem there is that when the business is incorporated the entire value of the shareholding is excluded from relief if it is deemed to be a 'holding investment'. However, for the sole trader the application of rules can be less harsh in that farm assets can be deemed to have failed in their qualification for BPR while the farming business assets can still qualify.

Another favourable case is that of *Furness v IRC [1999] STC (SCD) 232*. It is considered that what decides the availability of the BPR is not merely how much work is done but the nature of the work. Activities which are no more than a natural and necessary incidence of holding the property as an investment in order to derive rental income from it are the activities of holding investments. It is essential that diversifying farmers look at their activities and try and ensure that future claims for IHT relief are not lost.

With the current crisis in farming twinned with an increase in value of land and buildings there has been a tendency towards a trading activity holding investments. This is discussed at some length in Toby Harris's book *Business and Agricultural Property Relief* (LexisNexis Butterworths Tolley) in Chapter 9. The detail is well worth considering.

The cases of *Martin (Moore's Executors) v IRC [1995] STC (SCD) 5, Burkinyoung v IRC [1995] STC (SCD) 29, Hall (Hall's Executors) v IRC [1997] STC (SCD) 126* and *Denekamp v Pearce (Inspector of Taxes) [1998] STC 1120* are all relevant and need to be looked at to see why they failed and how this can be avoided. It is also important to look at what can be considered the victories for the taxpayer, ie *Furness v IRC [1999] STC (SCD) 232*; and the case which is the main feature of this chapter, *Farmer (Farmer's Executors) v IRC [1999] STC (SCD) 321.* (These are looked at in more depth in CHAPTER **13**.)

It is interesting to note that in the case of *Furness* it was the sheer quantity of work involved in running the caravan site which was enough to take the business outside the scope of IHTA 1984 s 105(3). In this case the Special Commissioner examined the evidence and the source of net profit. Essentially, this book is focusing on farmers and land diversification and, although a caravan park is a diversification as such, the case of *Farmer v IRC* is of such importance as it actually does relate to a farmer. This main area of diversification was the letting out of redundant farm buildings and cottages which sets the current scene for many UK estates. It is therefore worth looking at in some detail, especially the factors which were reviewed and those which were deemed to be favourable (see CHAPTER **13**).

Life assurance — when all else fails

5.20   A whole chapter of this book is devoted to how the financial services industry can help with tax planning matters (see CHAPTER **19**). Also see **18.20**.

Life assurance can be a useful tool to help farming families. The classic problem of the farming family is that there is often a large valuable asset but low income. Equality of succession can be very difficult to achieve and life assurance can assist. It can be used to provide for members of the family who do not work on the farm or in the business. Also, where the inheritance structure is such that one farming child inherits the business and has to buy out the siblings at market value of the land, this can be financed by the remaining child taking out an insurance policy.

The right of 'unimpeded physical enjoyment' — vacant possession

5.21   This title is taken from *Cumberland Consolidated Holdings Ltd v Ireland [1946] KB 264*. It was used to assess whether vacant possession had been achieved or not in the purchase of a warehouse which was found to have its cellars full of rubbish on completion date. The analogy of unimpeded physical enjoyment is a useful summary of this chapter.

The theme of this chapter is about protecting the assets. It is ironic that the case used to determine vacant possession should use the phrase 'unimpeded enjoyment'. Farming is not just an income source, a way of feeding the family, a business venture solely for the purpose of profit. It encompasses a large number of other issues, which cannot be overlooked, such as tradition, way of life, responsibility and environmental awareness. Many people who undertake farming as a vocation cannot suddenly change direction. A lot do not want to change direction and in the most part it is a way of life following a long family tradition.

Looking at trying to trade profitably and to protect the assets from unnecessary tax is something that is imperative if this way of life is to continue. One of the clear tax planning points is that the clients must involve the tax planner, and often the land agent, before an action is taken as opposed to after it has happened and then asking what is the tax position. This should involve close links with the land agents, who should be naturally seeking tax advice on agreements entered into. There are many circumstances where the tax treatment will totally depend on the wording of agreements. It can be marginal whether something is of a capital or an income nature. It can be marginal as to whether it is taxed under Schedule D or Schedule A, but the long-term effects in tax saving can be quite dramatic and should be considered in advance.

Clearly planning ahead with farmers and landowners involving their tax planners at an early stage is the key to strong tax planning.

Woodlands and Heritage Property 6

Julie Butler

- **Woodlands — income tax benefits**
  There are tax planning opportunities in having the income from the occupation of woodlands exempt from income tax. However, Christmas trees and short rotation coppices are not exempt.

- **Woodlands — protect the inheritance tax (IHT) reliefs**
  In the desire to have income from woodlands tax-free, the inheritance tax reliefs of the land ownership (APR and BPR) must not be overlooked. IHT relief for woodlands is only deferral.

- **Heritage property — a relief not to be overlooked**
  For assets which do not qualify for the generous agricultural property relief (APR) and business property relief (BPR), an alternative could be a review of the heritage property reliefs. It is, however, a deferral of tax and given consideration as such.

Introduction

6.1 To quote from Stephen Judd of Independent Woodland Management:

> 'The idea of planting new native woodlands on the farm is ever growing in popularity. The current farming recession adds to this appeal because substantial grant aid is available from the first year and profitability measured over a fifteen year period is often substantially better than a stock of arable comparison.'

Woodlands

Income tax

6.2 Under Income and Corporation Taxes Act 1988 (ICTA 1988) s 53(4) the occupation of woodlands (or land being prepared for forestry purposes) is exempt from Schedule D Case 1. Under s 15(1) all occupation of land is excluded from Schedule A. The exemption from income tax includes land being prepared for forestry purposes.

The exemption does not include Christmas trees or short rotation coppice cultivation [Finance Act 1995 (FA 1995) s 154(1)], which are treated as farming not forestry. The definition of coppicing is defined in FA 1995 s 154(3) as a perennial crop of tree species planted at high density, the stems of which are harvested above the ground level at intervals of less than ten years. Examples are willow or poplar, which is being used for new 'green' power stations.

The annual stock valuation should include direct costs of weeding, disease prevention, harvesting and the cost of the first cut. The initial cultivation of the land includes spraying, ploughing, fencing and planting of the cuttings as capital expenditure.

The position concerning Christmas trees is set out in Inspector's Manual at IM2270c:

> 'The growing of Christmas trees is not covered by the exemption for commercial woodlands (see *Jaggers v Ellis [1996] STC (SCD) 440*). Nowadays most Christmas tree production is from specialist Christmas tree producers or from farmers who grow the trees as a crop. Where Christmas trees are grown on an ordinary farm the income may be included in the farm profits. Specialist "Christmas tree farms" are nurseries and thus fall within the definition of "market gardening" in ICTA 1988 s 832.'

Some poor-quality Christmas trees are produced by selling the tops of felled trees from commercial woodlands or the thinnings from land being prepared for forestry. In those cases the profits are covered by the woodlands exemption. The Forestry Authority does not give grants under the Woodland Grant Scheme (WGS) to Christmas tree plantations. If the taxpayer has received WGS grants in respect of the land concerned then it is likely that the woodlands exemption will apply, but ultimately it will always be a question to be decided on all the facts of the case concerned.

Likewise the position concerning receipts from sales of timber etc is set out in Inspector's Manual at IM2270b:

> 'Commercial woodland is not within the statutory definition of farming. Profits from the sale of timber from commercial wood-

land are outside tax, although annual payments received by farmers under certain grant schemes in respect of such woodland may be taxable. Some guidance on the distinction between woodland and farmland may be derived from *De Poix v Chapman 1947 28 TC 462* (see, in particular, Atkinson J's comments on page 470 above definite separation of woodland and farmland within permanence of purpose and use).

Receipts from sales by a farmer of hedgerow timber, and of old standing trees originally planted on this farmland for amenity or shelter purposes, may, if the timber was never normally intended for sale, be excluded in computing profits for taxation purposes. The expenses of felling, marketing etc should likewise be excluded.

Receipts from sales of other trees planted on farmland should be included as part of the farm receipts (see, for example, *Elmes v Trembath (1934) 19 TC 72)*.' (See **9.37.**)

The cultivation of short rotation coppices is treated as a farming activity within the scope of Schedule D Case 1 and is not exempt as woodlands income. The definition of short rotation coppice is 'a perennial crop of tree species planted at high density, the stems of which are harvested above ground level at intervals of less than ten years' [FA 1995 s 154(3)].

Capital gains tax

6.3 Under Taxation of Chargeable Gains Act 1992 (TCGA 1992) s 250(4)–(6) the part of the cost and sale proceeds of woodlands in the UK, which is attributed to underwood or trees growing on the land, is disregarded for capital gains tax (CGT). Under TCGA 1992 s 250(1)–(2) where woodlands are managed on a commercial basis with a view to the realisation of profits the proceeds are also disregarded. The proceeds could be the right to fell standing timber, the proceeds of felled timber or the insurance proceeds from their destruction.

These two provisions, in principle, ensure that where the income is exempt from income tax it is also exempt from CGT.

The problem arises on the disposal of the land as the sale and purchase price needs to be apportioned between the land and the growing timber. The former is taxable, the latter is not. Although the occupation of woodlands on a commercial basis is exempt from income tax it is still a business for CGT. There is still the ability to rollover for CGT purposes with the sale of business assets.

Grants

6.4 There are a large number of grants available under the Woodland Grant Scheme and Grant for Existing Woodland.

Annual payments under the Farm Woodland Premium Scheme (see **20.26**) and Livestock Exclusion Payments are subject to tax as they are compensation for lost revenue. Other grants are outside the scope of tax. These include grants for planting, restocking and natural regeneration, better land supplement, locational supplement, annual management, woodland improvement etc. Woodlands planted on eligible set-aside can count toward the set-aside obligation.

Commercial considerations

6.5 The choice of diversifying into woodlands might be grant led. However, it is not something that should be undertaken lightly – there is no room for error due to the long-term nature and lack of flexibility. Woodland planting can result in loss of value. However, a small percentage of woodland can help increase the value of the farm/estate with increased sporting rights as a benefit.

The increasing awareness of the environment makes woodlands very attractive. There is a market for wood as approximately 90% of the UK's needs are currently imported into this country.

The grants are complex, and the management and economics need careful understanding. Like all diversification projects they need careful research, and professional assistance with grants and quality management is essential. Additional training and equipment may be required if undertaken on a large scale.

Inheritance tax deferral relief — the principle

6.6 There is a deferral relief by which an election can be made within two years after death to leave the timber (but not the land) out of account when valuing the estate [Inheritance Tax Act 1984 (IHTA 1984) ss 125–130]. The deceased must have owned the woods for at least five years before death unless he became beneficially entitled to the woodlands by gift or inheritance without consideration. However, when the timber is subsequently disposed of, whether by sale or by gift, IHT is charged, with a deduction for allowable expenses (including replanting costs within three years). Much more favourable, however, than this deferral relief will be outright exemption at 100%; either agricultural property relief (APR) where woodlands are occupied with agricultural land (and are 'ancillary' to it) or business property relief (BPR) where the woodlands are managed on a commercial basis.

Inheritance tax — subsequent sale of timber/short rotation coppice

6.7 Where the person liable has elected to take the relief, IHT will become payable if there is a disposal of the timber before the next death, whether by sale for full consideration or not. Since the tax has merely been deferred since death, the tax will become payable on a subsequent disposal whether or not that disposal is itself a chargeable transfer. The only exception is that a disposal by a person to his spouse will not cause the charge to be triggered [IHTA 1984 s 126].

If the timber is sold, tax becomes payable on the net proceeds of the sale. The person exclusively liable is the person who is, or would be, entitled to the proceeds of sale. The IHT liability is calculated by adding the sale proceeds to the estate of the deceased and calculating the IHT liability thereon. No change is made to any tax liability in any other asset in the estate. The proceeds that are brought into charge are the net proceeds of sale or the net value. For the net proceeds of sale one must deduct from the proceeds certain expenses, namely those incurred in the disposal, in replanting within three years or such longer time as the Board may allow, and in replanting to replace earlier disposals so far as not allowable on those previous disposals [IHTA 1984 s 128]. These deductions, however, are not allowed if they are allowable for income tax, a phrase that presumably means theoretically allowable and so excludes deduction for IHT, whether or not there is sufficient income to absorb its expense. The net value is the value of the timber after allowing for these deductions.

Where the disposal is itself a chargeable transfer, two sets of liability to tax will arise: the first by reference to the previous death, the second by reference to the disposal. It is then provided that in computing the value transferred on the second transfer a deduction is made for the tax chargeable on the first [IHTA 1984 s 127]. The deduction is simply in valuing the transfer. It is not a credit of tax against tax. Where the second transfer is an occasion for business relief, the reduction under that relief is applied to the value as reduced by the tax paid in respect of the first death [IHTA 1984 s 114(2)].

Short rotation coppice is a perennial crop of willow or poplar tree species at high density (3,000–4,000 acres), the stems of which are harvested above ground level at intervals of less than ten years. The land on which short rotation coppice is cultivated becomes 'agricultural' and buildings used in connection with the cultivation become 'farm buildings' [FA 1995 s 154]. Therefore, APR applies.

General tax planning for woodlands

6.8   With farming in crisis and so many forms of diversification being considered the income tax benefit of woodlands should not be overlooked.

The ability to have the relevant element of income (and related expenses) removed from the business tax computation is a very attractive proposition as indeed is any 'tax-free' income. The problem arises that with the high value of land the inheritance tax (IHT) relief of agricultural property could be put at risk.

In order for land used for growing 'woodlands' to classify as eligible for APR it must be occupied with agricultural land and ancillary to it. As more land is used for non-agricultural purposes, the emphasis of IHT reliefs moves from APR to BPR and the picture becomes more complicated. As a general planning point, whilst the taxpayer should look to minimise income tax through exempt income from woodlands, the finer points of future IHT planning should not be overlooked. As with all land ownerships in these changing times of diversification it is imperative to look at the total ownership 'in the round' and to review the total interaction of income tax, CGT and IHT relief.

As mentioned above the ability to leave income from some woodlands activities out of the taxable profits of a farming business is very attractive to many farmers and landowners. However, the IHT position of the very high value of the land must not be overlooked. It would, for example, be a shame to jeopardise the claim for future IHT relief by a relatively small saving of income tax.

Every holding of land must be looked at in 'the round'. In order for woodlands deferral relief to be claimed it must be occupied with agricultural land ancillary to it, and as mentioned APR and BPR can be much more attractive to the landowner.

Heritage property

6.9   It might be questionable as to why heritage property features in a book on tax planning for farmers and landowners. Clearly, the heritage property includes land and buildings and the landowner might seek to claim IHT deferral relief in the appropriate manner. Obviously, tax planning exercises which include a claim under BPR and APR would be much more satisfactory as it is not a deferral. However, there would be circumstances where BPR/APR fail and the property might qualify as 'heritage' – the tax relief opportunities should not be overlooked if this occurs.

What property qualifies?

6.10 Relevant property should be one of the following [IHTA 1984 s 31(1) as amended by FA 1998]:

1 Pictures, prints, books, etc which (or collections of which) appear to the Board to be of pre-eminent value for their national, scientific, historic or artistic interest.
2 Land, which, in the opinion of the Board, is of outstanding scenic or scientific interest.
3 Any building for the preservation of which special steps should, in the opinion of the Board, be taken by reason of its outstanding historic or architectural interest.
4 Any area of land, which, in the opinion of the Board, is essential for the protection of the character and amenities of such as a building.
5 Any object which, in the opinion of the Board, is historically associated with such a building.

What is the relief?

6.11 As with woodlands relief, the relief for heritage property is a deferral of the charge, rather than the abolition of liability that arises from 100% BPR/APR. Unlike woodlands relief, relief for heritage property is available on lifetime transfers of value and transfers of value made by trustees, as well as the deemed transfer made by death.

The relief operates to make a transfer value an exempt transfer to the extent to which the value is attributable to property accepted as 'heritage property' [IHTA 1984 s 30]. In order to obtain this exemption, a claim must be made. A claim can be made in respect of:

- any transfer on death; and
- any other transfer of value provided that the transferor or his spouse, or the transferor and his spouse between them, have been beneficially entitled to the property throughout the six years ending with the transfer; or the transferor acquired the property on death and the property was then the subject of a conditionally exempt transfer [IHTA 1984 s 30(3)].

In the case of a PET of heritage property, no claim for conditional exemption can be made until the death of the transferor and no claim at all can be made if the property has been sold before then [IHTA 1984 ss 3A–C]. However, if the property has, between transfer and the transferred to the Government in satisfaction of IHT [IHTA 1984 s 230], the transfer becomes exempt [IHTA 1984 s 26A].

A similar exemption applies where there is an occasion giving rise to tax in relation to property held on discretionary trusts [IHTA 1984 s 78]. Exemption may be claimed both in respect of the ten-year charge [IHTA 1984 s 79A] and the exit charge.

The undertaking

6.12 Undertakings are required in respect of the maintenance of a building designated as heritage property for the repair and preservation of its character, for the retention of objects associated with the building concerned and, also, for reasonable access to allow viewing of the heritage property by the public [IHTA 1984 s 31(4)].

The disposal

6.13 Where there is a disposal of property that has been designated heritage property for the purpose of the IHT relief, the conditional exemption is reviewed. Current practice is that if the disposal does not materially affect the heritage entity, the designated heritage property status remains in force.

When a chargeable event occurs and the conditional exemption ceases, tax is charged on an amount equal to the value of the property at the time of the chargeable event [IHTA 1984 s 33(1)]. The value will be measured by the sale proceeds or market value as appropriate [IHTA 1984 s 33(3)].

The tax is calculated by reference to the circumstances of the 'relevant person'. This will be the person who made the last conditionally exempt transfer, save that where there have been two or more such transfers within the last 30 years the Inland Revenue may select whichever of the transferors they choose [IHTA 1984 s 33(5)].

Breach of undertaking

6.14 On a breach of undertaking (or expiry without a new undertaking, unless a disposal occurs to a defined heritage organisation) a charge to IHT crystallises on the basis of the then value of the property, but (broadly) by reference to the rate applicable to the person who made the last conditionally exempt transfer. However, where there has been more than one such transfer since 7 April 1976, the Inland Revenue can choose any of the transferors. Its is understood that in applying this rule, the Inland Revenue do not have regard to conditionally exempt transfers before 7 April 1976 (when the current regime broadly took effect).

Overall tax planning

6.15   The IHT reliefs associated with woodlands and heritage property are essentially deferral of liability and the ability to claim generous APR and BPR associated with land ownership and business activity should not be overlooked.

Plant, Machinery, Motor Vehicles and Agricultural Building Allowance 7

Julie Butler

- **Green expenditure**

  The Finance Act 2002 has introduced beneficial 100% first-year allowances on certain 'green expenditure' and the tax planning opportunities should not be overlooked. The tax position and benefits are looked at briefly.

- **When is a building a plant?**

  Elements of new (and old) buildings can be classified as plant and machinery and therefore attract much more favourable tax reliefs. 40% first-year allowances on plant and machinery can represent far better value than the 4% writing-down allowances associated with agricultural buildings. This presents great tax planning opportunities.

- **Changes in trade**

  Diversification can result in the cessation of a farming business or part of a business; it can also mean plant being used in more than one business and agricultural building allowance (ABA) status changing. The tax planner must look at the consequences of all these permutations and combinations.

Maximising the claim for plant and machinery

Definition

7.1   There is no statutory definition of plant or machinery, although the latter usually takes its everyday meaning.

In *Yarmouth v France (1887) 19 QBD 647*, plant was described as 'apparatus used by a businessman carrying on his business ... which he keeps for permanent employment in the business'. One dictionary definition of 'apparatus' includes 'a collection of equipment used for a particular purpose; a machine having a specific function'. Over the years case law has been developed on the principle which seeks to distinguish property that has a functional purpose, having the characteristic of apparatus, from property that is merely part of a setting in which the business is carried on.

It might be wondered why a book on tax planning for farmers and landowners is paying so much attention to the definition of plant and machinery. There are a number of reasons for this, the first being the relatively generous and complicated tax allowances available in certain situations. So, for example, can part of a building be redefined as plant? (See **7.7**.) There is also the desire to write expenditure off against revenue as an expense and obtain 100% relief, eg on repairs and renewals, and a clear understanding of the definition is important.

Additionally, the Finance Act 1994 inserted Capital Allowances Act 2001 (CAA 2001) s 21 into the legislation, which specifies the expenditure that does not qualify as plant in relation to buildings, structures and land. Expenditure that does not appear in the list of exclusions is not necessarily plant. This has to be decided by the traditional process of considering the facts with reference to decided cases. This means applying the 'function versus setting' test.

For capital allowances on animals see CHAPTER **8**.

The function test

7.2   The case of *Yarmouth v France* (see **7.1**) in fact concerned a vicious horse (defined as plant because it was used for haulage). A full consideration of what constitutes plant for capital allowances is outside the scope of this book but reference should be made to the following cases:

- *IRC v Barclay Curle & Co Ltd [1969] 1 WLR 675*: a dry dock.
- *IRC v Scottish and Newcastle Breweries Ltd [1982] STC 296*: light fittings, bagpipes and deerskins.
- *Haigh v Charles W Ireland Ltd [1974] 1 WLR 43*: not a safe; it was stock.
- *Benson v Yard Arm Club [1979] 1 WLR 347*: not a ship used as a restaurant.

The durability test

7.3   In the cases listed above the issue of whether an asset might be plant concerned the identification of the function of the asset. A separate line of cases considered whether the item was for long-term or short-term use. The principle has emerged that articles with a working life of two years or more may qualify as plant if they are of the right type. In *Rose & Co (Wallpaper and Paints) Ltd v Campbell [1968] 1 WLR 346* wallpaper pattern books failed the 'durability' test which had previously been established in *Hinton v Maden and Ireland Ltd [1959] 1 WLR 875,* which rejected as plant articles which might be consumed quickly or worn out after only being used a few times.

Rates of capital allowances

7.4   A first-year allowance of 40% is available for small and medium-sized businesses on the cost (net of certain grants and subsidies) of plant machinery used for the purposes of trade, with a 25% allowance being available on the unrelieved balance, for subsequent years calculated on a reducing balance basis. A Schedule A business (ie property letting) is treated as a trade for capital allowance purposes.

A first-year allowance of 100% is available for small businesses that invest in information and communications technology equipment in the period 1 April 2000 to 31 March 2003. The definition of small business is the same as in Companies Act 1985 s 247. The cost of software is also included together with the cost of designing a website.

The main rates are set out below.

Low emission motor cars* (see **7.6**)	100%	
Other motor cars	25%	Max £3,000 p.a. per car
Plant and machinery		
First-year allowance	40%	Small and medium-sized firms
Writing-down allowance	25%	On reducing balance
IT equipment (small firms) and energy-saving**	100%	First-year allowance
Industrial and agricultural buildings	4%	Of building cost

** A low emission car is one that is registered on or after 17 April 2002 and either emits not more than 120gm/km CO_2 or is electrically propelled (see **7.6**).*
** For expenditure on or after 17 April 2002, the 100% allowance for designated energy-saving technologies will also be available for assets used for leasing, letting or hire.

Finance Act 2002 — enhanced capital allowances

7.5 The Finance Act 2002 has introduced some very interesting potentially beneficial capital allowance claims. These are set out below.

Enhanced capital allowances

7.6 100% first-year capital allowances are to be introduced for expenditure incurred by businesses on:

- new low emission cars (ie cars which are either electrically pro-pelled or emit not more than 120g/km of CO_2) registered on or after 17 April 2002; and
- plant and machinery to refuel vehicles with natural gas or hydro-gen fuel (such as storage tanks, compressors, pumps, controls, gas connections and filling equipment).

In contrast to the position for existing first-year allowances (but see below), the enhanced allowances will be available where the asset is to be leased, let or hired. The restrictions on capital allowances and on the deduction of lease rentals for cars costing more than £12,000 will be removed for low emission cars. These measures will apply to expenditure incurred on or after 17 April 2002 and before 1 April 2008.

100% first-year allowances are also to be made available for expenditure incurred on or after 17 April 2002 on energy saving equipment within the enhanced capital allowances scheme introduced in Finance Act 2001 where the asset is for leasing, letting or hire.

There is great scope for the farmer/landowner to benefit from these new provisions. The classification of a motor vehicle as 'plant' and therefore entitled to 100% first-year allowances is of prime impor-tance. However, the potential element of private usage and the poss-ible reclassification as a vehicle, which would be subject to benefit in kind rules within a limited company (see **7.15–7.16**), should not be overlooked.

Advantages of definition of plant not building

7.7 A large amount of expenditure in relation to a modern building relates to items that can constitute plant or machinery. The farmer or landowner may identify such expenditure and claim the appropriate capital allowances. All appropriate conditions must be met. This applies as much to a second-hand building as a new one. The apportionment depends on valuation techniques and requires knowledge of building construction. The bold tax planner might look at building works over the last six years to see if claims have been overlooked and possibly consider the error or mistake claim route.

The after tax cost of funding a new diversified venture will be affected by whether expenditure is treated as buildings or plant. There may well be borderline cases where planned expenditure could be regarded as plant. However, there are certain items of expenditure where the legislation is clear as it deems to be plant such as alterations to buildings incidental to the installation plant [CAA 2001 s 25].

As mentioned in the introduction, buildings are not plant but there is often difficulty in distinguishing one from the other, especially where items are incorporated into buildings or the building has a functional purpose. This distinction may be important since expenditure on buildings will usually only qualify for 4% p.a. allowances or none at all, whereas plant could start at 40% followed by 25% p.a.

In *Gray v Seymours Garden Centre (Horticulture) [1995] STC 706*, a claim for plant and machinery allowances was denied in respect of a greenhouse with no mechanical controls, used to display plants for sale to the public. However, Vinelott J stated that a specialised glasshouse with integral heating, temperature and humidity controls, automatic ventilation, shade screens and other equipment could be considered plant.

Plant and machinery for inheritance tax

7.8   These terms are not specifically defined for inheritance tax. The capital allowances definition is used in practice, qualified slightly so as to exclude items which would qualify for capital allowances only on the renewals basis. However, that rule is not absolute: some latitude may be given. Thus, plant includes anything which the businessman uses to carry on his business, other than his stock in trade. It will include goods and chattels, fixed or movable, which he keeps for permanent employment in his business. It does not just mean 'machinery'. Provided that it is used in the business it should be eligible for 100% agricultural property relief or business property relief, as appropriate.

Farming business ceasing with plant being sold, scrapped or taken over personally

7.9   What is the situation where a farm ceases to trade?

Balancing allowances or charges will arise upon cessation of farming activities, usually based on the actual consideration limited to original cost, where disposal is at or above market value.

Where, however, the disposal is for less than the market value, market value is substituted unless the buyer's expenditure will be taken into account for capital allowances or there will be a taxable benefit on an employee under Schedule E. Assets taken over personally are accounted for at market value.

The same rules are applied to value assets on hand at the date of cessation even though the events take place after cessation (unless there is likely to be a long delay between date of cessation and the above events, in which case the Inland Revenue take market value at the date of cessation as being the disposal value (CCAB Memorandum, June 1971)).

Farming business ceasing with plant being transferred to new business

7.10 This situation is of prime importance when a farming business ceases and a new diversified business starts.

Certain items of the old trade might be used in the new trade (eg a tractor for contracting). Such items will be treated as a disposal at market value in the old trade with the same amount representing qualifying expenditure in the new trade (assuming no proceeds change hands, otherwise the price paid will be substituted if capital allowances will be claimed). It would appear that no first-year allowances are available in these circumstances. The proactive tax planner should look at maximising the tax reliefs on cessation or transfer. The allocation of allowances between the businesses can change subject to realistic price or market value and there could be the opportunity to claim allowances in the right business. It could be that the value of the plant and machinery has been virtually written down to £nil, which would then create a balancing charge in the old business which could be used efficiently as capital allowances in the new business.

Plant used by more one than one business

7.11 If the farming trade continues, certain items of plant and machinery may be used by more than one business (eg a digger). For new acquisitions, the cost can be apportioned on a reasonable basis (usually based on initial usage) with capital allowances being claimed by the respective businesses in the usual way. For existing items included in the farm general pool, the proportion relating to usage of the new business can be treated as a disposal at market value, with a corresponding entry as an addition in the new business.

Alternatively, the farm could invoice the other businesses for the use of the plant, which would potentially enable full capital allowances to be claimed by the farm, although the method of giving the capital allowances will differ. If plant is first let otherwise than in the course of trade, the expenditure is treated for capital allowances purposes as having been incurred for the purposes of a notional trade, and therefore included in a separate pool. An apportionment will be required where the farm also uses the item of plant. Relief for such an item of plant and machinery is only available against the leasing income from that item, and cannot be claimed against other income, with excess allowances being carried forward for offset against letting income of later periods.

Another alternative could be to form a separate entity and transfer the plant and machinery into it, for the purposes of leasing the plant and machinery to respective businesses. The problems surrounding the financing of plant and machinery are dealt with at **7.13**.

The VAT position will need to be considered carefully in the above situations.

Agricultural Building Allowances (ABAs)/Industrial Buildings Allowances (IBAs)

7.12   Agricultural building allowances (ABAs) are available to owners or tenants in respect of capital expenditure on agricultural buildings and works, including farm buildings, fences, drainage, power supplies etc. Agricultural land is defined by statute [CAA 2001 s 361(1)] and means land, houses and other buildings occupied wholly or mainly for the purposes of husbandry. Therefore, ABAs will not be available for new buildings not put to agricultural uses. However, industrial buildings allowance is available if used for industrial purposes, as set out below.

The allowance is currently an annual allowance of 4%. To qualify for allowances it must be shown that the expenditure is incurred for the purposes of husbandry on the land in question. A maximum of one-third of the expenditure on a farmhouse can qualify for relief. This is reduced in such proportion as the accommodation and amenities of the farmhouse relate to the nature and extent of the farm. Where expenditure on an asset is incurred partly for the purpose of husbandry and partly for some other purpose the expenditure must be apportioned in a 'just' manner.

Under diversification it is important to see what effect on ABAs a change of use will have. Change of use has no effect on entitlement to ABA if the expenditure qualified for ABA when it was incurred; writing-down allowances continue for the whole of the writing down period. They continue even if the building is destroyed (subject to CAA 2001 s 381, see below).

What happens therefore on cessation, eg the sale of a farm?

When an agricultural building, etc is sold, demolished or destroyed there are two possible treatments. Where the building is sold, the normal method is for the seller and the buyer to receive ABA's in the year of the sale on a time-apportioned basis by reference to each party's basis period. In this case a balancing event is avoided. In the case of tenant farmers, there is a transfer of an interest in the buildings to the immediate landlord when the tenancy comes to an end, in the absence of an incoming tenant, and therefore the landlord enjoys the remainder of the allowances.

Alternatively, the disposal may be treated as a balancing event by election [CAA 2001 s 381]. A joint election by both parties must be made in respect of a sale. However, only the former owner is required to elect where the building is demolished or destroyed. In practice, elections on a sale are rare but consideration ought to be given in cases of destruction etc where a balancing allowance is likely to arise. The latter situation may well arise where land is put to different use. It is important when dealing with sales of agricultural property to confirm the position on ABAs.

The important point for the diversifying landowner and farmer is that where an asset no longer qualifies for ABAs will it qualify as an industrial building? An industrial building allowance (IBA) is also 4% of the allowable qualifying expenditure.

In order to qualify the building must be used for the purposes of a trade (or part thereof) which is carried on in a mill, factory or similar premises, or for the manufacture of goods or materials or the storage of goods or materials used in manufacture. The trade of maintaining or repairing goods or materials is also included, as is the agricultural operation undertaken for another person.

It could be difficult to prove that new buildings that fail in a claim for ABAs will actually qualify for IBAs.

From a tax planning point there are two concerns for the diversifying farmer. Firstly, it is worth considering re-utilising existing buildings or to be sure to use the building for an agriculture purpose first. The claim for 4% ABA/IBA may not be the prime motivating reason. The second point is to see if the use will qualify for IBA and to try and maximise this claim. However, for the tax planners the reliefs available for careful classification of part of building as plant as opposed to building qualifying for ABA/IBA is more important.

From a tax planning viewpoint it is worth referring to the Inspector's Manual at IM2336b:

'Any agricultural buildings allowances due under CAA 1990 s 122 in respect of expenditure incurred before 1 April 1986 may still be relieved against general income as they are given by discharge or repayment and are not caught by ss 384 and 397.'

Agricultural buildings allowances due under CAA 2001 ss 361(1), 369(1), 370(1), 372(1), 372(2) and Sch 3 para 82 in respect of expenditure incurred on or after 1 April 1986 are given in taxing the trade and are caught by the legislation.

Financing the plant and machinery

7.13 There is no doubt that the financing of plant and machinery is complex. It is useful if all farms keep a fixed asset register and retain all the documents that support the finance. The alternatives for purchase are:

- outright purchase;
- hire purchase;
- finance lease; and
- operating leases (also known as contract hire).

Statement of Standard Accounting Practice 21 (SSAP 21) gives guidance on the difference between finance and operating leases.

The first three alternatives are the same as a purchase and qualify for capital allowances. Generally, the operating leases are a lease arrangement with low rentals (usually including a maintenance element) during the period of hire with a large balloon rental as the final payment. For accounting purposes the rental payments of operating leases are treated as rentals which are accounted for when they fall due.

Historically, finance agreements on the purchase of plant and machinery have been a cheap source of finance. It can sometimes be difficult to try and ascertain exactly what is the purchase price and what is the trade-in value. This can all be tied up with discounts on new machines.

From a tax planning point, the client should review the tax status on the new addition and the commercial viability of the alternatives should be linked to tax status.

Motor vehicles

7.14 In order to maximise the capital allowances on motor vehicles it is important to look at the Finance Act 2002 changes. The other angle for the farmer/landowner to be very aware of is the benefits in kind on motor vehicles. This can be very relevant to directors of limited companies, members of the family employed by the family farm and employees of the farm or estate provided with a vehicle. It is sometimes possible to say that the vehicle has no private usage and therefore no benefit in kind arises but it is essential to look at both the Finance Act 2002 effect on company cars and fuel together with the 100% capital allowances on green expenditure.

Company cars and fuel — Finance Act 2002

7.15 From 6 April 2002 a new scheme of taxing company cars based on CO_2 emissions was introduced. Although the benefit charge will still be calculated taking a percentage (between 15–35%) of the car's list price, the change to an emissions basis will favour the employee with a smaller car, compared to the employee who does high annual business mileage. There is a 3% supplement on diesel cars subject to a 35% cap.

Fuel scale charges for 2002–03 will be increased by 15%.

The Chancellor announced that from 6 April 2003 fuel scale charges will also be linked to CO_2 emissions. A percentage will be calculated from a minimum of 15% to a maximum of 35%. There will be a discount for alternative fuels and hybrid cars, which could bring the charge below 15%. To calculate the tax due, the percentage figure will be multiplied against a figure set for the year.

Where an employee opts out of free fuel during the year he will only be charged on the relevant proportion of the full amount, but if he opts back in during the year he will be taxed on the full annual charge.

Vehicle benefits

7.16 Benefits are chargeable on employees earning £8,500 or over (including benefits) and directors.

For motor vehicles the charge is a percentage of the list price. The percentage depends on the level of CO_2 emissions. The minimum charge is 15%: the maximum charge is 35%. CO_2 emission details (see **7.15** above) are available on the Society of Motor Manufacturers and Traders Ltd website at www.smmt.co.uk.

There are no longer reductions for business mileage or for older cars. The list price relates to the day before first registration and includes accessories. The price is subject to an upper limit of £80,000. The list price is reduced by the employee's capital contribution when the car is first made available, subject to a maximum deduction of £5,000. Payments by employees for private use may reduce the above benefits.

Van benefit

Van benefit	Vehicle under 4 years old	Vehicle 4 years old or over
Per vehicle, includes fuel for private use	£500	£350

Car fuel benefit

Car fuel benefit	2002–03		2001–02	
Engine size	*Petrol*	*Diesel*	*Petrol*	*Diesel*
Up to 1,400cc	£2,240	£2,850	£1,930	£2,460
1,401–2,000cc	£2,850	£2,850	£2,460	£2,460
Over 2,000cc	£4,200	£4,200	£3,620	£3,620

Car fuel benefit is reduced to nil if employee pays for all private fuel.

Vat due per quarter

Vat due per quarter	Scale charge		VAT due	
Per car	*Petrol*	*Diesel*	*Petrol*	*Diesel*
Up to 1,400cc	£226	£212	£33.65	£31.57
1,401–2,000cc	£286	£212	£42.59	£31.57
Over 2,000cc	£422	£268	£62.85	£39.91

These rates apply to the first accounting period beginning after 30 April 2002 and will be included in each quarterly VAT return thereafter.

As part of the tax planning review of all assets this should include all vehicles so as to try and ensure that they are tax, VAT and CO_2 emissions efficient. The automatic assumption that vehicles provided for farm workers just because they are, for example, a working Land Rover, does not mean that they do not have some private use, and the benefits issue should not be ignored. Ignore a potential PAYE inspection at your peril!

The green car

7.17   Car benefits have been the focus of a lot of people's attention of late. The recent increase in tax due on these has hit some taxpayers hard and everyone has been looking at ways of making sure that these costs are minimised.

The natural route is to check that cars are 'green' under the Finance Act 2002 and have the right emission controls in order to make sure that the benefit is as low as possible (see **7.14–7.16**).

It is not realised by all that when a 'green car' is taken on by an employer, the employer does get 100% first-year allowance on this car. This is set out in **7.6** and it could mean that the employee can negotiate with the employer some form of flexibility to try and help compensate for the extra benefit in kind.

In practical tax planning terms, the Chancellor announced a new 100% first-year allowance for low emission cars used in the business or by employees and refuelling equipment for vehicles using natural gas or hydrogen. Businesses can also claim 100% allowances on the cost of designated energy-saving technologies for leasing, letting or hire. To qualify, the vehicles must be registered on or after 17 April 2002 and either be electrically propelled or emit less than 120 grammes per kilometre (g/km) of CO_2.

In the desire to pay as little tax as possible on the benefit of a motor vehicle, taxpayers have even looked towards the van. The taxable benefit on a 'van' is £500. For a 40% taxpayer this means that £200 tax is payable. Now that 'white van man' has become part of the English language there are some who might squirm at the very prospect of such an idea, but it is important to look at what qualifies as a van.

There have been instances where the Inland Revenue have accepted that the twin cab (also known as crew cab or dual) pick-up does qualify as such. There are certain qualifications and as long as you can load more than 1,000 kilograms in the back of a pick-up then these could qualify. If pick-up owners are VAT registered they can reclaim the input VAT. To claim the VAT refund, owners must have businesses that require such vehicles. Again, the interpretation of the Customs & Excise can be inconsistent.

So for those pondering over whether or not to have a company car and, if so, which one, they should not dismiss green vehicles, the simple van or the twin cab pick-ups.

Tax planning

7.18   The tax planning surrounding the acquisition, disposal and review of all areas of plant, machinery, motor vehicles and buildings should not be dismissed. With 100% first-year allowances on computer and IT acquisitions, and also on acquisitions which under the Finance Act 2002 qualify as 'green', there is a lot of importance to be placed on the timing of acquisitions and disposals. This would also apply to large machinery such as tractors, combines, forklift trucks etc, which attract a 40% first-year allowance.

With low farming profits the timing of the claim for capital allowances can turn a profit into a tax loss. This could be utilised efficiently; however, it could mean the loss of personal allowances and the benefits of the income tax basic rate band. This does link to farmers averaging (see **20.1**), but with the move away from farming and diversified income not qualifying as farming income there will be less chance to use this and the timing of capital allowances could be critical.

Likewise, in difficult times it might be efficient to actually waive (ie not claim) some capital allowances so as to ensure that personal allowances are utilised. It can be seen that a lot of new building work can classify as plant, and again the tax planner must be involved before the building is built to ensure maximum tax efficiency from both a timing viewpoint and also the classification of plant and machinery.

In an ideal situation farm management accounts will be reviewed prior to the year-end, fixed asset needs reviewed and considered and the planning carried out accordingly.

It is understood that the response in the practical world of farming is likely to be reluctance but we should be training clients to treat their farming and diversified business like any normal commercial activity with management accounts and pre-year end decision making.

Livestock, Valuations and Quotas 8

Julie Butler

- **International Accounting Standard 41 (IAS 41) — fair value**
  IAS 41 states that for agriculture biological assets should be measured at their fair value. This will have an interesting impact on farm accounts and tax. Until the Inland Revenue give greater clarity on the tax angles of IAS 41, there is scope to keep closing stock 'low' for tax and 'high' for the balance sheet.

- **Herd basis**
  The principal advantage of the herd basis election has been that the increase in the value of the herd was effectively achieved 'tax-free'. However, there is no tax relief for reduction. With a very vulnerable livestock market tax planners must consider all angles before electing. With farms undergoing restructuring of the business, the need to make a fresh election on the change of the partnership must not be overlooked.

- **Quotas as a fungible asset**
  Tax advantages can be obtained by looking at how the disposal of quota should be treated. The fungible asset rules mean that a higher base cost can be achieved than previously, although with the annual exemption for capital gains tax (CGT) this might not be always be the preferred choice. Small disposals under the old rules did mean utilisation of the annual exemption.

International Accounting Standard 41 (IAS 41)

8.1 Although International Accounting Standards apply only to companies, and only shortly apply to companies after the UK governing bodies have 'sanctioned' them, they still give direction and guidance. How will IAS 41 be interpreted in the UK? How will the Inland Revenue react? What will happen to Inland Revenue Business Economic Note 19 (BEN 19)? For a discussion of these points see the article featured in the July 2001 edition of *Accountancy* 'A fair time for agriculture?' (See **A.1**.)

It might be questioned what is the relevance of this article to the tax planner. Firstly, the article shows the interaction of BEN 19 (which explains the Revenue's views on the valuation of stock) and this proposed standard. In view of the importance of BEN 19 to the industry, this is reproduced in full in APPENDIX **B**. Secondly, if BEN 19 is not changed there could be an opportunity to show a high figure for stock in the balance sheet but a reduced tax figure. It will be interesting to see the Inland Revenue reaction.

Herd basis and BEN 19

8.2 Stock in annual farm accounts will normally be valued in accordance with BEN 19, the basics of which are set out in APPENDIX **B**. For non-farming stocks it will be important to value them at the basic principle of the lower of cost and net realisable value. Herd basis is very complex and there is not the scope here to look at it in detail. The position was made more complicated by the foot and mouth provisions. The rules relating to the herd basis are contained in Income and Corporation Taxes Act 1988 (ICTA 1988) Sch 5 and are also available in the Inland Revenue booklet IR9. Herd basis allows the chosen classes of mature animals to be treated as assets and excluded from the trading stock valuation. The advantage of the herd basis is that changes in the value of the production animals does not distort taxable profit. If they are eventually sold without replacement, the proceeds are effectively tax free ie, not included in the computation of taxable profits.

The decision as to whether to elect or not will depend on the individual. One of the disadvantages of electing is that there will be no tax relief on any reduction in value of the animals. This has become more relevant in the current crisis where it is not so certain that values will increase. The time limit for making the election is within twelve months after the fixed filing date of the year of assessment in which the production herd is first kept. The election is irrevocable.

There are detailed notes in the Inspector's Manual at IM230–IM2318.

If within five years of the sale of the herd the seller begins to acquire a new production herd of the same class then they are treated as 'replacements' and replacement of whole herd.

Where the difference between the cost of animals in the herd is much less than their ultimate market value the election is more beneficial. Likewise in periods of inflation, the herd basis helped keep unrealised profit out of the tax computation. Changes in a partnership need a fresh election and with farmers looking at restructuring this is important. An election of the herd basis is complicated in a share farming arrangement (see CHAPTER **11**).

'Flying flocks', ie herds of cows and flocks of sheep, are sometimes kept with individual animals sold at the end of their production cycles. These are not eligible.

Whether treated as trading stock or on the herd basis farm animals are exempt from CGT. They are regarded as wasting assets which are 'tangible moveable property' [Taxation of Chargeable Gains Act 1992 (TCGA 1992) ss 44–45].

Horses working on a farm may be treated as either trading stock or as a fixed asset, providing the treatment is consistent.

The Inspector's Manual at IM2296a sets out the position on harvested crops arable areas payments:

'Farmers growing cereals, oilseeds and proteins can claim subsidies under the Arable Area Payment Scheme. In order to qualify, they must set aside a percentage of the total area on which they are claiming and they are paid compensation for the area set aside.'

The timing of recognition of payments under the scheme was considered in an article in the Inland Revenue *Tax Bulletin* No 10 (February 1994) at page 108. It stated that accounts would be acceptable in which Arable Area Payments were recognised as income of the accounting period to the extent that the crop has been sold by the balance sheet date.

Where this approach is adopted and the deemed cost method of valuation described in section 7.3 of BEN 19 (see APPENDIX **B** and Inspector's Manual at IM2292) is used, valuations should be based on 75% of the total of the market value at the valuation date plus the related Arable Area Payments (including payments in respect of the required level of set-aside). The Area Payments should also be taken into account when net realisable value is computed.

Stock valuation adjustments on cessation

8.3 With a move to diversification it could be that part of the farming activity has to cease. It is therefore worth considering the position of what happens to stock at cessation.

Stock in hand at the date of cessation of farming activities needs to be valued in accordance with ICTA 1988 s 100, ie market value. Where stock is to be sold to another UK trader, the general rule is that the price paid is adopted for tax purposes provided that the parties are not connected with each other. The ceasing farmer treats the monies as a trading receipt and the incoming farmer as a trading expense.

Where the parties are connected (ICTA 1988 s 839):

- stock is valued at open market value;
- however, where open market value is greater than:
  (a) the actual price agreed; and
  (b) the amount which would be taken into account when calculating profit as representing cost of the stock as sold in the ordinary course of trade,
  the parties can jointly elect to substitute the greater of (a) or (b) and must do so not later than 22 months from the end of the chargeable period in which the trade is discontinued.

Stock taken for personal use or use in another business before cessation of trading shall be treated as a sale at market value (*Sharkey v Wernher (1955) 36 TC 275*).

Animals' eligibility for capital allowances

8.4 In certain circumstances a claim for capital allowances is available on working animals and production livestock kept for the purposes of a business, and includes live animals kept for permanent employment in farming and which serve to produce saleable products. Capital Allowances Manual, at CA 1571, accepts that a horse used in a school or show jumping business is plant, as is a guard dog or circus animal.

Animals that are kept mainly for sale to provide a saleable product after slaughter are outside the description. Thus, there is a distinction between dairy cattle, which do qualify as 'production livestock', and beef cattle, which do not. Laying poultry are plant, but not broilers. Young animals not yet ready for use as production livestock do not qualify. The Capital Allowances Manual, at CA 1571, requires a dog to be working to qualify. Farm animals are normally trading stock such that their cost is a revenue item, thus barring a capital allowances claim.

Quotas

8.5 Quotas came into being when the regulatory system of which they are a part was introduced. Normally, a total quota for the UK is subdivided among existing producers according to their level of production at a certain date. A pool of reserve quota may also be created and held centrally for allocation to special cases such as new entrants. Each eligible producer thus receives an initial allocation of quota without payment. The quota is immediately of value to farmers because it enables them to carry on the particular farming activity more profitably than they would be able to without quota. One effect of the introduction of a quota system is therefore the creation of a new capital asset in the hands of farmers.

Quotas may be transferable between farmers by outright sale and purchase. As the quota is normally a fixed capital asset of a farmer's trade such transactions normally have no income tax consequences for the farmers concerned. In particular, there can be no question of farmers who have bought quota claiming a deduction for the amount of any expenditure such as levies or leasing charges, which they would have incurred if they had not bought it.

Introduced by European Economic Community Regulations in 1984 (EC Reg 857/84), milk quota is an arrangement which allows the wholesale milk producers to produce milk up to the quota threshold without attracting liability to supplementary levy. A quota is allocated to a particular holding of agricultural land.

- IHT – It has been Inland Revenue practice in the case of dairy farmers to combine the value of quota with the value of the agricultural land for agricultural property relief (APR) purposes. In any event APR (and business property relief) will not be due on milk quota where dairying activities cease ie, the quota is held without a trading activity and leased out. As shown below the practical approach for small disposals is as a separate asset.
- CGT – Does a milk quota comprise an interest in the underlying land or should be treated as a separate asset for capital gains tax purposes? The decision in *Faulks v Faulks [1992] 1 EGLR 9*, concerned a dispute between a surviving partner and the widow of a deceased former partner over the amount of compensation due to the estate. Comments made by Chadwick J suggested that a quota was indistinguishable from the underlying land. This approach, if well founded, could imply that the disposal of a milk quota should be treated as a part disposal of underlying land, with the need to apportion expenditure attributable to the acquisition cost. However, the capital gains tax case of *Cottle v Coldicott [1995] STC (SCD) 239* has cast doubt on this treatment, where it was held that milk quota is a separate asset.

The quota is a fixed capital asset. The Inspector's Manual at IM2286b describes quotas as follows:

'A farmer holds a quota primarily in order to make a profit from carrying on the particular farming activity which it covers. She or

111

he does not ordinarily buy and sell quota in the course of the farming trade. The quota has the character of an enduring asset of the farmer's business similar to the buildings or farm machinery. Quota is normally therefore a fixed capital asset of a farmer's business.'

Quotas treated by the Inland Revenue as capital assets are subject to CGT and IHT in the normal way.

Examples are:

- Suckler cow quota – allowing a producer to claim headage payments on suckler cows.
- Ewe premium quota – allowing a producer to claim headage payments on ewes and ewe lambs.

All quotas can be leased or sold between farmers. For tax purposes there are two types of transaction: temporary or permanent. 'Back-to-Back' transactions are increasingly used whereby 'dirty' (used) quota is sold and 'clean' (unused) quota purchased on the same day. A temporary transaction is known as leasing: the cost to the purchaser is a trading expense. If it is the lease of temporary surplus then it will be treated as Schedule D Case 1. However, if the enterprise has ceased that section of farming then the leased out income is Schedule D Case VI (see **15.24**).

From a tax planning point, potato quota now has £nil value, therefore a claim for the capital loss should be considered under TCGA 1982 s 24(2). The timing of the claim, as in all such claims, should be made where possible in the year of a gain above the annual exemption for CGT.

Milk quota — as a 'fungible' asset

8.6 Fungible assets are assets that are movable or perishable and are of a sort that can be estimated by weight. The disposal of quota is generally a capital disposal taking advantage of CGT reliefs. But what is the base cost? If no milk quota has been purchased it is £nil, but what if further quota has been bought? How is the cost allocated between the total holding? Prior to the fungible asset rules it was 'pooled' with the total holding therefore giving a low CGT base cost. See **A.5** for the article from *Taxation* that discusses the benefits that milk quota as a fungible asset could have for farmers.

It should be noted that the fungible asset rule does not apply to the limited company. As mentioned above, the tax planning point on quota is that there are times when both methods have advantage subject to the individual position. An aggressive tax planner could use this to best advantage. However, consistency should be applied.

Where possible the farmer should contact their tax adviser *before* the disposal of any quota.

Horses and stud farms

8.7   The stock valuation is set out in the Inspector's Manual at IM2350c and IM2350d. This is summarised as follows.

'Specialist advice on open market valuations of thoroughbred horses is available from the Bloodstock Section, Shares Valuation Division, Nottingham. Requests for advice should include:

- The name(s) of the horse(s) to be valued.
- The valuation dates.
- Any opinion of open market value together with reasoning, if supplied.

Except where the herd basis has been adopted, both stallions and mares should be dealt with as stock in trade and valued individually at the beginning and end of each year on the usual basis of cost or net realisable value (see IM2350c), whichever is the lower. Stock valuations should also include any foals and, where appropriate, stud fees paid (see below).

In the case of stallions (but not mares) we accept a rule of thumb method of valuation, whereby the cost of the animal is written off by equal annual instalments until it reaches the age of 15. This rule of thumb method is an attempt to arrive at an acceptable figure for net realisable value where this is less than cost. The rule of thumb method is not appropriate:

- where a better figure is available because the animal is valued at the balance sheet date, or
- where it would give an unreasonable result. For example, in those exceptional cases where the value of an animal increases, or drops at a rate significantly slower than that used in the rule of thumb, because, for example, of very successful progeny, the figure computed using the rule of thumb should be increased to an amount not exceeding cost.

Foals – When the foal is born the stud fee becomes part of its cost.

- Foals should normally be included in the stock valuation at cost.'

Practical tax planning

8.8 A move to diversification will mean a move away from the rural standards of BEN 19, IAS 41, the herd basis and worries over quota. More straightforward standards of the lower of cost and net realisable value will be important.

With falling values previous assumptions might be challenged, especially by a harsh bank manager. Changes in the basis of valuation will have to be considered carefully for contravention of consistency principles.

These are difficult times and the valuations must be given the due care they deserve for business assessment, consistency and tax planning.

Planning for VAT   9

Allison Broadey ATII
(The VAT Consultancy)

- **Diversification — a VAT shock for the farmer**
  Historically, farmers have had relatively straightforward VAT registration and return issues with output generally being zero-rated and an ability to claim input VAT. Greater consideration towards the charging of VAT must now be considered with such matters as annual accounting, flat-rate schemes for small businesses, partial exemption, capital good schemes and transfer of a going concern (TOGC). The emphasis has to be that VAT must be planned ahead in the same way as tax.

- **Land and property — maximising the VAT position**
  Areas that are most commonly encountered are options to tax, urban regeneration measures, listed buildings and land and property diversification activities. The VAT issues surrounding property can be very high value and it is imperative to plan in advance and look at all the alternatives.

- **Equestrian activities**
  The recent VAT case of *John Window* is discussed and VAT planning ideas to assist in minimising VAT changes in livery and stabling are considered. The registration scheme for racehorse owners is discussed.

Note from the Editor

9.1 It is impossible to consider land use and ownership of assets without considering the VAT position. This is a comprehensive chapter on VAT and the effect that this tax may have on the various diversification activities and organisational structures being considered.

Not only are the VAT issues discussed in plain English but they have been written to highlight the hidden pitfalls and promote areas in which advance planning can bring real savings. VAT remains an extremely complex and ever-changing subject, but Allison Broadey shares her technical knowledge with us with great enthusiasm and an understanding of the impact that this indirect tax burden has on us all.

Introduction

9.2 It is assumed that the VAT issues of day-to-day activities are likely to be understood and it will be the norm to complete VAT returns and deal with the input and output VAT in a routine way.

However, with the need for farmers and landowners to diversify their activities and to seek alternative sources of income, the business will find itself moving into uncharted waters in many areas. The pressures faced by a business wishing, or having, to diversify its activities are huge. Considerations such as whether the proposed trade is financially viable, whether planning permission is required or will be granted, the cost of diversification and the tax implications of doing so are all necessary well before the proposed plans can be put into practice. As if this is not enough there is also the often forgotten indirect tax implication of VAT.

VAT is, unfortunately, often an afterthought in the planning stages and, consequently, can be the downfall of many business ventures. As with all taxes, little can be done to mitigate a tax burden after the event but much can be done to prevent its cost by a little forward thinking and planning.

The aim of this chapter is to highlight the impact of VAT on the diversification of a business and to consider its effect on some of those activities that the reader may be considering.

VAT rates — the basic principles

9.3 Business supplies will be subject to VAT at either the standard (17.5%), reduced (5%) or zero rate. These rates are known as taxable rates and give the right to recover input VAT on any related purchases.

There are also exempt supplies, which do not carry VAT but which do not give the right to recover any VAT on related costs unless such

VAT is beneath a 'de-minimis limit'. When a mixture of exempt and taxable supplies are made the business will usually be 'partially exempt' and the best method of apportioning input VAT on overhead costs will need to be considered. The issue of partial exemption is considered in further detail at **9.39**.

One of the greatest VAT dangers is to confuse the making of zero-rated supplies with the making of exempt supplies. Whilst both are not liable to VAT on sales income received the exempt supply will not give right to VAT recovery on costs and may even mean that a VAT registration is invalid.

There may also be other sources of income, such as grants and compensation payments, which are 'non-business' and are outside the scope of VAT. HM Customs & Excise (Customs) are often quick to associate the receipt of non-business income with an automatic disallowance of some of the input VAT incurred by the business. This should be resisted as this disallowance should only follow when non-business supplies are actively undertaken or if VAT is borne on costs that wholly and directly relate to the receipt of non-business income.

One of the initial hurdles when changing business activities is to ensure that the correct VAT rate is applied and that the VAT implications are fully understood.

Diversification — is a VAT registration required?

9.4   If the new business is to be carried on by the same legal entity as that already VAT registered, then there is no need to inform Customs of a change – all supplies will automatically be covered by the existing registration. This is, though, an important point to remember. If a business is VAT registered then *any* business activity undertaken by that entity will be covered by the existing registration. How diverse those activities are does not matter.

Following this line of thought, if the activity is to be undertaken by a new legal entity – a partnership rather than a sole proprietor – then it should consider whether a new registration is required. If the income generated from the new activities is taxable, and exceeds the current VAT registration limit of £55,000, then a compulsory VAT registration is required. A voluntary registration can, however, be sought if this limit is not exceeded and can be beneficial if the sales are largely at the reduced rate or zero rate, or if significant VAT on set up costs has been incurred.

There is also a further category of registration, which is an 'Intending Registration'. For a business that is not VAT registered but which will incur costs relating to intended future taxable supplies, it can register for VAI and recover input VAT on those costs to assist with its cash flow. A classic example is woodland farming. A business will prepare the land and plant trees for felling and sale in 20 years time. No income will be received until such sales are made but VAT registration can be sought and VAT recovered on the costs of the enterprise from the outset. With any VAT registration it is normal for the business to be on quarterly VAT returns but if the activities will result in input VAT exceeding output VAT each quarter then consider asking for monthly returns to help the cash flow.

The voluntary and intending registrations are ideal if the business wants to recover VAT on costs but what if the business has little by way of taxable costs and wants to avoid registering and accounting for VAT until it absolutely has to?

It is possible to arrange the business activities to legitimately keep below the threshold providing that each is a genuinely separate commercial enterprise. If the existing business trades as a partnership then the new activities could be routed through a different legal entity. This could have the advantage of keeping exempt and taxable activities separate, to allow for individuals to maximise their personal tax allowances or to ensure that the new venture is kept out of the VAT net for as long as possible. There are several important considerations in creating separate legal entities and both VAT and tax planning feature most highly on the list. There is no point in creating a different entity for VAT purposes if the direct tax implications outweigh the VAT benefits and vice versa.

However, if the new activities are best carried out by the creation of a new or different legal entity then the simple rule is to ensure that these activities are operated and run on commercial lines and that it is a clear and distinct business in its own right. The greatest danger with family businesses is that what starts off to be a separate business activity often tends to merge back to the original business after a period of time. Costs start to be 'shared' and sales income is paid into joint or main accounts 'for ease'. Beware!

Customs are well aware that businesses will seek to split their activities in order to avoid VAT. This is known as disaggregation and legislation was introduced to enable Customs to direct that businesses should be treated as one legal entity. They will also critically review businesses to see whether, despite the use of two or several legal entities, there is in fact only one business activity which should always have been covered by one VAT registration. Should such a decision be made by Customs then this will have a catastrophic affect on the business as Customs will assess for VAT on previous income and a VAT registration can be backdated by as much as 20 years.

In order to successfully challenge a ruling the business must ensure that it is financially, economically and organisationally independent from any other business.

Grants and compensation payments — are they taxable?

9.5   Where grants are received then these will be outside the scope of VAT providing that nothing is given in return. Should the donor require a report on how the grant has been spent or to inspect premises as a condition of the grant then this is not considered to be consideration for the supply.

Equally, a compensation payment is outside the scope where it is given only as recompense for injury, inconvenience, loss or damage. It is important to identify whether the compensation is in return for a supply as, like grants, a VAT charge could then arise.

VAT on costs incurred directly in connection with the receipt of grants or compensation payments will not be recoverable as input VAT. However, such VAT is likely to be relatively small and might only include the costs of seeking professional advice in submitting a claim. The fact that grant monies are used to support a fledgling business venture or are used to modernise an existing business should not affect that business's overall right to recover VAT.

Special VAT schemes — the benefits and burdens

9.6   Assuming that the business will remain in the VAT net then there are several 'schemes' which Customs have introduced in order to reduce the burden of VAT upon certain activities. These include cash accounting, annual accounting, the flat-rate farmers' scheme, the registration scheme for racehorse owners, and the new flat-rate scheme for small businesses.

Cash and annual accounting

9.7   Most businesses will be familiar with the cash and annual accounting schemes and these can be used by any business with a taxable turnover of less than £600,000 per annum. The cash accounting scheme allows for VAT to be declared on sales only when the income is received (thereby assisting with cash flow) although VAT can only be recovered on costs when the purchases are paid for [Value Added Tax Regulations 1995 (SI 1995/2518) regs 56–6(4)].

Annual accounting allows for a business to complete an annual VAT return rather than quarterly returns [Value Added Tax Regulations 1995 (SI 1995/2518) regs 49–55(2)]. The level of turnover will determine whether a quarterly or monthly interim payment is required by Customs, but for businesses with a turnover of less than £100,000 and a VAT liability of less than £2,000 in the previous year an interim payment can be avoided altogether. There are, of course, conditions placed upon both schemes and whilst the cash accounting scheme is a popular choice there are relatively few who decide to use the annual accounting scheme.

Flat-rate farmers' scheme

9.8　The flat-rate scheme for farmers was introduced as an optional scheme for businesses [Value Added Tax Regulations 1995 (SI 1995/2518) regs 202–211(3)]. The scheme refers to supplies made by farmers, but the nature of activities included within the scheme means that any business supplying farming and agricultural goods and services could be eligible. By registering under the scheme the 'farmer' receives certification and is no longer VAT registered. The scheme can only be used for designated supplies and its use means that VAT is no longer due on sales and that there is no VAT recovery on costs. Instead, the farmer is able to add a 'flat-rate' charge of 4% on sales of designated produce to VAT registered customers. The farmer can retain this 4% addition and the VAT registered customer can recover it on his normal VAT return. As the farmer is able to sell to the public without the addition of either VAT or the flat-rate 4%, he can increase his sales price in order to make a little more profit whilst these prices still remain below his VAT registered competitors.

Unfortunately the scheme has never been popular, but for those farmers using the scheme, a diversification of business activities will require an overview of its continued use. For businesses that are diversifying into supplies covered by the scheme then its use may mean that a VAT registration can be avoided without the creation of separate legal entities.

The designated supplies covered by the scheme include crop production, stock farming, forestry, bee-keeping and silkworm farming, fisheries, certain processing of farm products and supplies of agricultural services. For supplies not covered by the scheme the normal VAT rules apply. This means that once the non-scheme supplies exceed the VAT threshold then the farmer must leave the scheme and a VAT registration is required to cover all supplies. The only exception to this is where the non-designated activities are either wholly zero-rated or exempt. There are of course always conditions to the use of the scheme and the farmer is not entitled to use the scheme where his retention of the flat-rate 4% would exceed previously recoverable input VAT by more than £3,000.

An example of where planning and the use of the scheme may be of benefit is shown below.

EXAMPLE

A business currently lets 50 acres of land to a tenant farmer (an exempt supply) and has 150 acres of arable land, which he farms. The sales of the produce are a mixture of zero-rated cereal and standard-rated linseed (grown for its oil). Currently the farmer is VAT registered and wants to increase his income by offering bed and breakfast accommodation and to sell nursery plants and cut flowers to guests and to the public. By using the flat-rate scheme the farmer could de-register from VAT until such time as the B&B income exceeded the current VAT threshold. He would need to charge VAT registered customers 4% flat-rate on the linseed sales and on any of the nursery plant sales. However, he can avoid accounting for 17.5% VAT on the B&B and on the nursery sales to the public. He needs to consider the loss of recoverable VAT on assets and overheads but, if these costs are low, and his nursery sales to the public are successful, then the benefits could be very welcome.

Registration scheme for racehorse owners

9.9 The registration scheme for racehorse owners was introduced following discussions between Customs and the horse racing and breeding industries. It has always been recognised that businesses were entitled to register for VAT where their activities were economically geared to the care, breeding and showing or riding of horses. However, the increase in the purchase of shares in, or the whole ownership of, bloodstock by individuals, partnerships and companies brought into question whether the investment was of an economic or private nature. The scheme is not a 'scheme' in the truest sense but more a statement of practice for the procedure adopted by Customs for the VAT registration of owners of racehorses.

Under the scheme it is accepted that a racehorse owner can register for VAT as long as he is registered as an owner with Weatherbys. He also needs to have a sponsorship agreement registered with Weatherbys or to have the benefit of continuing business income from the exploitation of the horse, such as appearance monies.

The part ownership of a racehorse requires VAT registration as a partnership with the other owners where the share is less than 50%.

The scheme only covers those entities that are not currently VAT registered. If a business is VAT registered and wishes to purchase an interest in a racehorse then, for VAT purposes, it will be entitled to VAT recovery only if it can demonstrate the 'business' sponsorship or use as mentioned above. The business must remember that, once included within the VAT registration, the income received from the horse, such as prize money, sponsorship or sale proceeds will need to be declared and VAT accounted for where appropriate.

For a business diversifying into the horse racing industry it is vital to ensure that there is sufficient evidence of the intention to treat the activities as a commercial enterprise. This will secure VAT recovery on costs and avoid arguments with Customs over the activity being one of mere pleasure or recreation. (See **20.3**.)

Flat-rate scheme for small businesses

9.10 In the 2001 Budget the Chancellor announced a consultation process for the introduction of a new flat-rate scheme for small businesses. In the recent Finance Act 2002 this scheme was approved and was introduced on 25 April 2002.

The scheme is designed for businesses with a taxable turnover of less than £100,000, although the inclusion of exempt supplies increases the threshold to £125,000. The aim of the scheme is to enable businesses to declare a flat-rate percentage of their turnover as VAT rather than having to calculate VAT on a transaction-by-transaction basis for both sales and purchases.

The business remains VAT registered and is required to complete and submit its regular VAT returns. Invoices are still issued to VAT registered customers and show VAT as normal. When the VAT return is completed the output VAT is calculated by taking the gross turnover in the period and multiplying it by the flat-rate percentage determined by the main activity of the business. As an example, the flat-rate for agricultural services is 9%, forestry and fishing is 10% and animal husbandry is 11%. The differing flat-rates are designed to take account of businesses whose sales are not all at 17.5%.

A business will benefit because where before it has accounted for VAT at 17.5% on all supplies it only needs to declare VAT to Customs on the flat-rate percentage of the gross sales. The difference between the flat-rate value and the VAT actually charged is retained by the business to compensate for VAT incurred on expenditure that is not recoverable under the scheme.

It should be noted that the flat-rate is calculated on all sales even where these sales would normally be liable at the reduced and zero rate or would be exempt. The business is also unable to recover input VAT on costs unless they are goods of a capital nature with a value in excess of £2,000 inclusive of VAT.

The scheme is only in its infancy and it may be some time before its practical benefits will become apparent. However, it is unlikely to benefit very many businesses as the loss of input VAT and the high flat-rate percentages may mean that there is more of a cost than a saving to its use. As with many tax schemes the business will need to consider its own status, customer base and activities before making a decision on its application.

Land and property — a summary of VAT issues

9.11   One asset, which the business is likely to want to exploit as fully as possible, is that of its land and buildings.

The value of these assets can create enormous financial gains to the owner when sold or leased but the danger of hidden taxes always follows closely on its heels. VAT is no exception to this.

In general terms property can be split into those that are commercial in design and use and those that are domestic. The sale or lease of commercial properties and land can be subject to VAT at the standard rate or be exempt whilst residential properties can fall into the zero rate or exempt categories. Work to commercial properties will almost certainly be standard-rated whereas work on residential properties could be at the zero or reduced or standard rate. The VAT legislation governing the rates of VAT applicable to land and property transactions can be found in Value Added Tax Act 1994 (VATA 1994) Sch 8 Group 5 (concerning zero-rating for the construction of residential buildings), Group 6 (concerning the zero-rating applicable to protected buildings), Sch 9 Group 1 (concerning the exemptions for land), Sch 10 (relevant residential and charitable buildings, elections to waive exemption and anti-avoidance legislation) and, most recently, Sch 7A Groups 6 and 7 (concerning the reduced rate for conversion, alteration and renovation of dwellings).

The disposal, leasing or improvements of land and buildings is one of the most complex areas of VAT and specialist advice should always be taken before entering into any contract or supply. The following paragraphs are designed to assist in the planning stages but the exact VAT treatment will usually also be influenced by the VAT status of the vendor and purchaser and of the building or land in question.

The tax implications of property disposals and property letting are set out in CHAPTERS **14** and **15** respectively.

Option to tax

9.12   Also known as 'waiving the exemption' the option to tax gives businesses the opportunity to standard-rate a supply of an interest in commercial property. Normally such an interest would be exempt, but the option enables the business to charge VAT on supplies of the property and to then recover input VAT on costs associated with such supplies – thus potentially avoiding partial exemption issues.

Legislative references to the election to waive exemption can be found in VATA 1994 Sch 10 paras 2(1)–3A(14). Customs have also issued an updated (March 2002) Notice 742A, entitled *Opting to Tax Land and Buildings*, which provides more information on the option and how to apply.

When the option to tax was introduced it was not possible to opt to tax specific parcels of land and Customs insisted that an option was effective in respect of all adjoining land under the same legal ownership. However, with effect from 1 March 1995 this rule was relaxed and options were accepted on specific parcels of agricultural land.

It is a misconception that the option to tax stays with the land or property once it has been made. The option only binds the VAT registered entity that makes the election. A business can therefore opt to tax on individual properties or on parcels of land which are registered separately under land registry. It is therefore possible for a business to own three commercial properties of which two are opted and one is exempt.

The following paragraphs highlight the most common issues affecting the option and some points that businesses may not be familiar with.

Who can make an option?

9.13 The option can be made by any VAT registered business over land and buildings for commercial use. An option can be made even though the business may not have a legal interest.

How do I make an option?

9.14 The option must be made in writing to the local VAT office of the business. In the case of a business that is applying for VAT registration because of the taxable supply of a property, the option should accompany the VAT application form.

Following the Tribunal decision of *Blythe Ltd Partnership [1999] BVC 2224* Customs recommend that the letter notifying an option and any accompanying list or schedule of properties, is signed as appropriate by a director, two or more partners (or trustees), an authorised administrator, or by a sole proprietor.

A third party can notify an option on a business's behalf but Customs will require written confirmation that this person is an authorised signatory.

When is an option valid?

9.15 An option must be notified within 30 days of the decision to opt to tax. Customs have no discretion to back date an option but they will generally accept that an option has been validly made in cases where a business has evidence to show that it made a conscious decision to opt and has charged and accounted for VAT on the relevant supplies.

In cases of a property transferring as a transfer of a going concern (TOGC), Customs now accept that the option is notified on the date that a notification is posted to them. This was established in the Tribunal case of *Chalegrove Properties Ltd [2001] BVC 2279.*

Once made an option can only be revoked within the first three months, providing no related input VAT has been recovered or supplies have been made, or after a period of 20 years.

Once it has been made the option applies to that legal entity and not to the property itself. If a partnership opts to tax a barn then any interest in that property will also be taxable. Should the partnership sell the barn to a limited company then that limited company can either opt to tax or can let the barn as an exempt supply. It does not inherit the option made by the partnership.

There are some supplies upon which the option, even when notified to Customs, has no effect. This means that the supplies will remain exempt:

- if land or buildings have previously been used by the business for exempt supplies then an option is not effective unless the business first asks Customs for permission to opt to tax;
- on any supply of a building intended for use as a dwelling, number of dwellings or relevant residential purpose;
- on any supply of a building to be used for relevant charitable purposes;
- on any supply of land for a residential caravan pitch, moorings for a residential houseboat or for land to be used by an individual for construction of his dwelling;
- on any supply of land to be used by a housing association for the construction of dwellings or for relevant residential purposes.

In addition to the above, anti-avoidance rules were introduced in March 1997, and amended in March 1999, in order to block an option to tax being made on certain supplies of land and buildings to connected parties, or persons responsible for financing the development of land and buildings, where it is the expectation or intention for that land or buildings to be used for exempt purposes. It is outside the scope of this chapter to give detail on these anti-avoidance measures [VATA 1994 Sch 10 paras 2(3AA)–2(3AAA), 3A(1)–3A(14)] but very great care should be taken to ensure that land and property transactions that fall within the scope of the capital items scheme are not affected by these rules.

Even though the option does not apply to the sale of a building intended for use as a dwelling, part of a dwelling or for a relevant residential purpose, this can be overridden if both purchaser and vendor agree, in writing, that VAT can be charged. In order for the supply to be standard-rated the purchaser must have the intention, at the time of the agreement, of making a zero-rated supply of the building.

Do I need permission before opting?

9.16 If a property has previously been used for making exempt supplies then Customs must normally be approached to ask for written permission before an option can be exercised. Customs do accept that in certain circumstances permission is not required but this is restricted to those situations outlined in Customs Notice 742A (March 2002 edition) s 5.2, which has legal force.

Where permission is required the business must write to Customs and disclose full details of the previous use of the property, why the option is now sought and how much input VAT is likely to be recovered once the option is accepted. Providing that Customs are satisfied with the proposals then they will give written 'permission' and the business must then write and formally opt the property. If permission is not obtained when it should have been, then any subsequent option will be deemed 'invalid'.

Is there a need to opt to tax?

9.17 There is no need to make an option on supplies that are automatically standard-rated. These supplies are listed in VATA 1994 Sch 9 Group 1 Item 1 and include the following:

- the sale of new commercial properties, ie properties which have been constructed within the last three years;
- gaming and fishing rights unless the fee simple in the land is given;
- the provision of hotel or similar sleeping accommodation;
- caravan, tent pitches and camping facilities held out for holiday use (see **5.19** and **15.17**);
- parking facilities;
- the right to fell or remove timber (see CHAPTER **6**);
- the grant or right to store, moor or house aircraft, ships and other vessels;
- the right to occupy a box or seat at a sporting event or place of entertainment; and
- sports facilities.

As the above are likely to be areas in which a farmer will consider diversification, each has been discussed in further detail later in this chapter.

If a business acquires land or buildings upon which VAT has been charged then this VAT can be recovered in full, providing that the business uses the asset for its fully taxable trading activities. There is no need for it to opt to tax. An example of this is the purchase or construction of a new barn for storage of its farming goods. If the business is fully taxable then the VAT incurred in purchasing the barn can be recovered automatically.

Why opt?

9.18   By opting to tax the business must charge 17.5% VAT on the letting or disposal of the opted property although (as mentioned above) there are some exceptions. As the option is largely irrecoverable it must be exercised with great care.

The main benefit of the option is that it reduces the need for the business to make exempt supplies and therefore the need to carry out complex partial exemption calculations. The consequence of an exempt supply is a loss in the amount of input VAT that can be recovered. By opting the input VAT is secured and thus it does not become a cost.

The disadvantages of the option are that the prospective purchaser or tenant must pay VAT. His ability to recover this VAT will then depend upon whether he is VAT registered and whether he is fully taxable. In selling an opted property it should be borne in mind that the purchaser is required to pay the VAT and this is therefore a cash flow issue as well as an actual cost in that stamp duty is calculated on the gross not the net cost of the purchase price.

Before an option is made the farmer must consider whether the making of an exempt supply will give rise to significant VAT loss on costs and administration. If it does then he should consider whether the option will put off prospective tenants or purchasers or whether, in his chosen market, this is not an issue.

Urban regeneration measures — the 5% reduced rate

9.19   With effect from 1 May 2001 a reduced rate of VAT of 5% was introduced for certain supplies of construction services. The reduced rate was a measure introduced in the Spring 2001 Budget under the banner of 'Urban Regeneration', but the title is misleading as the reduced rate has nothing to do with inner city rejuvenation. Instead, the measures apply across the board to dwellings, and conversions of properties to dwellings, throughout the UK.

The reduced rate lessens the cost of VAT for private individuals and businesses that are renovating, converting and extending dwellings either for own occupation or for letting. This is particularly relevant for farmers and landowners who wish to create new dwellings or to renovate old properties to let for residential purposes. As these lettings are exempt, and the VAT incurred on costs would therefore be irrecoverable, the reduction from 17.5% to 5% must help to make such ventures more economically viable.

The reduced rate applies to renovations of existing dwellings, residential conversions, houses for multiple occupancy and to relevant residential and charitable buildings. As the first three of these areas are likely to be the more relevant to the diversifying farmer and landowner, the measures are highlighted in further detail below. Customs have issued several documents on the measures but the most informative is that of Information Sheet 04/01 which contains full details of all the urban regeneration measures including relevant residential and charitable buildings.

Renovation of dwellings

9.20 The 5% rate is appropriate for the cost of renovation of dwellings that have been empty for at least three years.

Renovation services includes *any* works of repair, maintenance or improvements carried out to the fabric of the building. The reduced rate will apply to the services of redecoration, annexes or extensions, including conservatories, provision of all utilities and construction of new garages.

The property must have been empty for at least three years prior to the works commencing. As the property owner you will be required to obtain such evidence to satisfy the contractor that the works are liable to the reduced rate.

It is interesting to note that Customs will accept confirmation from an 'empty property officer' who is apparently located in each local authority division, but if this cannot be obtained then they will require other evidence such as electoral role and council tax information.

Note that the 5% rate applies to the services of the builder or contractor and the building materials supplied in the course of these services. The purchase of goods only will result in a 17.5% VAT charge. Wherever possible contracts should be on a 'supply and build' basis. Landowners intending to buy materials and carry out the work themselves will not benefit from the urban regeneration measures.

The reduced rate will also apply where an empty property is purchased and the new owner starts to occupy it whilst renovation services are carried out. However, the three-year 'empty property' rule must still be met, the occupier must be the recipient of the services and no renovations should have been carried out within three years prior to the occupier purchasing the property. It is also a condition that the services are supplied within one year of the date of completion of the property purchase.

Under these rules a contractor must ensure that no previous renovations have been carried out within the three years prior to the date of purchase. It is also important to note that the services provided by the contractor must be completed within one year of the date that the property has been purchased not within one year of the building work commencing.

Where contractors carry out work on a property that is unoccupied then this one-year 'grace period' does not apply.

Residential conversions

9.21 The reduced rate applies to the conversion of a non-residential building into a dwelling or the conversion of a residential building to change the number of single household dwellings. Essentially, this means that the reduced rate will apply to conversion services where the number of dwellings either reduces or increases when compared to the original number of dwellings.

This will assist a landowner who is considering the conversion of a barn (which is treated as a commercial property) to a new dwelling or number of dwellings. The work of conversion will be at the reduced 5% rate.

The reduced rate will apply to all works of repair, and maintenance or improvement to the fabric of the building where the work forms a fundamental part of the change in the number of dwellings. The creation of new garages, annexes and extensions to the property will also be covered by the reduced rate.

Customs also consider that a property designed as a dwelling that is then converted for commercial purposes should be treated as a non-residential building. The conversion back to a dwelling will now qualify for the reduced rate.

For a landowner that is converting a property from commercial to residential use for his own occupation, the 5% VAT charge can be recovered by the submission of a DIY Housebuilders claim. For a new conversion that will then create a dwelling to be sold as freehold or a major interest (a lease in excess of 21 years) the sale will be zero-rated and full VAT can be recovered on the normal VAT return.

If a new conversion is to be let as investment income, then consider the grant of a major interest or freehold to a connected third party first (thus crystallising the right of VAT recovery) and then the third party can let the properties as an exempt activity. As well as giving an absolute VAT saving this planning then removes a partial exemption issue from the original owner. Do, however, consider the costs of stamp duty and capital gains tax issues before proceeding!

House in multiple occupancy dwelling conversion

9.22 Where a property is converted from a dwelling, or several dwellings, into a property of multiple occupancy the reduced rate will apply to the costs of conversion. This will include for instance the conversion of a house into bedsits or a bed and breakfast establishment.

Customs have confirmed that the reduced rate for conversions does not include a conversion to a hotel, a dwelling with a granny annexe or accommodation for guests or lodgers so great care needs to be exercised in these areas.

Transitional rules

9.23 As the works of construction or conversion services are treated as continuous supplies for VAT purposes, there are special rules for tax points on-going projects.

For any work that was not complete as of 12 May 2001, the contractor, or subcontractor will be able to apply the reduced rate to the qualifying services. If invoices were issued, for instance for stage payments, then credit notes can be issued to correct the VAT liability. Where work was complete as of the 12 May but was invoiced later then the full standard rate of 17.5 % will still apply.

Extension of zero-rating

9.24 With effect from 1 August 2001 the urban regeneration measures also introduced zero-rating for the freehold sale or grant of a major interest in residential properties that have been renovated but were unoccupied for at least ten years prior to the grant.

This will enable full VAT recovery to be made on properties such as abandoned farm cottages that have been left empty for at least ten years. The renovation costs will be liable to 5% VAT but this will now be recoverable providing that the cottage is then the subject of the grant of a major interest.

Listed dwellings — zero-rating

9.25 Customs have always allowed a partial VAT recovery on the costs of maintaining the working farmhouse. This is usually allowed to a maximum of 70% but will depend upon the taxable level of business activities being carried out. However, for those businesses that are partially exempt or where maintenance or construction costs are not related to business activities the VAT recovery will be much lower or even non-existent.

In these circumstances it is important to ensure that maximum use is made of the reduced rate and, for listed dwellings, the zero rate.

Works to a listed building which is, or will become as a result of the work, a dwelling can be zero-rated providing that the work required, and received, listed planning consent and that the work amounts to alterations to the fabric of the building [VATA 1994 Sch 8 Group 6]. Unfortunately, repairs and maintenance are not eligible for zero-rating but it is often arguable whether the works are repairs or alterations so careful consideration needs to be given for the purpose of the works and the extent of the listed planning consent required.

The zero-rating does not apply to commercial properties or separate structures in the curtilage of a listed dwelling where those structures are not themselves dwellings.

Where work does qualify as an approved alteration then the zero-rating will also apply to the making good of the area surrounding the alteration. It is usual to find that works will comprise of a mixture of alterations and repairs and therefore an apportionment of the build contract should be made. A review of the nature of the work carried out will help to ensure that the lower VAT rates are applied wherever possible.

It should be noted that a contract builder will often err on the side of caution and charge standard-rated VAT on the majority of contracts. Only when provided with sufficient evidence of the applicability of the reduced or zero rate will they usually be willing to review the VAT position.

Land and property diversification activities

9.26   Whilst it is impossible to outline all the activities in which a farmer or landowner may seek to diversify, the following paragraphs highlight those that are likely to require the most VAT planning.

Commercial properties — sale

9.27   The sale of a commercial property ie barns, or land, will be exempt from VAT unless the owner has 'opted to tax'. One notable exception is that if a property is less than three years old then it is automatically standard-rated.

Assuming that the sale is exempt then the VAT registered entity will not be able to recover VAT on the sale costs (legal fees, estate agency costs) unless this VAT is below a de-minimis amount of £625 per month on average and that this is less than 50% of all input VAT incurred (see **9.39**).

If the owner has opted to tax then the sale of any commercial land and buildings will be standard-rated. This means that 17.5% must be charged and accounted for on disposal and will increase not only the cash flow cost to the purchaser but also the cost of stamp duty. (See CHAPTER **14** on property disposals.)

Commercial properties — letting

9.28 Similar to the sale of property and land, the letting of any buildings or land will also be exempt from VAT if the option to tax has not been made. The VAT implications on the letting costs are also the same in that there can be no VAT recovery on costs unless these fall within the de-minimis limits. The main difference is that the letting of a new property remains exempt unless the option is made – there is no automatic standard-rating.

If the letting is an exempt supply it should be remembered that VAT on the costs of maintenance and repairs to the property will also potentially be blocked so a tenant repairing lease becomes a strong recommendation. (See CHAPTER **15** on property letting.)

Residential properties — sale

9.29 The sale, ie freehold or leasehold interest in excess of 21 years, of a new residential property will be zero-rated. This means that any VAT incurred on the construction or development will be recoverable but no VAT will be due on the value of disposal.

'New' means either a new construction from foundations upwards or where no more than one wall has been retained as a condition of planning permission. Take care with the renovation of existing residential properties, as the disposal of such a property will still remain exempt unless the property has not been lived in or occupied for ten years or more – note that evidence is required to support this. If the property has been empty for this period then the sale after refurbishment will be zero-rated. The conversion of a commercial property to residential use will result in a new dwelling and its sale as new will therefore be zero-rated. The costs of conversion will be liable to the reduced rate of 5% (see **9.19** (urban regeneration measures – the 5% reduced rate)) but this VAT will be recoverable as long as it relates to the zero-rated disposal. This will apply particularly to barn conversions.

The zero-rating for new residential houses only applies where the dwelling is self-contained, there is no direct internal access between connected dwellings and there is no restriction on occupation or disposal (statutory or otherwise). The construction of a new dwelling in the curtilage of an existing property often gives rise to VAT issues. If the new dwelling does not meet the above requirements then its construction costs are standard-rated and the disposal exempt – thus the VAT becomes a cost. (See CHAPTER **14** on property disposals.)

Residential properties — letting

9.30 The letting of residential accommodation is exempt from VAT and, as mentioned previously, you cannot opt to tax a residential property. A distinction is drawn between a residential let and a holiday let – both having different VAT treatments.

A holiday let will be advertised as such and will normally only be available for short, ie weekly or monthly, durations. There may be a planning restriction on the occupancy of a property available for holiday let and the rates or council classification may also be different. By contrast a residential tenancy will be for any period of time but should be the main or only private residence of the tenant.

As residential lets are exempt, the VAT incurred on the cost of refurbishment, capital expenditure and overheads will be subject to partial exemption rules and it is unlikely that this VAT will be recoverable. In order to reduce this cost the business should check whether it could take advantage of the reduced rate or zero rate for supplies in connection with certain dwellings. (See **Chapter 15** on property letting.)

Bed and breakfast and holiday accommodation

9.31 The provision of bed and breakfast and holiday accommodation is always standard-rated. For VAT purposes there is a difference between residential lettings and holiday lettings and it is important to recognise this both in terms of setting prices and for recovery of VAT on costs. Where guests stay for a continuous period of four weeks or more then a reduced rate of VAT applies. This reflects a taxable charge for the catering and 'serviced' element but an exempt supply of letting accommodation. With effect from day 29 an apportionment must be made and VAT is only declared on the taxable part.

The conversion of a farmhouse to accommodate B&B guests is a business expense for VAT purposes so VAT on the purchase of linens, decorations and on a proportion of capital expenditure can be recovered. Equally, the conversion of a barn or the construction of a new property for holiday lets will incur considerable amounts of VAT and this should be recovered on the normal VAT return.

Do not overlook the fact that only the legal owner of the property can recover VAT on the capital costs. If the B&B business has been structured so that a wife runs the B&B and registers for VAT, then no VAT will be recoverable on property conversion costs if the farmhouse is in the name of the husband and wife. Even if the husband and wife are separately VAT registered then the costs will still not be recoverable as the partnership is not the entity supplying the B&B accommodation.

The sale of a holiday home will be standard-rated within the first three years of construction and exempt at any time after the three years have elapsed. If the property sale is exempt then consideration will need to be given to any capital goods scheme adjustments which may be required (see **9.42**). (Also see **15.10–15.13** on furnished holiday lets and **15.14** on bed and breakfast.)

Camping and caravan pitches

9.32 Camping and caravan pitches are also included within the definition of holiday accommodation so are automatically standard-rated. However, the legislation refers to seasonal pitches so that any pitches which are provided for 12 months or more and are not held out for holiday use are exempt. The provision of pitches for residential use and for travellers are considered to be exempt as long as they can be used for a person's principal private residence. (See **15.15–15.18.**)

Gaming and fishing rights

9.33 The granting of fishing and shooting rights are standard-rated but any additional charges for the actual taking of game or fish can be zero-rated as long as the produce are edible in nature.

If the fee simple in land includes the right to take game or fish then there must be an apportionment between the exempt land element (subject to the option to tax not having been made) and the taxable gaming and fishing rights. Customs accept that this apportionment will not be required where the rights are less than 10% of the value of the land.

The VAT liability of shooting rights does depend upon the status of the landowner and Customs accept that a charge by a landowner to guests in order to cover the costs of the shoot can be treated as a private and therefore non-business activity. However, it will be treated as a business activity if the shoot makes a profit at year-end, the shoot is advertised to the general public or where it is run on a similar commercial basis.

Grazing rights are zero-rated if the principal purpose is for animal feeding; where care is the principal purpose then the supply becomes standard-rated (but see further **9.38**).

Letting of sports facilities

9.34 The letting of sports facilities and sporting rights are automatically standard-rated. There are special rules for the use of sports facilities where there are lets in excess of 24 hours or for the hire of facilities to the same user for a regular series of events (both then become eligible for exemption but can be opted).

Within the definition of sports facilities Customs include swimming pools, tennis courts and croquet lawns and areas of land that have been specifically designed or adapted for sporting activities. However, if the sporting facilities are let for non-sporting purposes then the exemption will apply. An example of this will be the letting of a swimming pool for a fashion shoot.

Boxes and seats at events and admissions

9.35 Admissions to events, ie car boot sales and concerts, are standard-rated. There are exemptions available if such events are organised by a charity for charitable purposes but otherwise the supply remains taxable.

However, land leased or let to a tenant remains exempt (subject to the option) even if the tenant then organises and runs an entertainment or event.

The farmer may consider opening the farm for tours as an additional source of revenue. Such tours are likely to be attractive to schools and to tourists. However, the charges for such tours, for tractor rides or other similar entertainments will all be standard-rated.

Parking, mooring and storage of vehicles and vessels

9.36 Charges for the right to store, park or moor are standard-rated. The exemption will be available if a lease is given in a particular area of land. If a landowner allows people to park on his land for a charge then this will constitute a standard-rated supply.

If the mooring, storage or parking forms part of a residential lease then it always remains exempt as it is seen as incidental to the residential use.

Timber rights

9.37 The right to allow a person to fell timber is standard-rated. However, the sale or lease of land containing woodland is exempt subject to the option to tax. A distinction is drawn between the rights to the timber afforded by the landowner and the rights of the land. (See CHAPTER **6**.)

Equestrian activities

9.38 A recent VAT Tribunal case *John Window [2001] VTD 17186* confirmed that the stabling of horses will remain exempt from VAT unless the option to tax has been made. Where any livery is provided as an incidental part of that stabling charge then the whole supply can remain exempt. In the past Customs have always treated the supply of livery and stabling as a single standard-rated supply so this change in interpretation will mean that the VAT treatment of both past and future stabling supplies should be reviewed.

Care should be taken in determining the VAT liability, however, as the nature of the supplies made will vary from client to client – some clients may only require DIY livery services (clearly exempt subject to the option to tax) whereas others will request full livery such that the level of care becomes the most predominant part of the supply and therefore remains standard-rated. The supplies made by racehorse trainers, stud farms and breaking-in are therefore not considered to be exempt in nature.

The exemption gives rise to opportunity for keeping the charges at a competitive level but businesses must remember that the ability to recover VAT on costs is also lost.

The provision of grazing rights is a zero-rated supply providing that the right is for a specific area of land for the purposes of allowing animals to feed. If a significant element of care is provided then the supply will be standard-rated.

Commercial supplies of horse riding lessons and tuition are considered to be educational and will qualify for exemption when provided by a partner, sole proprietor or non-profit making organisation. Corporate entities should treat the supplies as standard-rated unless they are also non-profit making and plough any 'profit' from this educational activity back into the furtherance of those activities.

Hacking and treks remain standard-rated unless they can be directly linked to an educational supply.

With the increasing exemptions available for stabling and educational tuition the business will need to consider the benefits of structuring these activities to maximise the VAT position. Whilst exemption will bring savings to the consumer, the business must consider the loss of VAT on related and overhead costs. (See **15.19**.)

Partial exemption — calculating the cost of exempt supplies

9.39 Legislation governing the application of partial exemption can be found in Value Added Tax Regulations 1995 (SI 1995/2518) Part XIV and Customs' interpretation of this in Notice 706.

When a business makes a mixture of exempt and taxable supplies it will suffer a restriction on the amount of input VAT that it incurs. This restriction is known as partial exemption. VAT cannot be recovered on the costs of making an exempt supply unless this VAT is beneath a de-minimis limit.

Whilst the making of exempt supplies means that no VAT is chargeable to the customer there is a cost to the business in that it restricts the VAT recovery on directly related costs and also on a proportion of overhead costs.

Any business making a mixture of exempt and taxable supplies should carefully consider the impact of partial exemption so that it can determine how much VAT is likely to be lost as a result of making exempt supplies – or what planning can be put in place to ensure that any loss is mitigated.

For a farmer seeking to diversify his activities his biggest resource will be land and property. These are normally exempt from VAT so that a move into increased land and property transactions – be it selling or letting, may well give rise to a VAT cost. In some cases early planning can mean that an option to tax can be made or that a transaction is structured to ensure it remains taxable. However, most businesses will have a partial exemption issue at some time in its existence and advance knowledge of it will ensure that any cost is factored into the sale value of exempt supplies.

The basic rules for partial exemption are that all input VAT must first be attributed either directly to a taxable supply, directly to an exempt supply or to an overhead cost (such as telephone, professional costs and running costs). Having identified the overhead VAT it must be apportioned so that only the proportion relating to taxable supplies is recoverable. Any costs directly relating to an exempt supply and the exempt proportion of the overhead cost are added together and are known as exempt input VAT. If the total amount of this exempt VAT is less than the de minimis limit (£625 per month and less than 50% of all input VAT) then all VAT is recoverable. If this limit is exceeded then none of the exempt VAT can be claimed in the VAT quarter.

The apportionment of the overhead VAT is the key issue and often forms one of the best planning opportunities. The 'standard method' is the most common method and does not need the prior permission of Customs. It is the method that must be used if no other method is requested or granted. The amount of overhead VAT that can be recovered is determined by the percentage that taxable supplies bear to total (taxable plus exempt) supplies. This percentage is rounded to the next whole number. An example of the standard method is given below:

EXAMPLE

A business has taxable sales of bed and breakfast accommodation and cereal crops and exempt income from the letting of barns and a residential cottage.

1   Identify all input VAT wholly attributable to taxable (ie standard-rated, lower rate and zero rate) supplies – say £2,000 on B&B and agricultural costs.
2   Identify all input VAT wholly attributable to exempt supplies – say £550 on the letting agreements and repairs.
3   Identify the rest (ie overheads etc) as being attributable to both taxable and exempt supplies – say £4,800.

The amount of input VAT that may be recoverable under (3) can be calculated by reference to the percentage of taxable supplies to total supplies in the period concerned.

Taxable supplies	£5,000
Exempt supplies	£15,000
	£20,000

Amount of overhead VAT recoverable under point 3 is therefore 25% (£1,200) and the amount of VAT which is therefore deemed to be attributable to exempt supplies is 75% (£3,600).

The total amount of exempt VAT in the period is therefore £550 plus £3,600 a total of £4,150. The VAT recoverable in the period is £2,000 plus £1,200 a total of £3,200.

The business should then check whether the value of exempt VAT is beneath the de minimis limit – if it is then all the VAT can be recovered. However, in our example £3,600 is above the £625 per month on average (£1,875 per quarter) but below 50% of all input VAT. As both tests are not met then none of the exempt VAT can be recovered.

However, at the end of the year (usually March, April or May dependent upon the VAT return periods) an annual adjustment is carried out and the quarterly calculation is repeated but using the year's figures. This may give the opportunity to recover exempt VAT which might have been irrecoverable in a previous VAT return, as the de-minimis limit is multiplied to a threshold of £7,500 and less than 50% of all input VAT.

Alternative methods

9.40   If the standard method does not produce a fair and reasonable result then a business can apply in writing to Customs for approval to use a special method. Once accepted the special method can be applied to the start of the current partial exemption year or from the start of the next year.

A special method can take any form – some of the most common are inputs based, but others can be staff time spent on taxable activities or floor space used for the making of taxable supplies. In the example above the letting activities generate a high value of sales but the business does very little to achieve them. Under the standard method the value of exempt supplies restricts the proportion of recoverable overhead VAT considerably. By opting for a special method based on the percentage that wholly taxable input VAT represents of wholly taxable plus wholly exempt input VAT, the percentage will increase from 25% to 79%. An alternative would be to consider the number of staff or hours involved in the taxable business against the total staff or hours used in the whole business.

Exclusions

9.41 There are some activities which, although exempt in nature, should not be included in the denominator of any value based calculations [Value Added Tax Regulations 1995 (SI 1995/2518) reg 101(3)].

Examples include the sale of capital assets. If an exempt property is sold, and that property was a capital asset of the business, then any VAT on costs incurred in making the exempt supply are still treated as exempt input VAT. However, the sale value of the property need not be included within the denominator of a value based apportionment calculation as to do so would be distortive. Other supplies which can be excluded from the denominator include those which are incidental to the main business activity are specified in reg 101(3), such as the sale of a business or part of a business, self supplies and reverse charge services, supplies involving finance and certain grants in relation to land and buildings.

Capital goods scheme — the exempt use of capital assets

9.42 The capital goods scheme applies where a VAT registered business purchases certain computers, computer equipment, land or buildings for use in his business. The scheme requires the business to review the use of the assets on a year-by-year basis over a given period of time. [Value Added Tax Regulations 1995 (SI 1995/2518) regs 112–116 Pt XV and Customs Notice 706/2 (updated January 2002) give more detailed information].

The scheme only covers computers and items of computer equipment with a tax exclusive value of £50,000 or more, and land and buildings of a tax exclusive value of £250,000 or more where the business acquires these for use in the business. The adjustment intervals are five for computers and ten for land and buildings (approximately five and ten years respectively). The 'use' clause means that businesses buying and selling properties are excluded: only those goods that are retained as capital assets in the balance sheet are to be included.

A land or building acquisition is covered by the capital goods scheme if:

- it costs more than £250,000 and tax has been charged on its purchase, or it has been the subject of a self-supply charge; or
- the building has been constructed by the person using it and the aggregate value of the land and the standard rate of construction costs is £250,000 or more; or
- it has been altered, enlarged or extended so as to create 10% or more additional floor area, and the value of the standard-rated works in connection with the alteration, extension or enlargement is £250,000 or more.

Refurbishments or fitting out costs where the value of capital expenditure is in excess of £250,000 will also fall within the capital goods scheme.

Unfortunately, the £250,000 limit for land and buildings now means that any business purchasing such a taxable asset is likely to have to consider the impact of the capital goods scheme. The scheme requires the business to monitor the use of an asset and to pay VAT back to Customs, or recover additional VAT from Customs, if the use of that asset varies from the use when first purchased.

EXAMPLE

A landowner has several barns on his property and wishes to convert one of them so that he can use it for his own office accommodation. The renovation and refurbishment of the barn costs £275,000 plus VAT. As the landowner makes no exempt supplies he can recover all the VAT on the costs incurred. Four years later he decides to let part of the barn to a tenant. He has not opted to tax so the rental income is exempt. Under the standard method of partial exemption his level of taxable activity is now 83%.

As the barn conversion cost in excess of £250,000 it has become a capital goods scheme item. This has no effect whilst he continues to use the barn for taxable purposes, but now that exempt income has commenced, Customs will require a proportion of the VAT originally recovered to be repaid to them. The amount of VAT to be repaid will be calculated on the taxable percentage determined under the partial exemption calculations but Customs can also be asked to base the calculation on the actual use of the barn. If the business originally claimed 100% of the input VAT it will be required to pay back to Customs the difference between the 100% recovery and the

---

current 83% although the adjustment is restricted to one-tenth for each year.

£48,125 divided by 10 = £4,812.50 x (100% – 83%) = £818.12

The calculation needs to be carried out on a yearly basis until the item is sold or the ten-year period has lapsed. In our example £818.12 must be repaid in the year that the letting commenced although allowance will be given for lettings part way through the year. If the level of exempt and taxable supplies remained constant at 83% then £818.12 would need to be repaid each interval for approximately the next six years.

If the barn was sold in year 4 then the calculation would be the same except that the remaining six years are treated as being for wholly exempt use so that a payment of £4,908.72 (£818.12 x 6) would need to be made in the adjustment period following the sale.

In the above examples the landowner has to repay input VAT to Customs and this becomes a cost to him. Advance planning will enable the landowner to build this cost into either his rental charges or sales value. Alternatively, by opting to tax the barn the landowner can avoid the adjustments under the scheme as his use would remain fully taxable.

Should the barn continue to be used as the landowner's office then the capital goods scheme will also bite if the general business of the landowner becomes partially exempt. In our above example if the barn continues to be used as an office the costs will be treated as an overhead of the business. If the landowner's business becomes partially exempt, perhaps he receives rent from the letting of residential properties, then a proportion of the VAT on overhead costs must be restricted in accordance with his partial exemption calculations. Even if he remains within the de minimis limits he is still required to carry out a capital goods scheme adjustment.

Transfer of a going concern (TOGC) — is VAT due on the sale of a business?

9.43   The sale, or purchase, of business will not be subject to VAT if the TOGC conditions are met.

This can benefit both the purchaser and the vendor and should be used wherever possible. The TOGC conditions are as follows, ie that:

● the purchaser is VAT registered, or required to be VAT registered, at the time of purchase;

- the purchaser will continue to carry out the same business activities as the vendor;
- what is transferred is a 'business' in its own right;
- there must be no significant break in trading; and
- the transfer must not be one of consecutive transfers.

For instance, the sale of land planted with crops can be sold as a transfer of going concern ie outside the scope instead of exempt, provided that the purchaser is VAT registered and that he will continue to farm the crops. The 'business' does not need to be a whole business – as long as what is sold can be operated as a separate business then this condition will be met.

The advantage of the going concern provisions is that the purchaser will not have to fund any additional VAT thus also making an absolute cash saving on stamp duty. The VAT incurred on the costs of selling the business should be recovered in accordance with the nature of the business being transferred. Thus, the sale of our farmed land would have given rise to a zero-rated supply if the crops were sold and the costs of the sale can therefore be recovered in full as relating to a wholly taxable supply. If the business was exempt then no VAT on costs would be recoverable and if the business was partially exempt then the costs should be treated as overhead.

Opted land

9.44 If the business being transferred includes land on which the vendor has opted then the purchaser must also opt in order for the TOGC requirements to be met. This is especially important and the purchaser should ensure that his option is submitted to Customs prior to the payment of a deposit on exchange if such monies are available to the vendor ie held by a solicitor as agent. If the solicitor acts as stakeholder then the deposit does not create a tax point and the option should be submitted to Customs prior to the completion date. If the option is not made in time then the transfer will not be a TOGC even if all other conditions are met (*Higher Education Statistics Agency Ltd [2000] STC 332*).

TOGCs and auctions

9.45 If an opted property is sold, then the sale may qualify to be treated as a TOGC providing that the normal TOGC rules are met and that the 'business' transferring is one of property rental. In addition to the normal rules the purchaser must make an option to tax as mentioned above.

In the case of an auction it is important for a purchaser to be aware of the VAT status of a property prior to making any bids. If the property can be transferred as a TOGC then the purchaser should make an option and post it prior to bidding. Customs now accept that written notification of the option to tax will be 'made' when it is put in the post (*Chalegrove Properties Ltd [2001] BVC 2279*). If unsuccessful, the bidder can rescind the option by writing to Customs within the three-month deadline. If successful then the purchaser will gain not only a cash flow advantage as there will be no VAT to pay, but also a real saving in the reduction stamp duty.

Allison Broadey

Allison Broadey has over 16 years' experience as a VAT practitioner, initially as a VAT Inspector with HM Customs & Excise, and then as 'gamekeeper turned poacher' in commercial practice. Having qualified as a Chartered Tax Adviser specialising in VAT with Coopers & Lybrand, she is now a Senior Consultant with The VAT Consultancy. She has a diverse range of clients in the farming and private sector and specialises in planning for land and property. She lectures to associations, practitioners and private businesses on all VAT matters. Allison Broadey and The VAT Consultancy can be contacted via www.thevatconsultancy.com or ab@thevatconsultancy.com.

The Reluctant Farmer   **10**

Julie Butler

- **Reluctant farmer**
  The tax reliefs available to both the farming and diversifying businesses are so great that it is worth all landowners considering whether or not they should ensure that the activity carried out on their land qualifies for future business tax reliefs. Business asset taper relief (BATR) at an effective 10% rate of tax from 6 April 2002 cannot be overlooked.

- **Reluctant farm practitioner**
  There are many general practitioners who have few agricultural clients but they do have a number of landowners who could benefit from a careful review of the business tax advantages of the land being used for farming or diversification.

- **Ownership structure of assets**
  The business status of the asset should not be 'tainted' by previous periods of non-business usage or ownership. The tax planner should check the correct ownership structure achieved to either maximise the generous reliefs available or at least not jeopardise claims for future tax reliefs.

Introduction

10.1 Rupert Bates wrote in *The Field* (May 2002): 'Over half of farms sold by Knight Frank last year were to buyers who had "little or no background in agriculture".'

The current UK business tax reliefs are very attractive and place a lot of emphasis on farmers and landowners to ensure that business status is achieved and maintained. This creates a position both of complexity and opportunity. The complex issues are discussed at length throughout the book, as are the tax planning opportunities. There is also an opportunity to create business status from barren and redundant land and buildings, which has obvious advantages. These issues are raised in the *TAXline* article 'Farming and Business Asset Relief' (see **A.2** and **20.18**), which perhaps should have been titled the 'Reluctant Farm Practitioner'.

There are those who love farming, the countryside, agriculture and all that goes with it and those that do not. There are those practitioners who see it as a complex, unprofitable industry to be avoided at all costs.

Most practitioners have clients who own land but have no interest in farming and this must be linked to the very favourable tax reliefs available for involving the land in a trading business. Various chapters of the book show the rules to ensure a farming activity qualifies as a business. The next chapter (**Chapter 11**) is devoted to explaining the ways of establishing the 'business' of farming without too much involvement in the actual 'dirty bits', eg contract farming and provisions to establish grazing agreements as business.

Maximising 'reluctant' tax reliefs

10.2 A Schedule D trade should exist where there is any profit arising from the occupation of land on a commercial basis.

The valuable reliefs that the reluctant farmers are seeking to secure are potentially beneficial capital gains tax reliefs on any future disposal and the beneficial inheritance tax reliefs. The latter are dealt with in **Chapter 4**, **Chapter 5** and **Chapter 13** and the former in **Chapter 14** on Property Transactions. Just for good measure there can be some very beneficial income tax and corporation tax reliefs as set out in **Chapter 12** with the main focus on losses.

The scene has been further set in **Chapter 2**, which explains that the Government direction is towards rural development and not direct farm subsidy. The chapter tries to set out what Government assistance can be obtained in looking at alternative land use. The benefits of business asset taper relief and the serial entrepreneur are also set out at **2.11**; and the provisions of 'tainted taper' are examined at **2.12**. In the same way that all diversified projects qualify for business asset taper relief (BATR) and should not fall foul of the 'tainted taper' considerations so too must the reluctant farmer ensure that the land is 'clean' and the claim for any taper relief will not be adversely jeopardised.

Reluctant traditional farmer

10.3   Imagine the situation where the happy landowner decides to venture into the mysterious world of farming to try and achieve a commercial return thereon whilst benefiting from associated tax reliefs.

The first step has to be to engage the professional services of a good land agent who can explain the alternatives and help with choice, grants and local contacts. If the traditional routes are chosen the alternatives generally are:

- contract farming;
- grazing agreements established as business;
- share farming;
- farm business tenancies (although these have to do with restricted tax reliefs).

These are all explained in more detail in Chapter 11. It must be emphasised that whether the ultimate goal of the reluctant farmer is to achieve beneficial tax reliefs through possible development or other sale proceeds, any arrangement must be well drafted and subject to scrutiny by the Inland Revenue. It must not be artificial and if development proceeds are involved it must not insult a keen tax inspector. Professional help is essential. Any agreement must be drafted by an experienced agricultural solicitor. The ownership structure (to avoid any 'tainted taper') should be reviewed jointly with solicitor/tax adviser and the whole project must have a full tax report in 'the round' which covers all areas of the income tax/capital gains tax/inheritance tax/VAT together with commercial budget business plans, advice on proper record keeping, etc. If tax protected development gains are the long-term aim it is well worth the effort and attention to detail.

Reluctant diversifying landowner

10.4   It might be that the traditional trade of farming (even if neatly packaged in a well-drafted and structured contract farming agreement) might not be attractive and the benefit of schemes under the rural development packages would be more appealing. These could be more commercial and in theory produce a more profitable return, especially on a small holding of land. Again, the first point of call is the progressive land agent well versed in diversification projects, planning permission and Government grants and support, as mentioned in Chapter 2. The same requirement for ownership structure, complete tax report and business plans apply.

It has been argued that another practical point is to try and obtain some bank borrowings to fund the project. A well-chosen business bank manager should be able to help review the plan and add value to different areas of commerciality. This and one year's free banking (perhaps) for new businesses could be worth taking advantage of.

Reluctant farm practitioner

10.5 Abuse of the tax provisions is foolhardy in the extreme. Reluctant farmers must not become 'lets see how far we can push it' landowners. The recent case of *Dixon v IRC [2002] STC (SCD) 53* gives an interesting ruling in this area (see **4.25**).

In the same way that there are people who love farming and the countryside and those who do not, there are also practitioners who love working with agricultural and rural industries and those who do not. There are many practitioners who would actually actively try to avoid agricultural clients because they know the complexities surrounding farm and land management from a tax viewpoint. Unless they act for a large number of farming clients they feel that it is not worthwhile having a one-off client. Farmers' averaging, herd basis election, agricultural property relief (APR), Business Economic Note 19 (BEN 19) for stock valuations (see **Appendix B**) together with the complexities of trying to sort out farming income from non-farming income does not make it commercial to only act for a handful of farming clients.

However, land ownership is something that is common to all accountancy firms and with the move from farming to diversification it is likely to embrace far more practitioners than previously. The fact that so many agricultural properties are being bought by people with no previous agricultural experience and that the Government direction is towards a revival of the rural economy rather than farm subsidies points towards a new type of landowner and a new type of practitioner.

Many practitioners might find that their existing clients are buying land and they are forced to embrace the farming rules reluctantly. It could be that a new business venture is only semi-agricultural but there is still a need to understand the complexities. It could be that a reluctant farming practitioner has a reluctant farming client who owns land which needs to establish genuine business status in view of some future development or potential capital gain and establishing business usage of land could be more common to general practices than first considered.

Share Farming, Contract Farming, Farm Business Tenancies and Other Farming Agreements **11**

Julie Butler

- **Casual lettings**

  The tax disadvantages of land being 'let' as opposed to being utilised in a trading business has been emphasised through the chapters. Some tenancies such as farm business tenancies (FBTs) and grazing can still attract restricted tax reliefs. The chapter emphasises the need for all letting arrangements to be reviewed and formalised for maximum tax reliefs and protection.

- **Contract farming**

  Contract farming can be a very tax efficient method of farming the land without some of the complications of share farming. The advantage over an FBT is that capital gains tax (CGT) reliefs are still preserved. A well-drafted agreement supported by facts that would stand up to Inland Revenue scrutiny is essential.

- **The need for an agreement**

  It is important that the landowner reviews carefully all the options and chooses the option to suit their specific requirements. Whatever choices (or complex series of choices for each area) are made it is essential to ensure that current and future arrangements are reviewed for tax efficiency and protected by formal agreement.

Introduction

11.1 With the decline in farm profitability it has been important to try to control costs and keep overheads to a minimum whilst trying to achieve tax efficiency. One way of achieving this has been through share farming and contract farming agreements. Since 1 September 1995 advantage has also been made of the farm business tenancy (FBT) provisions. It is useful to look at each one in turn. The aim of these agreements must be that they are not only commercially viable but also tax efficient. The drafting of the correct agreement is all-important. This is set out very clearly in the article entitled 'Casual Lettings' published in *Taxation* on 11 April 2002. Some of the points of the article are further emphasised in the book. The problems surrounding casual lettings are set out in **11.2** below.

Casual lettings

11.2 In an effort to overcome the decline in farming incomes, many landowners are engaging in casual letting or grazing agreements. Likewise, farming units are trying to take on more land under management in order to take advantage of the economies of scale.

Many tenancy arrangements have arisen without the appropriate legal advice having been taken, and this can have unpleasant tax consequences. The introduction of the FBT from 1 September 1995 has placed the landowner in the apparently happy position of having 100% agricultural property relief (APR) available for inheritance tax (IHT) purposes. However, it must be remembered that a FBT does not attract capital gains tax (CGT) reliefs and can have restrictions for expenses, as essentially it should be taxed under Schedule A and not Schedule D Case 1. Furthermore, the farmhouse will probably not qualify for expenses claims under Schedule D, or claims for IHT relief where the farm has been let. This is currently very important with the increasing value of farmhouses in the UK.

It is often overlooked that the FBT (subject to previous tax status) will have to be in existence for seven years in order to qualify for IHT APR, whereas a contract farming arrangement which is properly constructed will give the landowner the ability to show that he is the main occupier and, therefore, bring himself within Inheritance Tax Act 1984 (IHTA 1984) s 117(a). The result is that the minimum period of occupation or ownership required to be eligible for APR is two years rather than seven.

Grazing rights

11.3 Where a landlord grants a FBT in relation to the farmland he is no longer a farmer of that parcel of land but a landlord. This can apply with grazing rights, unless he carries out the following functions:

1 he cultivates, sows and establishes the grass crop;
2 he harrows and rolls the grass as necessary;
3 he fertilises the grass crop in spring and through the season as necessary;
4 it is important that the owner should cut or spray all weeds to prevent seeding and the owner must do any mowing that may be required for whatever reason.

This has been looked at in **4.30** and again in **11.35**. The grazier must also covenant not to mow or cut the grass and the owner must do any hedging, fencing and ditching needed and any other work of a proprietorial nature.

If the landowner manages to achieve this he should then be deemed to be a Schedule D taxpayer with paramount occupancy and, therefore, eligible for not only the APR available on the land, but also the APR on the farmhouse. The period of occupancy could then also be reduced. There is also greater potential to claim business expenses and qualify for CGT relief.

Historically, many written and un-written tenancies have evolved within farming partnerships and farming arrangements between members of the family, and these could jeopardise the tax shelter the farmland should present. Likewise, diversification could move towards the claim for business property relief (BPR) and not APR and, again, jeopardise the claim for APR on the farmhouse (see **Chapter 4**).

Another problem facing the farming community arises where members of an arrangement with the advantage of a pre-1 September 1995 tenancy then wish to change it. This could give rise to serious tax consequences and problems, such as the surrender of the tenancy (see **11.18**).

Careful planning

11.4 The farming community is being forced to look more closely at contract and share farming arrangements, which will make available Schedule D Case 1 tax reliefs and the associated APR/BPR, and CGT reliefs. It is essential that these contract farming arrangements are carefully drafted so as to protect the landlord. The Country Land and Business Association (CLA) has a draft agreement for share farming and all landowners and farmers should look to the current structure of the farming agreement in place and ensure that they are not jeopardising very valuable reliefs (see www.cla.org.uk).

The number of farmers who die intestate is alarming and while looking at all matters such as partnership agreements, tenancy arrangements and the tax consequences, and ensuring that all major reliefs are protected, it is essential that this review is linked in with a good tax-efficient Will (see CHAPTER **18**).

Care needs to be taken where gratuitous licence situations might have arisen where partnerships occupy land. Examples of how licences and tenancies can cause problems on the restriction on future IHT relief were explained in *Taxation* (13 December 2001) when Matthew Hutton highlighted some of the planning points of the October 2001 Countryside Tax Conferences. He commented on the points raised by Adrian Baird concerning bare licences of land outside the partnership. It was stated that it was feared that the Capital Taxes Office (CTO) will deny 100% APR for IHT purposes to the interest of the landowner who owns land outside of the partnership which he makes available to the partnership on a bare licence in circumstances where there is no documentary evidence as to the terms of occupation.

This might sound a rare and obscure point but there are actually probably more circumstances where this actually happens than at first meets the eye. Matthew Hutton and Adrian Baird noted that because the landowner was not able to get vacant possession within 12 months he is not able to secure 100% relief under IHTA 1984 s 116(2)(a). Likewise, because there is no tenancy in place, the extension of 12–24 months by extra-statutory concession F17 did not apply.

Adrian Baird stated that subject to any agreement to the contrary among the parties the basic rule under Partnership Act 1890 s 26 is that retirement can be secured simply by notice. Adrian suggested that the easiest solution in such a case is to have a document confirming that the partnership can be dissolved and/or the owner can recover his land (or payment of appropriate compensation) within a period of less than 12 months to satisfy the IHT requirement.

It was stated that where there is currently no deed there could be evidence in the form of partnership minutes that the parties have agreed to a notice period by the landlord of less than 12 months, which should put paid to any suggestion following the landowner's death that he could not so recover vacant possession.

This gives another clear indication of the need to review all legal agreements currently in place with the farming family.

The question that presents itself most regularly in the review is that of who is the paramount user or occupier. Let us now review more of the detail of each of the alternatives.

Share farming

The concept

11.5   The principle of share farming should be to try and take advantage of the economies of scale. Where smaller farming units need only part of a machine it is possible to share equipment. It has also evolved into an arrangement whereby a landowning farmer 'shares' the farming and has time to seek other profit alternatives.

Each party should be conducting a separate business. There should be separate bank accounts, except perhaps for one into which gross takings are paid and then divided into agreed shares. Each party must keep their own accounting records. If there are meetings, as there should be, to decide farm policy there should be minutes of those meetings. Without such minutes it may well be very difficult to show that the landowner has taken any active part in the farming operation at all. Whilst this might be seen to be over protective the size and strength of the CGT and IHT reliefs must not be overlooked.

In a share farming agreement the landowner and the farming operator agree to split the sale proceeds in a particular ratio based on the relative values of their contribution to the venture. Examples of the contributions are as follows:

- The share farmer provides:
  - labour;
  - machinery – moveable plant and equipment;
  - management – liaison on the farm policy with the landowner;
  - working capital in the form of a share of variable costs;
  - a share in the livestock.
- The landowner provides:
  - farmland and buildings;
  - farmhouse;
  - fixed equipment such as milking parlours or grain dryers;
  - major property repairs;
  - working capital in the form of a share of variable costs;
  - a share in the livestock;
  - involvement in the decision-making of farming policy.

Accounts and tax

11.6   The share farming agreement should ensure that the two businesses are separate with their own VAT workings and tax assessments. It is essential to try and ensure that the arrangement is not constructed as a partnership otherwise the parties will be joint and severally liable for each other's debts. If there was a deemed partnership there will also have to be partnership accounts prepared with a partnership and the related self-assessment tax returns and all the problems that are associated with this.

It is also noted that no tenancy is created providing the operator does not enjoy exclusive possession of any part of the land and buildings.

Generally, it is not considered necessary to produce a full set of accounts for a share farming venture as both parties' tax returns will include the proportion of output rather than it just being linked to a profit figure. Generally, the annual accounts to be drawn up by the landowning share farmer will only include a proportion of the gross margin and will exclude the items of the overhead paid for by the share farmer.

It is generally considered that the growing crops will be the property of the landowner whilst in the ground but the cultivation which is carried out by the share farmer up to the end of the accounting period will have been carried out by the share farmer's own labour and machinery. The value of tillages will also be the property of the landowner at this stage with a corresponding amount owing to the share farmer.

Inheritance tax and capital gains tax planning

11.7   The aim is to establish the share farming agreement as a trade assessable under Schedule D. In practice, the amount of income assessable will be similar under Schedule D and Schedule A, but it is the reliefs from CGT and IHT that must be preserved. It might be that this question of CGT and IHT will not arise until the first capital disposal is made when the Inland Revenue might ask for a detailed examination of the agreement.

It is important to ensure that full business asset taper relief (BATR) is preserved and that problems of 'mixed usage' and 'tainted taper relief' are avoided (see CHAPTERS **12** and **14**).

In order to be sure that APR (and in some cases, BPR) is not lost, the landowner must show that he is the paramount occupier and, therefore, brings himself within IHTA 1984 s 117(a), with the result that the minimum period of occupation or ownership required to earn relief is two years rather than seven. Such a valuable relief as APR is worth the effort to comply strictly with statutory requirements. The success of the use of farmland as a tax shelter does lie extensively in the care with which the arrangements are drawn up.

Another important factor is that if the share farmer is genuinely in a Schedule D trade then the farmhouse is treated as being part of the farming unit and it should be a case that the tax relief on the farmhouse will be preserved (see CHAPTER **4**). A similar position concerning cottages will also apply and the use of this agreement is important.

The risks

11.8 The advantage of the above approach is that the landowner can retain a genuine interest and involvement in the farm. However, if the arrangements are not set up correctly there are risks involved:

1 the risk of classification as a partnership;
2 the risk of tenancy status; or
3 the risk of loss of trading status for IHT and CGT and income tax reliefs.

There is not enough room in this book to explore the full risks of partnership and tenancy status and these would be best explained by a legal practitioner.

These points emphasise the need to have a correctly drafted legal agreement. Alternative ways of farming could be reviewed, such as contract farming. With the current emphasis on the Inland Revenue looking at the 'true facts' and being concerned over 'fragility' and 'artificiality' of arrangements, sound legal drafting is not enough – the correct facts must be in place. The Inland Revenue take as much notice of what is actually happening as to what is supposed to be happening.

The need for an agreement

11.9 Whilst share farming is generally acceptable to the Inland Revenue as 'trading as a farmer', there have been occasions when the whole principle has been questioned. Again, it is very important that the agreement is correctly constructed to ensure that there is no partnership and that it will pass Inland Revenue scrutiny and be established as a Schedule D trade. It is recommended that share farming agreements follow the model agreements from the CLA, which have had Inland Revenue approval, and that legal advice is looked for when drafting the agreement.

If any element of the farm be disposed of (see Chapter **14**) then the importance of ensuring that the tax position is correct cannot be emphasised too greatly, especially with favourable CGT business asset taper reliefs from 6 April 2002. The Inland Revenue has agreed that under an agreement based on the model set out by the CLA the landowner may establish trading status. It is important that the farmer shows that he concerns himself with the details of farming policy. The farmer must go on to the land for a material purpose, eg inspect crops or stock and decide the farming policy in the light of that inspection. The CLA have undoubtedly done much good work in this area and this is reflected in their publication *Share Farming: The Practice*. Model forms of agreement can be obtained from the CLA (www.cla.org.uk).

Under share farming both the landowner and operator farm the land. The tenancy problem is avoided if neither the landowner nor the operator has exclusive possession. The landowner must retain occupation of the land and any buildings for CGT purposes. The operator should have a mere licence to occupy. A difficulty could arise where, for example, animals on the land are owned by one party or the other subject to agreement rather than shares. The occupation of the land by the animals might lead to the owner of the land being regarded as the occupier of the land. Again, the risk of inadvertently entering into partnership must be avoided.

Contract farming

The concept

11.10 A contract farming arrangement is essentially a landowner using the services of a contractor or another farmer to farm the land. The landowner supplies variable costs of seeds, fertilisers and sprays for growing the crops. The contracting farmer supplies labour, machinery and management.

Examples of when a contract farming arrangement can be used effectively would be at the time of retirement of a farm manager; or when a tenanted farm has fallen vacant due to the departure of the tenant and the landlord does not wish to farm the land himself: he may lack the capital or the inclination to do so but nonetheless wishes to retain vacant possession, having in mind that one of his family might wish to have a farming career in the future. Sometimes the contract farming arrangements are entered into following farming losses when the landowner will take the view that they cannot continue to incur losses and would want to try and make the outfit more productive, effectively sharing in economies of scale and reducing employment costs.

Generally, the contractor will receive a set fee for the services provided and a bonus as a percentage of the calculated surplus from the venture. The arrangement is suitable for both livestock and cropping enterprises. The contracting income received by the contractor must be reviewed carefully. Whereas it will qualify as income under Schedule D Case 1 for the contractor, it will often *not* qualify as farm income.

Accounts and tax

11.11 Contract farming agreements generally centre around a memorandum joint venture account, which is an arithmetical calculation to establish how much the contractor should be paid for the services. It is often advisable in a contract farming agreement to set up a separate bank account in the landowner's name with all transactions relating to the agreement going through the account. This would also automatically divide the interest calculation on working capital as the account becomes overdrawn to fund variable costs.

The funding of the variable costs in a cropping agreement can be provided by the contracting farmer. In this instance the contracting farmer is providing an interest-free loan to the landowner as the legal title to the crops always remains with the landowner. It is essential that a correctly drawn-up agreement should aim to enable a landowner to carry on the trade of farming and provide a reasonable return for both parties, even within the current falling income position in the UK. This should then ensure that the landowner will preserve the business reliefs for not just IHT but also for CGT. Additionally, the IHT reliefs on the farmhouse are also preserved as this is one of the assets provided in the arrangement (see **Chapter 4**).

Businesses with financial year-ends prior to the calculation of a memorandum account will not know how much to provide for the amount owing to the contracting farmer for the final profit share. There are two options available:

1   delay the preparation of the final accounts until the creditor is known (this would depend upon the time delay involved); or
2   include an estimated amount for the profit share, which will have to be adjusted the following year in the contract charge.

Many contract farming arrangements include an annual valuation of grain for sale, variable costs and cultivations in September.

Unless the financial year-end of the business is the same time as the valuation it has no practical use or relevance to the preparation of the annual accounts.

The total remuneration of the contractor consists of supplying the following services:

1   labour;
2   machinery; and
3   management.

The total amount is normally invoiced as contracting fees plus VAT. It must be noted that each party is treated as a separate business for VAT and tax (see **Chapter 9**).

With current farm cottage rents as high as they are the cost of a farm employee becomes greater and the employment law problems surrounding this become even more so. This has resulted in some radical redundancies and some sharp contract farm agreements. Sometimes contract farming arrangements are entered into out of the pure necessity that the landowner physically cannot continue to commercially farm with the more conventional method of employing a farm manager and staff living in farm cottages.

Inheritance tax and capital gains tax planning

11.12 The advantage of contract farming is that for income tax purposes the landowner preserves Schedule D Case 1 status and the position and ability to offset any losses against other income under ICTA 1988 s 380 (see **Chapter 12**). There is also a greater ability to claim for general overhead farming expenses than under a FBT (see **11.15**). The CGT reliefs available to the farm should be preserved under a contract farming arrangement. For example, rollover relief, retirement relief (until it is phased out) and the business assets rate of taper relief (which is so beneficial from 6 April 2002) should be available.

A key tax planning point is the benefit of BATR and the possibility of 'tainted taper relief' where there has been a change of business status, ie from tenancy to contract. This must be looked at very carefully and is dealt with in **Chapter 12** and **Chapter 14**.

Ideally, if both owner and contractor are carrying on separate farming businesses then BPR at the rate of 100% will be available on the business assets of both parties. The owner should be regarded as farming the land and, therefore, APR at a rate of 100% should be allowable. However, it must be noted that the relief will depend upon whether it can be said that the landowner has a right to vacant possession, which will in turn depend upon the construction of the contract farming agreement.

This is another clear example of where a farmer who provides contracting services must check their tax computation and the practitioner must give very careful consideration to the position (see **12.4**). Clients with substantial contract farming income should be warned that a proportion of their income may not be treated as the trade of farming and that contracting income may have to be excluded in any averaging calculation (see **11.14** and **20.1**).

The risks

11.13 The landowner involved in a contract management agreement will inevitably be exposed to an element of risk as the result of fluctuating production and prices. In essence the landowner will continue the trade of farming and the degree of risk will depend upon the structure of the actual agreement. In many contract management agreements the contractor is not paid a fixed fee in profit share until after all crop proceeds have been received by the landowner. At this stage the contractor is exposed to substantial risk, particularly if the variable cost has also been funded by the contractor.

To minimise the risk to the contractor it is preferable to include within the agreement a clause giving the contractor the option to purchase the grain at the prevailing market price. The grain can then be immediately sold by the contractor for the same prevailing market price. In practice, most agreements state that the contractor has full responsibility for marketing the grain as agent on behalf of the landowner.

As long as the contractor can show that he purchased the grain for the current market price he does not contravene the agreement. The contractor will have acted professionally and will be able to contra any amount owing from the landlord for work done from the payment for the grain.

It must be mentioned that in the current farming climate it is critical for commercial viability to ensure that a return will be made under the contract farming arrangements and some are obviously making losses. This is pushing clients towards the more attractive return in farm business tenancies and the merits and problems associated therewith are reviewed at **11.15**.

The need for an agreement

11.14 In practice, there are a multitude of agreements operating in the agricultural industry. Many of these are inadequate or with no written documentation. Unless the written agreements and their operation are very similar to the structures required to establish a trade then practitioners must warn clients that their farming business status may be questioned by the Inland Revenue. All clients should be encouraged to have agreements reviewed by a good agricultural lawyer.

A correctly constructed agreement for contract farming is more straightforward than with share farming. Essentially, one party is supplying contracting services to a landowner. From the contractors' viewpoint, in practice, most contractors involved in these arrangements also farm in their own right. Therefore, their contracting income in addition to their income from their farming trade (depending upon the relative amounts) will be accepted as farming income. However, in the case where contractors do not farm land and derive all their income from contract farming they will be treated by the Inland Revenue as contractors and not farmers (see **11.12**).

It is important that the contract farming arrangement will not be construed as a tenancy agreement. For this reason it might be best not to stipulate three-year reviews as creating an obvious analogy with the three-year reviews of agricultural rents (in England and Wales). It is desirable that the agreement operates for a limited period only so that this rental equivalent can be reviewed in line with current market rents. With regard to the latter it is possible to arrange to share out the profits of the enterprise in a variety of ways, but it is usual to reserve a slice of the profit for the owner corresponding to the amount he would have received had he let the farm in the normal way.

Care will be needed so that the arrangement is not construed as a partnership agreement or as creating the relationship of employer/employee, all of which might create tax consequences other than those intended. It is also important that the contract is drafted so that the owner does not inadvertently purport to transfer ownership of/or an interest in the farm property to the contractor.

The CLA do not actually have a model for contract farming as they do for share farming but it is essential to receive good legal advice to see if a correct drafting can be achieved.

Farm business tenancies (FBTs)

The concept

11.15   Farm business tenancies, also known as FBTs, were introduced on 1 September 1995 under the Agricultural Tenancies Act 1995. Any land let for agricultural purposes after this date will be subject to an FBT. The advantages are that FBTs give greater freedom of contract and tenancies of any length without security of tenure. Also, there are open market rent reviews (unless no review of formula) and compensation for improvements at value added to the land. In simple terms, the FBT may replace any of the following arrangements:

- seasonal cropping agreement;
- Ministry licences (usually five years);
- 'Gladstone & Bower' arrangements (usually 23 months);
- land let under the Agricultural Holdings Act 1986 (AHA 1986), which provided lifetime rights; or
- pre-AHA 1986 tenancy, which contained the right to succession.

However, it is noted that they *cannot* replace the following arrangements:

- grass keep arrangements;
- share farming; or
- contract management agreements.

All these are dealt with in detail in this chapter. It must also be noted that a FBT is not retrospective and it will not interfere with existing arrangements.

Accounts and tax

11.16 Farm accounts should show clearly the rental income and record the allowable expenses. Rental income under a FBT is treated as Schedule A for tax purposes, whereas the income of contract farming and share farming is assessable under Schedule D. Any Schedule D losses brought forward cannot be used against this income and can only be carried forward to be used against any future Schedule D farming income. The expenses that will be allowed against this Schedule A income will be restricted to the costs directly attributed to the land ownership; therefore many costs will not be eligible for tax relief, such as expenses relating to the farmhouse and motor vehicle of the landowner etc. The fact that the FBT is Schedule A income will also cause problems concerning pension payments. However, the new pension provisions will ease this situation to a small extent.

Inheritance tax and capital gains tax planning

The history

11.17 The introduction of FBTs was heralded as a point of golden opportunity for the landowner in that he had an opportunity to secure 100% APR where previously this had not been available. However, the income tax and CGT position of these tenancies should not be overlooked. When land is let under a FBT the landowner is deemed to be no longer trading. Rollover relief on any capital gain that may arise will usually be restricted on a time-apportioned basis. The whole position of eligibility should be reviewed.

Surrender of old tenancy

11.18 The creation of a new FBT is a relatively straightforward matter. Much greater complications arise where there is an existing tenancy under the AHA 1986 or there is no right to vacant possession within either 12 months or 24 months. In order for the landlord to achieve 100% APR the tenancy should come to an end. In order to achieve this there must be a clear surrender of the old tenancy and a grant of the new. In his book *Business and Agricultural Property Relief* (LexisNexis Butterworths Tolley), Toby Harris goes to some length into explaining the provisions of IHTA 1984 s 116(2) and explores the position where the tenant of an old tenancy dies and a new tenancy commences. For a landlord currently bound by the tenancy arrangements, there are lots of useful details contained within this book.

To try and put it in summary, provisions of IHTA 1984 s 116 apply to all land subject to a FBT. In addition, it would apply to land let subject to any succession tenancy granted on or after 1 September 1995 under AHA 1986. This is extended so that it can include cases where the land transferred is let under a tenancy granted before 1 September 1995 but where either:

- a valid retirement notice for succession has been made after that date; or
- the tenant has died after that date and the tenancy has become invested or obtained by another person as a consequence.

The full details are outside the scope of this book but the aim of this section is to set out the worries and concerns so that they can be looked at in more detail.

Defining the commencement date

11.19 It is important, therefore, to look at the question as to the precise circumstances where a tenancy can be correctly regarded as commencing after that date having regard to the old and new tenant legislation. Obviously the starting point is 1 September 1995, so tenancies falling under the new legislation will qualify for 100% relief. Some tenancies governed by the old legislation will qualify for 100% relief because the tenancy began on or after 1 September 1995, for example, a succession tenancy following the serving of a retirement notice or death of tenant in occupation on 31 August 1995. In succession cases it may be possible to qualify for 100% relief where the new tenancies have not yet begun at the date of transfer, for example, where the landlord dies before the commencement of the new succession tenancy but after the death of the tenant or the serving of a retirement notice.

At this stage it is wise to look at any cases where 100% relief was already available before 1 September 1995 for certain qualifying tenancies. These situations were where the landlord had the right to vacant possession or the right to obtain it within the following 12 months [IHTA 1984 s 116(2a)]. Also, by February 1995 let land will have had the right to qualify for relief where the landowner had the right to vacant possession within 24 months (Inland Revenue extra-statutory concession F17).

The surrender of tenancies does create some practical problems and these are set out in Oliver Stanley's book *Taxation of Farmers and Landowners* (LexisNexis Butterworths Tolley) sections 15.22–15.30.

Planning period of ownership

11.20 APR at 100% is available for land let under a FBT but in order to qualify the land must have been either owned for seven years or have been farmed in hand, ie under Schedule D Case 1, for at least two years ending in the year of transfer. Therefore, new owners of agricultural land should ideally farm the land themselves for two years or contract farm the land for the first seven years before letting it on a FBT to secure APR at the earliest opportunity.

Double discount

11.21   It is also important to look at the case of the double discount. This will be where the pre-1981 full-time working farmer relief provisions would have applied had they not been abolished and the transitional provisions are satisfied. The main example will be land continuously let to a partnership or a company since before 10 March 1981, which the transferor has previously farmed in some capacity.

Conclusion

11.22   Whilst a FBT is very attractive due to the IHT relief available to owners of tenanted land there are those who argue that more time will have to elapse before it can be seen exactly what will happen with regard to the reliefs theoretically available. It is for this reason that the contract farming arrangement has been so successful as it gives better tax reliefs for income tax and for CGT and, possibly, gives greater clarity for IHT. However, an FBT can have the advantage that they have less involvement and less management than, say, contract farming. A FBT can suit a wide range of enterprises. Enter into all agreements with eyes wide open and take good advice from an experienced land agent.

The risks

11.23   In order to qualify as a FBT it is essential that the land is farmed as a trade or business and that the use of the land and character of the tenancy is primarily and wholly agricultural. Fixed farm tenancies of two years or less will expire automatically at the end of the term but fixed tenancies of two years plus will continue as yearly tenancies until notices between one or two years expiring on the contractual term date have been served. Rents may be determined by agreement between the parties.

The tax risks are the potential loss of CGT reliefs, the loss of trading expenses and concerns over IHT complications. The other risks are the complexity of tenancy rules as set out above.

The need for an agreement

11.24   This chapter highlights the need for well-drafted agreements. It is hoped that the strength of the available tax reliefs shows the need to use an agricultural specialist to draft the agreement and a tax specialist to ensure the tax treatment is correct.

Farming partnership/farming the land as a licensee/tenancies

The history

11.25 Historically, many farming partnerships have actually farmed the land that they jointly owned under a tenancy. This may present substantial tax problems. The tax planner must carefully review the IHT and CGT implications.

Tenancy compared with licensee

11.26 There are those who would argue that where there is an existing family farming tenancy it should be brought to an end. If this is the case it is not just the tax costs of making the change that should be considered but what are the advantages of the existing structure and what new structure could be substituted. It is, therefore, important to look at the tax consequences of having any form of agricultural tenancy in place as opposed to a licence. Once the licence is put in place it must be capable of being achieved that the owners interest in the land carries the right to vacant possession so that APR at 100% will be secured. The effect on any change of status on business asset taper relief with the impact of 'tainted taper' relief must be considered.

The disadvantages of tenancies

11.27 The tax disadvantages of any form of tenancy are as follows.

- The creation of a tenancy can give the tenanted land a lower base cost for CGT purposes where there is a death intervening. This is because on the first death the IHT value will be reduced by the tenancy and this will be the base cost of CGT. Obviously, the age of the landowners for proposed future sales should be considered.
- APR might be put in jeopardy because of a failure to complete the stipulated seven-year ownership requirement.
- CGT reliefs of rollover (and to be phased out, retirement relief) could be lost. However, there could be an ability to secure business asset taper relief. This should be reviewed in each specific case.

Changing the current structure

11.28 A lot of farmers who are working within a family structure will be reluctant to change arrangements which are currently working well, both from a farming and a business standpoint, simply to try and obtain better tax relief. Nevertheless, it is essential that tax drawbacks are pointed out, at the very least, for consideration of protection under professional indemnity insurance. Likewise, it should be noted that any change in the partnership arrangements is likely to involve legal costs. Again the position of tainted taper relief must be considered.

Consideration must be given to the changes in the legal structure of the partnership, which could in themselves give rise to CGT. It should also be considered that there is a possibility of CGT arising on the termination of a tenancy. The tenant will be making a disposal of an asset, which may be regarded as significant capital value. It could be deemed that the tenant has potential IHT problems. The tenant will need to consider whether, on a surrender of his tenancy, he is making a transfer of value for IHT purposes and, if so, what is the value of such a transfer and whether the transfer qualifies for APR.

Surrender of old tenancy

11.29 It should be noted that the surrender of the old tenancy by a tenant certainly does diminish the estate by value. Clearly, from case law such as *Baird v IRC [1991] 1 EGLR 201* a non-assignable agricultural tenancy has a value for IHT. It must be questioned, therefore, that where a landlord and tenant are in negotiations to surrender an old tenancy, with a view to bringing in a FBT, the Inland Revenue might argue that the old tenancy has a significant value, due to the landlord and the tenant wanting to extinguish it, and consideration must be given to the value of the land being greater once the old tenancy has been removed. The Capital Taxes Office has indicated that it intends to construe IHTA 1984 s 124A(3)(a) strictly.

A solution to this would appear that it is the surrender of the tenancy made for no consideration. Any gain should be capable of being held over. The tenancy is a qualifying asset within Taxation of Chargeable Gains Act 1992 (TCGA 1992) s 165(2)(a). The problem arises where there are monies paid for the transfer, as the surrender of an existing tenancy for consideration is the disposal of a chargeable asset for CGT purposes. The tenant will be deemed to receive the open market value of the tenancy as consideration [TCGA 1992 ss 17–18].

Review of all tenancy situations

11.30 There has been a large amount of coverage in the Farming Press recently about landlords wishing to change to FBTs from the old tenancies, and the tenants receiving quite a considerable sum of money for this. This has helped some parties considerably in that the landlord has a chance for better APR and greater security over his own land, and the tenant receives a considerable sum, which in these difficult farming times can be the difference between failing or surviving.

It is essential in any circumstance to clearly weigh up the tax consequences and it is advised that all landholding operations involving third parties, that could in any way be considered a tenancy situation, be assessed as part of the current review of assets.

Casual letting, grazing tenancies and income from grasslands

Casual letting of land

11.31   The casual letting of land does not spoil the qualification of the landowner to be regarded as the occupier. The cases of *IRC v Forsythe Grant (1943) 25 TC 369* and *Mitchell v IRC (1943) 25 TC 380* give examples of this. Problems can arise when there is a significant interval between one casual letting and another and whether the land used has been for the purposes of agriculture in the intervening time. Problems also arise where one grazing agreement after another, or one 'Gladstone and Bower' agreement after another, has been entered into over a period of time. It could well be argued by the Inland Revenue that the taxpayer has effectively let the land. Care must be taken on the drafting of agreements and the structure of the arrangement to ensure tax efficiency.

Grazing tenancies

11.32   The position of grazing tenancies needs to be looked at very carefully to see whether it is actually the trade of farming or Schedule A. If the latter applies there is jeopardy to all the tax reliefs that have been discussed previously. Obviously, the owner of the land which is let for grazing and who manages to secure that the income be treated as farming income can obtain many of the tax advantages of business reliefs for CGT, of the IHT reliefs both APR and BPR, together with income tax expenses. The CLA has recommended a form of deed to grant a right of herbage, which has been approved by the Inland Revenue (see www.cla.org.uk).

With regard to IHT the Inland Revenue have agreed that a landowner who continues to occupy a farmhouse on a farm which is grazed by tenants may still be in agricultural occupation of the farmhouse, provided the income from grazing is farming income, and hence will potentially qualify for APR (see Cʜᴀᴘᴛᴇʀ **4**). If, on the other hand, grazing income is purely Schedule A income and there are no other farming activities undertaken, there is a risk that the APR on the farmhouse will be lost. There are also VAT advantages on grassland, which is deemed to be a zero-rated trade supply and the VAT can be claimed against it (see Cʜᴀᴘᴛᴇʀ **9**).

It is essential that a landowner who wishes to secure these tax advantages is meticulous in their approach to the nature of the grazing agreement and the activities they agree to undertake. It is important that, under ICTA 1988 s 832 (see **1.3**), the farmer is proved to be occupying the land for the purposes of husbandry so as to preserve APR.

Paramount user

11.33   In order to achieve the maximum tax relief it is vital to establish who the paramount user of the land is. The courts have approved the view that the occupier for tax purposes will normally be the same as the occupier for rating purposes. This is found in *Dawson v Counsell (Inspector of Taxes) [1938] 3 All ER 5, 22 TC 149*. In the case of grazing of grassland the courts have been prepared to accept that the landowner can be the person who is using the land in a paramount position. In *IRC v Forsythe-Grant (1943) 25 TC 369* it was noted by Lord Clarmont that the laying down of grass in suitable parts, the manuring of land so as to produce a good crop and the arrangement for the seasonal grazing of the grass by cattle brought to the land are operations of husbandry. The parks are being used for the purposes of husbandry by the proprietor who is occupying them. The tax advantages of this are obvious.

It was also noted that the growth of grass in a grass park does not require cultivation in the same sense as grain crops do, as such agricultural operations on the land as are necessary to promote its growth, namely manuring, are performed by the landowner and not by the grazier. On the assumption that the landowner is the occupier the agreement between him and the grazier may be regarded as the sale of growing crop rather than the let of land.

Grazing as a tenancy

11.34   There are two Scottish cases, *Mitchell v IRC (1943) 25 TC 380* and *Drummond v IRC (1951) 32 TC 263*, which held the landowner was not farming the grasslands. The *Drummond* case put forward the point that the top dressing was not applied to the land by the owner. It was found that the landowner was not a farmer, primarily because the grazing agreements were in reality a type of tenancy rather than merely a seasonal let for grazing. Obviously, if a grazing agreement is regarded by the courts as a tenancy it will result in the landowner not being regarded as a farmer. In the case of *Bennion v Roper (1970) 46 TC 613* the court was influenced by the fact that the grazing agreement was seen to be 'a perfectly ordinary tenancy agreement'. The essential ingredient of a grazing agreement is to ensure that the landowner qualifies as a farmer. The landowner and not the grazier should be responsible for growing the crops of grass. In Oliver Stanley's book *Taxation of Farmers and Landowners* (LexisNexis Butterworths Tolley) a model example of pasture agreement can be found in Appendix 1.

Clearly, a FBT for grazing should not be employed if the landowner wishes to be in the business of farming. Again, attention is drawn to the CLA sample agreement to 'grant a right of herbage' as proved by the Inland Revenue.

Provisions to establish grazing agreements as business

11.35 In order to establish the tax efficient grazing agreement it is essential that the landowner should:

1 cultivate, sow and establish the grass crop;
2 harrow and roll the grass where necessary;
3 fertilise the grass crop in the spring and through the season as necessary;
4 cut or spray all weeds to prevent seeding;
5 perform mowing as required;
6 provide hedging, fencing and ditching where needed.

These are set out in more detail at **4.30** and reviewed at **11.3**.

The grazier must in fact covenant not to mow or cut the grass. Some landowners have thought to employ contractors to perform all the acts of actual husbandry, who are distinct and totally at arm's length from the grazier, in order to establish the Schedule D case status of the income and not the Schedule A status. At this point the distinction between Schedule D and Schedule A becomes very borderline as do all the associated tax reliefs.

It is generally considered that where the landowner is actively farming other land and provides only some of his land for seasonal grazing he will be regarded as the farmer of the grasslands, even where he contracts others to fertilise weeds, seed etc, particularly if these people are working on his own land. However, a landowner who only has grasslands would be in a much stronger position if he carries out all the duties himself.

It goes without saying that in every case it would be better if the duties are physically carried out by the landowner but the next best thing would be an independent contractor.

Tax planning

11.36   The message of this chapter has to be that landowners and farmers should enter into all new agreements and arrangements with their eyes wide open. All existing agreements must be reviewed and all verbal arrangements should be made formal, in writing, and tax efficient. Legal help should be sought.

The tax reliefs associated with genuine farming status are too great to overlook. Review all assets and arrangements as the tax reliefs could mean the difference between surviving and not surviving.

Hobby and Recreational Farming and Use of Farming Losses **12**

Julie Butler

- **Hobby and recreational farming**

  If the 'five-year' loss rule applies to a farm, ie it is deemed non-commercial, it is not just the income tax loss relief that is at risk but also future inheritance tax (IHT) and capital gains tax (CGT) reliefs. The need to review the tax computation, diversification income and commerciality are of utmost importance to the tax planner. There is a lot at stake.

- **The use of losses**

  Farm losses cannot just be carried forward or carried back in the opening years and offset against total income. They can also be off-set against capital gains. Farm losses can be claimed independently of the averaging claim and there is great scope for the tax planner to use losses carefully.

- **High land prices**

  Despite the farming crisis farmland is holding its value and in certain sectors prices have increased substantially over recent years. A lot of purchasers have no interest in agriculture. Reasons behind the strength of the prices being commanded are the combination of generous tax reliefs, development/diversification hope value and the undiminished pleasure of a country estate. It is only the fool-hardy who would risk these tax reliefs by bad planning.

Introduction

12.1 With the decline in farming income, a section which looks at the use of farm losses, their computation, the risk associated therewith and the future of agriculture would seem appropriate.

It may seem obvious to state, but it is essential to establish the amount of the loss before considering the alternatives of how to deal with it, such as which reliefs to seek and so on. Consideration should be made, amongst other things, of the hobby farming rules and how these could affect, at some time in the future, or even now, a history of farming losses.

The starting point is identifying the extent of the loss. It is imperative that the tax computation is clearly sorted out between farming and non-farming profitability with possible apportionments of overheads etc. The question of what is Schedule A and what is Schedule D Case 1 income has been mentioned when looking at agricultural property relief (APR), business property relief (BPR) and the potential to claim capital gains tax (CGT) reliefs. A large number of farming tax computations are now including a significant amount of diversification income which should, strictly speaking, be extracted from the tax computation, thus possibly increasing the farming loss and the profit from other activities (see **1.9**).

Hobby and recreational farming — the facts

12.2 Farming has its own set of 'hobby farming rules' which historically have stated that a profit must be made every six years. This again can be seen as an over-simplification and must be looked at carefully.

The hobby farming rules were introduced in 1960 due to concerns over taxpayers farming for recreational purposes and not for commercial reasons. The original intention was to restrict loss relief in 'extreme cases' where the trading activities bore no relationship to the criteria of a commercial trade. The so-called 'five-year rule' was introduced as an extension to the original rules, ie as a further test it must be shown that the business is capable of making a profit [Income and Corporation Taxes Act 1988 (ICTA 1988) s 397]. Similar provisions for the restriction of corporation tax relief are included in ICTA 1988 s 393A(3). There are provisions introduced to prevent the formation of a company or a change of partnership breaking the five-year rule. In the latter case example, husband and wife are treated as the same person.

The Inspector's Manual at IM2340a states the position is as follows:

'ICTA 1988 s 397 denies relief against general income etc in respect of a farming or market gardening loss where a loss computed without regard to capital allowances was also incurred in each of the five years of assessment preceding that in which the claimed loss was incurred.'

The section only applies to losses sustained in trades of farming or market gardening, but for this purpose the definitions of those trades are extended, by sub-section (5), to include activities carried on outside the UK. It is worth referring direct to the Inspector's Manual at IM2336a.

Claims for tax relief in respect of farming losses can present particular difficulty because:

- farming is regarded by many people as an attractive activity in its own right. Taxpayers with substantial income from other sources may take up farming for the sake of recreation or the lifestyle or status which it offers rather than for genuinely commercial reasons; and yet
- all UK farming is treated as the carrying on of a trade by virtue of ICTA 1988 s 53(1) – and is thus eligible for the loss relief provisions applying to trades – whether or not it meets the normal commercial criteria of trading (see Inspector's Manual at IM2262).

Special legislation therefore exists to prevent losses from farming activities which lack commercial inspiration being relieved against non-farming income.

Where losses are sustained in farming activities of an essentially non-commercial nature, relief under ICTA 1988 s 380 may fall to be restricted under either:

- ICTA 1988 s 384 – which restricts relief (see Inspector's Manual at IM2336b) where the trade was not run on a commercial basis and with a view to the realisation of profits (see Inspector's Manual at IM2338 and IM3375); or
- ICTA 1988 s 397 – which restricts relief (see IM2336b) where losses were incurred in each of the five previous years (see Inspector's Manual at IM2340a onwards).

Section 397 of ICTA 1988 is generally more straightforward to use as it involves an objective test. It should be applied, subject to Inspector's Manual at IM2341a and IM2341b, in all cases where the conditions are satisfied (see Inspector's Manual at IM2340a onwards). Cases where ICTA 1988 s 397 does not apply, but where the activities appear clearly non-commercial, should be considered for challenge under ICTA 1988 s 384, subject to Inspector's Manual at IM2338 and IM3375 onwards.

Where relief by way of carry back in respect of losses sustained in the commencing years of a trade is claimed under ICTA 1988 s 381 the test of commerciality is provided by s 381(4) and is stricter than that of s 384 (see Inspector's Manual at IM3507).

Those who have owned farms and estates for a number of years and have had difficulties in making profits must have taken great heart from the extra-statutory concession made in December 2000 for the loss period to be extended for 2000–01 and 2001–02. It is interesting that the extra-statutory concession for this loss extension was actually granted prior to the arrival of the foot and mouth crisis in February 2001. It must also be noted that the conditions of extension come with a provision for there having been profits previously.

Outsiders looking at the tax position of a farm or estate held as a pleasure activity, rather than as a genuine working farm, would say that all that has to be achieved is a profit every six years and there is great scope for claiming what could only be termed as 'quasi-business expenses', to subsidise an enjoyable country life. However, anybody contemplating undertaking the purchase of a country estate or following in the steps of the TV comedy *The Good Life* must embrace the hobby farming rules with eyes wide open. With the move to diversification they must also look at standard commerciality rules.

Tax planners must be aware of what would happen if a farm or holding were deemed to be trading as a hobby. Not only would income tax losses no longer be available under ICTA 1988 s 380 but it could lead to a large potential denial of other tax reliefs. If the farm is deemed to be a hobby then the assets used therein would not have business status which could put in jeopardy previous rollover claims for CGT, and future claims for CGT and inheritance tax (IHT) relief. The loss of BPR for IHT, where income tax loss relief has been denied under the hobby farming rules, is a matter on which opinions differ.

A large number of enterprises have had to look seriously at diversification in order to ensure that there is a profit. Some of these activities do not come under the farming definition. As a result the Inland Revenue have a right to apply to some or the whole of the trade not just the hobby farming rules but the normal commerciality rules. In the current climate those involved with the farming industry are painfully aware that it is very difficult to make a profit from pure farming and it has been difficult for a number of years. As set out in Chapter 1, strictly the tax computation of the business should be separated between farming and non-farming (see **12.4**) and the tax implications of the hobby farming/commerciality rules dealt with accordingly.

It is vital, therefore, that anyone contemplating entering into such a venture, or advising clients about entering into such a venture, should look carefully at the definition of what is and what is not farming (see Chapter 1).

Anybody contemplating the purchase of a farm should do everything in their power to ensure that the hobby farming rules will not apply. Review of farming methods such as the choices between share farming, contract farming and farm business tenancies (FBTs) (as set out in Chapter **11**) is a prime example: whereas the FBT does not qualify for business reliefs for CGT, it can result in a higher return. It is a question of personal choice.

Hobby and recreational farming — the good life or a nightmare?

12.3   The desire for many people to return to 'the country' has, over the years, been given much media publicity. The recent re-runs of the TV comedy *The Good Life* set a picture at one end of the scale, whereas stars of the music and TV industries buying very expensive estates in beautiful parts of the West Country presents a picture at the other. Likewise, with the recent fashion for tracing family roots back several generations via the internet, people are more aware than ever of the UK's strong agricultural history. Prior to the Industrial Revolution, which in the grand scheme of things is not that long ago, over 70% of the UK population earned their living from the land. Hence, the desire to own a small farm or estate is a dream of many hardworking town and country dwellers alike.

The above factors could link quite closely to the interesting current position in the UK whereby, despite falling farm incomes, the foot and mouth crisis and the farming industry very much in decline, land prices are still maintaining their high levels and in some instances still increasing in value. To an 'outsider' this might appear an anomaly rather like houses in mining villages going up in price at the time of the collapse of the mining industry. However, there are a large number of other factors which underpin the current strong land prices.

In the Home Counties where a large percentage of the workforce is based in the City or the prosperous large towns surrounding London, the increase in land prices is not that surprising. There are the underlying factors of 'hope value' for development, the laws of supply and demand (there is an undeniable shortage of houses, as borne out by documents such as the Hampshire Structure Plan) and the desire to enjoy the pleasures of a shooting estate, of being surrounded by your own land and the tax advantages that can be linked with 'the good life'.

At the risk of repetition from other chapters, a summary of the tax advantages are set out below.

- The ability to rollover gains from business assets into another business asset, and the potential for business asset taper relief for CGT should part of the land be sold or developed within the allowed timescale. This is even more attractive post Finance Act 2002.
- Business and agricultural property reliefs for IHT.

- The allowability to claim income tax relief where losses are sustained.
- The ability to repair and improve the property whilst claiming maximum allowable input VAT and, where possible, maximum income tax relief.

All reliefs must be carefully scrutinised and it is essential that all the relevant conditions are met so as to take full advantage of each and every one of them.

As with any business all expense claims must be wholly, necessarily and exclusively for the purpose of the farming trade or estate enterprise and the operation must be commercial and must be shown to be commercial.

The terms of any contract farming agreement must be carefully reviewed (see CHAPTER 11). Some agreements are no more than tenancies 'dressed up' as farming arrangements. Some arrangements are fragile and could fail Inland Revenue scrutiny. It is imperative to have a well-drafted agreement.

Another area of concern is where 'recreational activities' are blatantly incorporated into the farming activities and subjective decisions have to be made between the allocation of expenses between business and private. Clear examples are shooting estates and farms that incorporate the stabling of private horses.

There can be examples where the owners/taxpayers can be greedy in their claim for business expenses, such as those creating large losses for income tax purposes but jeopardising the five-year rule and capital gains and IHT reliefs. The expenditure and income of recreational activities should be excluded except for the element of control of vermin. Professionals must not only warn their clients of the potential problems of trying to claim such expenses but evidence it in writing.

The need to review the tax computation

12.4   With the farming industry moving towards greater diversification there is a need to consider carefully how business tax computations are prepared and to plan for future reliefs.

It is interesting to note that the Country Land and Business Association (CLA) document *A Tax Framework for Jobs and Enterprise in the Rural Economy*, published prior to the Finance Act 2002, included the request for one set of tax rules for all rural activities managed as one business, which they consider would be a useful tool for diversification. The CLA follow-up document *Reform to Perform* suggests that income from diversification such as let office space in farm buildings should be taxed as farming income.

When practitioners prepare the farm tax computation, the correct procedure is to remove non-farming income items and also to match the non-farming expenses to the income. In practice, a lot of accountancy and tax practitioners are just preparing a computation which arrives at an accurate Schedule D Case 1 net profit or loss, and which has little regard for the allocation of expenses and income. It could be that income from items such as quota leasing and grazing by horses are inflating the profit to assist with the avoidance of the hobby farming rules.

Oliver Stanley, in his book *Taxation of Farmers and Landowners* (LexisNexis Butterworths Tolley), states of the hobby farming rules:

> 'To state the rule cynically, a profit once every six years is sufficient to avoid the effect of the section. This can sometimes be secured by correct apportionment of expenditure amongst the years in question.'

Nevertheless, abuse of the 'hobby farming' provisions is foolhardy in the extreme, partly in view of the current high values of the farmland and, above all, farmhouses and their associated IHT reliefs.

As a practical tax planning point, the affairs of all clients who are associated with farming must be reviewed to ensure the correct treatment of income and expenses. It will also be essential to review what future reliefs the client may need to claim, eg is there a question of the 'commerciality' of the farm or the business. It is also useful to ask such questions as does the client intend to claim APR for IHT purposes? If APR is lost will BPR still be available? This is dealt with in **CHAPTER 13**. Could the eligibility for retirement relief be utilised before it disappears?

Another reason to check the tax computation is clearly divided between 'farming' and 'non-farming profit' is because of the farmer's average claims (see **20.1**). The latter only relates to farming income. The importance of the classification of diversification in mentioned in a number of chapters.

Whilst reviewing the tax computation it is essential to ensure that our clients are still eligible for tax reliefs that are dependent on 'business/commercial' status. Examples of reliefs which could be lost are business asset taper relief and rollover relief for CGT.

It is worth considering the position where taxpayers might try to trigger notional cessations and recommencements in order to preserve the use of the losses. The Inspector's Manual at IM2340d sets out the effective anti-avoidance position as follows:

> 'Section 397 does not deny relief where the trade was set up and commenced within the five years prior to the year of claim. This includes a notional cessation and recommencement under ICTA

1988 s 113 where there has been a change in the persons carrying on the trade, but subject to the following modifications:

- The application of section 113(4) does not affect the operation of section 397 in relation to any person who is engaged in carrying on the trade before and after the change.
- Husband and wife are to be treated as if they were the same person. Any transfer of the trade between them will, therefore, not affect the operation of section 397. A widow is not, however, to be treated for these purposes as a wife, so that when a trade passes to a widow on the death of her husband, a new run of losses must accrue before section 397 becomes effective to deny loss relief.
- If a husband and wife, or either of them, control a farming or market gardening company and succeed to the company's trade, or if they, or either of them, carry on a trade which is taken over by the company the trade is to be regarded as a continuous trade for section 397 purposes. (In this connection, 'control' has the meaning given by ICTA 1988 s 416.)'

How can the trading losses be used?

12.5 The first point is to identify the genuine Schedule D loss. Expenditure will be disallowed if it is not deductible in arriving at the true commercial profit on business or accounting principles. Attention needs to be directed towards the underlying purpose. Does the expenditure promote the business and earn profits from it? The test is always commercial advantage, not moral interest. It is essential to establish the validity of the loss and to ensure that it is not restricted. Once the exact amount has been confirmed the destination must be decided.

A large number of farming reliefs can be overlooked by non-farming accountants such as the ability to exclude woodland income (see CHAPTER 6) when appropriate. It is hoped that this book helps to focus on these.

Loss reliefs that can be available to the farming business are as follows.

- Set-off against total income in the year of the loss or total income of the following year [ICTA 1988 s 380].
- Relief for losses in earlier years of trade carried back to the three years of assessment preceding the year of loss [ICTA 1988 s 381]. Earliest years are taken first.
- Carry forward against subsequent profits of the same trade (indefinitely) [ICTA 1988 s 385].
- Terminal loss relief on cessation, applied against earlier profits for the three years of assessment [ICTA 1988 s 388].

- Relief pre-trading expenditure is set against income of year of assessment in which trade is newly set up [ICTA 1988 s 401].
- Relief for losses on unquoted shares in trading companies [ICTA 1988 s 574].
- Furnished holiday letting and property letting losses [ICTA 1988 ss 380–390, 393, 394]. See further **12.7**.

For the treatment of losses in a farmer's averaging claim see CHAPTER **20**.

Income tax losses can be set against CGT of the individual under FA 1991 s 72. It is only the trading losses for the year of sale or preceding the year of sale, which are available to offset against the capital gain. In-depth planning is required in respect of the timing of the disposal of assets to coincide with difficult years of trading. Section 72 of FA 1991 was introduced to bring unincorporated businesses in line with companies which could already set trading losses against income and capital gains under ICTA 1988 s 345(1). Any trading loss which is not set against income or gains for current or preceding years is available to carry forward and set against future trading profits.

Relief against gains is given in priority to relief for CGT losses brought forward from earlier years and in priority to annual exemption, which is therefore sometimes lost. So-called hobby farming losses do not qualify for relief against CGT, ie if they are disallowed for offset against total income and only carried forward against future profits (ICTA 1988 s 385) then likewise they are not allowed under FA 1991 s 72.

There is obviously great scope for the tax planner to utilise losses efficiently and structure timing of expenditure to maximum use. Clearly, as part of the review of asset ownership, and tax efficiency, there is a need to review all proposals and plans to utilise the timing of the losses. The timing of property disposal for CGT is of prime importance as, under Taxation of Chargeable Gains Act 1992 (TCGA 1992) s 28(1), it is the date the contract is entered into, not the date of the conveyance, which is significant. If the contract is conditional it is the date the condition is satisfied under TCGA 1992 s 28(2), and hence this conditional element is vital when reviewing the exercise of an option (see CHAPTER **14**).

Letting income assessable as trading income

12.6 CHAPTER **15** sets out the practical considerations of letting income with consideration for the associated IHT angles.

It is considered appropriate to deal with Schedule A losses in this chapter. However, before this is looked at in depth it is necessary to see how rents can be assessable as trading income, ie under Schedule D Case 1. This is of prime importance for loss management and links closely to the hobby farming rules. The ability to reclassify rents as Schedule D can be the difference between making a trading profit or not in a year.

So when is rent trading income? First, when a trader's business premises is sub-let and the second is where services provided by the landlord are of sufficient substance that the landlord is carrying on the trade of providing serviced accommodation. This would be a vital tax planning tool to the diversifying farmer who is looking to maximise income from buildings. To qualify for sub-let of farmer's business premises the accommodation must be temporarily surplus to business requirements and the property must be used partly for the business and partly let. In addition, the rental income must be comparatively small, although the definition of this is not clear.

A prime example would be the subletting of part of a barn or building for another trade. Most farmers currently have this type of income in their accounts and the tax planner should ensure that it is assessed under Schedule D.

The next stage is to look at the provision of serviced accommodation. Generally, following the decisions in *Gittos v Barclay [1982] STC 390* and *Griffiths v Jackson [1983] STC 184* the Inland Revenue try to move the status from Schedule D Case 1 to Schedule D Case VI. The VAT treatment of serviced accommodation cannot be overlooked, as rents from letting residential accommodation are normally exempt from VAT but serviced accommodation could be liable to VAT at 17.5% (see **CHAPTER 9**).

There is the dilemma, as so often, of choosing between a possibly more beneficial tax treatment and a possibly disadvantageous VAT position (see **CHAPTER 15**).

Losses from rents received and furnished holiday letting

12.7   Schedule A income tax losses are carried forward against any future income from the Schedule A business [ICTA 1988 s 379(A)(1)].

Schedule A corporation tax losses of a company arising after 1 April 1998 can be set against total profits for the accounting period [ICTA 1988 s 392A(1), inserted by FA 1998 Sch 5 para 28]. As an alternative the loss can be carried forward and treated as a Schedule A loss in the next accounting period [ICTA 1988 s 392(A)(2)]. The loss can be surrendered to another group company under the group relief rules but it cannot be surrendered as group relief in that later period.

Losses from furnished holiday lettings are allowable under the provisions of ICTA 1988 ss 380–390, 393, 394. This means that, in principle, they can be offset against total income in the year of the loss and the following year. In the opening years they can be offset against total income of the three years of assessment preceding that in which the loss was suffered [ICTA 1988 ss 380 and 381].

Many diversifying farmers and property owners will look to maximising their returns by moving from furnished letting income to furnished holiday lets. The advantage of the latter is the ability to claim losses under ss 380 and 381 of ICTA 1988, ie against total income in the year of the loss and the following year with all the advantages of the opening year's losses. Where furnished holiday accommodation was first let as furnished accommodation there can be a restriction under s 381, ie the holiday accommodation is deemed for s 381 to start when furnished lettings began not when lettings as holiday accommodation began. (See also CHAPTER 15.)

Losses in stud farming

12.8   Reference should be made to the Inspector's Manual at IM2350g.

Following discussions with the Thoroughbred Breeder's Association in 1982, Policy Division wrote to the association as follows:

> 'It has always been recognised that some ventures are by their nature unlikely to show a profit by the sixth year of trading and s 397(3) provides for loss relief to be continued after the fifth year where the claimant is engaged in a particular farming activity of an intrinsically long term profit making nature we have long accepted that the breeding of thoroughbred horses is such a long term venture, and provided that a stud farming business is potentially profit making, we would not normally seek to invoke s 397(1) until after 11 years from the start of the business.'

The Thoroughbred Breeder's Association have circulated this text to their members.

This letter does not mean, however, that all stud farming losses are relievable against other income up to 11 years from commencement. The requirement that the business should be potentially profitable (in other words, the question of whether ICTA 1988 s 397(3)(a) is satisfied) should be checked in suitable cases. Nor should the letter be interpreted as meaning that the five-year period is extended in cases where a run of losses arises in periods after a year in which a profit has been made, or in cases where a business is taken over as a going concern. Such cases should be dealt with individually on their merits.

Where the enterprise is clearly not running on a commercial basis and with a view to the realisation of profits, a challenge under ICTA 1988 s 384 should be considered. See also **20.3** on stud farms.

Farming losses — test of commerciality

12.9 The tests for commerciality are very well set out in the Inspector's Manual at IM2338.

> 'ICTA 1988 s 384 denies relief against general income etc unless the taxpayer can show that, during the period when the loss was sustained, the trade was being carried on on a commercial basis with a view to the realisation of profit. The fact that a trade was being carried on so as to afford a reasonable expectation of profit is taken as conclusive evidence that it was being carried on with a view to the realisation of profit.'

As mentioned in **12.2**, the provision was first introduced in 1960. The Chancellor of the day stated in the course of a parliamentary debate on the section:

> 'We are after the extreme cases ... in which expenditure very greatly exceeds income or any possible income which can ever be made and in which, however long the period, no degree of profitability can ever be reached.'

These words should be borne in mind when considering the application of the section to farming cases. The small farmer and the farmer with marginal land who are genuinely trying to make a living from their farms in difficult circumstances are not caught.

Nor should the section be used to deny the relief to a farmer who incurs temporary losses while establishing an enterprise, for instance by building up a production herd or bringing land back into fertility, provided the enterprise in which he is engaged is likely in due course to become an economic undertaking. For example, it may take a farmer five years to clear and work land infested with bracken before there can be an expectation of profit. Relief under ICTA 1988 s 380 should not be refused on the initial losses in such a case.

General guidance on ICTA 1988 s 384 may be found in the Inspector's Manual at IM3375 onwards. Where the application of the section is contested in a case involving a farming loss, the Inland Revenue should make a report to the Business Profits Division (Farming) before listing the claim for hearing by the Commissioners.

There is a let-out where farming is part of a large undertaking. This is set out in IM2341b as follows:

> 'Section 397(4) provides that relief is not to be denied where the loss-making farm or market garden is part of, and ancillary to, a larger trading undertaking. The sub-section is designed to meet cases such as that of a butcher who makes a practice of fattening

bullocks for his business, or a manufacturer who grows his own raw materials, or a seedsman or chemical manufacturer who runs a farm for testing or improving his products.'

The phrase, 'part of, and ancillary to' should be interpreted strictly. 'Ancillary' means 'subservient and annexed to' (see Croom-Johnson J in *Cross v Emery (1949) 31 TC 194 at 198*). It implies a close operating link with and contribution to the larger undertaking.

The Inspector's Manual also sets out the principle on how the Revenue look for avoidance with regard to tax losses. This is set out at IM2342 as follows:

'Taxpayers may attempt to avoid the operation of section 397 by ensuring that the farming enterprise periodically makes an isolated profit. The most obvious year to pick for this purpose would be the sixth year, and then every sixth year thereafter.'

Obviously, there is nothing to say that a farm which has been unprofitable for five years could not make a profit in the sixth year. Furthermore, it may be possible for a taxpayer to arrange his affairs in a way that leads to the making of a genuine one-off profit. The Inland Revenue will check to ensure that the profit has not been manufactured by means of artificial transactions or devices, particularly in a case where substantial farming losses have been relieved against the income of an otherwise wealthy taxpayer. The Inland Revenue will look for the following examples:

● charging business expenses (especially interest paid) to the farmer's capital account or not including them in the accounts at all;
● recognising sales and/or expenses in the wrong year; or
● manipulating opening of closing stock valuations.

The Revenue naturally consider these and similar methods as unacceptable and enquiries could be made, in worthwhile cases, to ensure that the accounts include all the business income and expenses for the period concerned but only the business income and expenses for the period.

Agriculture — more than just a profit

12.10   The theme of this book is not 'Agriculture is dead; long live diversification'.

It has been said by Elliot Morley that tourism was more important to the countryside than farming. In response to this Willy Poole MBE of the CLA states:

'It is this countryside that brings in the tourists. Tourism may be a larger industry than farming but it rides on the farmer's back. A well farmed countryside that maintains its ancient traditions and people who make it work are, or should be, treasured national assets.'

The Deputy President of the CLA, Mark Hudson, has equally strong views on future conservation policy being underpinned by profitability. In a speech given to a public policy seminar he stressed the need to reform current measures, many of which prevent good conservation management. Mr Hudson gave full backing to the Curry Report's recommendations on profitability and warned that for farmers to deliver the countryside that the public wants on a sustainable basis, they must be able to derive profit from conservation activities. He said:

'Land managers and woodland owners need to make a profit for the same reasons as companies that sell medical equipment to the NHS. Nobody would ever suggest that medical companies should supply the NHS at their own cost, so it is equally unreasonable to ask farmers and land managers to undertake conservation at their own cost.'

Whilst reviewing the profitability of diversification, the profitability of pure agriculture must not be overlooked. All those involved in farming and land ownership need to keep updated with what farming policy is together with the outcome of CLA and National Farmers' Union (NFU) lobbying. If profit is to be achieved action has to be taken and the farming accountants have to act promptly on that action.

It seems ironic to long-time farmers that they could be caught under the hobby farming rules purely due to the farming crisis.

How to prevent a real farmer being classified as a hobby farmer

12.11   There is no doubt that in the current economic climate it is difficult to make a profit from true farming after all overheads have been correctly allocated. This is particularly so if a farming unit has borrowings, staff commitments or rent to pay. Unless the word agriculture is broadened it could be that a lot of farming units will be showing profits from diversification such as let property and losses on the actual farming activities. If these losses continue on the farming activity then the hobby farming rules might have to come into play.

It is imperative that costs are allocated correctly and that non-farming income such as let property does have its full share of overheads allocated to it. This could cause arbitrary calculation and some negotiation with the Inland Revenue. The CLA are lobbying for a broadening of the definition of agriculture to prevent this, but in the meantime the tax planner must take care when reviewing tax computations.

At the other end of the scale is the recreational landowner who enjoys the lifestyle and would like to embrace the tax reliefs as a side issue. The tax planner must point out all the benefits but at every stage warn of commerciality.

Planning the Best Use of Agricultural and Business Property Reliefs for Inheritance Tax 13

Julie Butler

- **Maximising agricultural property relief (APR) and business property relief (BPR)**
  This chapter goes into more detail on this subject following on from CHAPTER 4 and CHAPTER 5. The problems of agricultural value and the risk of tax relief being reduced to 50% are looked at in some detail. The problems of limited companies are also considered.

- **Avoiding failed potentially exempt transfers (PETS)**
  The subject of 'gifting now' is mentioned in CHAPTER 5 and this chapter looks in detail at how to avoid 'failed PETS'. With farming in decline and going through significant transformation with diversification there are worries that business gifts might 'fail' if the transferor dies within seven years and there is a change of business status.

- **The case of *Farmer* — protection of the let property**
  The author considers this a significant case for the purposes of the diversifying farmer and landowner. The business of letting cottages and redundant farm buildings can be an integral part of the business of farming and land management. The successful claim for BPR against the element of the farm business that involved the letting out of farm assets has to be reviewed in detail. There is no

doubt that the *Farmer* case receives a lot of attention from this book but this is in direct proportion to the impact the decision could have on this form of diversification. The case cannot be looked at in a superficial way.

- **The case of *Farmer* — looking at the farm in 'the round'**
  One of the principles arising from the *Farmer* case is not just the ability to claim BPR on the business of letting farm properties but the need to look at every case 'in the round'. From a tax planning viewpoint one aspect or element of a business looked at in isolation is dangerous without the whole picture. It is the latter that the Revenue will be interested in.

- **IHTA 1984 s 105(3) — is there a business or is there a holding of investments?**
  This is a question that every tax practitioner has to consider for all businesses. How often are the updated facts looked at on a regular basis?

Too valuable to put at risk

13.1 An introduction to the issues discussed in this chapter has been approached in Cʜᴀᴘᴛᴇʀ 5. In addition, the inheritance tax (IHT) reliefs on farmhouses have been set out in Cʜᴀᴘᴛᴇʀ 4. It is hoped that this has emphasised the benefits to the landowner that can be attributed to IHT reliefs for the farm and surrounding land. The case of *Dixon v IRC [2002] STC (SCD) 53* gave some interesting insight into the attempt to claim agricultural property relief (APR) on a very small holding.

There are considerable complexities surrounding business and agricultural property reliefs (BPR and APR). Essentially, the full details surrounding this can be found in *Business and Agricultural Property Relief* by Toby Harris (LexisNexis Butterworths Tolley).

The purpose of this chapter is to emphasise how IHT reliefs are at risk with a move towards diversification. The tax planner must be aware of the difference between APR and BPR, their interaction and also the major concerns surrounding the reliefs.

It is essential to look at cases where relief might be lost through diversification and therefore what action can be taken to ensure that IHT relief is given where possible. The Country Land and Business Association (CLA) document *A Tax Framework for Jobs and Enterprise in the Rural Economy* shows that various ideas to benefit the rural economy are being promoted, including the reform of IHT, as the current rules impede diversification on agricultural holdings.

The conclusion of this chapter is to look at the case of *Farmer (Farmer's Executors) v IRC [1999] STC (SCD) 321* as it involved a successful claim for BPR on a diversified farm, which in this case was the business of let property.

Agricultural value

13.2   This subject is first looked at in **4.31** on the agricultural value of the farmhouse. When reviewing APR claims an understanding of the definition of agricultural value is vital. It is limited by Inheritance Tax Act 1984 (IHTA 1984) s 115(3): 'The value which would be the value of the property if the property was subject to a perpetual covenant prohibiting its use otherwise than as agricultural property'. Priority is given to APR under s 116(1) of IHTA 1984 before BPR, ie when property qualifies for both reliefs APR is given first.

The first point that any tax planner would worry about (as indeed would their clients) is the fact that the market value of agricultural property might well exceed its agricultural value and there could, therefore, be a differential which would be chargeable to IHT over and above the APR claim. It is useful at this point to look at the scope of the claim for BPR as it may be that the relief could be claimed against the difference.

Differences in value could be caused by such factors as the granting of sporting rights, which would have a considerable influence on the value of agricultural land. As the raising of pheasants is not deemed to be (in most instances) for the purpose of the production of food then this would not qualify as 'agricultural' activity, and so a business relief claim could be pursued. In these instances, as with any form of diversification, it will be necessary to examine just exactly how the shoot is run and how it is managed as a business. Thus, the landowner might not secure APR on the value of the sporting rights but it could well be that BPR would be claimed on the business element of the shoot, ie the exploitation of those rights. It is vital that there is evidence that the business has been commercial in this instance.

As a practical planning point it is advisable to see that every asset owned by landowning clients is reviewed and consideration must be given to whether APR can still be claimed. If APR is going to be lost due to diversification careful consideration must be given to ensure that BPR can be claimed. The BPR claim depends on the existence of a commercial business. The previous chapter (**Chapter 12**) on recreational hobby farming gives direction in this connection. VAT and case law should be reviewed when considering this.

The problem with defining 'agricultural value' is that there has been very little market evidence of the value for property subject to such a covenant. Any restrictive covenant must make that property worth at least 'one bid' less than an unencumbered property. Claims of up to 30% discount have been made. See **13.7** on lotting.

When does agricultural property relief (APR) apply?

13.3 APR does not just apply on death. It also applies to settling on discretionary trusts (see Chapter **17**), transfer of value by a close company and lifetime potentially exempt transfers (PETs). APR also applies to the Channel Islands and the Isle of Man under IHTA 1984 s 115(5).

What categories of property attract 100% relief?

13.4 This subject is first discussed in **5.2** on protecting the farm assets. The following categories can be considered in more detail here.

1   Property where the transferor has the right to vacant possession or can obtain vacant possession within 12 months [IHTA 1984 s 116(2)(a) extended to 24 months by Inland Revenue Extra-Statutory Concession (ESC F17)]. Where there are joint owners of the land, the conditions are held to be satisfied where the aggregate of their interest carries the right to vacant possession [IHTA 1984 s 116(6)]. See **5.21** on vacant possession.

2   Property let on a tenancy that began on or after 1 September 1995, irrespective of the terms of that tenancy [IHTA 1984 s 116(2)(c)]. This date was the date on which the provisions of Agricultural Tenancies Act 1995 came into effect. In repealing Agricultural Holdings Act 1986, a landlord is entitled, from that date, to give a tenant farmer a farm business tenancy (FBT), with whatever security is agreed between the parties and without an automatic right for the tenant farmer to renew the lease or pass the tenancy to his successor.

3   Let agricultural land where the terms of the tenancy are such that the value of the land is not diminished by the tenancy, notwithstanding the freeholder's inability to obtain vacant possession (ESC F17).

4   The land has been owned since before 10 March 1981 and satisfies the conditions for APR that applied under the pre-1981 rules [IHTA 1984 ss 116(2)(b) and 116(3)]. This gives relief for a 'working farmer' where the tenant is a company controlled by the taxpayer or a partnership of which he was a member, or the tenant was an employer or relative. However, relief is restricted to the lower of £250,000 of agricultural value or 1,000 acres of land [FA 1975 Sch 8 para 5(1)].

The period of ownership for APR must be considered under IHTA 1984 s 117. One of the following two rules must apply: (1) the required occupation must exist throughout the two years before the transfer and must be by the transferor; (2) the required occupation must exist throughout seven years before the transfer, during which period the transferor must own the property.

What categories of property attract 50% relief?

13.5   Relief at 50% is given against the agricultural value of land that is let on a tenancy that commenced prior to 1 September 1995 and does not allow the landlord vacant possession within 24 months [IHTA 1984 s 116(2)]. Where the lease commenced before 1 September 1995 but the current tenant did not become entitled to the lease until after that date (perhaps as a result of statutory succession to an old Agricultural Holdings Act tenancy), relief is provided at 100% (Inland Revenue Interpretation R121).

Where a tenancy is acquired by succession, succession is treated as taking place at the death of the tenant from whom the succession occurs [FA 1996 s 185(5)–(6)].

BPR of 50% is given against the value of the following categories of business property.

1   Any land, building, machinery or plant used wholly or mainly for a business carried on by a company controlled by the transferor [IHTA 1984 s 105(1)(d)].
2   Any land, building, machinery or plant used wholly or mainly for a business carried on by a partnership in which the transferor is the partner [IHTA 1984 s 105(1)(d)].
3   Land, building, machinery or plant held by trustees in which there is an interest in possession and the asset and the property was used wholly or mainly for the purposes of a business carried on by the beneficiary entitled to the interest in possession [IHTA 1984 s 105(1)(e)].
4   Quoted shares in a company that does not carry on an excluded business [IHTA 1984 s 105(1)(cc)].
5   Quoted securities in a company that does not carry on an excluded business [IHTA 1984 s 105(1)(cc)].

Definition of 'agricultural property'

13.6   In order for the tax planner to make use of the maximum IHT reliefs it is essential that there is a clear understanding of what the definition of agricultural property is for APR. It is a 'property' based relief and in most farm businesses it must be clear where BPR will apply when APR does not apply.

'Agricultural property' is defined as:

- agricultural land or pasture [IHTA 1984 s 115(2)];
- woodland (as distinct from timber) [IHTA 1984 s 115(2)] (see Chapter 6);
- buildings occupied with agricultural land or pasture and use for arable farming, livestock rearing or intensive fish farming [IHTA 1984 s 115(2)];
- such cottages together with land occupied with them as are of a character appropriate to the property (see **5.4**);
- such farm buildings together with land occupied with them that are of a character appropriate to the property;
- such a farmhouse together with land occupied with it which is of a character appropriate to the property (see Chapter 4);
- short rotational coppice [FA 1995 s 154(2)] (see Chapter 6);
- stud farms [IHTA 1984 s 115(4)] (see **20.3**); and
- land in habitat schemes [IHTA 1984 s 124C].

APR is only provided on land and other property in the UK and the Channel Islands but it does include the Isle of Man. The provision for this is found in s 115(5) of IHTA 1984.

As mentioned earlier, the granting of sporting rights is generally considered as a business and not agricultural activity. The case which gives clarity to this is *Earl of Normanton v Giles [1980] 1 WLR 28.*

Lotting

13.7 The Valuation Office Agency (VOA) Manual CH1B para 9.3 sets out the principles that relate to what is known as lotting, ie consideration for the valuation of agricultural property where different areas would be sold as separate lots. If one or more of the lots is wholly exempt from IHT then it is unnecessary to value that lot. However, where a lot is partially exempt this gives rise to an interesting tax planning point with regard to valuations.

When considering valuations it must be assumed that the seller marketed the property in a way which produced the best selling price. If appropriate, it must be divided into lots or assembling those items to sell them together. This can be of importance in relation to farmhouses and consideration to the case of *Earl of Ellesmere v IRC [1918] 2 KB 735.* In the *Duke of Buccleuch v IRC [1967] 1 AC 506* case the general principle is that there is no obligation that there should be lotting into natural units but the property should be marketed in such a way as to produce the largest price provided that it did not involve excessive time or effort (see **5.9**).

Inheritance tax (IHT) — interaction with capital gains tax (CGT)

13.8 A landowner's adviser should bear in mind that death is not a chargeable event for capital gains tax (CGT) purposes. It is generally accepted that values which attract 100% APR vary enormously due to different circumstances. It is essential that a tax planner is involved in the valuation and the client's circumstances and, above all, future plans are given consideration.

Concerns over future CGT are overcome when it is clear that the client wants to hold on to the family property (hopefully) forever. However, if it is obvious that the beneficiaries cannot afford to maintain the estate as it stands and might have to dispose of certain assets then the whole interaction with CGT and IHT relief is of prime importance.

Where future disposals are intended the tax planner should try to argue high values for IHT and therefore CGT at death. Examples to test the tax planner are as follows.

- 'Hope value', ie land used for farming which has planning potential. Ideally, BPR can be claimed on the difference between the agricultural and hope values.
- The valuation of related property. As defined by IHTA 1984 s 161(2), the concern here rests that an artificial assumption can be made in order to determine the value of property for tax purposes. Related property rules are of wide application as must be given consideration by the practitioner in a large number of cases (see **5.11–5.13**).
- Restrictions on disposal of the asset.
- Unquoted shares and securities.
- A lease being treated as a settlement.
- The interaction of debts (see **5.14**).
- Farm cottages (see **5.4**).

It has often been argued that the concept of an open market is a hypothetical one. It is generally considered that the market which is perceived is one where the property is offered for sale to the world at large and that all potential purchasers have an equal opportunity to make an offer and it is widely known it is for sale. Reference can be found in *Lynell v IRC [1972] AC 680*.

Assets not qualifying for relief

13.9 The tax planner should be aware of what assets *might* not qualify for APR to see if they in turn would attract other forms of relief such as BPR. Some of these points were touched upon in Cʜᴀᴘᴛᴇʀ 4 and Cʜᴀᴘᴛᴇʀ 5. Problem areas for APR are listed as follows:

- farmhouses, the ownership of which has been separated from the land or where the land is not held by a company controlled by the owner of the house (see Cʜᴀᴘᴛᴇʀ **4**);
- very large farmhouses or mansions occupied with small let acreages (see Cʜᴀᴘᴛᴇʀ **4**);
- non-commercial agricultural units (see Cʜᴀᴘᴛᴇʀ **12**);
- land used for non-agricultural purposes as set out in Cʜᴀᴘᴛᴇʀ **1**. Examples of this are grazing by horses, income from industrial units, share farming agreements with minimum return etc;
- buildings used for rearing birds or fish;
- farm cottages that are not occupied by farm workers or former farm workers nor their dependants (see *Farmer (Farmer's Executors) v IRC [1999] STC (SCD) 321* at **13.26**).

If the APR claim fails then a BPR claim should be researched.

Interaction of agricultural property relief (APR) and business property relief (BPR)

Priority of APR

13.10   As mentioned previously, under IHTA 1984 s 116(1) APR takes precedence over BPR. In the situation where both of these are available in respect of a single asset APR is given first and BPR is given second. This can often happen in the case of farmland left in the estate of a deceased person. If the relevant conditions are fulfilled APR will remove from charge the value of the land, valued for agricultural purposes, and the balance could form a claim for BPR provided the relevant conditions are satisfied. It is therefore essential to see what constitutes BPR.

BPR at 100%

13.11   Further to Cʜᴀᴘᴛᴇʀ 5, which showed examples of 100% BPR at **5.2**, further detailed conditions for 100% BPR are as follows:

1   a business carried on as a sole trader or the partners' interest in a business carried on in partnership [IHTA 1984 s 105(1)(a), (3)];
2   any unquoted shares in a company that does not carry on an 'excluded business' [IHTA 1984 ss 105(1)(bb), (3)]; or

3   unquoted securities (opposed to shares) in a company that was controlled by the transferor before the transfer [IHTA 1984 s 105(1)(b)].

For BPR to be available, the business concerned must not consist 'wholly or mainly' of any of the 'excluded businesses', which are:

• dealing in securities, stocks or shares;
• dealing in land or buildings;
• making or holding investments [IHTA 1984 s 105(3)].

For tax planning purposes these definitions are of great importance for the diversifying business including the limited company. As the nature of farmland and buildings move from trading property to possible investment properties with diversification, eg let industrial building, there is risk of not qualifying for BPR. Likewise, the farmer who decides to move from 'growing crops to growing houses' (see CHAPTER 14).

BPR more favourable than APR

13.12   In what circumstances is BPR available because APR does not fully cover the liability?

1   Businesses or shares attributable to agricultural property where the ownership requirement is not yet sufficient for APR but which replace non-agricultural business assets (so that the assets qualify for BPR under the replacement property rules).
2   Non-controlling unquoted shareholdings in a farming company.
3   The assets of a farming business other than land and buildings.

It should also be noted that BPR does not have the territorial limits of APR, ie it is not restricted to the UK, the Channel Islands and the Isle of Man.

Replacement property — period of ownership

13.13   The tax planner should be aware of the definition of replacement property. In order to understand these rules it is necessary to review the rules regarding the period of ownership. No BPR is available unless the property or replacement property has been owned by the deceased throughout the two years immediately preceding his death or by the transferor throughout the two years immediately preceding a chargeable lifetime transfer [IHTA 1984 s 106]. In very exceptional cases BPR is available on property which is owned for less than two years.

The property concerned can satisfy the period of ownership if it is a replacement for a property which has previously qualified for BPR [IHTA 1984 s 107]. The test that is applied is whether BPR would have been available on the property previously owned if there had been a transfer of value immediately before it was replaced [IHTA 1984 s 107(1)(b)]. It is interesting to note that there can, in principle, be any number of replacements that together make up the two-year qualifying period of ownership. The eligibility for BPR on a property that has been replaced necessitates a two-year period of ownership for that original property [IHTA 1984 s 107(2)], unless it would, itself, qualify as replacement property for the property transferred on an earlier disposal.

The limited company

13.14   It would be impossible for a book such as this to have a chapter on maximising BPR and APR without mentioning the problems of the limited company and IHT reliefs. The book does not have the scope to go into the full detail but aims to highlight the problem to the tax planner.

The EIS position of limited companies is set out in **14.61–14.65** and in **20.33–20.36**. The BATR position is set out in **14.5**.

In **2.13** the advantages of the choice of limited company as a trading vehicle are set out. However, the IHT problems must never be overlooked. This can be emphasised in **Chapter 4** on protecting the farmhouse (at **4.35**)

This raises the question can the limited company ever win? If the farmhouse is held outside of the limited company (the trading business), the IHT relief is restricted to 50%. However, if the farmhouse is included in the limited company there is a problem of whether it qualifies as a business asset or as an investment within the meaning of 'making or holding investments' found in IHTA 1984 s 105(3). See further **4.33**.

Farming companies

13.15   Only controlling interests qualify for APR [IHTA 1984 s 122], though a minority interest may attract BPR.

Section 122 allows APR on the value of shares in or securities of a company if, and only if:

1   the agricultural property forms part of the assets of a company and part of the value of the shares or securities can be attributed to the agricultural value of that agricultural property; and

2   the shares or securities gave the transferor control of the company immediately before the transfer.

The problems with limited companies — cases where BPR will be denied

13.16   Where the company assets consist of shares or securities of another company they are not relevant business property for BPR if the business of that company is of an excluded nature. Therefore, if the company in which the shares are held is an investment company then no BPR would be available.

In addition, BPR is denied in respect of a shareholding if, at the relevant date, a winding up order has been made in respect of the company or the company has passed a resolution for a voluntary winding up or is otherwise in the process of liquidation, unless the business of the company is to continue (whether carried on by the company or by another entity) after a reconstruction or amalgamation, which is the purpose of the winding up or liquidation, and does, in fact, so continue or resume not later than one year after the transfer of value [IHTA 1984 s 105(5)].

BPR is, similarly, denied where, at the date of the transfer, the shares are subject to a binding contract for sale [IHTA 1984 s 113] (see **5.7**).

Any company that holds land or farming assets should be reviewed for future IHT relief with attention to not only the assets contained therein but the structure of the share holdings. For problems on reorganisation see **13.21**.

What is a 'failed potentially exempt transfer' (PET)?

13.17   As mentioned in Chapter 5 on protecting the assets, the current re-structuring of the ownership of farmland and farming business units under diversification can include gifting to the next generation. Largely this involves making a gift now under the PET rules. Consideration must be given to not only CGT on this gift, or potential CGT, but whether there will be BPR or APR on a 'failed' PET. These situations are set out below.

Definition

13.18   Where there has been a PET followed by the donor's death less than seven years later, no tax would have been payable at the time of the transfer but IHT may become due by virtue of the death. This is known as a 'failed potentially exempt transfer'. BPR is available against the PET if the conditions for obtaining a relief were fulfilled at both the date of the PET and the date of the subsequent death [IHTA 1984 s 113A(1)]. Similar rules apply to transfers to discretionary trusts [IHTA 1984 s 113A(2)].

In order for BPR to be available on the failed PET, or the recalculation of the lifetime chargeable transfer, two conditions must be satisfied:

1   the property must qualify as a 'relevant business property' for BPR at the time of the death [IHTA 1984 s 113A(3)(b)]; and
2   the recipient of the lifetime gift must have retained the property given until the death of the transferor or, if earlier, his own death [IHTA 1984 s 113A(3)].

The conditions are applied strictly. Although property moving between an individual and a settlement in which he has an interest in possession is ignored for this purpose, as for all other purposes of IHT [IHTA 1984 s 49], any other change in ownership denies the relief. Hence, a transfer of property between spouses, whilst an exempt transfer for IHT purposes, would cause any BPR on a PET to be removed if the donor dies within seven years.

How can a failed PET be avoided?

13.19   In the same way that BPR is available on a PET that becomes chargeable by virtue of the death of the donor within seven years, APR is also available [IHTA 1984 s 124A].

Obviously, one factor that cannot be planned exactly is the *date* of death. Carrying out tax planning around ill or very ill clients requires great sensitivity. Practical work can involve a regular review of the lifetime gifts and, of course, warning the transferor and transferee at the point of transfer. There are a large number of changes to the gift that can take place over the seven years and not all landowners and donors may be aware of them. The aim of this section is to highlight the fact that, where gifts that should qualify for BPR or APR are made, it is vital that any predictable changes over the next seven years are planned for tax purposes.

Agricultural property replaced by agricultural property

13.20   In a similar position to BPR, there is provision to cover the situation in which the agricultural property that was gifted is sold and replaced by other agricultural property that is owned at the date of death [IHTA 1984 s 124B]. APR and BPR reliefs are only available where both the disposal of the original property and the acquisition of the replacement are made in a bargain at arm's length or on such terms as would be contained in such a bargain [IHTA 1984 s 124B(2)]. Clearly, this means that disposals and subsequent purchases must be carefully monitored between family members and associates. The time limit of three years or such longer period as the Inland Revenue may allow is also the same [IHTA 1984 s 124B(2)(a), (5)(b)]. The conditions for the relief are then applied to the original and replacement property so that the transferee must have owned the original property at the date of the disposal and the replacement as from the date of the acquisition. The properties must have been occupied for purposes of agriculture during these times and the replacement property must be agricultural property immediately before the death [IHTA 1984 s 124B(3)]. As with BPR, where the donee dies before the donor, the rules are applied at the death of the donee [IHTA 1984 s 124B(5)].

The similar position is when business property replaces agricultural property. The donee should ideally check with the donor's tax adviser before the replacement.

Reorganisation of the share capital of a farming company

13.21 Where there has been a reorganisation of the share capital of a farming company, within the APR qualifications, or where the property held at the date of death consists of shares of a farming company, for which the original property was exchanged, the shares held at death are treated as if they had been the subject of the PET [IHTA 1984 s 124A(6)]. APR is made available by deeming the owner of the shares to be the owner of the original agricultural land.

Length of occupation or ownership

13.22 There are provisions for BPR where the conditions as to length of occupation or ownership are not satisfied but the farm was acquired on a previous transfer that did qualify for relief. It is further necessary that it should be only these conditions that prevent relief on this occasion and that one of the transfers should be on death [IHTA 1984 s 121]. Provision is made for the replacement of property between the two transfers. As with the general replacement rule, relief is restricted to the lower of the agricultural values of the replaced and present farms [IHTA 1984 s 121(2)]. Where, on the previous transfer, only a part of the value qualified for relief as where the earlier transfer was a part purchase, only a like part can be reduced on the present transfer [IHTA 1984 s 121(3)].

Transferee retaining ownership

13.23 In a similar position to BPR, there is a condition that the original property transferred must be owned by the transferee from the time of the transfer to the death of the transferor (or the earlier death of the transferee) [IHTA 1984 ss 124A(3)(a), (4)]. Where property is settled on trusts in which there is no interest in possession, the trustees are to be treated as the transferee [IHTA 1984 s 124A(8)]. It is imperative that transferees keep the transferor and their tax adviser fully aware of all changes of ownership and occupation and ideally before the change.

Continuing agricultural use by the transferee

13.24 It is essential that where the original property is agricultural property prior to the death (of the transferor or, if earlier, that of the transferee) that it should have been occupied by the transferee (or another) for the purpose of agriculture throughout the relevant period [IHTA 1984 s 124A(3)(b)]. Care must be taken where the original property consists of shares in a farming company and so, in this instance, it will suffice that the company that owned the land and farm was occupied for the purposes of agriculture throughout the period [IHTA 1984 s 124A(3)(c)]. The replacement by agricultural property is mentioned above. Satisfaction of the tax rules should also be achieved by replacement with business property (see **13.20**). BPR criteria are essential (see below).

Business gift sold and agricultural property purchased

13.25 What happens when a gift of a BPR property is sold and an agricultural property purchased? If the donor then dies within seven years of making the gift, is any relief available on the failed PET? In the Inland Revenue's view, BPR is available if the agricultural property satisfies the requirements for business property (such as, it is farmland farmed by the donee) but neither relief is available if it does not satisfy the BPR criteria (such as if it is farmland let to another person) (Inland Revenue Interpretation RI95).

The tax planner must review all gifts in the last seven years to ensure that any potential risk of the loss of BPR/APR is highlighted to the parties concerned and such rescue action as is required is taken. Once again this highlights the need for agricultural property to embrace all 'business' not 'letting criteria'.

Farmer (Farmer's Executors) v IRC

Introduction

13.26 The case of *Farmer (Farmer's Executors) v IRC [1999] STC (SCD) 321* is worth looking at in full detail. Not only is the case considered to be very helpful to the diversifying farmer but it also gives the reader an example of how an appeal is dealt with. It highlights which sections of the Taxes Act and which other cases are relevant.

Areas that are focused on are the basis of appeal, the facts and the issues of the case, together with the evidence and arguments produced by the executors. In addition, the history and structure of the farm and lettings are looked at. Finally, there is an examination of the Inland Revenue's arguments and the reasons behind the final decision.

This case has already been looked at briefly in **5.4** in the section on farm cottages maximising the claim for IHT. It is also dealt with in **15.2** in relation to letting income.

Considering the position 'in the round'

13.27 One of the principles arising from the case is that when the factors have been considered it is necessary to stand back and consider the position 'in the round'. In this case this included deciding on whether the business was trading or consisted mainly of making or holding investments.

Let us look at the basis of the appeal. Mr A B Farmer and Mr C D E Giles, the executors of Frederick Farmer (the deceased), appealed against a notice of determination dated 30 April 1998 that the business known as Home Farm, which formed part of the estate of the deceased at his death on 17 February 1997, consisted mainly of making or holding investments within the meaning of s 105(3) of IHTA 1984 and so was not relevant business property for the purposes of s 104 of the Act.

Chapter 1 of Pt V of IHTA 1984 (ss 103–114) gives relief for relevant business property by providing for a percentage reduction in the value transferred. At the date of the death of the deceased the relevant parts of ss 103, 104, 110 and 114 provided:

> '103...(3) In this chapter "business" includes a business carried on in the exercise of a profession or vocation, but does not include a business carried on otherwise than for gain.
>
> 104...(1) Where the whole or part of the value transferred by a transfer of value is attributable to the value of any relevant business property, the whole or that part of the value transferred shall be treated as reduced – (a) in the case of property falling within section 105 (1) (a) below, by 100%...

105...(1) Subject to the following provisions of this section...in this chapter "relevant business property" means , in relation to any transfer of value, – (a) property consisting of a business or interest in a business...(3) A business or interest in a business...are not relevant business property if the business...consists wholly or mainly of one or more of the following, that is to say, dealing in securities, stocks or shares, land or buildings or making or holding investments...

110...For the purposes of this chapter – (a) the value of a business or an interest in a business shall be taken to be its net value; (b) the net value of a business is the value of the assets used in the business (including goodwill) reduced by the aggregate amount of any liabilities incurred for the purposes of the business...

114...(1) Where any part of the value transferred by a transfer of value is reduced under chapter II of this part of this act by reference to the agricultural value of any property...such part of the value transferred as is...so reduced under that chapter shall not be reduced under this chapter.'

Chapter II of Pt V of IHTA 1984 (ss 115–124) gives relief for agricultural property by providing for a percentage reduction in the value transferred.

The facts and issue of the case

13.28   At the date of his death the deceased owned the freehold of Home Farm at which he carried on a farming business. He also let properties at Home Farm which were surplus to the requirements of the farm. The Inland Revenue accepted that the business carried on by the deceased did not consist *wholly* of making or holding investments but argued that it did consist *mainly* of making or holding investments, with the result that relief for relevant business property was excluded by IHTA 1984 s 105(3). The executors accepted, on the authority of *Martin (Moore's Executors) v IRC [1995] STC (SCD) 5*, that the letting of property consisted of making and holding investments but they argued that the business carried on by the deceased consisted mainly of farming with the result that the relief given by IHTA 1984 s 104(1)(a) applied, and was not excluded by s 105(3) of IHTA 1984.

Accordingly, the issue for determination in the appeal was whether the business carried on by the deceased consisted mainly of farming (as argued by the executors) or mainly of making or holding investments (as argued by the Inland Revenue). The net value of the business, as referred to in s 110 of IHTA 1984, had not been formally agreed and the parties requested a decision in principle.

Evidence presented by the taxpayer

13.29 A bundle of documents were produced by the executors. The bundle included copies of the accounts of the business for the seven years ending on 31 December 1995 and for the period from 1 January 1996 to 17 February 1997 (the latter being the date of death of the deceased). The bundle also included a plan of Home Farm. In addition, a large framed aerial photograph of Home Farm was produced at the hearing by Mr A B Farmer. Oral evidence was given on behalf of the executors by Mr A B Farmer, the son of the deceased, and one of his executors, and by Mr Gerard Hanley Carter, the farm manager of Home Farm.

Structure of the farm

13.30 In about 1969 the deceased purchased the freehold of Home Farm. At that time the deceased was about 60 years old and had already succeeded in a number of other businesses. He continued to be involved with at least one other business, a countryside park, but no business other than that carried on at Home Farm was in issue in the present appeal.

Home Farm had a total area of about 449 acres, broken down as follows:

Arable land	274 acres
Grassland	60 acres
Farmhouse, farm buildings, their curtilages etc	9 acres
Woodland	98 acres
Rented properties and their curtilages and tracks	8 acres
Total	449 acres

The area of Home Farm remained unchanged during the eight years prior to the death of the deceased. At the time of its purchase by the deceased, Home Farm had the benefit of a planning permission for a dwelling house and the deceased subsequently built the dwelling house. The deceased managed Home Farm on a businesslike basis. He instructed a firm of agricultural consultants and had regular meetings with them. Representatives of the agricultural consultants visited the farm and looked at the crops and machinery. The deceased had a business plan and budgets were produced to monitor profitability. He was also registered for value added tax. The deceased liked his farm to be well equipped with machinery, which was maintained to a high standard and replaced regularly. He also let out any buildings which were not required for use by the farm. He treated the whole of Home Farm as a single business of which he was the sole proprietor. He operated one bank account into which all receipts were paid.

Each year a firm of chartered accountants prepared a 'Balance Sheet and Trading and Profit and Loss Account' for 'F Farmer Esquire trading as Home Farm'. These were unaudited accounts compiled from records, information and explanations supplied to the chartered accountants. They related to the single business which included the farm and the lettings. In this decision they are referred to as 'the business accounts'.

History of the farm

13.31   Home Farm is on sand and so needs treatment to make it productive as a farm. It is, however, good for root crops. At the relevant time the main crop was wheat but some root crops (potatoes and carrots) were grown as well. In evidence Mr Carter said that one-fifth was potatoes from which it was assumed that one-fifth of the acreage which was farmed was used to grow potatoes. Because yields were low the farm aimed at the quality market.

Although Home Farm employed a number of employees in earlier years, by 1989 there were only two full-time employees, namely a farm manager and an assistant farm manager. Mr Carter was appointed as farm manager as from 10 April 1989. The terms of his appointment were set out in a letter to him from the agricultural consultants which said that, in addition to his salary, he would be paid a percentage of the farm profits which included the estate rentals. An assistant farm manager was appointed in 1992 on similar terms. Casual labour was employed for seasonal tasks such as bagging and grading potatoes and for estate maintenance work such as fencing. In evidence Mr Carter estimated that there would be four or five casual staff in a year.

Before his appointment as farm manager at Home Farm, Mr Carter had had a lifetime's experience in farming and had been employed as assistant farm manager at another estate of 250 acres which had grown vegetables and seed crops and which had a staff of ten. At Home Farm Mr Carter's responsibilities included everything that happened on the estate including cropping, selling, buying in seed vegetables, seed contracts, liaison with markets, overseeing the shoot, safety, tracks, fences, cottages, and 'keeping the tenants happy': if a tenant had a problem he went to Mr Carter to sort it out. In evidence Mr Carter estimated that he spent 90% of his time on the farm and 10% of his time on the lettings; the assistant farm manager spent 95% of his time on the farm and 5% on the lettings; and the casual staff did not spend any time on the lettings with the possible exception of 'a bit of painting or mowing'.

The deceased and Mr Carter used to meet once a week and go

round the estate. Mr Carter prepared a weekly report which mentioned matters such as the weather, prices, etc. The deceased and Mr Carter had meetings with the agricultural consultants three times a year. There was one such meeting at the end of each year when they discussed results and forecasts; there was another meeting in May; and another at harvest time. At each meeting the budgets were checked and rechecked and the agricultural consultants advised on European Union provisions.

Facts and history surrounding the lettings

13.32   Mr A B Farmer (the son of the deceased) has a BSc degree in estate management. In 1971 he qualified as a solicitor and thereafter practised in a firm of solicitors. In 1989 his firm merged with another firm and Mr A B Farmer then retired from practice as a solicitor. In the same year Mr A B Farmer's mother died. The deceased was then about 80 years of age and so Mr A B Farmer assisted his father with his business interests. He was not employed by his father but rendered monthly invoices for his services as a consultant; these payments were shown in the business accounts as professional fees. In 1989 Mr A B Farmer reviewed all the lettings and ensured that future lettings were on a commercial basis. Later, he looked after the renewals of the leases and licences and completed forms for the Ministry of Agriculture, Fisheries and Food (now DEFRA). He spent about a day and a half each week on work connected with Home Farm and, of that, about 30% was spent on the farm and about 70% on the lettings.

At the date of the death of the deceased there were 23 tenancies. One was an agricultural tenancy of a farm cottage occupied by a former farm worker and it emerged at the hearing that the value of that property was probably entitled to APR. Of the remaining 22 tenancies, six were of original farm cottages; four were of original farm buildings or barns converted for use by small businesses; four were of original farm buildings used for storage; three were of mobile homes placed by the deceased; two were of stable blocks, one of which was let with some grazing land; one was of a staff bungalow which was let with some stables and grazing land; one was of a pre-fabricated bungalow built by the deceased; and one was of redundant land for the storage of timber. The plan of Home Farm showed that the buildings which were let were grouped in two main clusters towards the centre of the estate and the grazing areas which were let were contiguous to the clusters of let buildings.

Most of the residential lettings were shorthold tenancies for either six months or one year; the other lettings were either by licence by letter for one year or by leases for one year which excluded the provisions of ss 24–28 of the Landlord and Tenant Act 1954. There was one licence of a converted barn for commercial use which was, exceptionally, for five years; this longer term was granted because, although the deceased had provided the materials for the conversion, the tenants had provided the labour to produce a purpose-built gymnasium and the deceased therefore wished to give them a longer licence than usual. In evidence Mr A B Farmer said that his father and himself did not want to grant long-term leases which might affect the future use of the estate. The cottages had not been let to individual tenants until the shorthold legislation had come into force.

In respect of the let properties the deceased was responsible for landlord's repairs as required by statute and also provided water for which tenants paid. If a tenant had a problem which required immediate attention, such as a blocked drain, then the tenant approached Mr Carter or the assistant farm manager. Mr A B Farmer dealt with the renewals of the leases and licences.

Contents of the business accounts

13.33 The business accounts related to the activity of a single business carried on by the deceased. The following details have been extracted from the business accounts:

Year ending	Total turnover	Non-rental turnover		Rents received	
31.12.89	£216,065	£142,254	(65.84%)	£73,811	(34.16%)
31.12.90	£210,421	£115,134	(54.72%)	£95,287	(45.28%)
31.12.91	£270,108	£175,488	(64.97%)	£94,620	(35.03%)
31.12.92	£182,928	£ 87,264	(47.71%)	£95,664	(52.29%)
31.12.93	£258,168	£139,791	(54.15%)	£118,377	(45.85%)
31.12.94	£340,089	£218,612	(64.28%)	£121,477	(35.72%)
31.12.95	£386,289	£258,802	(67.00%)	£127,487	(33.00%)
01.01.96 to 17.02.97	£285,280	£134,113	(47.01%)	£151,167	(52.99%)

The non-rental turnover includes sales of farm produce, revenue grants received from the Ministry of Agriculture, Fisheries and Food (now DEFRA), and profit on the sale of fixed assets used in the farm.

The business accounts showed separately the direct cost of farm sales but the overhead expenses did not differentiate between expenses relating to the farm and expenses relating to the lettings. Mr A B Farmer stated that his father had not been interested in breaking down the expenses between the farm and the lettings.

Probate values

13.34 The deceased died on 17 February 1997 and Home Farm was included in his estate at the date of his death. The probate value of Home Farm was agreed at £3.5 million. Of that, £2.25 million related to the farmhouse, farm buildings and farmland and it was agreed that that value qualified for 100% APR. The sum of £2.25 million included £600,000 for the farmhouse which was used as an office for the entire estate and £145,000 for the house occupied by Mr Carter, the farm manager. The other £1.25 million related to the let properties.

Arguments put forward by the executors

13.35 For the executors Mr Tallon first argued that, in reaching a decision, it was necessary to consider all the circumstances over a period of time and not to take an arbitrary date or a 'snapshot': he cited *FPH Finance Trust Ltd v IRC [1944] AC 285, 26 TC 131* and also *Martin (Moore's Executors) v IRC [1995] STC (SCD) 5*.

Next, Mr Tallon argued that the word 'mainly' in IHTA 1984 s 105(3) was used in its ordinary everyday sense of 'chiefly' or 'principally' and involved no more than deciding whether the letting activities predominated. He cited *Miller v Owners of the Ship Ottilie [1944] KB 188 at 190 and 191, Minister of Agriculture, Fisheries and Food v Mason [1969] 1 QB 399 at 404*, and *Hall (Hall's Executors) v IRC [1997] STC (SCD) 126 at 129 and 131*. He also cited *Furness v IRC [1999] STC (SCD) 232* as authority for the view that it was necessary to look at the business in the round. He distinguished *Sywell Aerodrome Ltd v Croft (Inspector of Taxes)[1942] 1 KB 317, 24 TC 126* which, he argued, was not concerned with the meaning of the word 'mainly'.

In deciding which of two activities of a single business constituted the main part of that business, Mr Tallon proposed four relevant tests, which he placed in order of priority.

1   The first test was the extent to which the proprietor and his employees were engaged in each activity. In this appeal there were only two full-time employees and Mr Carter spent 90% of his time on the farm and the assistant farm manager spent 95% of his time on such activities.
2   The second test was the amount of income or turnover produced by each activity; in this appeal the farm turnover exceeded the letting turnover for six out of eight years.
3   The third test was the amount of capital employed in each activity. In this appeal £2.25 million of capital was employed in the farm and £1.25 million in the lettings; although the figure of £2.25 million included the dwelling house it was used as an office and so

was used for agricultural purposes; the figure of £2.25 million also included the sum of £145,000 for the farm manager's house and that was also used for agricultural purposes.

4   The last test was the contribution of each activity to the overall profit of the single business. Mr Tallon argued that one reason why profit was the least important test was because different activities could have different profit margins and profits from some activities, such as farming, could be very volatile.

In *Furness v IRC [1999] STC (SCD) 232*, the Court had considered both gross and net profit but Mr Tallon argued that gross profit was a better indicator, especially in this appeal where farm prices were so volatile. In *Hall (Hall's Executors) v IRC [1997] STC (SCD) 126* there had been no mention of profits, just of turnover. Section 103(3) of IHTA 1984 merely provided that the business had to be 'carried on . . . for gain' and did not provide that there was no relief if there were losses.

Mr Tallon concluded by arguing that the single business carried on by the deceased at Home Farm qualified for 100% BPR, although the provisions of IHTA 1984 s 114(1) operated to restrict the BPR to that part of the value which was not entitled to APR.

Arguments put forward by the Inland Revenue

13.36   For the Inland Revenue Mr Twiddy accepted that it was necessary to look at the business over a period of time and he also accepted that the period from 1989 to 1997 was representative.

However, Mr Twiddy went on to argue that IHTA 1984 s 103(3) defined a business for the purpose of the relief as a business 'carried on . . . for gain' which, in the present context, meant profit: accordingly, the whole thrust of the legislation was geared to looking at profits and so, in considering what a business 'mainly' consisted of it was primarily necessary to have regard to the profits. In *FPH Finance Trust Ltd v IRC [1944] AC 285 at 303, 26 TC 131 at 149* Viscount Maugham indicated that 'mainly' related to more than half the income. In *Hall (Hall's Executors) v IRC [1997] STC (SCD) 126 at 129* the Special Commissioner had directed his mind to profit and not to turnover and had asked whether the activity made a profit. In *Furness v IRC [1999] STC (SCD) 232 at 237*, although the Special Commissioner had said that he had looked at the business in the round, he had then gone on to base his decision on the allocation of the net profits. Mr Twiddy also cited *Sywell Aerodrome Ltd v Croft (Inspector of Taxes) [1942] 1 KB 317 at 328, 24 TC 126 at 137* and went on to argue that certain figures which he had produced demonstrated that the net profits (or losses in four years out of eight) of the farming business were swamped by the net profits of the lettings.

Finally, Mr Twiddy argued that, in applying the capital test, it was necessary to look at the use of the capital. He argued that, although the sum of £2.25 million had been granted APR, it included the dwelling house built by the deceased which was valued at £600,000 and that was not capital employed in the agricultural activities. There was also the farm manager's house valued at £145,000, and a cottage valued at £60,000 and neither represented capital employed in agricultural activities.

Reasons behind the decision

13.37 In considering the arguments of the parties it is convenient first to consider the point made by Mr Twiddy that, because IHTA 1984 s 103(3) refers to a business carried on for gain, the principal factor to be considered, when deciding if a business consists 'mainly' of making or holding investments, is the net profit of each part of the business. In this connection the decisions in *Miller v Owners of the Ship Ottilie [1944] KB 188* and *Minister of Agriculture, Fisheries and Food v Mason [1969] 1 QB 399* are of assistance.

The issue in *Miller* was whether a cook employed on board a fishing trawler, who suffered an injury by accident, was entitled to compensation under the Workmen's Compensation Act 1925. Section 35(2) of that Act provided that it did not apply to such members of the crew of a fishing vessel who were remunerated 'wholly or mainly' by shares in the profits. The appellant was paid a weekly basic wage of £2 3s 9d, risk money of £1 5s 0d and food valued at 18s, making a total of £4 6s 9d. In addition, he was entitled to a share in the profits which amounted in his case to £7 9s 0d per week. The Court of Appeal held that as three-fifths of his remuneration was derived from a share in the profits the only possible conclusion was that he was remunerated 'mainly' by shares in the profits and so the Act did not apply to him.

From this authority the principle can be derived that the word 'mainly' has to be considered within the statutory context in which it appears: in *Miller* the statutory context required a decision as to how a person was remunerated and the fact that more than half of his remuneration came from a share in the profits meant that he was 'mainly' remunerated by shares in the profits.

The issue in *Minister of Agriculture, Fisheries and Food v Mason [1969] 1 QB 399* was whether an employer was entitled to a repayment of selective employment tax. Section 2 of the Selective Employment Payments Act 1966 provides that a repayment is due if the establishment was engaged by way of business in certain activities and if more than half the employees were employed 'wholly or mainly' in connection with those activities. The employer owned a house and employed a gardener to look after the flower garden and the vegetable garden. As more vegetables were grown than the owner could use some were sold: the gardener spent between 10% and 15% of his time on the commercial side of the vegetable garden. In deciding that the repayment was not due the Divisional Court held that the requirement that an employee should be employed 'wholly or mainly' in connection with certain business activities meant that the employee must devote more than 50% of his time to those activities.

Again, in *Mason* the word 'mainly' took its meaning from the statutory context in which it appeared. The statute required that the employee had to be employed 'mainly' in connection with certain business activities and that meant that he had to spend more than half of his time on them.

Applying the principles in *Miller* and *Mason* to the facts of the present appeal, the statutory context of IHTA 1984 s 105(3) requires a decision to be made as to whether a 'business consists' mainly of making or holding investments: s 105(3) does not limit the decision to one particular factor of a business, for example, whether the gains of a business are derived mainly from making or holding investments; the decision must be of what 'the business consists'. That indicates that all the relevant factors of what a business consists require consideration.

If IHTA 1984 ss 103(3) and 105(3) are considered within their statutory context, it appears that s 103(3) defines the type of business which can obtain relief for relevant business property, namely, a business carried on for gain; whilst s 105(3) provides that, where there is such a business, it is not relevant business property if it consists wholly or mainly of making or holding investments. Hence, it does not appear to necessarily follow that, because the making of net profits is part of the definition of a business, the level of net profits is to be the only, or principal, test for determining whether 'the business consists' mainly of making or holding investments.

Neither party argued that s 110(a), which refers to the net value of a business, was relevant for the purposes of interpreting s 105(3); but if s 103(3) were thought to be relevant then the same could be said for s 110(a).

Factors surrounding definition of 'the business . . . consists'

13.38 Having considered the statutory context of IHTA 1984 ss 103(3) and 105(3), the conclusion is that the level of net profits is not the only, or even the principal, factor in deciding whether a business consists mainly of making or holding investments: all the factors of which a 'business consists' require consideration.

That leaves open the question as to what factors should be considered in deciding whether a business consists mainly of making or holding investments and to answer that question a reference is now made to the other authorities cited by the parties to see what principles they establish.

The decision in *Sywell Aerodrome Ltd v Croft (Inspector of Taxes) [1942] 1 KB 317, 24 TC 126* is of limited assistance in this appeal because it concerned the issue as to whether profits which arose wholly from the ownership and occupation of land, which was assessed under Schedules A and B, were also assessable under Schedule D. The decision that they were not was reached on the grounds that Schedules A and B taxed the deemed income from ownership and occupation of land by reference to its annual value and no further tax was payable in respect of any income referable to the same property.

In *FPH Finance Trust Ltd v IRC [1944] AC 285, 26 TC 131* the issue was whether the income of a company 'consisted mainly of investment income' because that determined whether it was an investment company for surtax purposes. The company dealt in stocks and shares and in earlier years profits from its business were very much larger than its income from investments. Later, however, it had trading losses and its investment income was its only income. Viscount Maugham stated (*[1944] AC 285 at 305, 26 TC 131 at 150*) that it was wrong to take a period of great losses in trade without also considering the results of the preceding periods: if the periods when the company had trading income were also considered the conclusion must be that the company was not an investment company.

Authority given by the case

13.39 That decision is, therefore, authority for the view that consideration should be given to the overall picture. Also, the phrase requiring interpretation in that appeal was 'the income whereof consists mainly of investment income'. That is not the issue in the present appeal where the phrase requiring interpretation is whether 'the business ... consists ... mainly of ... making or holding investments'.

The decisions in *Hall (Hall's Executors) v IRC [1997] STC (SCD) 126* and *Furness v IRC [1999] STC (SCD) 232* were both concerned with the same issue as this appeal, namely whether a business consisted wholly or mainly of making or holding investments. They were both decisions of the Special Commissioners and were, therefore, decisions on their own facts. In one the appeal failed but in the other the appeal succeeded.

In *Hall* the deceased had owned and managed a caravan park. Lots for caravans were let to tenants who owned the caravans, but the caravans had to be bought and sold through the deceased, who received commissions on the sales. There were also some holiday chalets let on leases for 45 years. The rents and standing charges totalled a little less than 84% of the total income of the business and the Special Commissioners held that the activities of the business consisted mainly of making or holding investments.

It is interesting that in *Hall* the leases were for 45 years, which can be distinguished from the short leases in the present appeal. Also, the Special Commissioners considered what 'the activities of the business consisted of' and regarded income as the relevant factor on the facts of that appeal.

Furness v IRC [1999] STC (SCD) 232 also concerned a caravan park which was licensed for 218 static caravans and eight touring ones. There were also about seven rallies each year. The static caravans were owned by the residents but had to be purchased from, and sold to, the owner of the site. Various facilities were provided at the park for entertainment and amusement. The owner of the park, and three full-time employees, carried out a considerable amount of office and maintenance work including the cleaning and repairing of caravans, maintenance of the grounds, and servicing of the drains. The profits from the sales of the caravans, together with sundry sales and rally charges, exceeded the profits from the rentals, from the caravans.

The Special Commissioner held that the business *did not* consist 'wholly or mainly of holding investments' because the net profits of the caravan sales exceeded the caravan pitch rentals. Also, the owner and his employees undertook a very considerable amount of work in maintaining the park and its structures, a level of activity not normally found in a business which consisted wholly or mainly of the holding of investments. From that decision the principle can be derived that it is necessary to look at the business and its activities in the round and to consider *all* the relevant factors.

Factors relevant to the decision

13.40 Applying the principles derived from the authorities to the facts of *Farmer (Farmer's Executors) v IRC [1999] STC (SCD) 321*, the following factors can be identified as being relevant when determining of what the business consists:

- the overall context of the business;
- the capital employed;
- the time spent by employees in making the business function;
- the turnover; and
- the profit.

These factors will now be considered in turn.

Overall context of the business

13.41   In considering the overall context of the business, it is relevant that the business of Home Farm is that of a landed estate and that most of the land is used for farming. The area occupied by the let properties is a small proportion of the total area. Also, most of the let properties are of buildings which were formerly used by the farm but are now superfluous to the requirements of the farm. They are located towards the centre of the land which comprises the estate: most of them would not exist if it had not been for their previous connection with the farm. To that extent it could be said that the let properties are subsidiary in function to the main function of the estate which is its use as a farm. In this connection it is also relevant that the terms of the leases and licences are short and that is unusual for properties which are used for investment purposes. It is also relevant that the farming business was conducted in a businesslike way with the help of agricultural consultants, professional farm managers, business plans and budgets. By contrast, the lettings appear to have been conducted personally by the deceased, with the assistance after 1989 of Mr A B Farmer.

Capital employed in the business

13.42   The next relevant factor is the capital employed in the business. It was agreed that, of the total probate value of £3.5 million, £2.25 million obtained APR and £1.25 million represented the value of the let properties. However, Mr Twiddy sought to argue that the value of the dwelling house (£600,000) and of the farm manager's house (£145,000) should be deducted from the amount of capital employed in the farm for the purposes of the present calculations. As the farm manager's house was occupied by Mr Carter, who devoted 90% of his time to the farm, it would appear that, at the most, 10% of the value of his house might be treated as capital employed in the lettings. As far as the dwelling house is concerned, the evidence was that the value included some woodland, which was managed on a commercial basis; also that it was used as an office for the whole business. It may be that some reallocation of the capital value should be made for such part of the office use as related to the lettings but there was no evidence as to the extent of such use. On the other hand, it emerged at the hearing that one of the cottages valued at £60,000, and included in the figure of £1.25 million for let property, was occupied by an agricultural tenant and might therefore be entitled to APR.

It was decided that the evidence was not sufficient to establish that any alteration should be made in the probate values. That means that, for the purposes of this appeal, £2.25 million was the capital employed by the farm and £1.25 million was the capital employed by the lettings.

Time spent by the employees

13.43 The third relevant factor is the time spent by the employees and consultants in making the business function. Here the evidence was that Mr Carter spent 90% of his time on the farm; the assistant farm manager spent 95% of his time on the farm; and the five casual workers spent all their time on the farm. Mr A B Farmer spent one-and-a-half days each week on estate business of which about 70% was concerned with the lettings. The exact time spent by the agricultural consultants was not known but the evidence was that it was all connected with the farm.

Turnover

13.44 The fourth relevant factor is the turnover. In two years out of the eight (1992 and the last period) under consideration the non-rental turnover exceeded the lettings turnover. The evidence of Mr A B Farmer and of Mr Carter that the explanation for the fluctuations in the farming turnover, and for the very low farming turnover in 1992, was primarily related to the volatility of the potato market was accepted. Mr Carter mentioned that the price of potatoes ranged from £150 per ton in 1995 to £30–£50 per ton in 1996. Another factor was that the price of cereals fluctuated with the weather. The last period (1 January 1996–17 February 1997) was not typical as there was an oversupply of potatoes in October 1996 and prices became depressed. Also, that period included rents for 14 months whereas there would have been little in the nature of farm sales in January and February 1997.

Profit

13.45 The final factor is profit. The business accounts showed the farming sales separately from the rental income and also showed the direct cost of the farming sales from which it was possible to calculate the gross profit of the farming sales. However, because the business accounts did not distinguish between the overhead expenses relating to the farm on the one hand and the overhead expenses relating to the lettings on the other, the business accounts did not give figures for the net profit of the farm and the net profit of the lettings.

At the hearing Mr Twiddy produced some figures which assumed that all the depreciation and vehicle expenses were incurred by the farm and that one-quarter of the professional fees related to the farm and three-quarters to the lettings. The result of these assumptions was that the farming activities either made a net loss or a small net profit, whereas the letting activities made a substantial net profit. The following is an extract from Mr Twiddy's figures:

Year ending	Agricultural gross profit	Agricultural net profit [loss]	Lettings net profit
31.12.89	£46,600	[£1,120]	£70,637
31.12.90	£38,541	[£7,684]	£89,298
31.12.91	£65,757	£28,470	£86,602
31.12.92	£11,189	[£30,250]	£86,185
31.12.93	£46,895	£16,313	£107,699
31.12.94	£132,537	£88,475	£105,435
31.12.95	£162,560	£112,276	£114,576
01.01.96 to 17.02.97	£16,256	[£46,680]	£132,901

The agricultural gross profit was derived by deducting the cost of farm sales from the figure for farm sales and then adding revenue grants received and the profit on the sale of fixed assets. The agricultural net profit was derived by deducting all the depreciation, all the vehicle expenses, and 25% of the professional fees from the agricultural gross profits. The lettings net profit was derived by deducting 75% of the professional fees from the rental income.

On Mr Twiddy's figures the agricultural gross profit was the following percentage of total gross profit:

Year ending	Agricultural gross profit as a percentage of total gross profit
31.12.89	38.7
31.12.90	28.8
31.12.91	41.0
31.12.92	10.5
31.12.93	28.4
31.12.94	52.2
31.12.95	56.1
1996–97	9.7

On Mr Twiddy's figures the lettings net profit was the following percentage of total net profit. For these purposes any loss is ignored.

Year ending	Lettings net profit	Lettings net profit as a percentage of total net profit	Total net profit
31.12.89	£70,637	100	£70,637
31.12.90	£89,298	100	£89,298
31.12.91	£86,602	75	£115,072
31.12.92	£86,185	100	£86,185
31.12.93	£107,669	87	£124,012
31.12.94	£105,435	54	£193,910
31.12.95	£114,576	50.5	£226,852
1996–97	£132,901	100	£132,901

When Mr Twiddy's figures were put to Mr A B Farmer in cross-examination he accepted that they were feasible and that he could not dispute them. However, the assumptions on which the figures are based did not accord with the oral evidence of Mr A B Farmer which is more probable. Mr Farmer said that some of the depreciation related to the let buildings and he also said that about 70% of his fees related to the lettings.

Mr Twiddy's figures only give deductions for depreciation, vehicle expenses and professional fees and not for the other overhead expenses which included bank charges, rates, insurance, heating, lighting, telephone, repairs, renewals, upkeep and other sundry expenses. Also, Mr Twiddy's figures do not give any deduction for depreciation of the let buildings; they assume that Mr A B Farmer spent 75% (and not 70%) of his time on the lettings; and they make no allowance for the fact that most probably all the fees of the agricultural consultants (which were also professional fees) related to the farm. There were one or two computational errors in Mr Twiddy's figures (in particular the transposition of the depreciation figures for 1991 and 1992 which made the net profit of 1991 look better than it should have been and the loss in 1992 look worse than it should have been) which meant that his figures could not be treated as wholly accurate. Nevertheless, even bearing in mind those reservations, the figures do show that the lettings were more profitable than the farm. In only two years out of the eight did the agricultural gross profit exceed the lettings gross profit and in all years the net profit of the lettings exceeded the net profits of the farm: in some years (for example, 1994 and 1995) the difference was small but in other years (for example, in 1992 and 1996) the difference was large. The explanations for the low performance of the farm in 1992 and 1996 have already been considered.

The decision and the way forward

13.46   Mr A B Farmer gave evidence that the farm was run for a profit but that it is very difficult to make a farming profit without the subsidies from the European Union. The evidence of Mr Carter was that the farm could have been run at a profit if there had been no lettings: there would not be a large profit but the farm could be self-supporting and there would be a healthy profit in some years. Over a ten-year period the farm would be viable.

It is now time to stand back and to consider the business in the round. Of the five relevant factors four, namely, the overall context of the business, the capital employed, the time spent by the employees and consultants and the levels of turnover, all support the conclusion that the business consisted mainly of farming. The profit figures, and more particularly the net profit figures, on the other hand, support the opposite view. Taking the whole business in the round, and without giving predominance to any one factor, the conclusion is that the business consisted mainly of farming.

The decision on the issue for determination in the appeal was that the business did not 'consist mainly of making or holding investments'. The appeal was, therefore, allowed. The Inland Revenue, at the date of writing, have not taken this case further which made the decision even more significant when advising clients.

The theme of *Farmer* and the significance to the tax planner is that of 'unified management' with all aspects of the business being examined. The consideration of the fact that *surplus* properties were let is relevant. Until further cases emerge it will be essential for the tax planner advising mixed rural estates to work very closely with the land agent and the farmer. The action to be taken could be beyond tax advice and linked to the reality of good land management. Key factors appear to be:

- ensuring that the letting of surplus farm buildings is incorporated into the farm as one unit;
- ensuring integrated accounts of one unit;
- recording time spent on let properties;
- using organisations such as the CLA, the National Farmers' Union (NFU) and the farming and rural business group of the Institute of Chartered Accountants to monitor APR/BPR claims and to report back on successes and failures.

Mr Carter's statement that it '*could have* been run at a profit if there had been no lettings' is of interest. Could this statement still be made in 2002? Also, the business 'consisted mainly of farming'. Is this still the case? Hopefully, direction from case law or the Government will give future clarity, but in the meantime the tax planner should utilise the main points as far as possible and work together for a common aim of achieving maximum tax reliefs.

Furnished holiday letting

13.47   It is a convenient point to move away from consideration of the IHT position in *Farmer (Farmer's Executors) v IRC [1999] STC (SCD) 321* and to look at the IHT position on furnished holiday lettings. The income tax position is dealt with in Chapter **15**.

The IHT position regarding this was set out in an article by the author in *TAXline* 'Furnished Holiday Letting' (March 2002). (See **A.4**.)

The conclusion appears to be resting with the interpretation of IHTA 1984 s 105(3) and the criteria not that dissimilar to the points raised in *Farmer (Farmer's Executors) v IRC [1999] STC (SCD) 321*. 'Is there a business or is there a holding of investments?'

The Inland Revenue's solicitor has advised the Capital Taxes Office (CTO) that many more such businesses would *not* be excluded by IHTA 1984 s 105(3) than the CTO had previously thought. The criteria is where the owner (either himself or through agents) '... was substantially involved with the holidaymaker(s) in terms of their activities on and from the premises'.

Risk areas are:

- where no services are provided to holidaymakers;
- where lettings are to friends and relatives;
- longer-term lettings (including assured shortholds).

Bed and breakfast

13.48   The inheritance position on the diversified business of bed and breakfast is interesting and one that should be handled with care by the tax planner. It is not an agricultural activity and therefore will not qualify for APR. If the activity is carried out from the farmhouse then the notes on the IHT position on the farmhouse should be reviewed (see **4.22**).

The correct procedure should be to claim APR on the agricultural element of the farmhouse and BPR on that part carried out by the business of bed and breakfast. The exact distinction could prove difficult subject to the size of the operation and the size of the farmhouse. The tax planners could argue that with the claim for full APR on the farmhouse being at risk then the bed and breakfast business should help in the claim for BPR. As with any BPR claim there must be clear evidence of a genuine business being carried on. In order to qualify for relief part of the farmhouse must be used 'wholly or mainly' for the purpose of a business.

Another area of problem is if the bed and breakfast is a partnership and the asset is not in that business there could be a restriction to 50% relief.

There are a multitude of permutations and combinations of complexity, eg the farm partnership which does not include the member of the family who carries out the bed and breakfast.

A bed and breakfast business carried out in property other than a farmhouse should qualify for 100% BPR provided the business conditions are met and the ownership requirements that ensure the 100% and not the 50% relief is available should be reviewed. Again, for maximising IHT reliefs the tax planner must review asset ownership and the interaction to the business structure and the other farming business activities.

The practical planning point is that the move towards diversification such as bed and breakfast should not be entered into lightly without the review of all the IHT considerations. Sometimes the desire to minimise the charging of VAT (see **CHAPTER 9**) could have more complexities than originally envisaged. Proceed with caution – you have been warned. (The income tax position is dealt with in **15.14**.)

Property Disposals and Capital Gains Tax

14

Julie Butler

- **Capital gains tax (CGT) reliefs**
  On the assumption that the disposal of farm or diversified land is classified as a capital disposal this chapter looks at maximising all the reliefs.

- **Trading in land**
  There could be situations where the disposal of farm or diversified land is deemed to be trading in land or an artificial transaction in land. This chapter warns against the problems whilst showing how they can be embraced by the tax planner should the development route be followed.

- **General tax planning opportunities relating to land**
  Consideration for the sundry points of options, reinvestment relief, enterprise investment scheme (EIS) deferral relief and the burden of stamp duty.

Looking at tax planning opportunities

14.1   It is probably this chapter more than any other that will be the most read in the current crisis. Sadly, some farmers will be forced to sell the whole farm and it is essential that they minimise the tax liabilities and plan in advance to maximise the tax reliefs. Forward planning and full understanding of the reliefs available is essential.

This book does not have the scope to go into too much technical detail on the tax points raised. However, more detail can be found in the titles *Property Taxes* by Robert W Maas and *Taper Relief* by F Michael Cochrane (both published by LexisNexis Butterworths Tolley).

It is also likely that many farmers and landowners will have to sell *part* of the farm in order to support the struggling farm income. It might well be that part of the farm or estate is very suitable for a diversification project that would add considerable value to the land or buildings in question but the landowner does not feel able to see the project through himself, and would do better to dispose of the site and use the funds to support the farming enterprise.

Planning consent details are dealt with by James Cleary in CHAPTER 3 and the rural development details (as far as they are known) are set out in CHAPTER 2.

Capital gains tax (CGT) — Finance Act 2002

14.2 It is important to review all the capital gains tax (CGT) changes introduced by the Finance Act 2002.

Table of exemption and rates

14.3 As the replacement to the indexation allowance, business asset taper relief (BATR) now affects all non-corporate farming and landowning individuals. It has an increasing importance on what decisions are made with regard to disposals. A substantial change to taper relief came into effect from 6 April 2002. Set out below are the Finance Act 2002 changes to all the relevant angles of CGT.

	2002–03	*2001–02*
Taxed as top slice of income		
Annual exemption		
individual	£7,700	£7,500
settlement	£3,850	£3,750
Retirement relief (maximum)		
exempt, first	£50,000	£100,000
50% exempt, next	£150,000	£300,000

Transfers between husband and wife living together are exempt.

Non-business asset taper relief

14.4 Taper relief is given on a sliding scale. After ten years maximum relief is reached with only 60% of the gain chargeable. There are special rules where an asset is eligible for business asset relief for part only of the period of ownership. There are no proposed changes to the rates of taper relief for non-business assets.

Business asset taper relief (BATR)

14.5 It is this relief that will be the main focus for the diversifying landowner and farmer. Prior to 6 April 2002, the maximum taper was achieved after holding business assets for four years. Since 6 April 2002 this has been reduced to two years. Broadly, business assets include:

- assets used in an individual's trade;
- shares in any unquoted trading company;
- shares in a quoted trading company where the shareholder can exercise at least 5% of the voting rights;
- shares held by an employee in a trading company by which he is employed; and
- shares held by an employee in a non-trading company by which he is employed, provided he does not have an interest of more than 10% in the company.

It will be appreciated from the above that assets held within a limited company do not qualify for BATR. From 6 April 2002, gains will be tapered in accordance with the table below.

Number of complete years for which asset held	Percentage of gain chargeable	Effective tax rate for higher rate taxpayer
0	100%	40%
1	50%	20%
2 or more	25%	10%

Trading losses and taper relief

14.6 Under FA 1991 s 72 a claim to set trading losses against general income may be extended to cover capital gains as well as income. Currently, the maximum amount of gains that can be covered by trading losses in this way is the amount of gains *after* taper relief. In future, the maximum amount will be the amount of gains *before* taper relief. This new rule will apply automatically in relation to trading losses incurred in 2004–05 and subsequent years, but taxpayers can elect to apply it in relation to trading losses incurred in 2002–03 or 2003–04, such election to be made by 31 January 2005 or 31 January 2006 respectively.

Taper relief anti-avoidance

14.7   Schedule A1 para 11 of Taxation of Chargeable Gains Act 1992 (TCGA 1992) (the so-called anti-avoidance rule) will not apply to disposals on or after 17 April 2002 and, in relation to such disposals, will not apply in determining the status of an asset (ie business asset or non-business asset) at any time after 5 April 1998. This rule provided for the taper relief clock to be reset on a relevant change of activity by a closely-controlled company. It will be replaced by a rule to the effect that any period of time after 5 April 1998 during which such a company is not 'active' will not count towards the qualifying holding period or the relevant period of ownership of shares and securities in that company for taper relief purposes.

Definition of taper relief

14.8   For disposals on or after 17 April 2002, and in relation to holding periods from that date, certain definitions applying for taper relief purposes are to be brought in line with those applicable for the purposes of the new exemption for substantial shareholdings of companies. For example, the special treatment of company shareholdings in joint venture companies and joint enterprise companies will apply in relation to shareholdings of at least 10% (as opposed to 30% as at present).

Personal losses set against attributed trust gains

14.9   At present, it is not possible for a settlor to set a personal capital loss against a capital gain attributed to him under the special rules for both UK-resident and non-resident settlements in which he has an interest. For 2003–04 onwards, the gain attributed to the settlor will be computed *before* taper relief (in contrast to current rules), and the settlor will set personal losses firstly against his personal gains (if any) and then against attributed gains. The taper relief that would otherwise have been applied by the trustees is then applied to the *net* attributed gains. This new rule will not apply in certain cases where the settlor has been temporarily non-UK resident and returns to the UK. In other cases, a settlor may elect for the new rule to have effect for any of the tax years 2000–01, 2001–02 or 2002–03, such election to be made by 31 January 2005 in each case. If the election would result in the trustees having to reimburse the settlor a greater aggregate amount for those three years than would otherwise have been the case, the election must be made jointly by the settlor and the trustees. For more details on trusts see CHAPTER 17.

Business asset taper relief (BATR)

Need to review assets

14.10 Although BATR is an exceedingly beneficial relief to the farming and landowning community it is equally complicated. It has already been mentioned that there is a whole book on the subject, *Taper Relief* by F Michael Cochrane (LexisNexis Butterworths Tolley).

It is the consideration of many practitioners that every business asset belonging to each client should be reviewed for its eligibility for BATR, and any problems associated therewith should be reported to the client and suitable action taken. Obviously, if the landowner or farmer is to make a substantial gain on land disposal the benefit of this review will be enormous.

Shares in unquoted company — 'wholly' for the purpose of carrying on a trade

14.11 There are problems with diversification in that since 6 April 2000 shares in any unquoted company are now business assets and a company must exist *wholly* for the purpose of carrying on a trade. It is likely that if there is a substantial increase in the holding and investments that this could be caught by TCGA 1992 Sch A1 para 11.

Maximising the generous reliefs

14.12 As mentioned in **14.5**, BATR is a generous relief that is available for business assets with a prospect of 10% CGT rate after just two years of ownership following the Finance Act 2002. It is, therefore, necessary to define what is a business asset. It is also essential to ensure, as mentioned above, substantial farming and business assets do qualify for the generous BATR.

It is sufficient to say that all capital gains realised by non-corporate entities, ie individuals and partnerships, on the disposal of assets, business and non-business, qualify for taper relief. Business assets qualify for far greater, and more easily achieved, rates of relief.

The fundamental position is that where an individual carrying on a trade (or a partner in a business carrying on a trade) and an asset wholly or partly being used for the purpose of that trade BATR is available under the TCGA 1992 Sch A1 para 5(2)(A).

There are, however, a number of problems with BATR, as discussed below.

Mixed use period

14.13   This is the situation in which an asset is simultaneously used for more than one purpose, one of which would qualify the asset as a business asset and the other not as a business asset. In a farming situation a typical example would be where a sole trader farmer owns a barn and one part of it is used for the purposes of the farm and the other part is let out. Where this is the case TCGA 1992 Sch A1 para 9 introduces an apportionment calculation. This is a very complex calculation where it is necessary to calculate the relevant fraction of each mixed use period for which the asset is used for a non-qualifying purpose. Such a calculation shall be made on a just and reasonable basis. The relevant fraction represents the proportion that uses the asset for non-qualifying purposes. For the tax planner it is essential to identify mixed use assets and inform the client accordingly. This is of most relevance where there is a potential disposal.

Tainted taper relief

14.14   A complex situation arises where there are consecutive periods or periods of simultaneous business and non-business, ie mixed use. This is linked to another area of taper relief problem known as 'tainted taper relief'. There are several situations in which an asset becomes tainted. Earlier non-qualifying periods will prejudice the eventual taper relief and the question arises as to what can be done about it.

Alternative land use — non-trading activity

14.15   With diversification it is important to see what would trigger non-trading activity. Care should be taken not to leave farm buildings empty for periods between use in the old farming trade and the new non-farming trade, or for periods when they are apparently temporarily surplus to the requirements of the old farming trade. The Inland Revenue will argue that a period when a building has stood empty is a period of non-business use for taper relief purposes.

Where an asset has been used consecutively for business and non-business use the gain is apportioned on a time basis over the relevant period of ownership [TCGA 1992 Sch A1 para 3(2)(3)]. Each part of the apportioned gain is then treated as though it had arisen from the disposal of a separate asset [TCGA 1992 Sch A1 para 3(5)(a)]. Note, however, that the qualifying holding period and relevant period of ownership of each notional asset is the same as the qualifying holding period and relevant period of ownership of the real single asset.

Farmers have traditionally looked to rollover relief (see **14.19**) to assist them in tax saving and the interaction must be carefully reviewed. Rollover relief may still be the best relief to use, unless a further sale of the new assets, without further reinvestment, is contemplated with the next two years. In such a case the period of ownership of the old asset is ignored when calculating taper relief on the gain arising on the sale of the new replacement asset. It will be necessary in such a case to look at how taper relief will operate to reduce gains on the sale of the old assets and the hypothetical sale of the new assets.

The section on rollover relief looks at a tax planning opportunity through separating land and buildings (see **14.21**).

Tenanted farmland

Periods between 6 April 1998–5 April 2000

14.16 Tenanted farmland will not be a business asset for taper relief purposes for any period from 6 April 1998 to 5 April 2000 unless:

1 the tenant is a partnership of which the landowner is a partner [TCGA 1992 Sch A1 para 5(2)(a)]; or
2 the land is used by a company which is a qualifying company in relation to the landowner [TCGA 1992 Sch A1 para 5(b)]; or
3 the asset is used within a group (51% subsidiary test) where the holding company of that group itself qualifies as a holding company of a trading group [TCGA 1992 Sch A1 para 22].

For the company to be a qualifying company in relation to the landowner it must be a trading company, or the holding company of a trading group, and the landowner must either hold shares with 25% of the voting rights, or 5% of the voting rights if he is a full time working officer, or employee, of the company, or of a company that has a relevant connection with it.

Periods after 5 April 2000

14.17 For periods after 5 April 2000 it is sufficient for the land to be let to any unlisted trading company (or holding company of a trading group) to qualify for BATR.

For other unincorporated tenants, for periods after 5 April 2000, the landlord will still have to be in partnership with them, or for a listed company he will need to be employed by the company, or hold 5% of the voting rights in the company. The relief will not be reduced if the tenant pays a full market rent.

Compare this position to retirement relief where:

1 there would be no relief at all if the land was let to either a partnership or a company of which the landlord was neither a partner nor a shareholder; and
2 there would be a restriction to the relief, and no relief at all, if the land was let to a partnership in which the landlord was a partner, or to a company in which the landlord was a shareholder, and the rent paid was a full market rent.

Compare the position further to rollover relief where there will be a restriction of relief for periods when the land is occupied by others [TCGA 1992 s 152(7)].

In search of capital

14.18   Using BATR etc, CGT may be minimised by careful planning, thus providing the landowner with liquid funds, which might not have been available previously. There are a multitude of possible complications in this scenario, however, and the combinations are endless: it is sufficient to say that there are significant advantages in managing to define the disposal of assets as a capital gain as opposed to assessable under Schedule D and to use the many CGT reliefs that are available, particularly BATR.

To summarise, make sure the assets qualify as a business asset, check for tainted taper, check for mixed use and check for interaction with other reliefs.

Rollover relief

Alternative land use

14.19   Where the new diversified activity involves the cessation of the farming business and the commencement of a new non-farming business, there may be a change in the use of the farmland or the farm buildings.

A common solution where a farm business cannot make a profit is for the farm land to be contract farmed, for example, by a neighbour, or even let to a neighbour, and for the farm buildings to be put to some other non-farming business use (see **Chapter 11**). A point that needs to be considered is whether the buildings used in the new business, if sold at some point in the future, would then qualify for rollover relief. The tax planning point is that non-farming does not necessarily mean non-trading.

Relief is not lost if the buildings were originally used for a farming purpose, but have become assets of a new non-farming business after the cessation of the farming enterprise [TCGA 1992 s 152(8)]. The test is that the assets disposed of must have been used throughout the period of ownership only for the purposes of 'a business'. However, this rule is relaxed where a person carries on two businesses 'successively' and they are treated as one.

If there is an interval between the cessation of one trade and the commencement of another, the two trades are treated as being carried on 'successively', providing the interval does not exceed three years. If there is a disposal of assets, and reinvestment in new assets, for rollover relief purposes it will not matter if the old trade and the new trade are different in nature, as long as both the old and new assets fall within the headings at Classes 1–8 of TCGA 1992 s 155.

Be careful, though, if the disposal of the old assets and the acquisition of the new assets takes place during the interval between the old business ceasing and the new one starting. Relief is not lost, provided the asset is not used for any other purpose before the commencement of the new business and is used for the new business after it has commenced.

The time limits are of course subject to the overriding rule that the acquisition of the new asset must take place within a four-year period starting one year before and ending three years after the disposal of the old asset.

Replacement of business assets

The whole proceeds

14.20 One of the most frequently utilised CGT reliefs by the landowner is that of replacement of business assets. However, a common problem for the unwary arises in that the owner of the old asset is not the owner of the new asset. This is a particular problem on setting up or disbanding a partnership or where a new partner is added or leaves a partnership. If the asset is owned by the partnership these changes can trigger a loss of relief. Another problem arises in that a requirement for full rollover relief to be allowed the entire proceeds of the old asset must be reinvested in the new qualifying asset. This is set out in s 153 of TCGA 1992. It must be noted that any proceeds not so applied will be charged to CGT.

As mentioned above, the interaction of taper relief introduces a further complication. The principle of replacement of business asset is that the gain arising on the disposal of the land may be rolled over and subtracted from the cost of acquiring the new asset. Additionally, both the disposal and the corresponding acquisition must be made by the same person and with the assets being used for the purpose of a trade or other qualifying activity. Due to this, land sales can be rolled over into non-farming activities. This can be a diversified farming activity or a completely separate business activity.

The fact that the gain that has been rolled over due to this has only been *deferred*, and hence a subsequent sale could be a crystallisation of that gain, makes the taper relief in its recent form more and more attractive. The BATR position should be looked at and planned on the final sale without rollover. When would BATR be most useful?

Separate land and buildings — tax planning

14.21   For rollover relief purposes, 'buildings' and 'land' are the most widely used class of assets [TCGA 1992 s 155]. They are defined as:

1 *Building*: Any building or a part of a building and any permanent or semi-permanent structure and the nature of a building occupied (as well as used) only for the purpose of the trade.
2 *Land*: Any land occupied (as well as used) only for the purpose of the trade. Schedule 1 of the Interpretation Act 1978 requires that unless the contrary intention appears the word land includes 'buildings and other structures, lands covered with water and any estate interest, servitude or right in or over land'. This approach is somewhat modified by s 288(1) of TCGA 1992 which defines land as including 'messuages, tenements and hereditaments house and buildings of the tenure'.

There is a tax planning advantage identified here in that buildings and land are separate, ie there are people who strongly argue that land should not be given an extended meaning and must exclude buildings together with permanent, semi-permanent structures in the nature of buildings. It can be extremely useful with matching acquisitions, disposals and support of the claim for rollover relief. If land is sold with a building erected on that land, the sale proceeds may be apportioned between two different assets, ie the building and the land separately. A similar approach may be used when land and buildings are purchased.

It may, therefore, be possible to rollover the gain arising on disposal of only one of the two assets leaving the gain on the other asset to absorb the annual exemption or perhaps losses. This could also interact with taper relief.

What are the requirements?

14.22 What are the requirements to qualify for rollover relief? Section 152(1) of TCGA 1992 states:

'... the consideration which a person carrying on a trade obtained from the disposal of or of his interest in assets used and used only for the purpose of the trade throughout the period of ownership is applied by him in acquiring other assets, on interest in other assets which on the acquisition are taken into use and used only for the purpose of the trade, and the old assets and new assets are within the classes of assets listed in s 155.'

The requirements can be summarised as follows.

1   The old assets and new assets must fall within the classes of assets listed in s 155 of TCGA 1992.
2   The person must be carrying on a trade.
3   The person disposing of the asset must obtain consideration from the disposal of that asset or an interest in an asset.
4   The consideration obtained must be applied in acquiring other assets or an interest in other assets (the new asset).
5   On acquisition, the new assets must be taken into use and used only for the purpose of the trade.
6   The asset being disposed of must have been used and used only for the purpose of the trade.

Let property

14.23   The position of the tenanted farmer is discussed with regard to BATR at **14.16**. There are a number of definitions which must be looked at, such as the difference between trade and income derived from property that is let out. Although it has been defined previously, some further direction has been given in the case of *Griffiths v Jackson & Pearman [1983] STC 184*. The decision in this case confirmed the profits derived from property which is let out (in this case furnished) are not the profits of a trade and assessable under Schedule A or Schedule D Case VI. It was defined that:

'... income derived by the owner of a property from letting the property furnished whether for a short or a long term and whether in small or large units and whether in self-contained units or to tenants who share a bathroom or kitchen or the like is not income derived from carrying on a trade.'

There are some exceptions: the letting out of industrial units and distinct office complexes converted from farm buildings are not the profits of a trade; the other exceptions are dealt with in the section on furnished holiday accommodation under TCGA 1992 s 241(3). The activity must be carried on commercially (see CHAPTER 15).

The CLA are currently lobbying for let property to be an asset that qualifies as an asset for rollover purposes. It has been suggested that provisions should include low cost residential accommodation in rural areas. The advantage of rollover into refurbished farm buildings, which are used for either commercial or residential lets, would have obvious advantages for the rural economy.

Partial business use

14.24   As with BATR, one section of the replacement of business assets which is important to the farming and landowning community is where there is partial business use of an asset. This is dealt with under TCGA 1992 s 152(6) where, over the period of ownership or any substantial part of that period, part of a building or structure is not used for the purposes of a trade. There is no direct definition of the word 'substantial'. It is agreed that if part of a building is not used for purposes of trade throughout the whole, or substantial part, of the period of ownership the asset must effectively be divided into two parts for rollover relief: there must be the part which represents the business use, and the other representing the non-qualifying use. Each part will then be treated as a separate asset with rollover being confined to the chargeable gain allocated to the business use element.

Mixed use

14.25   Again, as with BATR for the replacement of business assets, another point to check is where the old asset was not used for the purposes of the landowner's trade throughout the period of ownership. This is covered in TCGA 1992 s 152(7). It is accepted that this deals with the situation where at some stage within the ownership period there was no qualifying use whatsoever. For disposals taking place after 5 April 1988 the period of ownership cannot commence earlier than 31 March 1982. When this situation is in existence the old asset is effectively divided into two different parts as follows:

1   the element representing the non-trading use; and
2   the element representing the use of the purpose of the trade.

It is generally accepted that the apportionment of costs and disposal proceeds will be undertaken on a just and reasonable basis, as there will be periods of both use and non-use. Time apportionment may well produce an acceptable solution to this problem.

With the generous BATR rules post-5 April 2002, there are strong arguments for forsaking rollover relief in favour of BATR to ensure that there is a change of ownership to start the new two-year taper relief clock ticking. There are a multitude of concerns such as will the first change trigger CGT? Is the payment of some CGT acceptable? The answer is that all future disposals should be reviewed with a complete understanding of all available reliefs and what the farmer or landowner is wanting to achieve.

Further, where there is prior cessation of use, ie the asset ceases to be used in the business prior to disposal, there are concerns that the ability to claim rollover relief will be lost because the old asset ceased to be used for the purpose of a continuing trade before being sold. There is a clear decision in the case of *Richard v J Lyons & Co Ltd (1989) 62 TC 261*, which shows that the relief is *not* lost, but it might be restricted. It does give confirmation that an asset need not actually be used for a qualifying purpose at the time of disposal before a claim for rollover relief can be made.

Is it worth making the rollover claim?

14.26 Unlike indexation allowance, taper relief does not actually enter into the calculation of the chargeable gain: it only assumes significance once the amount of the gain has been determined. In view of this there are many other considerations which compete. It is essential to look at the interaction of BATR and rollover relief very carefully to the extent that it is increasingly relevant to consider whether it is worth making a rollover relief claim? Examples can be shown where a substantial gain may arise on the disposal of an asset which has been owned for several years after 5 April 1998 and thereby qualifies for considerable taper relief. However, the gain is rolled over against the cost of acquiring a second asset which is then sold after a short period of ownership and not replaced. It is the period during which the second asset has been owned which governs the percentage of available taper relief.

The elimination of liability otherwise arising on the disposal of the old asset may well have secured a cashflow advantage but this advantage could be more than offset should a substantial loss of taper relief arise on the disposal of a replacement asset.

There have been numerous articles on the possible complications arising from the interaction between rollover relief and BATR and it is vital to point out at this stage that they should be weighed up very carefully. A better result may be obtained by using taper relief in relation to the disposal of both the old and the new asset, rather than claiming rollover relief. This is of particular relevance if the owner wants to 'bank' some of the proceeds without being tied down to a rollover of possibly all the proceeds.

Detailed 'what if' calculations are essential if it is known that there

will be a sale of the new assets within four or five years. The real difficulty of course arises where rollover relief has been claimed, instead of
taper relief, because no sale was contemplated within four or five years,
but the new venture does not take off and the new assets have to be sold.

Rollover into a depreciating asset

14.27 It is possible to postpone a gain by holding it over into a depreciating asset (for example, plant and machinery). This would appear in
the balance sheet as fixed assets. This is found in s 154 of TCGA 1992.
A non-depreciating asset can be acquired within the ten-year period
and again held in suspense and the gain can be rolled over.

A depreciating asset is one with a useful life of 60 years or less at the
date of acquisition. The standard rollover rules bring the deferred gain
back into charge on the earliest of:

1 ten years elapsing;
2 the second asset being disposed of; or
3 the second asset being used for the purposes of the trade.

When the postponed gain becomes chargeable to tax BATR is calculated according to the period and nature of ownership of the original
asset only. As mentioned under TCGA 1992 s 154 it is possible to
make a rollover claim relating to a depreciating asset to be withdrawn,
if a further rollover takes place before the gain falls back into charge.
This third asset must *not* be a depreciating one. Taper relief relating to
asset one is again lost. The need for clear calculations is essential.

Commerciality test

14.28 One of the clear factors to be considered is that difficulties
may be experienced in securing entitlement to CGT reliefs following a
change of trade if the new or the old trade were not carried on
commercially and with a view to profit. The existence of a commercial
trade is an essential requirement before any entitlement to rollover
relief or BATR can arise.

Holdover relief

Gift to family members

14.29 A gift, although potentially free of inheritance tax (IHT), may
still trigger a CGT charge. The provisions of TCGA 1992 s 165 may be
used to holdover the gain arising on a gift made directly to a family

member. If the gift is made into a discretionary trust, TCGA 1992 s 260 will achieve the same result (see **CHAPTER 17**). It should be noted that these holdover provisions can apply equally to the gift of let land if it falls within the definition of agricultural property for IHT purposes [TCGA 1992 Sch 7].

Note, however, when making gifts that separate the ownership of buildings from the ownership of land with which they have been historically associated, right to agricultural property relief (APR) on the buildings may be lost.

Holdover relief is preserved if the asset continues to be used for the purposes of a trade carried on by the transferor. This means that it has to have been in trade use just before it is gifted. The fact that there may be a change in the nature of the trade should not affect the operation of the relief. However, if there is a period of non-business use (including any gap period between successive trades), or part of the asset is not used for business purposes, apportionments will have to be made so that only part of the gain will qualify.

Agricultural property qualifying for APR for IHT purposes qualifies for holdover relief where it is not used for the purposes of trade carried on by the transferor, or his personal company [TCGA 1992 Sch 7 Pt I]. This effectively means that relief is available on the gift of let land even where the transferee does not actually use the property. Switching to non-agricultural lets, eg industrial units will mean relief is lost. It is the gift of let agricultural property that can be the most beneficial.

The conversion of a barn for residential use, which was previously used for trade purposes by the transferor, will not qualify as it would neither be used for the purposes of trade nor be occupied for the purposes of agriculture at the time of a subsequent gift.

Qualifying assets

14.30 Under the current rules for transactions carried out after 13 March 1989 a claim for holdover relief can be made under s 165 of TCGA 1992. In order to make a claim for holdover relief it is important to identify persons involved that are eligible and also the assets which are capable of supporting a claim for holdover relief.

There are principally three groups of qualifying assets, as discussed below.

Assets used for the purpose of trade

14.31 First is under TCGA 1992 s 165(2) which is an asset or an interest in an asset used for the purpose of a trade, profession or vocation, by the transferor's personal company or a member of the trading group of which the holding company is the transferor's personal company. This also includes shares or securities of a trading company or the holding company of a trading group where:

1 shares or securities are neither listed on or recognised by the Stock Exchange nor dealt with on the unlisted securities market; or
2 the trading company or holding company is the transferor's personal company.

Note that the unlisted securities market ceased at the end of 1996.

Agricultural property

14.32 The second group of assets that qualify for holdover relief is agricultural property. This is limited to disposals by an individual otherwise than by way of a bargain at arms length. In order to qualify as an asset for the holdover provision agricultural property must come within the meaning of Inheritance Tax Act 1984 (IHTA 1984) Ch II Pt V. In addition, it must be shown that the disposal does not otherwise fall within s 165(1).

For this purpose s 115(2) of IHTA 1984 defines agricultural property (see **1.6**) as meaning:

> '... agricultural land or pasture and includes woodland and any building used in connection with the intensive rearing of livestock or fish if the woodland or building is occupied with agricultural land or pasture and the occupation is ancillary to that of the agricultural land or pasture; and also includes such cottages, farm buildings and farmhouses, together with land occupied with them, as are of a character appropriate to the property.'

The land used for the breeding and rearing of horses on the stud farm and the grazing of horses in connection with those activities is treated as agricultural property, and any buildings used in connection with those activities are also treated as farm buildings. It can also be noted that land and buildings used for the cultivation of short rotation coppices can be treated as agricultural property from 6 April 1995.

Section 115(2) of IHTA 1984 means that agricultural property can be divided into three different categories:

1 agricultural land or pasture;
2 woodland and any building used in connection with the intensive rearing of livestock or fish if the woodland or building is occupied with agricultural land or pasture and the occupation is ancillary to that of the agricultural land or pasture; and

3 such cottages, farm buildings and farmhouses together with the land occupied with them as are of a character appropriate to the property.

In the case of *Starke v IRC [1995] STC 689* it was defined that 2.5 acres added on to a six-bedroom farmhouse which had previously been an agricultural holding did not comprise agricultural land or pasture and it was not agricultural property within the meaning of s 115(2) of IHTA 1984.

Transfers by trustees

14.33 The third class of assets which can qualify for holdover relief are transfers by trustees into discretionary and life interest trusts. In order to qualify for inclusion in this group it must be demonstrable that the trustees undertake the disposal of specific assets otherwise than by way of a bargain at arm's length. This is covered by TCGA 1992 7 Sch 2(1).

The assets must comprise:

1 assets, or an interest in assets, used for the purpose of a trade or professional vocation carried on by:
   — the trustees making the disposal; or
   — a beneficiary who has an interest in possession in the settled property immediately before disposal; or
2 shares or securities of a trading company or a holding company of a trading group where:
   — the shares or securities are neither listed on a recognised stock exchange or dealt with on the unlisted securities market at the time of the disposal; or
   — not less than 25% of the voting right exercised by shareholders of the company and general meeting are excisable by the trustees at the time of the disposal.

There are various references which have been defined in other sections of the book including 'trade', 'profession', 'vocation', 'trading company', 'holding company of a trading group' and 'listed'.

The claim for holdover relief is not mandatory and a formal claim is required. The claim must be made jointly by the transferor and the transferee unless the transferees are trustees of the administering of the settled property when the claim may be made by the transferor only.

The time limit specified for the submission of a claim and the normal time limits recorded in the Taxes Management Act 1970 will apply in this case. These require that in the case of a transaction taking place a claim had to be made within a period of six years following the end of the year assessment in which the disposal occurred. This is applicable for a disposal taking place before 6 April 1996. After this date the time limit is shortened slightly to five years and ten months, ending on 31 January where the disposal occurs on or after 6 April 1996.

In order to understand the holdover gain position it is essential to look at the steps which may be necessary to calculate the amount of the holdover gain which can then qualify for holdover relief. These are as follows:

1   calculate the chargeable gain arising on disposal using normal CGT rules, ignoring taper relief;
2   reduce the amount of that gain if necessary where actual consideration is received by the transferor;
3   reduce the holdover gain where an asset has been subject to partial use or a company or group retains disqualified assets;
4   further reduce the gain where there has been any partial retirement relief.

It could well be that steps 2, 3 and 4 are not needed, but it is necessary to consider these points to see whether or not they should be taken into account. It is important also to look at the interaction with holdover relief and taper relief. Taper relief will not directly affect the calculations required for the application of holdover relief.

It is only to the extent that any part of a chargeable gain remains after applying holdover relief, and where appropriate retirement relief also, that the remaining part becomes vulnerable to CGT. Taper relief will then be applied to the remaining part in the normal manner.

Retirement relief

Catch it while you can — deadline 5 April 2003

14.34   With a lot of farming activities ceasing totally or in part changing in structure there are still opportunities to use retirement relief, especially with regard to land sales. Retirement relief ceases to be available for disposals from 5 April 2003 and it is important to note that the application of these rules is limited. However, there are those ardent tax planners who think that it should be looked at and claimed where possible prior to its departure.

The tax position on the retirement of a partner due to the breakdown of a marriage is looked at in **16.25**. The VAT implications of the sale of a business (transfer of a going concern (TOGC)) are dealt with in **9.43–9.45**.

Change of activity

14.35   Retirement relief is available on the disposal of assets after the cessation of farming activities even if those assets are retained for use in the new activity. However, it is more difficult to achieve relief in cases where farming continues alongside the new activity. Mere scaling down in farming activities does not constitute disposal of part of the farming business and this was set out in the cases of *McGregor v Adcock [1977] STC 206* and *Atkinson v Dancer [1988] STC 758* and *Mannion v Johntson [1988] STC 758* (see **14.37**). It could well be that one part of the activity is due to change and a land/property sale will arise. Retirement relief in these circumstances cannot be overlooked.

However, there is a case which works in favour of the taxpayer and this is *Jarmin v Rawlings [1994]*. Here it was demonstrated that a particular farming activity, in this case dairy, had ceased even where another kind of farming, such as beef rearing, had been taken up. In this case the Commissioners found that dairy farming was a separate part of the taxpayer's farming business. It, therefore, differed from the activities of rearing and finishing store cattle. This case does suggest the useful approach for farmers who are, for example, giving up dairy farming and make a gain from the disposal of land, buildings and milk quotas arising therefrom.

Another case involving a farmer was *Barret v Powell [1998] STC 283*. In this case retirement relief was denied because it was pointed out that the disposal of the agricultural tenancy was effectively the disposal of an asset used for the purpose of the business and not the disposal of whole or part of a business of farming which clearly continued until a much later date.

It should be noted that under s 163(2)(b) of TCGA 1992 it is easier to secure upon complete cessation of farming and that it would not apply where activities have merely been scaled down. However, it may be available where a particular activity has ceased, as mentioned, and with changes to the farming activities and diversification there are arguments to say that an active tax planner should look at the ability to claim retirement relief before it disappears into the distance.

Tax planning requirements

14.36   There is a section on retirement relief in K R Tingley's *Tolley's Roll-over, Hold-over and Retirement Relief* (LexisNexis Butterworths Tolley). It goes into great length explaining what retirement relief is, definition of the business interest, the points regarding age, demonstration of ill health, the whole or part of the business is looked at in detail. There are detailed notes on the basic requirements for retirement relief to apply to shares and securities which look at various matters including the singleton company, the holding company, capital distributions, offices and employment, settled property, associated disposals and give examples of how to calculate the relief.

In addition to a section on planning for retirement relief there are sections explaining how to deal with associated disposals, increasing the qualifying period where there are several disposals, the division concerning husband and wife and the complications concerning an organisation's reconstruction. It explains the relationship with other reliefs such as taper, rollover, reinvestment, deferral, holdover etc. It also sets out the position concerning earlier disposals and partnerships.

It is, however, worth taking a brief look at this so that it can be seen in principle whether it is worth claiming. The new provisions became effective for disposals made after 5 April 1995. In order to make a claim for retirement relief an individual must be aged over 50 and there is relief where they have had to retire early on ill health grounds. It must be noted that whilst retirement relief is being phased out between 1999 and 2003, it is only the amount of available relief which is changing as the main conditions are staying in force (ie the conditions such as age, length of business use etc still apply, irrespective of the reduction of the relief) [TCGA 1992 s 163].

The underlying principle of these cases is that ideally for retirement relief claims to be successful there should be sale of the whole business. As mentioned scaling down should be looked at carefully. Likewise, it can be argued that where the farmer is over 50 and there is still an opportunity to claim before 5 April 2003 and various assets might be sold with the move to diversification, there are considerable tax planning opportunities.

Before the introduction of taper relief, when retirement relief was available in larger amounts, there existed various schemes which enabled the taxpayer to claim retirement relief without retiring and without selling part of the business. Hence, any scheme should be looked at carefully.

Within TCGA 1992 ss 163–164, there are different rules for retirement relief for individuals and for partnerships; different rules for assets owned by an individual and used by a partnership of which he is a member; and different rules for assets owned by an individual and used by a company of which he is an office holder, employee or shareholder.

The disposal need not be a sale. A gift to the next generation of a family farming partnership, forming part of a planned succession strategy, may be an ideal opportunity to trigger the relief.

Scaling down of activity

14.37 At the time of disposal the individual must have reached the age of 50 or have retired on ill health grounds, as mentioned previously. There are a large number of cases, which help with the finding of disposal of a partial interest for the claim of retirement relief. In addition to those mentioned there is *Pepper v Daffurn [1993] STC 466*; *Wase v Bourke [1996] STC 18*; *Barret v Powell [1998] STC 283* and *Purves v Harrison [2001] STC 267*.

Pepper v Daffurn, which was decided in 1993, is worth mentioning as it was disposal of part of a business undertaken by a farmer. In this case retirement relief was rejected on the conclusion that 'to categorise a third of land in those circumstances as a third of part of his business seems to me ... to be the antithesis of the true position'.

In this case the farmer had, prior to 1986, farmed a holding of some 113 acres. The holding comprised a farmhouse and a number of out-buildings, including a covered yard. For many years the taxpayer had kept cattle in these sheds. The cattle side of the business consisted of buying and rearing calves, which were over-wintered in the covered yard. In September 1986 the taxpayer sold 83 acres of the farm together with the farmhouse and claimed retirement relief for gains arising on the disposal. He retained the remaining 30 acres including the covered yard. It was considered that the yard retained had development potential, although an application for planning permission to develop had been refused. From the end of 1985 to early 1986 the cattle herd was reduced in anticipation of receiving planning permission. Planning permission was due to be granted in September 1987 and no calves were purchased after 1985 and all had been sold by 5 April 1989. The covered yard was sold for a substantial consideration in September 1988.

On appeal, Jonathan Parker J observed that with a view to the eventual sale of the covered yard, the taxpayer changed the nature of his business with the result that the yard was no longer required for the purpose of his business. The entitlement to retirement relief was rejected. Hence, great care needs to be taken in structuring disposals correctly, especially where only part of a farming business is sold.

The retirement relief route may be of particular interest to those leaving the rigours, and early mornings, of dairy farming to, say, the comparative ease of raising a few pedigree heifers while others contract farm or take grazing from the majority of the acres that were grazed by the dairy herd.

Change of trade prior to disposal

14.38 For this purpose it is not necessary that the business carried on throughout the ten-year period should be the same business as that carried on when the CGT disposal takes place. Thus, a change of business from farming to, say, a caravan site (where that activity is treated as a Schedule D trade and not a Schedule A business) ending in a disposal of the caravan site business on retirement would not affect the retirement relief due. However, there would be a reduction of relief if there was a time gap between the two business periods. If that time gap was greater than two years, the earlier period in business would cease to qualify for relief, even though it fell within the ten-year period.

If the time gap between the two businesses was less than two years, the earlier business period would continue to qualify, but the intervening period would not qualify for relief and a proportionate reduction in the maximum relief would fall to be made [TCGA 1992 Sch 6].

On a change of land use, therefore, preservation of retirement relief requires that the interval of time between the two activities be reduced to a minimum.

As noted earlier, where farming ceases, and all the other conditions for retirement relief are satisfied, there is nothing to prevent a claim for retirement relief merely because it is intended to use those assets not sold, but retained, in some alternative activity. In these circumstances there would be retirement relief on one disposal and then a claim for relief on a subsequent disposal, when there may be relief restrictions having regard to the previous disposal.

Life interest trust

14.39   Where no succession is planned but the client wants to trigger retirement relief before it disappears, a disposal into a life interest trust may provide the answer and may be worth considering, eg client and wife both over 50 wish to sell part of the farmyard and buildings for housing. The proceeds will be used to refurbish other farm buildings and then let them as office buildings. The gains on the sale of the farmyard and buildings cannot be rolled over into the refurbishment of the office buildings, as the letting of the offices will not be a trade. Retirement relief cannot be claimed in the ordinary way as the farming trade is continuing. A solution may be to dispose of the whole of the farmland and buildings into a life interest trust, claiming retirement relief, and for the trustees to dispose of the office buildings.

Maximum retirement relief is due where the client has carried on a qualifying business for a period of ten years. Where the business has been carried on for less than ten years, a proportion of the full amount of relief is due, computed on a time apportionment basis. However, such tax planning should not be undertaken without specialist advice. The whole issue of the setting up of a trust cannot be looked at in isolation. (The subject of trusts is dealt with in **Chapter 17**.)

Part disposals and small part disposals

Part disposal rule

14.40   There is a statement of practice issued by the Inland Revenue that states that where part of an estate is disposed of, for example, the sale of a field, the Inland Revenue will accept that such part disposal can be regarded as a separate asset and any fair and reasonable method of apportioning the total cost will be accepted by them. This cost is then deducted from the original cost or March 1982 value.

The Inland Revenue is not, however, forced into using the part disposal basis: the estate may still be treated as a single asset. However, a decision will normally have to be made on the timing of the first disposal out of an estate and then use the same basis for subsequent sales etc.

The advantage of the part disposal rule is that there can be short-term benefits in reducing the chargeable gain by being able to allocate a higher base cost against the gain, which can be very beneficial. However, like all the disposals that have been discussed it is the interaction with other reliefs and the interaction of future disposals and the interaction of what future tax reliefs will be.

Interaction with business asset taper relief

14.41   The end result that the decision is an application of the part disposal rule or not must depend very heavily on the current and future plans of the farmer. It is imperative that the practitioner does note these down. The interaction of BATR has made (in some circumstances) the use of the part disposal rule less attractive. It was considered that it was really a short-term benefit so as to reduce the gain down and pay the minimum amount of CGT now and leave a lower base cost for capital gains. Items to be considered are as follows.

1   Death is not a chargeable event, ie there is no CGT payable on death and so short-term CGT benefits should be weighed against long-term aims.
2   BATR post-5 April 2002, ie very favourable rates.

The timing of disposals will be important when looking at this if the part disposal rule gives the tax practitioner and the landowner some degree of choice over what the base cost is. There will be great scope for timing of reliefs, interaction of taper relief and interaction of retirement relief, before it is phased out. Whilst it could be considered an enticing exercise for the tax planner, for the hard-working practitioner it could be considered quite a nightmare.

Small part disposal rule

14.42   Another element of the part disposal rule is that known as the small part disposal rule and the use of this cannot be challenged by the Inland Revenue. Under s 242 of TCGA 1992 the transferor may claim that the sale of land does not constitute a disposal where the following conditions are met:

1   the consideration does not exceed £20,000;
2   the consideration does not exceed 20% of the market value of the entire holding at the time of transfer; and
3   the consideration for all transfers of land made by the taxpayer in the year in question does not exceed £20,000. In this instance the sale proceeds would be deducted from the base cost.

Once again, both tax planning and tax calculation in relation to disposals of land is not straightforward and there are some factors, which could influence the decision-making process surrounding the disposal. These would include the use of annual exemptions and the use of BATR.

Now that BATR has come into full effect from 6 April 2003, provided the conditions are met, this must bring into question other CGT reliefs which interact with the BATR calculation.

Is it still relevant after 6 April 2002?

14.43   Of particular concern must be the small part disposal of land advantage given under s 242 of TCGA 1992. Under this provision proceeds from a small part disposal of land used to finance new ventures can be maximised by taking advantage of the relief. The transferor may claim that the sale of the land does not constitute a disposal where the conditions as set out above (see **14.42**) are met.

If a piece of land were to be sold, for example, by a husband and wife trading, there would be a clear need to check the use of the annual exemption for CGT. Now, it will also be relevant to look at the BATR calculation. There could be strong advantages in not claiming the relief so as to secure a higher base cost for future use. Again, this is not an exact science as it would depend what the future use of the taxpayer's base cost will be. As death is not a chargeable event some would argue that the effect on the future base cost is irrelevant. However, some taxpayers who have another disposal intended would have to look at how they could use the base cost, how it would interact with future taper relief and a number of combinations arise.

This does show what a nightmare time the tax planner faces. When looking at combinations of CGT relief, large amounts have been written on tainted taper and the like, and from 6 April 2003, when more beneficial rates of BATR are effective, it will present even more choices to the tax practitioner. There are many clients who have fallen into the habit of needing to make business decisions very promptly demanding almost immediate, over-the-telephone, advice: 'Do I buy now? 'Do I sell now?' etc. It will be a practical point for the practitioner to make sure the client realises that, with the complexity of the CGT reliefs, there is no such thing as a quick over-the-telephone answer. From a practice management point of view this highlights the need for the tax practitioner to document the choices clearly. Ultimately, the decision on which action to take rests with the taxpayer, and all options must have been thoroughly explained to him, and documentary evidence of this will be required. This additional paperwork adds costs to the process, which should be built into the fee structures.

Farmland disposals — trading in land?

Alternatives available

14.44   With the acute housing shortage and the large demand for development land, farmers have in some cases turned to land sales and building development for survival. As mentioned in the introduction the tax planner must ensure that these are taxed in the most efficient way.

Property transactions have a very high unit cost and, therefore, there is scope to look at individual transactions rather than the whole. Also a very large profit on a single transaction could arise giving the Inland Revenue great incentive to try to tax the profit as trading rather than capital. With the very beneficial BATR rates from 6 April 2002 the tax planner must ensure that this is not the case. Likewise, there are other CGT reliefs to lose, such as annual exemption, rollover, retirement relief before phasing out and indexation for earlier acquisitions if the asset is treated as a trading activity.

It is possible for a gain arising on the disposal of land to be taxed under one of three heads.

1   CGT (see **14.45**).
2   Schedule D Case 1 – 'trading in land' (see **14.46**).
3   ICTA 1988 s 776 – 'artificial transactions in land' (see **14.48**).

The VAT position on the disposal of land is dealt with at **9.11–9.18**. The tax implications of selling land for development should be considered before the sale is agreed because if the gain is not subject to CGT any contemplated relief such as business asset taper or rollover would be lost, and this could destroy the whole economic purpose of the sale as approximately only 60% of the proceeds would be left. The whole matter should be planned now and the status of all land and future transactions reviewed.

Capital gains tax (CGT)

14.45   A gain on the disposal of land will be taxed under this head where it can be demonstrated that the taxpayer is not dealing in land. Likewise, it will be taxed under the CGT provisions provided that the anti-avoidance legislation of ICTA 1988 s 776 does not come into play. This classification is generally the most advantageous with all the generous tax reliefs.

Trading in land

14.46   It can be argued that if the farmer/landowner carries out any work to the property to promote the development/sale other than by just obtaining planning permission then he is trading in land. It is possible that if a farmer/landowner makes frequent disposals or buys to sell-on he could be caught under the trading in land provisions. Trading is defined in s 832(1) of ICTA 1988 as including 'every trade, manufacture, adventure or concern in the nature of trade'. This does not really define trading at all and, therefore, the so-called 'badges of trade' have been formulated. It is not necessary to show that all badges of trade are present for an activity to be assessed as a trade; however, a profit-seeking motive at the time of acquisition is the most persuasive, which is often confirmed by the existence of other badges.

Let us look at what makes up the trading emblems known as the badges of trade.

1   *Motive*: This is classically illustrated where land has been acquired for the purposes of resale. The land has not been acquired as fixed capital but rather as stock in trade and will usually be confirmed if there is a short interval of time between the acquisition and sale. File notes and documentation should support the capital disposal motive not the trading motive. Document also that the land has been used for dedicated farm purposes or diversification purposes.
2   *Trading interests in a similar field*: Is the taxpayer involved in similar ventures that have been admitted as trading or do other capital disposals in the light of the current disposal connect the transactions as trading after taking account of the other badges?
3   *Frequency of transactions*: A number of similar transactions may indicate a continuous activity. Transactions normally treated as of a capital nature in isolation, acquire the characteristic of income due to the frequency of the transactions. This would apply to a farmer who sells a number of areas of land over a short period of time. Again, it would be looked at 'in the round'. Was this merely

a disposal of long held farmland in a number of transactions or was it frequent disposals of newly acquired sites which scarcely saw a farm animal nor a plough?

4   *Circumstances of acquisition:* It is difficult for the Inland Revenue to demonstrate that the sale of land acquired by gift or inheritance amounts to an adventure in the nature of trade, as intention of resale will not necessarily be in mind at the time of acquisition. Again, if it can be shown it was acquired to improve the farming trade.

5   *Subject matter:* Is it genuine farmland? Has it been farmed or stored for resale? This badge of trade tends to be unhelpful in land cases since land can be acquired as an investment, own occupation and resale. Links to motive are relevant here. Was it bought as farmland as well as being farmland?

6   *Time interval:* Holding the land for a number of years may point to a lack of profit-motive when the land was acquired. However, the factor is not considered conclusive by the Inland Revenue. In *Cooksey and Bibbey v Rednall (1949) 30 TC 514*, the taxpayer successfully argued that there was a lack of profit-motive, but the case still went to the High Court even though the land in question had been held for 15 years.

7   *Supplementary work:* This applies where work is done to the property to make it more marketable (eg in cases of development) or where the taxpayer actively takes steps to find purchasers. However, there may be circumstances where cash needs to be raised as soon as possible. The more development work carried out the more likely the trading clarification.

8   *Method of finance:* The purchaser may have purchased the land with the assistance of a loan that has been made on terms requiring repayment upon resale. This gives a clear indication of intention as demonstrated in *Turner v Last (1965) 42 TC 517*. It is one point amongst a large number of others.

The tax planner must ascertain what the intention is on acquisition. Of crucial importance is the acquirer's *intention* at the moment of the acquisition of the land: see *Lionel Simmons Properties Ltd v IRC [1980] STC 350*, in which Lord Wilberforce said at p 491:

'Trading requires an intention to trade: normally the question to be asked is whether this intention existed at the time of the acquisition of the asset.'

In land transactions, the moment of acquisition is defined as the moment of exchange of contracts for purchase and not the moment of completion. The simple task of obtaining planning permission does not constitute development.

Tenants disposal of superior interest in land

14.47 Where a tenant buys and immediately resells a superior interest in the land he occupies (usually his landlord's freehold) it may be possible to argue that the transaction amounts to an adventure in the nature of trade. This is so whether the tenant is a residential, commercial, industrial or agricultural tenant.

In order to quantify the Case 1 profit relating to the purchase and sale of the freehold, the market value of the tenancy at the time the freehold was acquired must be established. The tenancy is then treated as if it were appropriated from fixed assets to trading stock thereby invoking TCGA 1992 s 161 (*Bath and West Counties Property Trust Ltd v Thomas [1978] STC 30*).

This market value constitutes the 'consideration' on which the capital gain is computed. It also constitutes a deduction in the computation of the Case 1 profit.

The basic trading principles apply in determining whether the transaction is a trading transaction. Common features of such transactions are prearranged or early sales and funding of the purchase to be reimbursed from the proceeds of sale. Such transactions merit close scrutiny to see whether a trading argument is appropriate.

The Inland Revenue argument is that:

- such transactions involve two separate assets – the tenancy and the freehold;
- the tenancy is a capital asset and any gain on that asset will be a capital gain;
- the freehold was not acquired with the intention to retain but to sell at profit;
- the freehold was therefore never part of the taxpayer's capital structure and is not consequently a capital asset;
- it is the profit on the freehold alone that the Inland Revenue wish to isolate, and tax as the profit of an adventure in the nature of trade;
- that profit is part of a marriage profit which is generated when the tenancy and the freehold merge.

Artificial transactions in land

Definition

14.48 Developers are usually caught under the terms of ICTA 1988 s 776(2)(c), which encompasses cases where: 'land is developed with the sole or main object of realising a gain from disposing of the land when developed'. The aim of this section is for the Inland Revenue to prevent property dealing profits being treated as capital.

It has been said that some farmers and landowners enjoy 'growing houses' more than growing crops and after one genuine disposal they start to 'trade' in land. The purpose is to prevent property dealing profits being disguised as capital. The circumstances are clear and likely to be kept to two situations:

- the disposal of shares in a property company (*Yuill v Wilson [1980] STC 460*); or
- where a UK resident passes the opportunity to make a trading profit on UK land to an overseas company.

The scope of s 776 of ICTA 1988 is broad and catches transactions which have little or no element of artificiality; therefore the avoidance can be accidental or unwitting by the landowner. With the current shortage of houses there could be farmers and landowners who are caught in these provisions.

The rules apply in the following circumstances:

1   land is developed with the sole or main object of realising a gain from disposal later;
2   land is held as trading stock; or
3   the land or any interest that has its value derived from it (eg shares in a landowning company, interests in partnerships, etc) is acquired with the sole or main object of realising a gain on disposal.

In order for ICTA 1988 s 776 to apply a gain of a *capital nature* must result. This means that the gain must not be chargeable as income under any of the Taxes Acts if it is trade. If a trade exists it will be caught in the trading in land provisions.

'Slice of the action' schemes

14.49   One of the most common applications of ICTA 1988 s 776 arises under point 1 at **14.48** involving 'slice of the action' schemes. These schemes involve the landowner selling surplus land to a developer, receiving a fixed sum, followed by future contingent payments based upon the success of the development. The developer himself will be trading and will, in effect, be passing some of the trading profits on to the former landowner. The receipt will be of a capital nature in the landowner's hands and accordingly will be caught by s 776 as a Schedule D Case 1 profit has emerged in a capital form. The Inland Revenue's authority for treating additional payments in this way can be found in *Page v Lowther (1983) STC 61*. The fixed sum, however, will remain chargeable to CGT. It is the contingent payments that must be taxable as trading profit.

Section 776 cannot be invoked where the landowner could be charged under Schedule D Case 1 – refer to the 'badges of trade' to see if it is pure trading.

Section 776 cannot apply in respect of the disposal of a main residence which is exempt from CGT [TCGA 1992 s 222] or would be if it were not for s 224(3) of TCGA 1992, regarding residences acquired wholly or partly for the purpose of realising a gain from the disposal.

Non-resident company

14.50   Other schemes involved are normally intentional rather than unwitting. A common device involves structuring what is, in essence, a trading transaction in land in such a way that the gain is realised by a person who is not within a charge to UK income tax. This can be done by diverting profits into non-resident companies, as was the case in *Sugarwhite v Budd [1988] STC 533*. It was held that a person, who provides the opportunity of making a gain to someone else (who is non-taxable), can be assessed under ICTA 1988 s 776.

First intention date

14.51   When ICTA 1988 s 776 applies, the gain is taxed under Schedule D Case VI, but there is a restriction of the charge [ICTA 1988 s 776(7)]. The effect is that the gain attributable to the period before the intention to develop the land was formed, is excluded. Any gain that has arisen while the land was being used as a capital asset is chargeable to CGT, not ICTA 1988 s 776. This requires the land to be valued at 'the first intention date'. The amount chargeable under s 776 will normally be the difference between the total proceeds (that is fixed sum + contingent payments) and the market value of the land at the 'first intention date'. The latter is used as the disposal proceeds in the CGT computation.

The 'first intention date' is a question of fact.

Advance clearance procedures

14.52   A formal Inland Revenue advance clearance procedure is available in respect of transactions potentially falling within points 1 or 3 at **14.48** [ICTA 1988 s 776(11)]. This can be made before or after the relevant transaction. However, it is rarely used in practice since disclosure puts the inspector on notice, and there is a tendency for inspectors to 'play safe' if there are any doubts, knowing full well that an enquiry can be raised once the tax return has been submitted.

Freehold reversion

14.53 An interesting case to look at is where a sitting tenant will want to acquire the freehold reversion from the landlord in order to unlock the marriage value. What are the tax implications if the tenant sells part of the freehold after acquiring the reversion? Has he entered into a trading transaction or will he be able to use the shelter of CGT?

The answer to this will often depend on how the acquisition is financed. A common arrangement in these circumstances will be the provision of funds in the form of a bridging loan. The loan will be conditional on it being repaid shortly after the purchase and the lender will usually expect that there is a willing buyer of the freehold land already lined up. The transaction is likely to be viewed as trading.

This will result in the tenancy being appropriated from fixed assets to trading stock [TCGA 1992 s 161(1)], which will represent a deemed disposal at market value for CGT purposes. This same value will then be deductible in computing the Schedule D Case 1 profit.

However, the deemed disposal of the tenancy could give rise to significant gains (especially if the tenancy was not in existence on 31 March 1982). However, the tenant can elect for no capital gains to arise [TCGA 1992 s 161(3)] and the value of the tenancy acquired as trading stock will be such that produces neither a gain nor a loss on appropriation. This would avoid valuing the tenancy where it has commenced after 31 March 1982.

Diversification into the trade of property developer

14.54 It might well be that the farmer/landowner wishes to diversify into the trade of property/developer. Development can be an investment operation and it can be a trading activity. It depends whether it is intended to retain or sell the property. If the intention is to try and obtain a rental income from the property then it is an investment. The IHT angles of the investment have already been looked at. The problems of development are dealt with in Robert W Maas's book *Property Taxes* (LexisNexis Butterworths Tolley) (see also **14.11**).

Option agreements

History

14.55 In a lot of cases the farmer will sell his land to a professional developer, and this will be classed as a CGT disposal.

However, the possibility of progressive and deferred sales and the use of option agreements should be considered. In the nature of things developers are often only too ready to defer completion of transactions, and this readiness needs to be taken advantage of in terms of tax planning.

If a series of options are entered into with the sole aim of obtaining CGT annual exemptions then the basic principles of *Ramsay*, with extension by *Furniss v Dawson* (see **19.44**), cannot be overlooked, ie the inspector will be very aware of general anti-avoidance rules.

Business usage

14.56 So as to avoid the loss of retirement relief, or restriction of rollover or business asset taper relief, ensure that land over which a client has granted an option to a developer does not stand unused, or becomes incapable of use because it is inaccessible as a result of work that the developer has started on adjacent land.

This can happen during the construction of motorways or other developments. All the problems raised in the book on failure to qualify as a business asset apply in this case. *Tax Bulletin* No 2 (February 1992) set out the position that the Inland Revenue accept that rollover relief on replacement of business assets is available in respect of grants on the option over land by reference to the underlying land.

It may be prudent to preserve photographic or other evidence of farming use of the land right up to the day when the option is exercised.

Deferred consideration may fail to qualify for rollover relief, and the timing of both the grant and likely exercise of option agreements requires careful consideration in conjunction with time limits for reinvestment (see **14.34**).

Does the option qualify for business asset taper relief (BATR)?

14.57 An option is not a part disposal of the underlying land over which the option is granted [TCGA 1992 s 144]. The grant of the option is the disposal of a separate asset, the option itself. Because it is not a part disposal, it does not matter how long the underlying land has been held by the person granting the option.

In a straightforward situation where the option is never exercised the capital gain arises on the grant of the option and no BATR will be due.

Once the option is exercised the disposal created by the grant of the option is cancelled [TCGA 1992, s 144(2) and (3)] and the sums received for both the grant and the exercise of the option are aggregated in one disposal at the time of the exercise. Taper relief then applies to the aggregated consideration, and is determined by reference to the date of the exercise, and by reference to the period of ownership of the underlying asset disposed of [TCGA 1992 Sch A1 para 13].

If the asset changes status from being a business asset to a non-business asset between the date of the grant and exercise of the option the apportionment rules will apply to the whole gain and part of the gain will lose favourable business asset status. Similar restrictions apply where there is partial non-business use of the asset between the grant of the option and its exercise.

Where either change is unavoidable a contract that crystallises accrued gains at the date the change of status in the asset occurs will ensure the whole gain to date qualifies for the higher business rate of taper relief.

Where it is known that it will take time to move into profit it will be prudent to preserve evidence of both commerciality and profit seeking motive (business plans, budgets and cash flow projections).

This will give the opportunity to claim Schedule D Case 1 losses now in anticipation of future trading profit.

Problems of development — alternative land use

14.58   Planning consent for residential development may be difficult to obtain, but in terms of the value involved, this may be the most substantial category of diversification. There is all the more reason to review the tax consideration. James Cleary explains the process of obtaining planning permissions in Chapter **3**.

Commercially, it may be beneficial to retain some right over the land in order to keep some control over future development. Ransom strips or covenants can be used to protect the landowner. Ransom strips result in part disposal rules (see **14.40**). Covenants are a capital asset and so again result in a part disposal. Their value will be difficult to ascertain and so will have negligible cost.

New trade as a developer of land

14.59   Development is not defined by statute. The Inland Revenue interpretation is any physical adaptation or preparation for new use of land.

The increase in value created by planning consent, representing the difference between agricultural value and development value can raise problems if matters are not thought through first.

The development by the farmer himself of houses for sale will be an adventure in the nature of trade as a developer or property dealer. The question of whether or not there is a trade is dealt with at **14.46**.

If the landowner becomes a developer, land previously held as a farm asset will be appropriated to the trading stock of the new trade. On this change of status, CGT arises on a deemed disposal at market value [TCGA 1992 s 161]. An election under TCGA 1992 s 161(3) will normally be sensible. However, a person who has owned land with no intention of selling does not necessarily become a property developer merely because he takes steps to enhance the value of the property in the eyes of a developer who might want to acquire the land for development (*Taylor v Good [1973] STC 383*).

There are circumstances where it must be accepted that the trade of property developer has started and the eligibility to CGT reliefs ceases. As mentioned previously, this must be planned accordingly.

Owner of tenanted land with development value

14.60   Tenanted land with development value will constitute a non-business asset for taper relief purposes – not much help if the land later gets sold for development. The landowner should , therefore, consider securing the status of farming by entering into a partnership or share farming agreement. This will not be possible unless something is done about the tenancy. Bear in mind that an incontestable notice to quit can be served by the landlord under Case B (s 26 and Sch 3) of the Agricultural Holdings Act 1986, although this can be time consuming. It would probably be better to offer an incentive to procure a surrender of the tenancy. Such a transaction should not be entered into without the help of a lawyer.

Reinvestment relief and Enterprise Investment Schemes (EIS) deferral relief

Corporate structure

14.61   Most farming businesses have operated historically without the need to adopt corporate structures (see **13.14–13.15**).

The exceptions are the very largest businesses where the protection of limited liability was needed, or family situations where company and tenancy structures were adopted to try and devalue the asset value of the farmland in an estate for capital taxes planning purposes. Generally, though most farming families have avoided the use of companies.

There was a period from 29 September 1994 until 6 April 1998, when reinvestment relief was abolished, when it was possible to roll over gains on the disposal of any asset into a subscription for shares in a farming company [TCGA 1992 ss 164A–N].

Capital gains tax (CGT) deferral relief

14.62 Reinvestment relief was replaced by the CGT deferral relief, introduced as part of the Enterprise Investment Scheme arrangements. Farming is specifically excluded from the trades that qualify for deferral relief after 5 April 1998.

Reinvestment relief

14.63 Although the repeal of the reinvestment relief legislation has effect in relation to share acquisitions made on or after 6 April 1998, this does not imply that the entire reinvestment relief legislation ceases to have effect on that date.

Events taking place after 5 April 1998 can still result in a clawback of reinvestment relief granted for acquisitions of shares made before that date.

Two of the events that can result in a clawback of relief would be if the company in which the acquired holding subsists ceased to be a qualifying company, or if the shares ceased to be eligible shares.

Clawback

14.64 A company may lose its qualifying status as a result of a change in its business activities, involving the introduction of some precluded trade. The shares may cease to be eligible shares where rights attached to the shares are varied, or where there is a reorganisation of share capital or a return of value to the investor.

In most farming companies cases, the three-year relevant period for clawback will have expired on 5 April 2001. Any variation in a company's trade after that date as a result of diversification is, therefore, unlikely to result in clawback of reinvestment relief.

If diversification realises large gains that cannot be relieved in any other way, for example, on the sale of land with development value, the form of CGT deferral relief introduced for periods after 5 April 1998 [TCGA 1992 Sch 5B] may provide a tax-free route into a new trade through a subscription for eligible shares.

The conditions to be satisfied to qualify for the relief, and the actions to avoid to avoid the claw-back or loss of relief already given are complex.

The trades precluded from relief include asset backed trades such as farming, dealing in land, property development, holding, managing and occupying woodlands and leasing [ICTA 1988 s 297(2)] (see **20.33–20.35**).

Enterprise Investment Schemes (EIS)

14.65   EIS can be used as a method to defer capital gains. If a farm unit trades as a limited company it would be very attractive to raise capital through the tax efficiency of EIS. Farming is *not* a qualifying trade, *nor* is trading in land. Diversified activities *might* qualify and should be looked at as a tax planning tool. Andrew Miles covers this in some detail at **19.60**. (See **20.33–20.35** on changing the EIS rules.)

Diversification — gifts to family members

14.66   There will be cases where as part of the diversification process it may be timely to make gifts of land or buildings to other family members, as part of a planned programme of succession.

Suggested action may be to put the assets in the same hands as the son/daughter who is going to carry on the new diversified business; or the timing may reflect a belief held by the client that the current generous IHT regime, including potentially exempt transfers, and APR at 100%, cannot last forever. This has been looked at in CHAPTER **13**.

Other angles which need to be looked at are:

1   CGT (see **14.29**);
2   possibility of a 'failed potentially exempt transfer' (see **13.17–13.25**);
3   gifts with reservation of benefit (see **5.10**).

Stamp duty — Finance Act 2002

Transfer of goodwill and debts

14.67   In any property transaction the position concerning stamp duty always has to be taken into account. This is often an overlooked tax. There have been changes in the Finance Act 2002 and these are set out below. Stamp duty is an extremely complex subject and this book has not got the scope to deal with it in detail. The title *Property Taxes,* by Robert W Maas (LexisNexis Butterworths Tolley), devotes a whole chapter to stamp duty and is worth reading, especially in anticipation of large property transactions.

With effect from November 2001, all transfers of property of no more than £150,000 in the most disadvantaged parts of the UK have been exempted from stamp duty. This exemption will be extended, subject to approval from the European Union, to cover all transfers of non-residential property in disadvantaged areas. The change will take effect from a date yet to be announced.

With effect for all documents executed after 22 April 2002, transfers of goodwill will be exempt from stamp duty. This means that transfer documents relating only to goodwill no longer need to be stamped. If the transfer document relates to property that consists partly of goodwill and partly of chargeable property, it will be necessary to apportion the sale price, on a just and reasonable basis, to determine the correct amount of chargeable duty.

Transfers of debts will also be removed from stamp duty, but this change will not take effect until late 2003. This measure is intended to make it easier for companies to raise finance through debt factoring and the issue of bonds secured on debt portfolios.

Anti-avoidance

14.68 A series of measures have been included in the Finance Act 2002 which are intended to counter avoidance of stamp duty on commercial property transactions. The measures include to:

- clawback group relief where UK property has been transferred between intra-group companies, and the recipient company subsequently leaves the group within two years;
- clawback partial relief under FA 1986 s 76 where a company acquires the whole or part of an undertaking of another company in exchange for shares in the acquiring company, and the acquiring company passes it to a third party within two years;
- deny relief under FA 1986 s 76 where, in respect of an instrument transferring UK land, the acquiring company is under the control of a third party at the time the whole or part undertaking is transferred to the acquiring company, and arrangements exist for the third party to receive the shares that are issued to the target company;
- extend the penalty rules for documents executed in the UK to documents relating to UK land or buildings that are executed outside the UK; and
- bring contracts for the sale of interests in land for a consideration in excess of £10 million into charge.

Proposed reform of stamp duty on land and buildings

14.69 The Chancellor has also launched a major reform of stamp duty on land and buildings in the UK. Stamp duty is over 300 years old and the legislation was last consolidated in 1891, over 111 years ago. It is a charge on documents which transfer property. The majority of stamp duty arises on conveyances of land and transfers of shares. The reform announced in Finance Act 2000 focuses on transactions in UK land and buildings.

A primary reason for modernisation is to introduce a regime that can support wider Government plans to facilitate e-business. When duty is paid, stamps are still physically impressed on the relevant document. The main sanction for not paying is that the document cannot be registered or used as evidence in court. A tax on paper documents is not well suited to modern commercial practice, e-business or future developments in the house buying process.

The Inland Revenue has, therefore, issued a consultative document and the main features of the proposals are as follows.

- For commercial property a move away from a tax on documents to a tax levied when a significant payment is made to satisfy a contractual obligation.
- The reporting and paying of stamp duty electronically, eventually via the electronic conveyancing systems to be introduced by the Land Registries over the next five years or so.

Rates of duty

14.70   Stamp duty is an ad valorem duty (% of the consideration for the sale). Rates are as follows:

Consideration up to £250,000	1%
Consideration between £250,000 and £500,000	3%
Consideration in excess of £500,000	4%

No duty is chargeable if the value of the consideration is £60,000 or under, provided the instrument contains a statement certifying that the transaction effected by it does not form part of a larger transaction or series of transactions in respect of which the aggregate amount of value of the consideration exceeds £60,000.

Property transactions in general

14.71   As stated in **14.1**, it is probably this chapter that will be read the most. There is an inescapable fact facing farmers – whilst incomes drop, property values increase. This, together with the emphasis on the reluctant farmer (see CHAPTER 10) – ie the landowner who can embrace business tax reliefs through farming – makes the whole question of property tax relief very relevant. Whether it is the protection (as set out in CHAPTER 5) or the disposal (as set out in this chapter), the subject is complex and with potentially large tax reliefs at risk. The aim of this publication is to help consider the alternatives for both protection and planning.

Property Letting and Associated Activities

15

Julie Butler

- **Furnished lets**

  This is possibly the most basic form of property diversification and a welcome income stream to property owners. For income tax purposes ensure that the interaction of Schedule D and Schedule A is considered and that maximum expenses are claimed. The further impact of the *Farmer* case was looked at in great detail in Chapter 13.

- **Furnished holiday lets (FHLs)**

  This is potentially a very tax efficient form of diversification for the farmer/landowner and should not be overlooked.

- **Caravan sites**

  The whole area of the assessment of income and future inheritance tax (IHT) reliefs must be looked at with great care before this form of diversification is undertaken.

Furnished lets

History

15.1 One of the first forms of diversification of the farming industry was the letting out of 'redundant' farm cottages. Traditional farming units contained a large number of cottages for farm workers but, as farm machinery improved and fewer workers were required, so more and more cottages became available to let out. In addition, various redundant traditional farm buildings originally designed for smaller equipment have been converted into residential accommodation, which has the potential of being let out.

In the current climate rental income is at a height where many landowners and farmers are looking to maximise their income from property. The planning permission angles are set out by James Cleary in Chapter **3**.

The inheritance tax position is set out in Chapter **13** (see *Farmer (Farmer's Executors) v IRC [1999] STC (SCD) 321*).

Tax treatment — the impact of Farmer v IRC

15.2 The general position with regard to rents received from farm cottage letting is that they are assessed under Schedule A. The letting income should be included in the main farm accounts and the management of the properties incorporated in the management of the farm accounts (see *Farmer (Farmer's Executors) v IRC [1999] STC (SCD) 321* at **13.26–13.46**).

In sorting out the division between Schedule D and Schedule A, the income and expenses must be deducted in the business tax computation. As mentioned previously the income should be integrated in the accounts. It is imperative to claim the correct expenses against the correct source of income. There are tax planning implications where there are trading tax losses brought forward. Advantages in maximising 'trading' (Schedule D) profits and minimising Schedule A should be looked into. Each individual, partnership or limited company's tax position is different but the planning implications of expenses allocation should be considered.

Capital allowances

15.3 No capital allowances are available on machinery or plant (eg furniture, fixtures and fittings) let for use in a dwelling house. For example, if a house is let furnished, no capital allowances are given on the furniture (wear-and-tear/renewals allowances are available instead). However, where furnished holiday lets (FHLs) are treated as if a trade, capital allowances are available on items of furniture etc.

Capital allowances are available for machinery or plant used or provided for use for the purpose of a Schedule A business and are deductible as a business expense.

Wear-and-tear allowances

15.4   Expenditure on furniture etc that would otherwise be disallowed, qualifies for wear-and-tear allowances calculated on 10% of the rents less any expenditure that the landlord meets which would normally be the tenant's responsibility, eg water, council tax etc.

The wear-and-tear allowance is intended to cover furniture and furnishings, and fixtures of a type which, in unfurnished accommodation, a tenant would normally provide for himself (for example, cookers, washing machines, dishwashers). It only applies to furnished residential accommodation (not commercial/industrial property where capital allowances are available). Additionally, the accommodation must be fully furnished so that the tenant could occupy the accommodation without necessarily having to provide any of his/her own furniture etc. Wear-and-tear allowances cannot be claimed in respect of qualifying holiday lets (as capital allowances will be available).

Renewal basis

The principle

15.5   As an alternative to the wear-and-tear allowance, the cost of the renewal of furnishings, fixtures etc, may be claimed. The conditions that must be met are:

- there should be no deduction for the original expenditure (disadvantageous for long-life assets);
- no claim should be made for the cost of any improvement element (a more expensive item does not necessarily constitute an improvement);
- the old asset should be definitely discarded before renewals allowance on its replacement is due; the old asset cannot be kept as a reserve.

Renewal of fixtures that are an integral part of the building

15.6   The landlord can claim the cost of renewing fixtures which are an integral part of the building which would not normally be removed by either tenant or owner if the property were vacated or sold (eg baths, washbasins, toilets). Expenditure on renewing such items may be treated as expenditure on repairs in addition to the 10% wear-and-tear allowance.

One estate election

15.7   The 'one estate election' allows an owner-occupier of a mansion house to deduct excess allowable expenses over a notional rent against rents received from other properties on the estate [Income and Corporation Taxes Act 1988 (ICTA 1988) s 26].

Note, however, that the one estate election has been repealed as from 2001–02 (from 1 April 2001 for companies).

Rent-a-room exemption

15.8 Rent-a-room applies to income from providing furnished residential accommodation in the owner or tenant's main residence. This applies whether the rent would be assessable under Schedule A or Schedule D Case 1. It can, therefore, apply to bed and breakfast accommodation but not where any part of the residence is let out as unfurnished (eg let as office accommodation).

The scheme is for qualifying individuals and does not apply to companies or partnerships. However, it can apply when individuals have the income jointly (for instance, husband and wife where there is no partnership).

It is not necessary for the residence to be the individual's only or main residence throughout the whole of the basis period. Occupation as the main residence at some time during the basis period is sufficient.

Gross annual receipts of £4,250 are exempt from tax under the scheme which include additional services eg meals as well as rent. Where receipts are in excess of £4,250, the taxpayer has a choice of:

- preparing an income and expenditure account and being taxed on any profit; or
- being assessed on the excess gross rents over £4,250 with no relief for expenses being available.

An election is required for the latter, which must be made within one year after the 31 January following the relevant tax year. Once an election is made it remains in force until it is withdrawn. The time limits for a withdrawal are the same as for the election. It is, therefore, possible to apply or disapply the exemption on a year-by-year basis.

Business property relief (BPR) — let property

15.9 So what is the inheritance tax position on let property qualifying for business property relief (BPR)? This is discussed in great depth in *Farmer (Farmer's Executors) v IRC [1999] STC (SCD) 321* (see **13.26–13.46**), but not all landowning situations can relate to this case. For example, let us look at the limited company. The commercial terms are more important than the detail of the analysis of rental income and business income. The interesting question is the interpretation of wholly or mainly in a case where a company has both a trading and an investment arm – should one look primarily at turnover, profitability, underlying asset values or some other criteria? Probably all three are relevant. It is understood that the CTO interpret 'mainly' as more than 50%. Section L.97 of the Advanced CTO Instruction manual on the meaning of 'wholly or mainly' says to the inspectors:

> 'In practice you should have regard to the preponderant activities of the business, and to its assets and sources of income or gains, over a reasonable period preceding the relevant transfer.'

There is no doubt that currently the letting out of property is one of the most efficient uses of assets available to the landowner and farmer. However, as with all areas of diversification, the tax efficiency and implications must be fully considered. The short-term income advantages must not be taken without fully protecting the income tax, IHT and CGT advantages.

Furnished holiday lets (FHLs)

The qualification

15.10   The diversifying farmer has for some time looked to furnished holiday lets as the tax efficient and relatively straightforward source of additional income.

Income from furnishing holiday accommodation is now taxable under Schedule A (*Gittos v Barclay [1982] STC 390*) unless the landlord remains in occupation of the property and provides services over and above those usually provided by the landlord, in which case Schedule D Case 1 could apply. However, in any case, the activity can be treated as if it was a trade for the following areas of tax relief, provided certain conditions are met [ICTA 1988 s 504]:

- loss relief;
- capital allowances;
- relevant earnings re pension contributions;
- capital gains business asset taper relief;
- capital gains holdover relief;
- capital gains rollover relief;
- capital gains retirement relief (until it is phased out).

This is a very extensive list of tax reliefs and allowances, which have distinct advantages over the letting out of redundant farm cottages. However, in affluent locations the return received from a normal let property can be so beneficial that to go through all the aggravation of a holiday let seems less attractive.

The conditions set out in s 504 of ICTA 1988 are:

1   it must be available for commercial letting to the public as holiday accommodation for at least 140 days; and
2   it must actually be let for at least 70 days; and
3   for the period of at least seven months (not necessarily continuous but including any months in which holiday letting takes place), it must not normally be in the same occupation for a continuous period exceeding 31 days.

The letting of furnished holiday accommodation is treated as a trade for income tax loss purposes, provided the activity satisfies the tests in respect of occupation, letting and availability for the letting that are explained in paras 415–422 of booklet IR150 *Taxation of Rents*.

The above tests are normally applied on a tax year basis, except on commencement and cessation, where the first and last 12 months are looked at. For companies it is by reference to a 12-month accounting period.

The test to ensure that the ICTA 1988 s 504 conditions are relevant must be applied on a property-by-property basis where a person has a number of units of accommodation, which are let for holiday purposes. However, it is possible to for a specific property that has failed that 70-day test to nevertheless qualify on the making of a claim for averaging treatment [ICTA 1988 s 504(6)]. A claim can be made where the average period of letting for all properties is at least 70 days.

All qualifying properties will be treated as one single letting activity. If there are non-qualifying properties then Schedule A accounts should be prepared.

Foot and mouth special bulletin

15.11   Where an established FHL business is prevented by the foot and mouth restrictions from satisfying these conditions any loss would normally have to be dealt with under the less advantageous Schedule A rules. For tax years 2000–01 and 2001–02 the tests are being relaxed as follows. If the FHL business satisfies the tests in 1999–2000 or 2000–01 but is prevented from doing so, by foot and mouth, in 2000–01 or 2001–02 then the failure will be disregarded and the FHL rules will be deemed to be satisfied. This concession will enable losses to be offset against other income.

VAT

15.12   Rents from holiday accommodation in buildings, huts, caravans, houseboats or tents are standard-rated for VAT provided that the accommodation is advertised and held out as such. Holiday accommodation advertised or offered at lower rates during the off season can be treated as residential accommodation, where it is let for that purpose for more than four weeks, and the property is situated in a holiday resort where trade is clearly seasonal. In such cases the whole let, including the first four weeks, is an exempt supply. The 'season' in such resorts would normally be expected to be at least from Easter to the end of September.

Inheritance tax

15.13 This is dealt with in **13.47**. Business property relief can be claimed in certain circumstances.

Bed and breakfast

15.14 The whole activity of bed and breakfast is only likely to amount to a trade where the owner remains in occupation of the property and services are provided substantially beyond those normally offered by a landlord. The key factor for assessment under Schedule D, and therefore greater chance of BPR, is the provision of services. For longer term lets, the Inland Revenue tend to argue that there are two sources of income: one of rent (Schedule A) and the other relating to the provision of services where significant, and including meals (Schedule D Case 1). However, the landlord will usually not be in occupation of his own property in these cases (the tenant will). The Inland Revenue publication IR150 *A guide to property income* is a helpful source of information on this subject. The supply of bed and breakfast accommodation is standard-rated VAT.

The inheritance tax position on bed and breakfast activities is looked at in **13.48**.

Caravan sites

15.15 Income from letting caravan pitches is chargeable under Schedule A. However, where the site proprietor carries on associated activities (eg shops), which constitute trading and account for a substantial part of the income, the letting income may be included as receipts of the trading under Schedule D Case 1. This applies regardless of whether the letting is for permanent or touring caravans.

Capital allowances

15.16 With regard to caravan sites, capital allowances can be claimed as plant. This will depend on the definition of plant as follows.

- Caravans occupying residential sites do not qualify as plant.
- Expenditure on the provision mainly for holiday lettings of a caravan (as defined in s 29(1) of Caravan Sites and Control of Development Act 1960) on a holiday caravan site qualifies as plant.
- Caravan park swimming pool – held to be plant (*Cooke v Beach Station Caravans Ltd [1974] STC 402*).

VAT

15.17 Seasonal pitches (ie those provided for less than one year, or provided for more than one year where permanent residence is prohibited) are standard-rated. This includes the supply of any pitch for erecting tents or parking caravans. Pitches for permanent residential caravans are exempt. The charge for additional services will also be standard-rated.

Business property relief (BPR)

15.18 There have been a number of cases on this subject in relation to caravan sites, as there is inherently a mixture of trading and letting activities. It is a question of whether the business as a whole constitutes one of mainly holding investments.

- *Furness v IRC [1999] STC (SCD) 232* – relief allowed. The activities of the owner and his staff were greatly in excess of what would be the norm in a business concerned wholly or mainly of the holding of investments.
- *Weston v IRC [2000] STC (SCD) 30* – relief denied – sale of caravans were ancillary to the pitch fees. The employees spent 111 hours a week on park maintenance and 37 hours on sales activities.
- *Hall v IRC [1997] STC (SCD) 126* – relief denied – almost 84% of the income from the park consisted of rent and standing charges.
- *Powell v IRC [1997] STC (SCD) 181* – relief denied even though income had been assessed under Schedule D Case 1.

These are reviewed in **5.19** when considering protecting business property against disallowance.

Horse livery — trading status

15.19   Schedule D Case 1 status will usually apply where an element of care is provided by the stable owner, eg feeding, mucking-out, putting out to graze, arranging for veterinary and farriery services, etc. However, this may not be so sustainable where the stables are merely rented out (Schedule A) for DIY livery, where the horse owner has exclusive use of the stable. There may be a mixture of DIY and non-DIY activities with Schedule D status being secured on the basis that both activities will usually also involve a supply of feed to the stable owner (by the fact that the horse will be put out to graze in any event). It will, therefore, be necessary to consider each case on its own facts. BPR should be available provided that the stable rent is not the main activity. The businesses of riding schools and horse trekking will be assessable under Schedule D Case 1 and not as let income.

Wayleaves and receipts for grants of easements

15.20   An easement is the right to use, or to restrict the use of, the land of another person in some way. A wayleave is the right to use a defined area of land for purposes unrelated to its primary use.

Landowners may receive payments for easements from electricity and gas concerns, or other similar undertakings, for easements in connection with cables, pylons etc on or over their land. The types of payment which may be made include:

1   yearly payments for easements;
2   single lump sum payments for grants in perpetuity or for a specified number of years;
3   yearly or lump sum payments for disturbance arising from the erection of pylons, relaying of mains etc.

A lump sum payment to a farmer for the granting of an easement or wayleave (whether in perpetuity or for a term of years, and whether or not under an enactment incorporating compulsory powers of purchase) to place, construct or maintain a pipe, main, cable etc in, on, over or under land should be dealt with in accordance with the instructions at IM363. Thus, any element of compensation received for temporary loss of profit, or for damage to crops or to reimburse revenue expenditure on the repair of damage to land or buildings falls to be included as a receipt taxable under Case 1 of Schedule D.

Costs of re-instatement of land

15.21   Where there is expenditure on repairs of damage to land or buildings etc covered by the compensation payment, this will be an allowable deduction either for Schedule D Case 1 or Schedule A if the compensation is chargeable to income tax. Where a lump sum payment is regarded as capital, any corresponding expenditure should be excluded from the computations under Schedule D Case 1 or Schedule A.

How are they treated (1997–98 onwards)?

15.22

- The requirement to deduct tax at source under ICTA 1988 s 120 from electricity wayleave payments was abolished with effect from 6 April 1997 (FA 1997 s 60).
- Where a payment can be regarded as a trading receipt it will be assessable under Case 1 of Schedule D.
- Where the electricity wayleave payments are received for wires and cables running over or under land which gives rise to property income assessable under Schedule A, the wayleave payments should be treated as a Schedule A receipt – see ICTA 1988 s 53 below (see **15.23**).
- Otherwise the wayleave payments will be assessable under Case VI of Schedule D.

ICTA 1988 s 53

15.23

- Profits derived from the occupation of land. The charge under Schedule A is essentially derived from the exploitation of an interest in land and not a charge on profits derived from what happens on the land.

Once-and-for-all receipts for permanent easements will have the characteristics of capital and will not be liable to income tax, but to capital gains tax. If the consideration receivable does not exceed £20,000 in any one year of assessment, the recipient may claim that the receipt should not be treated as giving rise to a charge but should be deducted from his base cost for the purpose of computing liability on a future disposal. This is on the assumption that the disposal is 'small in value', which will normally be so for the owner of even a modest farm or estate. For this purpose 20% or less by comparison with the value of the total holding is regarded as small (TCGA 1992 s 242).

The practical planning point for farmers and landowners about to enter into a wayleave agreement or, indeed any grant of easements, is to be aware of the tax consequences and the final decision as to the tax treatment can depend upon the wording of the agreement. Whilst the income from the rental might seem attractive, it might seem less so when it is subject to income tax. A capital sum could be more attractive and worth negotiating for.

Quota leasing

15.24   Most types of quota can be leased by one farmer to another for a fixed period, usually a year. In particular, there is a very active market in the leasing of milk quota. The essential difference between leasing and sale is the temporary nature of the leasing arrangement with the quota reverting back to the original owner at the end of the agreement. This leads to a difference in the tax treatment. Payments for quota leasing are allowable expenses in the farmer's accounts. Similarly, receipts from the leasing of quota which is temporarily surplus to the requirements of a particular activity carried on by a farmer may be regarded as part of the farming income within Case 1 of Schedule D. But income from leasing of quota which is not required because the activity to which the quota relates has ceased or substantially reduced should be dealt with under Case VI of Schedule D.

Where quota is leased out by a non-farmer (including an ex-farmer who has retained quota), the income is chargeable under Case VI of Schedule D. It is highly unlikely that there would be evidence to justify Case 1 treatment.

The tax consequences of selling quota or leasing quota should be considered when looking at the commercial alternatives. CHAPTER **8** (see **8.5–8.6**) deals with the capital position concerning quotas and the article on quotas as fungible assets does make them more attractive as capital disposals. For unincorporated businesses with the ability to use the fungible asset rule, the use of annual exemptions etc the tax advantage of disposals should be built in when trying to weigh up disposal or leasing.

Mobile phone masts

15.25   It is impossible to pick up a farming magazine and not be made aware of the need for mobile phone masts. The tax treatment principles are essentially similar to those of wayleaves and will very much depend upon the agreement that is entered into. The difference is that there is a far greater chance of selling the land that the mobile phone mast is on and therefore realising a capital sum (see CHAPTER **15**) and there can be capital advantages.

The key to the tax planning lies in the agreement that is negotiated, the wording thereof and the tax treatment that results. It is advisable to use a land agent to negotiate the alternatives and it might well be that the interest in a mobile phone mast has arisen due to seeing an advert in the farming press and therefore an agent is already involved. It is possible to re-negotiate existing arrangements and the tax consequences should not be overlooked.

Divorce and Farming   **16**

Michael Gouriet and Suzy Ashworth
(Withers^{LLP})

- **The impact on the farming community and land owners of *White v White***
  Review of the Court's approach to the division of assets on divorce and consideration of the implications of *White v White*.

- **Divorce issues of particular relevance to farming cases**
  Consideration is given to liquidity, valuations, deferred charge/postponed interest and property acquired prior to the marriage or inherited during the course of it.

- **Protecting the assets**
  The chapter considers ways of protecting assets, for example, by use of pre-nuptial agreements, trusts, ante-nuptial or post-nuptial settlements. Consideration is also given to the preservation of confidentiality.

- **Tax implications**
  An overview of all tax considerations surrounding a divorce including income tax, capital gains tax (CGT) and inheritance tax (IHT). The chapter also reviews the tax treatment of maintenance payments, business partnerships and the availability of tax allowances.

Note from the Editor

16.1   As the main theme of this book is the protection of assets for the farmer and the landowner, it would be incomplete if mention was not made of the potential issues and pitfalls that can surround divorce and farming. It is a particularly complicated subject, with asset values increasing and income reducing, and there is no-one better than the family law specialists at Withers[LLP] to highlight the cases that are of particular relevance to farming; to consider how the assets are divided on divorce (with particular consideration of the impact of *White v White*); to look at possible ways of protecting assets with trusts and pre-nuptial agreements; and to consider the various tax implications.

Michael Gouriet and Suzy Ashworth have extensive knowledge on the financial ramifications of divorce. They have the added advantage of immediate access within the firm to leading experts specialising in trust and tax law and agricultural, commercial and residential property, all of whom have a wealth of experience in dealing with and advising on land-related issues. They are particularly well placed to produce this informative chapter.

Introduction

16.2   This chapter will look at the potential impact of divorce on a farming family, steps which might be taken to reduce the impact of a divorce, and tax considerations arising on divorce. It is instructive to consider the general approach of the Family Court to the division of assets on divorce before looking at the particular issues which are likely to have significance in farming cases.

Division of assets on divorce — the Court's approach

16.3   On divorce, the Court has an extremely wide jurisdiction to make appropriate financial provision between the parties as it sees fit. When exercising its discretion in considering what order to make, the Court has to take into account a number of factors prescribed by the law. These are set out in s 25 of the Matrimonial Causes Act 1973 (MCA 1973) as follows:

> 'The court has a duty in deciding whether, and how, to exercise these powers to have regard to all the circumstances of the case and to give first consideration to the welfare of any child of the family under 18. The court shall, in particular, have regard to:

(a) the income, earning capacity, property and other financial resources which each of the parties to the marriage has or is likely to have in the foreseeable future, including in the case of earning capacity any increase in that capacity which it would in the opinion of the court be reasonable to expect a party to the marriage to take steps to acquire;

(b) the financial needs, obligations and responsibilities which each of the parties to the marriage has or is likely to have in the foreseeable future;

(c) the standard of living enjoyed by the family before the break-down of the marriage;

(d) the age of each party to the marriage and the duration of the marriage;

(e) any physical or mental disability of either of the parties to the marriage;

(f) the contributions which each of the parties has made or is likely in the foreseeable future to make to the welfare of the family, including any contribution by looking after the home or caring for the family;

(g) the conduct of each of the parties, if that conduct is such that it would in the opinion of the court be inequitable to disregard it;

(h) the value to each of the parties to the marriage of any benefit (for example, a pension) which, by reason of the dissolution or annulment of the marriage, that party will lose the chance of acquiring.'

16.4   The basic guidelines found in s 25 of the MCA 1973 were originally introduced in 1969, and have not changed significantly since then despite the rapid and significant changes in society in the intervening period. One important statutory development has been that since the mid-1980s the courts have had a duty to consider whether or not in the circumstances of the particular case a clean break can be effected between the parties so as to terminate their respective financial dependence on the other.

The interpretation by the courts of the statutory rules has developed over the last three decades. In the early 1970s, the tendency was to award one third of the joint capital and of the joint income to the financially dependent party (usually the wife), leaving the breadwinner or wealth-holder (usually the husband) with the lion's share of the assets.

This gave way in the 1980s to a propensity of the courts to seek to meet the reasonable requirements of the wife (or financially weaker party) in terms of both capital and income. The motives were sound, but the effect was that the more money there was the less equal the settlement. This was particularly so in cases where there were sufficient resources to enable a husband to pay a capital sum to his wife by way of a clean break in settlement of her maintenance claims. By reference to what are known as 'Duxbury tables' (which make actuarial assumptions as to life expectancy, capital growth, income yield and inflation), the courts can calculate the level of lump sum which a wife would need in order to meet her income requirements for the rest of her life – assuming that she will draw down on the capital as well as the income produced so that at the end of her life expectancy that sum would be exhausted.

A fundamental flaw in this approach was that it appeared to penalise the long-serving wife since the younger the wife and the shorter the marriage the higher the Duxbury award, whereas the older the wife and the longer the marriage the lower the Duxbury award. This led to wives sometimes concocting large inflated budgets to boost their claims, eg Mrs Flick in *F v F [1995] 2 FLR 45* argued that as part of her annual budget she 'reasonably required' £4,000 p.a in order to maintain her Labrador dog in the manner to which the dog had become accustomed, and £5,000 p.a. to stock a drinks tray for casual visitors.

In October 2000 the House of Lords was given its first opportunity to consider the exercise of discretion and the interpretation of the statutory criteria set out in s 25 of MCA 1973 since the legislation was introduced. The case which came before the House of Lords (*White v White [2001] 1 AC 596*) involved a farming family.

White v White

The facts

16.5   Martin and Pamela White had married in 1961 when he was 24 and she was 26. They had three children. At the time of the hearing before the House of Lords they were in their sixties. They both came from farming families.

Following their marriage they formed a farming partnership pursuant to an oral agreement between them. At the outset each of them contributed a similar amount of capital (£1,884 from Mrs White and £1,135 from Mr White).

In October 1961 Mr and Mrs White acquired the former matrimonial home (Blagroves Farm with 160 acres) for £32,000. This was mainly borrowed on mortgage but supplemented by what was effectively a gift of £14,000 from the husband's father to the young couple jointly. In 1974 Mr White's father released his loan of £14,000.

Initially, this was reflected by an increase in Mr White's partnership capital account but ten years on Mr and Mrs White's capital accounts were merged into a single joint capital account.

Various land purchases over the years saw Blagroves Farm expand to 339 acres (acquired by the parties through the partnership).

In April 1971 the opportunity arose to acquire the Willett Estate which was largely tenanted by Mr White's father. It was a joint purchase by Mr White and his brother at an advantageous price reflecting their father's tenancy and with the aid of an advantageous mortgage. The three brothers farmed separate portions of the Willett Estate individually. Mr White's portion was Rexton Farm which was, effectively, farmed by the husband and wife partnership together with Blagroves Farm as a single unit. Both farms were dairy farms.

In 1993 the White brothers entered into a Deed of Partition of the Willett Estate so that in place of joint ownership of the whole each brother took his individual share – Mr White taking Rexton Farm, which was then registered in his sole name.

After 33 years of marriage the wife left Blagroves Farm in August 1994 and petitioned for divorce in December of that year. Her financial application followed in March 1995. That came before Bristol County Court in September 1996.

Judgment

16.6 The judge (Holman J) determined that the net total assets amounted to £4.6 million made up as follows:

- approximately £185,000 in the sole name of the wife;
- approximately £1,730,000 in the sole name of the husband;
- £1,343,000 being the wife's share of the assets held in joint names; and
- £1,343,000 being the husband's share of the assets held in joint names.

The judge identified two fundamental issues:

1   whether the wife should be entitled to fulfil her desire to continue to farm; and
2   whether in a case such as this it would be right to make a net transfer of assets from the wife to the husband.

On contributions the judge made the following finding:

> 'Each party contributed a great deal of effort to this marriage and to the welfare of the family. Within the home it was the wife who

primarily brought up the children. I am also quite satisfied that she worked hard in all sorts of ways on the farm.

I am quite satisfied that the husband has been a hard working, active farmer. In truth this was a marital and also a business partnership in which, by their efforts and commitment, each contributed to their full for 33 years and any attempt to weigh the respective contributions of their effort is idle and unreal.'

However, having regard to financial needs, he said:

'In my judgment it would be unwise, and not justifiable on the facts of this case, to break up an existing, established farming enterprise so that the wife, at 61, can embark much more speculatively, on another. Her claim has strong emotional, but little financial sense.'

He focused on the wife's reasonable requirements and assessed that she needed £425,000 to purchase and equip a house and he capitalised her income needs (by reference to the Duxbury tables) at £555,000, thereby giving her a total of approximately £980,000. He concluded that it was justifiable in this case that the wife should receive a lesser lump sum than the paper value of the assets currently in her name.

He recognised that the wife's share on his judgment would amount to only 20% of the whole. He said:

'I acknowledge that a final result which accords to this wife only one-fifth of the total wealth seems low in proportion to the length of the marriage and her contributions. That is, in part, a result of the well-known paradox that the longer the marriage and hence the older the wife, the less the capital sum required for a Duxbury type fund. But one-fifth is not so low as to be manifestly wrong or unfair.'

Mrs White, who had contended that her contributions to the marriage and the length of it should result in an equal division of the assets, appealed to the Court of Appeal.

Appeal to the Court of Appeal

16.7 The Court of Appeal concentrated on the wife's legal entitlement. Thorpe LJ said that the dominant feature of the case was that the parties traded as equal partners and that had the partnership been dissolved by the death of either of them the extent of the estate of the deceased partner would have been established according to the law of partnership. He said that equally, the wife was in law entitled to her share on dissolution of the partnership by mutual agreement. He concluded that in his opinion once the financial worth of each of the parties had been determined on the immediate dissolution of the existing farm partnership the next issue was to decide whether or not the Court should exercise its powers to increase or reduce the parties' respective shares. Thorpe LJ raised the pertinent question that if it was reasonable for the husband to be able to continue farming in a worthwhile way why was it not equally reasonable for the wife to require to be able to continue farming in a worthwhile way?

The original judgment of Holman J was set aside and the wife was awarded a lump sum of £1.5 million in addition to her own assets of £185,000.

Appeal to the House of Lords

16.8   Both Mr and Mrs White were unhappy with the ruling of the Court of Appeal. They both appealed to the House of Lords. Mrs White sought an equal share of the assets contending that the correct starting point was equality of entitlement. Mr White sought to reverse the Court of Appeal's decision and restore the order of Holman J.

The House of Lords took the view that the approach of the Court of Appeal in focusing on the parties' respective entitlements under the partnership was not the correct approach.

Principles

16.9   The guiding principles which have emanated from the House of Lords judgment in *White v White [2001] 1 AC 596* are as follows.

- The Court must consider each and every section 25 (MCA 1973) factor. There is no hierarchy in those criteria. In certain cases some of those criteria will carry more weight than others depending on the circumstances of the case in question.
- The Court must look to achieve a fair outcome. In seeking to reach that objective there is no place for discrimination between a husband and wife and their respective roles. There should be no bias in favour of the money-earner and against the home-maker and the child-carer.
- Before reaching a firm conclusion a judge should check his tentative views against 'the yardstick of equal division'.
- There is no presumption of equal division but as a guide equality should be departed from only if, and to the extent that, there is good reason for doing so. The need to consider and articulate reasons for departing from equality would help the parties and the

Court to focus on the need to ensure the absence of discrimination. Equality should be a check and not a presumption.

The House of Lords rejected the judicially developed concept of 'reasonable requirements' and held that there was nothing in the statutory provisions or in the underlying objective of securing fair financial arrangements to say that the available assets become immaterial once the wife's financial needs are satisfied. In the leading judgment, Lord Nicholls asked, rhetorically, 'where assets exceed the financial needs of both parties why should the surplus belong solely to the husband?'

Although the House of Lords did not agree with the approach which the Court of Appeal had adopted in reaching its conclusion, their lordships did not alter the resultant figure (£1.5 million) as this was within the ambit of what a Court might reasonably award and therefore the result could not be challenged on the ground that it was plainly wrong. The Court of Appeal had taken into account all of the available assets and the significant contributions made by the husband's father. The House of Lords found no ground to interfere with the Court of Appeal's exercise of discretion.

Since White v White

16.10   The House of Lords decision in *White v White [2001] 1 AC 596* has provoked huge debate and raised many questions about its application in a variety of circumstances. With the glass ceiling of 'reasonable requirements' having been smashed by the House of Lords the more difficult it is for practitioners to advise clients on the likely outcome of cases with any degree of certainty. This is particularly so in 'big money' cases where assets exceed needs as the concept of fairness is in part a subjective one. This was acknowledged by Lord Nicholls at the start of his judgment in *White*, when he made the following comment:

> 'Everyone's life is different. Features which are important when assessing fairness differ in each case. And, sometimes, different minds can reach conclusions on what fairness requires. Then fairness, like beauty, lies in the eye of the beholder.'

Since *White* there have been a number of cases where the principles espoused in *White* have been applied. It is worth reflecting on three of these.

1   *Cowan v Cowan [2001] 2 FLR 192*. This is a case where the total assets amounted to approximately £11.5 million, and the parties

had been married for over 30 years. The Court of Appeal assessed that the husband and wife had equal needs in terms of capital and income amounting to £3 million. The Court of Appeal justified the unequal division of the surplus of £5.5 million as to 25% to the wife and 75% to the husband giving him a total of £7.1 million and her a total of £4.4m million, on the basis of Mr Cowan's 'stellar' contribution to the creation of their wealth notwithstanding that all of the assets had been built up during the marriage.

2   *H-J v H-J [2002] 1 FLR 415.* This is a case involving a marriage of approximately 25 years and total assets of approximately £2.7 million, in which Coleridge J (on appeal) held that the wife should have 50% of the net assets. He stated:

'(i) The significance attaching to a particular fraction or percentage is more than merely the monetary value it represents. It goes to the core of the parties' understanding of fairness. So 50/50 resonates with fairness (as the House of Lords has identified); both parties depart with the sense of being equally valued. There are no winners or losers. Once there is a departure from equality, as there often has to be, however small that departure, one party (more often the wife) is left with a sense of grievance, of her efforts having been undervalued. Understandably, at the time of divorce, these considerations matter a great deal to the parties.

(ii) In this case, after a marriage which lasted in excess of 25 years, net assets, after deduction of notional sales costs and capital gains tax, have been accumulated amounting to more than £2.7 million. Accordingly, there is ample to go round. It would indeed be sad if, in this category of cases (as opposed to those cases where the overall means are less than sufficient and so the needs of children and their carers must inevitably remain predominant), the broad and sweeping reform underlying the speeches in *White* was to become bogged down in a welter of zealous, over-sophisticated and costly forensic analysis, or watered down by judicial reticence.'

3   *N v N (financial provision: sale of company) [2001] 2 FLR 69.* This is a case concerning a 14-year marriage with three children and total net assets of approximately £2,575,000. The wife was 35. There were substantial liquidity problems in that the vast majority of the family wealth was represented by the value of the husband's business interests in two companies and various partnerships. The only immediately available funds amounted to approximately £200,000.

The husband argued for a substantial departure from equality relying on the fact that a considerable part of the value of the two companies had accrued after the parties had separated; that illiquidity should constrain the Court downwards; that the wife was young, the marriage not very long; and that his contributions were more valuable than hers. The wife argued for 50%.

In his judgment, Coleridge J stated that:

(i) The accrual of assets after separation might be a relevant factor if the increase was referable to specific contributions on the part of the husband rather than the effects of inflation, increase in land prices or general market forces. However, the significance of that factor would be diminished by the contributions of a non-financial nature (such as looking after the children) made by the wife after separation.

(ii) The division of the assets would be based on the value of the assets at the time of the hearing.

(iii) Most significantly, the judge decided that the wife should not be prejudiced on the grounds of liquidity but acknowledged that husbands should be given a realistic period of time in order to effect an orderly realisation of assets.

In a well-publicised extract of his judgment he said:

'It must now be taken that those old taboos against selling the goose that lays the golden eggs have largely been laid to rest; some would say not before time. Nowadays the goose may well have to go to market for sale, but if it is necessary to sell her it is essential that her condition be such that her egg-laying abilities are damaged as little as possible in the process. Otherwise, there is a danger that the full value of the goose will not be achieved and the underlying basis of any order will turn out to be flawed.'

The impact of White v White

16.11   The case of *White v White [2001] 1 AC 596* and the cases decided since then reflect a sea-change in treatment across the whole range of ancillary relief cases. It would appear that judges and practitioners alike are focusing on percentages and, in particular, what in the circumstances of each case is a fair percentage distribution and whether or not a special contribution has been made by one party or the other so as to suppress the other's entitlement. The cross-check of equality of outcome is not a starting point but intended to be a safeguard against discrimination.

The decisions of the courts since *White* have meant that in general where resources exceed needs it is likely that wives, particularly those in long marriages, can now expect to be awarded a substantially larger share of the parties' combined wealth on the dissolution of their marriage than previously.

Issues of particular relevance to farming cases

Liquidity

16.12   The main difficulty created by farming cases is the illiquidity of assets since capital is usually locked away in the form of land, livestock and machinery. Also, income yield is usually relatively modest. Often, in the pre-*White* era it was very difficult to provide adequate compensation for an outgoing spouse as the Court set its face against breaking up a business which would have an adverse effect on the livelihood of the parties.

A good example of this was the case of *P v P (financial provision: lump sum) [1978] 1 WLR 483*, where the farm had been purchased shortly after the marriage by the wife's father, which he eventually conveyed to the wife. The farm was run down at the time when it was acquired and the husband put in a great deal of effort in improving the farmhouse and the land and building up a successful farming business, which the husband and wife ran as partners. On divorce, the husband was awarded a small lump sum of £15,000 payable in three instalments of £5,000. His appeal was dismissed by the Court of Appeal as the wife would have to provide the money for bringing up the children and, therefore, she must be allowed to keep the farm in order to derive an income from it for that purpose. £15,000 was held to be the largest capital sum that she could reasonably be expected to raise from the farm business without being obliged to sell it. As the sum of £15,000 would satisfy the husband's principal requirement of a home that was held to be a practical and realistic figure.

It was a similar approach and similar outcome (one party being allowed to continue farming at the apparent expense of the other) which led Mrs White to appeal on the first instance decision of Holman J (as related at **16.7**).

There have, however, been cases in the past where the courts have decided that the farm should be sold: for example, *Moorish v Moorish [1984] Fam Law 26* where it transpired that the farm had been seriously mismanaged by the husband.

Alternatively, courts have directed that part of the land (or livestock) be sold where it does not seriously affect the viability of the business itself: for example, *S v S (1980) Times, 10 May*. In that case it was directed that three smaller farms should be sold in order to provide a lump sum for the wife. The main farm unit was retained as a viable one to permit the husband to continue farming.

Valuations

16.13   Whereas in the pre-*White* era the Court was resistant to applications for expensive and detailed valuations in cases where the business (as the source of income for the family) was not going to be sold, now the value of the farm business assumes a far greater significance whether or not any part of it is to be liquidated. The value needs to be ascertained to enable the Court to assess whether or not the outcome is a fair one.

When looking at valuation, first consideration has to be given to the structure of the business: for example, whether it is sole proprietorship, partnership, company, subject to share farming or contract farming schemes.

Consideration then needs to be given to the ownership of farm assets: for example, if the assets are owned by a company then consideration has to be given to the size, ownership and structure of shareholding and whether or not control is affected by relationships with family or third parties.

If the assets are held in trust then the trust instrument needs to be considered as to the identity of the trustees and beneficiaries; the powers of the trustees and how those powers have been exercised in the past; as well as the timing of the creation of the trust and the purpose for which it was established.

Other issues to investigate include:

- whether or not the land has vacant possession and, if not, what the tenanted values might be and whether or not the existing tenancies are valid and are capable of assignment. If the tenant is a limited liability company the tenancy value is likely to be high which would have a detrimental impact on the value of the freehold;
- the value of livestock, farm machinery and equipment needs to be determined and consideration as to whether or not any part can be sold without materially affecting the business once ownership has been established. For example, equipment may be shared or leased;
- the timing and saleability of growing crops and harvested crops (considering also actual and projected yields) and whether or not income is awaited on crops already sold;
- the value of quotas;
- the value of Government grants or subsidies;
- whether or not there is value in timber or minerals and also whether the farm or any part of it has development potential (residential or commercial development including the sale of surplus farm buildings and conversion of those into houses or industrial units), particularly in view of any local development plans;
- whether or not revenue of the farm business can be increased, for example, by the letting of land under farm business tenancies or cottages (as, for example, holiday cottages).

Consideration also needs to be given as to the type of expert to be instructed in assisting in valuation (chartered and/or rural surveyors or farm management consultants) and whether or not such experts should be instructed by the parties jointly so as to minimise the cost of each party having their own expert valuers. Disagreements between experts will necessarily increase the costs and matters in issue and extend the Court's time for the hearing of expert evidence and adjudication. The appointment of joint experts is encouraged by the courts.

Although valuations are required to enable the Court to carry out its function, in the case of *White v White [2001] 1 AC 596* Lord Nicholls (in the House of Lords) made it clear that where parties are in business together there should be a broad assessment of the financial position and not a detailed partnership account. He said there did not need to be a full and detailed investigation in order to assess precisely each party's proprietorial interests. Specifically, Lord Nicholls commented as follows:

> '... If a strict valuation of the parties' shares on a dissolution of the partnership were needed several disputes would have to be resolved: disputes about the assets and liabilities of the partnership, a dispute about the value of the milk quota, and a dispute over the proper interpretation of the somewhat obscure retirement provisions in the partnership agreement. I do not think any of these differences need to be resolved.'

Deferred charge/postponed interest

16.14 Depending on the circumstances of the case it might be appropriate, in order to achieve fairness, to give one party a deferred charge over part of the land or property. Inevitably, it would prevent a clean break between the parties but it has been a solution which the Court has been prepared to consider in the past. For example, *Webber v Webber (1982) 12 Fam Law 179* in which the wife was awarded a 25% share by way of a charge on the farm business which was to vest in her on the husband's sixty-fifth birthday; but which charge was to lapse in the event of her remarriage or death. Also the deferred charge route was followed in *Robinson v Robinson (1983) 4 FLR 102*. Alternatively, the Court might be prepared to consider adjourning the financial application if there was a realistic prospect of the farm (or part of it) being sold or one party being bought out by business partners (eg *Davies v Davies [1986] 1 FLR 497*).

The Court adopts a flexible approach in exercising its discretion and in an appropriate case it may take account of the assistance of third parties. For example, in *B v B (Financial Provision) [1990] 1 FLR 20*, the Court was informed that trustees would co-operate with the husband to enable him to raise money from farmland held in trust.

Further consideration will be given to the use of trusts at **16.16**.

Property acquired prior to the marriage or inherited during the course of it

16.15   In contrast to certain countries (such as New Zealand and Scotland) the basic rule is that there is no distinction in the matrimonial legislation in England and Wales between:

1   inherited property and property owned before the marriage on the one hand; and
2   matrimonial property on the other hand.

During the course of his judgment in *White v White [2001] 1 AC 596* Lord Nicholls hinted that inherited property should not necessarily be treated in the same way as 'marital property'. He said that property which had been acquired by way of an inheritance by one spouse should be one of the circumstances of the case to be considered by the Court. It represents a contribution made to the welfare of the family by one of the parties to the marriage. The judge had to take it into account. He should decide how important it is in a particular case. The nature and value of the property and the time when and circumstances in which the property was acquired, are among the relevant matters to be considered. However, in an ordinary course, this factor can be expected to carry little weight, if any, in a case where the claimant's financial needs cannot be met without recourse to this property.

Although it does not as yet appear to have been tested by the courts since *White*, the view of the writer is that in the circumstances of a particular case the Court may well decide that it is in the interest of fairness that the spouse who came into the inheritance be allowed to retain it provided that no prejudice is caused to the other spouse in doing so. It may be possible, therefore, to employ this argument to seek to retain the farming business where it has passed down generations of the same family in seeking to minimise the other spouse's claim to it. The retention line of argument might also be assisted where there is a child of the family who is already involved in the farm or undergoing training in farming, providing, once again, that that argument does not prejudice the non-retaining spouse's needs.

In *White*, Lord Nicholls said that a parent's wish to be in a position to leave assets to his or her children would not normally fall within the statutory criteria of financial needs (under MCA 1973 s 25), either of a husband or of a wife. He added, however, that that wish is not wholly irrelevant to the section 25 exercise in considering all of the circumstances in a case where resources exceed the parties' financial needs.

The principal concern for farming families on divorce is that, since the case of *White* and the cases which have followed it (for example, *N v N* at **16.10**), in contrast to the past, the issues of illiquidity and inherited property are not likely to prevent the sale of the farm or part of it if to do so would obstruct a fair outcome between the spouses. Therefore, it is likely to prove much more difficult to resist the sale of a farm, or part of it, in order to raise the requisite funds to meet the claims of the other spouse unless there are cogent reasons for doing so (such as ability to satisfy the claim from other resources; relatively short marriage; the farm has been in the family for generations) which will not prejudice the other party. The argument against realisation becomes more difficult when regard is had to the amount of capital tied up in the farm proportionate to the income produced by it.

Protecting assets

Trusts

Generally

16.16 Although in certain circumstances a trust may be a useful device to seek to protect family wealth from a divorcing spouse, the Family Courts do have jurisdiction to vary or look straight through certain types of trust on divorce. (**CHAPTER 17** explains the creation of the trust, the administration and the tax treatment.)

Ante-nuptial or post-nuptial settlements

16.17 Trusts which constitute an ante-nuptial or post-nuptial settlement of property within the MCA 1973 are capable of variation by the Court on a financial application within the context of a divorce. To be capable of variation there has to be a nuptial element to the settlement, but the word 'settlement' is given a wide meaning in that context.

The settlement has to be upon the husband or the wife or both in the character of spouses – with reference to their married state. However, even in a long-standing family trust, where there is a power to appoint a life interest to a spouse on a beneficiary's death and that power is exercised, the trust may become (albeit inadvertently) a post-nuptial settlement capable of variation on divorce.

One example of the Court's approach on variation of an ante-nuptial settlement is the case of *E v E [1990] 2 FLR 233*. The husband's father was paymaster throughout the marriage and provided funds to set up an offshore discretionary trust to hold shares in a Panamanian company, which in turn held the title to the matrimonial home. The property was worth £1.25 million at the date of the hearing. The husband, wife and the children were members of the class of beneficiaries and the husband's father was protector. The powers of the trustees were only exercisable with the consent of the protector. Ewbank J varied the settlement by removing the husband's father as protector, removing the trust company acting as trustees and granting the wife £50,000 outright from the settlement, with a life interest in £200,000 from it and the remainder to the children. The award to the wife in that case may have been higher had she not abandoned the children and engaged in serial adultery.

Where possible, therefore, in order to seek to maximise protection any settlement of property on trust should be made well outside the context of marriage. It would be more difficult on a divorce to argue that a settlement of property should be excluded from consideration if the settlement or re-settlement of assets took place when the marriage was in prospect or after the marriage. Also, if the class of beneficiaries is broad it is likely to be more difficult to link the settlement with a particular marriage, particularly if the class of potential beneficiaries specifically excludes any prospective spouse but includes future generations of the family creating the trust.

Other trust interests

16.18   Even if the trust in question is not an ante-nuptial or post-nuptial settlement (as defined in the matrimonial legislation) and thus capable of variation, if a spouse has an interest under a trust that interest will be taken into account when assessing the resources of parties.

Both parties have a duty to give full and frank disclosure of their financial means, resources and other relevant circumstances within divorce-related financial proceedings and that duty to make full disclosure includes the valuation of any interests in a trust.

As the limitation of a wife's claim to her reasonable requirements has been disapproved of by the House of Lords in *White v White* *[2001] 1 AC 596* the value of one party's trust interests could prove to be a very significant factor in assessing the overall resources and deciding what is a fair outcome in a particular case. The financially weaker party (and his/her lawyer) will be aiming to maximise the value of assets available for division.

Trustees may be joined to divorce proceedings. They may be asked to explain the practice of distribution, or to produce accounts, deeds and records of distributions which the Court considers may be necessary for the purpose of dealing fairly with a financial application.

In *T v T (joinder of third parties) [1996] 2 FLR 357* the husband had transferred his interest in the business which he had set up to a Jersey trust of which he was a beneficiary. His spouse was also a beneficiary. When the wife applied for an injunction against the trust the husband argued that he had no effective control over the trust assets. The trustees were directed to be joined as parties to the proceedings. The trustees applied to set aside the order under which they were joined.

They were concerned about submission to a foreign court and were concerned also that they may be criticised for being parties to proceedings which might result in a depletion of trust assets.

The trustees' application to set aside the court order was refused and it was held that there were various benefits enjoining the trustees. Those benefits included assisting the Court with discovery and the provision of evidence; assisting the enforcement of any financial order; and the obtaining of a mirror or supplementary order in Jersey if required.

It is important that trustees are separately represented so that they can seek to minimise the allegations that they might be 'in the pocket' of the husband or wife (as the case may be).

The courts are particularly suspicious of discretionary trusts in the context of divorce. Every judge will have heard many times the arguments of wealthy spouses who say that a trust is wholly discretionary and entirely beyond their control when in fact it has been utilised as a personal cash fund or credit facility for the duration of the marriage. If the trust has generally advanced money regularly or on request this situation will be assumed by the courts to continue in the future, even though the beneficiary may only be one of a class of discretionary beneficiaries.

The case of *Thomas v Thomas [1995] 2 FLR 668* is interesting in the way in which it afforded judicious encouragement to third parties to provide a spouse with the means to comply with the Court's view of justice in the case. Here, the majority of the husband's wealth was tied up in a shareholding in a family company whose policy it was to pay relatively low salaries to directors and plough the profits back into the company. There were heavy charges to the company on the family home to cover a mortgage, a bank guarantee covering contingent liability to Lloyd's as well as loans for Lloyd's losses. Lord Justice Glidewell reached the following conclusions:

> '(a)   Where a husband can only raise further capital, or additional income, as the result of a decision made at the discretion of trustees, the court should not put improper pressure on the trustees to exercise that discretion for the benefit of the wife.
>
> (b)   The court should not, however, be "misled by appearances"; it should "look at the reality of the situation".
>
> (c)   If on the balance of probability the evidence shows that, if trustees exercise their discretion to release more capital or income to a husband, the interests of the trust or of other beneficiaries would not be appreciably damaged, the court can assume that a genuine request for the exercise of such discretion would probably be met by a favourable response. In that situation if the court decides that it would be reasonable for a husband to seek

> to persuade trustees to release more capital or income to him to enable him to make proper financial provision for his children and his former wife, the court would not in so deciding be putting improper pressure on the trustees.
>
> In relation to the facts of the present case, I would apply these principles to the family company as if it were a trust, and the shareholders (the husband, his mother and brother) the trustees.'

The Court is not obliged to limit its orders exclusively to resources of capital or income which are shown actually to exist. The Court can draw inference from a spouse's expenditure or lifestyle or from his inability or unwillingness to allow the complexity of his financial affairs to be investigated in a way necessary to ascertain his actual wealth or the degree of liquidity of his assets.

As in *Thomas v Thomas*, the Court may make assumptions about funds being made available to the beneficiary which would have the effect of making the beneficiary bankrupt if the trustees refuse to co-operate.

See also *Browne v Browne [1989] 1 FLR 291*, another case in which the Court seized on the practice of distribution. Mr Browne was the former MP for Winchester who was making financial claims against his wife. She was the sole beneficiary of a Jersey trust. The Court made an order in the husband's favour, which the wife could only meet by drawing from the trust. The reason for this order was that the pattern of distributions was such that whenever the wife requested a distribution for almost any purpose sums were advanced. On that basis Butler-Sloss LJ concluded that the wife in effect had immediate access to the funds. The fact that the trustees objected to future distributions (which would in effect pass to the husband) was not held to be decisive. When the husband applied to commit the wife to prison for failure to comply with the Court order the lump sum appeared.

The recent case of *Mubarak v Mubarak [2001] 1 FLR 673* has thrown third-party interests into the spotlight. As a result of that case the Court may be more reluctant to look through trust arrangements where there are genuine third party interests. In that case, in the context of enforcement proceedings where the husband had not complied with the Court order to pay a lump sum to his wife, the Court ruled that to attack the trust by lifting the corporate veil would prejudice the interests of the third parties involved. In that case assets were kept out of reach of the wife by being held in trust through underlying trading companies. The Court did say, however, that it would have no hesitation in attacking the trust structure if it had been set up or used as a sham or a device with the intention of diminishing the claims of the other spouse.

Pre-nuptial agreements

16.19   At present, the Courts in England and Wales do not recognise a pre-nuptial agreement which seeks to limit or oust the Court's jurisdiction to make financial orders on divorce. Such an agreement is not, therefore, legally binding.

That is not to say that parties should not have a pre-nuptial agreement. It will be one of the circumstances that the Court has to take into account when determining applications for financial provision. The weight which an agreement will carry will depend on all of the circumstances of the case including the circumstances in which the agreement was created, the length of the marriage and the extent to which provision under the agreement is deemed fair.

There has not yet been a reported case where the parties have been held by the English Court to the financial terms of a pre-nuptial agreement. However, they have been influential in certain cases, as discussed below:

- In *F v F (ancillary relief: substantial assets) [1995] 2 FLR 45*, where the provision made by the pre-nuptial was extremely limited, Thorpe LJ pronounced that 'in this jurisdiction pre-nuptial agreements must be of very limited significance'.
- However, in *S v S (matrimonial proceedings: appropriate forum) [1997] 2 FLR 100*, Wilson J held the parties to a term of their pre-nuptial agreement which provided that proceedings should take place in New York.
- More recently, in *M v M (pre-nuptial agreement) [2002] 1 FLR 654*, the Court said that it would be as unjust to the husband to ignore the existence of the agreement and its terms as it would have been to the wife to hold her strictly to the terms of it. Although the wife was not held to the terms of the pre-nuptial agreement in that case the existence of it was one of the more relevant circumstances which had tended to guide the Court to a more modest award than might have been made without it. Other relevant factors in departing from equality were the comparative shortness of the marriage and the fact that the husband had created the family wealth.

The Government has indicated support for the concept of pre-nuptial agreements in a consultation document produced in November 1998 entitled *Supporting Families*. However, that consultation document has not yet developed into legislation. In that consultation paper it was stated that:

'... the Government is considering whether there would be advantages in allowing couples either before or during their marriage to make written agreements dealing with their financial affairs which would be legally binding on divorce. This could give more people more choice and allow them to take more responsibility for ordering their own lives.'

Safeguards proposed in the consultation paper, which, if found to apply, would render any such agreement not binding, included:

- the existence of children;
- the absence of legal advice;
- the lack of disclosure;
- when signed less than 21 days before the wedding;
- if there is significant injustice; and
- where agreement would be unenforceable under contract law.

Therefore, if parties to a marriage wish to have a pre-nuptial agreement then in order to give it as much persuasive weight as possible in the event of a divorce the following factors should apply:

- each party must take separate independent legal advice;
- there must be full and frank disclosure of the assets and resources available to each party, including any trusts of which either party is a beneficiary;
- the agreement should be executed as far in advance of the wedding day as possible, so that neither party can subsequently claim they were under undue circumstantial pressure to agree terms in the hope of avoiding its effects;
- the agreement must be fair, ie within the general sphere of what a Court might award each party in the event of a divorce; and
- there should be evidence of genuine negotiation of terms to avoid a challenge on the basis that the 'agreement' was in fact simply a dictat from the financially stronger party to the weaker.

Generally, it is in the interests of the financially stronger party to have a pre-nuptial agreement as the terms may be influential, particularly in the early years of a childless relationship. If nothing else, it shows the Court the intention of both parties when they embarked on the marriage.

Confidentiality considerations

16.20 In the recent Court of Appeal judgment in the case of *Clibbery v Allan (2002)*, the Court considered the issues of privacy and confidentiality in family proceedings. Miss Clibbery and Mr Allan were not married but had a relationship for about 14 years. When the relationship ended, Miss Clibbery applied to the Court for an occupation order in respect of one of the properties owned by Mr Allan which they had occasionally used. Her application failed, and she approached a national newspaper which later published an interview with her and extracts from Mr Allan's sworn statement to the Court.

Mr Allan obtained an injunction against further publication of details of or documents from the hearing, but this injunction was overturned. The following points arise from the case.

- There is a fundamental 'implied undertaking' or duty to the Court to the effect that 'a party who seeks discovery of documents gets it on condition that he will make use of them only for the purposes of that action, and no other purpose' (Lord Denning MR in *Riddick v Thames Board Mills Ltd [1977] QB 881*). This implied undertaking applies even where documents have been read out in open Court.
- There is no duty of confidentiality between unmarried partners, save for the general 'implied undertaking' referred to above in relation to documents disclosed under compulsion.
- No subsequent publication of information is allowed in a case that concerns children.
- In ancillary relief proceedings, the implied undertaking applies and covers information disclosed 'before, during and after the proceedings', including that disclosed voluntarily. However, questions remain about whether the implied undertaking applies before divorce or ancillary relief proceedings have been commenced and, therefore, if confidentiality is likely to be a concern, an express undertaking to that end should be considered.

It should be noted that the publication of an order – and probably a judgment – given by the Court in private is not contempt of Court unless there is an express prohibition against it.

Tax implications

Income tax

16.21 Since 1990–91 husbands and wives have been (in almost all respects) subject to independent taxation. This means that each is entitled to a single person's allowance regardless of their marital status.

Married couples' allowance and children's tax credit

16.22 Until April 2000 the married couples' allowance provided some tax relief to married couples. However, on 6 April 2000 that allowance was abolished, except for those couples born prior to

6 April 1935 (based on the age of the oldest spouse). For 2002–03 the maximum tax saving (at 10%) is £5,465 where the eldest spouse was born before 6 April 1935, rising to £5,535 where the eldest spouse is over 75. The minimum tax allowance is currently £2,110.

Additional child allowance was also repealed in the Finance Act 1999 – being replaced by a children's tax credit (CTC). The full allowance under this credit is currently £5,290 and is given in the form of a reduction in income tax liability at a rate of 10%. The maximum available relief for 2002–03 is, therefore, £529. The CTC applies to those who have a child under the age of 16 years living with them.

The CTC is normally allocated to the higher earning partner/spouse unless an election is made by the lower earning partner to claim half of the CTC or a joint election is made to give the whole of the CTC to that partner.

Tax treatment of maintenance payments

16.23 The basic rules are as follows.

- Maintenance payments have no tax consequences for either the payer or the payee. They are paid gross and are not treated as taxable income in the hands of the recipient. No tax relief is available to the payer unless either party was born prior to 6 April 1935 when limited relief is available (by way of a reduction in the payer's income tax liability at the rate of 10%, on a maximum amount of £2,070 (2002–03)).
- Neutral tax treatment of maintenance payments referred to above applies whether the payments are made to a spouse or to a child [Income and Corporation Taxes Act 1988 (ICTA 1988) s 347A].
- Previously, tax relief was available for maintenance payments made under Court orders or written agreements made prior to 15 March 1988. However, since 6 April 2000 such relief is no longer available unless, as above, either of the parties is over 65.

Secured maintenance

16.24 The tax treatment of secured maintenance orders is different.

Secured maintenance orders are rare. However, it may be appropriate for there to be a secured maintenance order where there is a doubt as to the paying spouse's commitment to pay maintenance on an ongoing basis or, for example, where that spouse resides abroad.

Under a secured maintenance order, usually one spouse places assets in trust to provide for payments of maintenance to be made to the other spouse out of income arising from those assets. Such an arrangement would usually be caught by the settlement provisions (under which the settlor is taxed on the income arising) except that arrangements in favour of a divorced or separated spouse are specifically excluded [ICTA 1988 s 660A].

As payments of maintenance under a secured maintenance order are not annual payments they are not qualifying maintenance payments. Instead, the recipient spouse will be taxed on any income paid from the settlement for his or her maintenance. The paying spouse will only be taxed on income returned to him or her as surplus to the maintenance requirements.

Secured maintenance orders in favour of a child are caught by the settlement anti-avoidance provisions and, therefore, the income remains taxable on the settlor spouse.

Business partnerships

16.25 If the spouses are in partnership together the breakdown of the marriage more often than not will result in a breakdown of the partnership. If the business ceases, the normal income tax rules for the cessation of a business will apply.

If the business continues there are separate rules for retiring and continuing partners.

The retiring spouse is treated as if he or she had ceased trading on the date of retirement and the profits are apportioned to that spouse in accordance with the profit-sharing agreement of the partnership [ICTA 1988 ss 63 and 63A].

The continuing spouse is taxed on the basis that his or her business continues. Profits accrued prior to the other spouse's retirement are apportioned in accordance with any profit-sharing agreement whilst the profits arising subsequently accrue and are taxable to the continuing partner.

Capital gains tax (CGT)

General

16.26 As with income tax, as husbands and wives are subject to independent taxation they are each entitled to an annual exemption (£7,700 in 2002–03) on chargeable gains. Capital gains tax (CGT) payable is computed separately for each spouse using their own income tax bands and applying indexation allowance and taper relief, where appropriate, without reference to the CGT liability of the other spouse.

Consequently, allowable losses of one spouse may only be deducted from that spouse's deductible gains and unrelieved losses may only be carried forward and relieved against future gains of the same spouse, not the other spouse.

The key event for CGT purposes when a relationship breaks down is not the date of the divorce but the date when the married couple cease to be living together as 'man and wife'.

Under Taxation of Chargeable Gains Act 1992 (TCGA 1992) s 288, spouses are considered to be living together for the purposes of capital gains unless they are separated under a court order or a deed of separation or are separated in circumstances where the separation appears to be permanent. It is possible for a couple to live separately even under the same roof (*Holmes v Mitchell [1991] STC 25*).

Whilst the husband and wife are still living together a transfer of assets between them will be deemed to be on a no gain/no loss basis. In the first tax year of permanent separation any such transfer will also be on a no gain/no loss basis [TCGA 1992 s 58].

The recipient takes the donor's cost base as the acquisition cost for any subsequent disposal. On the eventual disposal of the asset the recipient is then taxed on the total gain (subject to indexation) over the combined period of ownership since the asset was first acquired by the donor spouse (or 31 March 1982, if later).

Spouses remain connected persons for capital gains purposes. Transfers between connected persons are not regarded as transfers at arm's length [TCGA 1992 s 18]. This means that where an asset is transferred between connected persons the market value at the date of disposal will be the deemed consideration when computing the capital gain made by the donor spouse. Chargeable gains can therefore arise on gifts of assets or on sales at an under value. If a loss accrues on such disposal the loss can only be set against gains made on the transfer of assets between the same connected persons.

Assets which are transferred pursuant to a divorce settlement are not usually made for consideration and therefore market value of the asset transferred will be substituted for the consideration.

The date of transfer between husband and wife is important. If the transfer is subject to a court order the date of the court order will be taken as the date of the transfer. If the court order is made by consent then the date of transfer is likely to be treated by the Inland Revenue as the date of the consent agreement if there is no other contract under which the asset is being transferred.

Careful consideration needs to be given, therefore, to the timing of disposals in order to minimise potential CGT liability. Chapter 13 looks at property disposals and CGT.

Transfer of the matrimonial home

16.27 On a divorce the home is likely to be transferred between spouses or sold.

A house which has been occupied by the owner as his or her main residence throughout the period of ownership will be wholly exempt from CGT [TCGA 1992 ss 222–224]. The last three years of ownership will be treated as a period of occupation even if another main residence has been acquired in that period.

If there have been periods of non-occupation during the period of ownership then only the appropriate proportion of the gain will be exempt.

Often it will be the case that on the breakdown of a marriage one spouse will leave the matrimonial home whilst the other remains in occupation. If the departing spouse transfers his or her interest in the property to the remaining spouse within three years of having left the property, his or her gain will be covered by the principal private residence (PPR) exemption. This exemption from CGT will apply even if the departing spouse has acquired another property in the meantime. The exemption will also apply if the property was sold rather than transferred.

A more detailed analysis of the PPR exemption and the extent to which it may apply to a farmhouse and its surrounding land and buildings is considered in Chapter 4 (Protecting the Farmhouse).

If the spouse who has an interest in the former matrimonial home has left the property more than three years prior to the transfer or sale of his interest in it, further relief may be available in the form of extra-statutory concession D6 which will allow exemption from the gain provided that he has not acquired a new main residence in the meantime and elected for that residence to be his principal home. If a new house has been acquired consideration should be given to the CGT consequences of electing which one should be treated as his main residence. Election for the extra-statutory concession will prevent that spouse from subsequently claiming PPR on another property for the period for which the extra-statutory concession is sought.

The extra-statutory concession D6 applies only to a transfer of a matrimonial home to a spouse. It does not apply where the home is sold.

Deferred charge or postponed interest in the home

16.28 As indicated above, in order to achieve fairness between spouses in the post-*White* era it may be appropriate for the departing spouse to retain an interest in the home to be realised at a later date, for example, when the youngest child reaches a certain age or completes full-time education. This may be done in one of two ways: by a postponed interest or a deferred charge.

1 *Deferred charge.* The home would be transferred to the remaining spouse (assuming that it is not already in that spouse's sole name).

At the date of transfer if the PPR exemption (with extra-statutory concession D6 if applicable) is available then there will be no CGT to pay by the transferring spouse.

The home would be subject to a charge in favour of the departing spouse (either for a fixed sum or a percentage share of the proceeds). However, the CGT position is different depending on which option is taken.

If the deferred charge is for a specific amount of money (for example, £50,000) then it is regarded as a debt and there will be no chargeable gain on the repayment of that charge to the departing spouse [TCGA 1992 s 251].

However, where the deferred charge is represented by a percentage of the value of the property it is not a debt as the amount cannot be ascertained until the date of repayment. The increase in value between the date that the charge was created and the date that it was repaid will, therefore, be subject to CGT on the spouse who has the benefit of the charge.

2 *Postponed interest.* An alternative to a deferred charge is where the home is retained in (or transferred to) the joint names of the spouses or to trustees on their behalf. This is known as a 'Mesher' order. The Inland Revenue regards a 'Mesher' order as a settlement and the CGT consequences are generally favourable. The initial transfer into joint names or to trustees will usually be exempt under the PPR rules for the spouse remaining in occupation and also for the departing spouse if the PPR rules (and extra-statutory concession D6, if applicable) apply.

When the date of realisation of the interest is reached the trustees are treated as selling the property and reacquiring for themselves as bare trustees [TCGA 1992 s 71]. The trustees will be able to claim the PPR exemption on the deemed disposal assuming that the remaining spouse has continued to live in the property since the original order was made [TCGA 1992 s 225].

Secured maintenance orders

16.29 Assets transferred into a settlement in order to secure the payment of maintenance will give rise to a charge to CGT [TCGA 1992 s 70]. As the settlor and the trustees will be regarded as connected persons the consideration for the transfer will be the market value of the underlying assets [TCGA 1992 ss 18 and 286].

Gains realised by the trustees during the settlement will be taxable on the settlor as a beneficiary of the settlement [TCGA 1992 s 77] although CGT paid can be recovered by the settlor from the trustees of the settlement [TCGA 1992 s 78].

If a secured maintenance settlement terminates during the lifetime of the non-settlor spouse, the settlement will come to an end and there will be a deemed disposal of the assets at market value. The gain will be taxable on the settlor (if he/she is still alive) as he/she retained an interest in the settlement.

If, however, the settlement terminates on the death of the non-settlor spouse there is a deemed disposal of the assets. In that situation, if determination occurs while the settlor is still alive the assets revert to him at a consideration such that no gain/no loss arises on the disposal [TCGA 1992 s 73]. However, if the settlor is dead the consideration will be the market value of the assets at the date of determination but any gain arising will not be liable to CGT [TCGA 1992 ss 72 and 73].

Transfers of business assets — holdover, taper and retirement reliefs

16.30   As above, timing of transfers between spouses is crucial.

If the transfer can be made before the end of the tax year of separation the transfer will be made on a no gain/no loss basis and no CGT will arise on the transfer. In contrast, transfers made after the end of the year of separation are chargeable to CGT.

A disposal of an asset which is not a bargain at arm's length is treated as a disposal at the open market value and the donor is deemed to have received the market value of the property even if he has received nothing in return for it.

It may be possible for such a gain to be held over where the disposal is a gift of business assets [TCGA 1992 s 165] or a gift to discretionary trust [TCGA 1992 s 260].

Although transfers between spouses made after the tax year of separation or under a court order after divorce may potentially be eligible for holdover relief the Inland Revenue does not accept that it is available. The Inland Revenue argues that consideration is given for the transfer since the donor spouse is being relieved of the obligation to make other financial arrangements. The value of the consideration (the rights being given up by the recipient spouse) reduces the gain which would be eligible for holdover relief to nil and thus the deemed gain is immediately chargeable to CGT.

In order to persuade the Inland Revenue otherwise the donor and the recipient spouse would have to prove to the satisfaction of the Inland Revenue that the transfer was made wholly or partly with gratuitous intent.

As holdover relief is unlikely to apply, the application of taper relief to business assets (referred to in Chapter 2) may play an important role in structuring a financial settlement on divorce. This is looked at in Chapter 14 on property disposals.

Retirement relief may be available (where a spouse who is disposing of the whole or part of a business has attained the age of 50, or has retired under that age due to ill health, where he owns at least 5% of the share capital or partnership interest and is a full-time working director or employee). However, retirement relief is in the process of being phased out. In the tax year 2001–02 100% relief was available on gains up to £100,000 and 50% relief on gains between £100,000–£400,000. However, in 2002–03 the 100% gain is limited to £50,000 and 50% relief is limited to gains between £50,000–£200,000.

Tax indemnity

16.31 It is important to note that where potential CGT issues exist as a consequence of transfers made in connection with a divorce the recipient spouse is likely to seek tax indemnities and it may well be appropriate for the transferor spouse to give such indemnities.

As the provision of such indemnities is likely to impact on the structure of a financial settlement it is important that they are not overlooked in negotiations.

Inheritance tax (IHT)

16.32 Whilst the parties are married any gifts made by one to the other (whether during lifetime or on death) will be exempt under IHTA 1984 s 18. That exemption is limited to £55,000 if the recipient spouse is not domiciled in the UK but the transferor spouse is so domiciled. The exemption for gifts between spouses is not conditional on the couple living together and, therefore, it will apply to gifts made after separation but not to gifts made after divorce.

Inheritance tax (IHT) is not usually a problem for divorcing couples. The Inland Revenue usually accepts that a divorce settlement is covered by s 10 of IHTA 1984 which excludes from a charge from IHT a transfer made at arm's length which is not intended to confer any gratuitous benefit. That overrides the exemption for potentially exempt transfers (PETs) and there is, therefore, usually no risk of an IHT charge if the transferor dies within seven years.

The payment of maintenance (for a spouse or for children) is specifically exempted from IHT [IHTA 1984 s 11] and will not be regarded as a transfer of value provided it is for the maintenance of the other party or for the maintenance, education or training of the child no longer than the year in which the child becomes 18 or ceases full-time education or training.

Other payments to or for a child will normally be PETs and there will be no IHT liability unless the transferor dies within seven years after the date of the gift.

A settlement created to secure maintenance will, unless covered by the maintenance exemption, represent a PET as it constitutes a settlement. If the settlor dies before the termination of that settlement his or her reversionary interest will be included in his or her estate for IHT purposes as it does not constitute excluded property [IHTA 1984 s 48].

Other reliefs from inheritance tax (in particular agricultural property relief) are considered in detail in CHAPTER 4 and CHAPTER 5.

As indicated above, it is essential that specialist advice is sought in order to ascertain and seek to minimise the potential adverse tax consequences which may arise in connection with a divorce.

Michael Gouriet

Michael Gouriet has been with Withers[LLP] *since 1993 (where he did his training), moving into the firm's Family Law Department on qualification in 1995. He was made a partner in January 2002. He advises on all aspects of private family law with a particular emphasis on the resolution of financial issues on separation and divorce (including those involving farms and landed estates). Many of the cases he advises on have an international element.*

He has had various family law articles published – both in the national press and in legal journals. He has lectured on family law issues in the UK and abroad, and he has also appeared on TV and on radio.

Suzy Ashworth

Suzy Ashworth has been with Withers[LLP] *since September 2000 and is a solicitor in the Family Law Department. She previously worked in the Property and Trusts Reform team at the Law Commission for England and Wales. She advises on all areas of family law.*

Trusts $\qquad$ **17**

Jane Dearle
(Withers^{LLP})

- **The creation of a trust**
  Generous reliefs are currently available to the owners of agricultural and business property. In an uncertain world crystallising these reliefs has become a priority for many taxpayers. The creation of a trust is one way of doing this without loss of control.
- **The administration of a trust**
  Understanding the legal formalities and complying with them is an essential pre-requisite to the creation of an effective trust. Equally important is knowledge of the obligations and duties of trustees during the continuance of the trust.
- **Uses of trusts**
  Trusts are an obvious vehicle for controlling devolution, securing succession and maintaining farms and estates as single, viable entities; but they can also play a major role in ensuring tax efficient pension provision, life assurance and school fees planning.

Note from the Editor

17.1 The tax planning benefits of trusts have been mentioned throughout the book. In CHAPTER 5 we look at the bold step of gifting the assets now, and consideration is given to gifts with reservation of benefit. The links with holdover reliefs are set out in CHAPTER 14. The use of trusts to prevent a failed potentially exempt transfer (PET) is set out in CHAPTER 13.

The book's theme is to look carefully at the ownership structure and vehicle for holding land and business assets. Every situation has to be tailor-made to the circumstances and the future plans and aims of the taxpayer.

This chapter outlines the formalities needed to create a trust, the role of trustees, different types of trust and their tax treatment. An in-depth analysis of trust and tax law is outside the scope of this book and specialist advice should be sought. Withers[LLP] advises both domestic and international clients on a range of trust and tax issues. The specialist Landed Estates group is comprised of lawyers drawn from the private client, property, family and corporate departments.

Introduction

17.2 The law of trusts is one of the UK's greatest exports. Jurisdictions across the Globe have adopted the concept of equity with enthusiasm and vigour. Many of the world's trust laws follow the English model – a model which has been revised, extended and adapted over the years to suit particular needs and different markets.

It is from a common law base that the law of trusts has developed in England and Wales. Its roots lie in the concept of the 'use', which as long ago as the fourteenth century was used as a means of avoiding restrictions on the alienation of land. Trusts still offer opportunities for tax efficient estate planning for landowners and farmers. A trust can control the devolution of a large parcel of land, but a discretionary trust set up to receive the death benefits payable under a life policy can also secure significant inheritance tax (IHT) savings.

The law of trusts is contained in legislation and case law, the principal statutes being the Trustee Act 1925, the Settled Land Act 1925, the Variation of Trusts Act 1958, the Perpetuities and Accumulations Act 1964, the Trusts of Land and Appointment of Trustees Act 1996 and, most recently, the Trustee Act 2000, which came into force on 1 February 2001.

Whilst statute governs the structure of a trust and the duties of trustees, the trust is above all a creature of equity and as such is ruled by equitable principles. These are founded on a distinction between legal rights and equitable interests. Where property is held in trust, the trustees have the legal rights of ownership over the property, but the beneficiaries on whose behalf the trustees hold that property enjoy the equitable interests. Trustees must administer trust assets in the best interests of the beneficiaries and must have regard to the nature of the beneficiaries' interests, balancing the interests of those presently entitled with those of future beneficiaries, such as the unborn.

Trustees are subject to stringent duties and responsibilities and risk personal liability if they fail to carry out their duties in a proper manner. These are considered later in this chapter. The Trustee Act 1925 contains the principal duties and powers of trustees but those powers are usually extended specifically in the trust instrument. The Trusts of Land and Appointment of Trustees Act 1996 and the Trustee Act 2000 further enhance the duty of trustees to consult and act in accordance with the wishes of beneficiaries, and widen trustees' powers of delegation.

The creation of a trust

17.3   A trust can be created by deed during lifetime by an oral declaration, or by Will. Certain formalities are required to establish a trust.

The individual wishing to create the trust (the 'settlor') must demonstrate an express intention to do so and, where land is involved, that intention must be evidenced in writing. The asset, subject to the trust, must be vested in the names of the trustees and put under their control. The trust only becomes operative when the property is vested in the trustees. Very often trusts are established with a nominal sum of say £10 with other property being added in due course when the formalities necessary to transfer that property have been complied with.

Different types of property entail different formalities, for instance chattels vest on delivery, shares must be re-registered into the names of the trustees and a transfer of legal title to land must be effected by deed.

Alongside the formalities for creating a trust, the trust itself must comply with the three certainties:

1   words;
2   objects; and
3   subject matter.

It must be clear from the wording that the settlor intends to establish a trust. The individuals for whose benefit the trust is intended must be ascertained or ascertainable and the property subject to the trust and the beneficial interests in it must be certain.

In addition to satisfying the three certainties, the trust must not infringe the rule against perpetuities and excessive accumulations. These rules are designed to ensure that property cannot be tied up in trust indefinitely. All the interests under the trust must vest, ie cease to be contingent, within the perpetuity period (commonly called the trust period). If this is not the case, the trust will be void.

The trust period is prescribed by law. It is usual to specify the period in the trust instrument. The three most commonly selected periods being:

1 a period based on the life of someone alive at the date the trust
   instrument takes effect plus 21 years;
2 a period based on the lives of members of the Royal Family; or
3 80 years.

The latter is the period most commonly incorporated into modern trust
instruments, as it has the advantage of certainty.

Alongside the rule against perpetuities is the common law principle
against excessive accumulations of income. This reflects the principle
that the trust assets are intended for the benefit of certain individuals.
The ability to have the use or enjoyment of the income, at some point
in time, is an essential part of this.

The Law of Property Act 1925 provides that income may not be
accumulated for any period longer than the following:

1 the life of the settlor;
2 21 years from the death of the settlor or testator;
3 the duration of the minorities of any persons living or 'en ventre sa
   mere' (an unborn child) at the date of the death of the settlor or testator; or
4 the duration of the minorities of any person who would be entitled
   to receive the income being accumulated if of full age.

Two further categories were added by the Perpetuities and
Accumulations Act 1964:

5 21 years from the date of the settlement; and
6 the minority of any person or persons in being at the date of the
   settlement.

The period of 21 years from the date of the settlement is typically
selected in modern trust instruments on the grounds of clarity and
certainty.

The choice of trustees

17.4 The office of trustee involves the assumption of onerous duties
and obligations. As well as individuals a corporate entity or a trust corporation may be appointed. There is no limit to the number of trustees
although the maximum number permitted to hold a legal estate in land
is four, and for administrative convenience it is usually preferable to
appoint no more than this number.

A sole individual trustee may act, but will not be able to give a good
receipt for the proceeds of sale or other capital money arising from the
sale of land. It is therefore usual to appoint at least two individual

trustees. A corporate trustee can act alone but must be a trust corporation if it is to give a valid receipt for capital monies. In practice, only corporate entities with substantial capital backing will be eligible for designation as trust corporations.

The Trusts of Land and Appointment of Trustees Act 1996 has eased the rule that a retiring trustee could only be discharged from his office if two 'individuals' remained in office after his retirement. Under the 1996 Act, a retiring trustee can be discharged if two 'persons' or a trust corporation remain as trustees.

The settlor may choose to appoint trustees resident in the UK or outside the UK. The residence of the trustees and the beneficiaries, the tax status of the settlor, the location of the trust assets and the geographical forum for the administration of the trust will all influence the tax regime which applies to the trust.

The English Court will accept jurisdiction over a trust where there is a proven connection with the jurisdiction. The location of the trust assets in England and Wales or the residence of the trustees or beneficiaries in England and Wales will usually be a sufficient connection.

The administration of a trust

17.5 Trustees are under a duty to file annual tax returns where chargeability to UK tax exists. They must account for UK basic rate tax and in some circumstances, depending on the type of trust, additional rate income tax.

Trustees must keep adequate records of their running of the trust so that they are in a position to produce accounts on request by the beneficiaries.

Where a trust is dormant, for instance a trust established to receive the death benefits payable under a policy of life assurance, the Inland Revenue may be willing to dispense with the need for annual returns on application by the trustees but this will usually only be on the basis that the trustees undertake to submit returns as soon as the proceeds from the policy are received and chargeability to tax therefore arises.

Types of UK trusts

17.6 The current UK tax regime distinguishes between trusts with, and trusts without, an interest in possession. The definition of an interest in possession is the 'present right to present enjoyment of the trust property' (see *Pearson v IRC [1981] AC 753*), and a trust with an interest in possession is therefore one in which one or more beneficiaries has such an interest.

An interest in possession can take a number of forms, the most common being a lifetime right to enjoy the income arising from the trust assets. This is commonly called a life interest. A beneficiary may also acquire such an interest when, for example, he is given the exclusive right to occupy a trust property.

Trusts without an interest in possession are usually categorised as discretionary trusts. The trustees have complete discretion to determine when, and if, a particular beneficiary should be given an absolute or limited interest in some or all of the trust assets. Limitations can be put on the trustees' discretion, but as a rule it is preferable to give the trustees wide unfettered powers to apply the trust assets in the interests of some or all of the beneficiaries as and when they think fit. Notes of wishes from the settlor can, however, provide helpful guidance to the trustees.

In addition to the standard discretionary trust, tax legislation allows for certain other types of discretionary trust. These comprise:

- accumulation and maintenance trusts designed to allow property to be held on flexible trusts for persons aged under 25. These trusts benefit from their own tax regime, which is considered later in this chapter. They must satisfy the conditions set out in Inheritance Tax Act 1984 (IHTA 1984) s 71 which broadly require that a beneficiary attains an interest in possession in the trust property on or prior to his twenty-fifth birthday. In the meantime, the income from the trust assets can be accumulated to the extent that it is not applied for the beneficiaries' maintenance or education;
- charitable trusts;
- trusts for disabled persons; and
- trusts for employees.

The tax treatment of the three commonest types of trust, namely discretionary, life interest and accumulation and maintenance trusts, is considered below.

The tax treatment of trusts

17.7 When looking at the tax treatment of trusts three stages should be considered:

1 the creation of the trust;
2 the continuance of the trust; and
3 the termination of the trust.

Different types of trust enjoy different tax treatment. The creation of the trust requires the transfer of property from the settlor to the trustees. This will be a disposal by the settlor for the purposes of capital gains tax (CGT), which may or may not give rise to a chargeable gain. That said certain types of property (principally business and agricultural property) can qualify for holdover relief. Where a settlor transfers such assets to trustees and elects to hold over the gain, the trustees will take the assets at the settlor's base cost and no charge to CGT will arise on the disposal by the settlor. A similar relief can be obtained where the settlor passes any type of property to trustees to be held on discretionary trusts.

The creation of a trust will also entail a transfer of value by the settlor for the purposes of IHT. As with CGT, the IHT treatment of the transfer will vary depending on the type of trust involved. A transfer to a life interest or accumulation and maintenance trust will be a potentially exempt transfer, which will only become chargeable to IHT if the settlor fails to survive it by seven years. A transfer to a discretionary trust will, however, be a chargeable transfer, with IHT presently being levied at the rate of 20% for transfers in excess of the settlor's nil-rate band. Certain types of agricultural and business property can, however, benefit from relief from IHT and a transfer of such property to a discretionary trust can therefore be made free of IHT (see Chapter 13).

During the continuance of the trust, the trustees are treated as a single and continuing body of persons. All trusts pay CGT at the rate applicable to trusts. The annual exemption from CGT is set at one half of the exemption available to individuals, but trusts made after 6 June 1978 by the same settlor share one annual exemption. Chargeable gains made by trustees are calculated in the same way as for individuals.

Trustees are deemed to dispose of trust assets in two situations:

1 when a person becomes absolutely entitled to all or part of the trust assets as against the trustees; and
2 where an interest in possession in trust property terminates on the death of the person entitled to the interest, but the property remains settled. In such circumstances there is, however, a tax-free uplift and no chargeable gain arises, except to the extent that any gain was held over on the creation of the trust.

The distinction in tax terms between the different types of trust is most marked in the context of IHT. During the continuance of a discretionary trust the legislation provides for two occasions of charge to IHT.

- The ten-year anniversary charge entails a charge to IHT on each tenth anniversary of the date the settlement commenced. The formula for calculating the charge is complex and will usually necessitate taking professional advice.
- The exit charge arises whenever trust assets cease to be 'relevant property' within the definition in the legislation. This is broadly

when the property ceases to be held on discretionary trusts, for instance if a beneficiary becomes absolutely entitled to it or becomes entitled to a life interest in it. As with the ten-year anniversary charge, the calculation of the exit charge is complex and professional advice is usually necessary.

Other types of trust, such as accumulation and maintenance trusts and life interest trusts, do not suffer the IHT charges outlined above during their continuance on the basis that a beneficiary with an interest in possession in trust property is deemed to own the underlying capital with the result that a charge to IHT arises on the beneficiary's death. The Inland Revenue is therefore assured a charge to IHT once a generation. This is not the case with a discretionary trust. The combination of the ten-year anniversary and exit charge is designed to ensure a full charge to IHT on the trust assets once each generation.

The termination of a trust involves a deemed disposal by the trustees for the purposes of CGT. This may arise where a beneficiary becomes absolutely entitled as against the trustees, but can also arise where trust property is resettled on new trusts. The termination of a discretionary trust will also entail a charge to IHT (an exit charge) unlike the termination of a life interest or accumulation and maintenance trust when no IHT charge arises.

Uses of trusts

17.8   What role can trusts play in modern day life for landowners and farmers? Trusts are an obvious vehicle for controlling devolution, securing succession and ultimately maintaining estates or farms as single viable entities, but trusts can also play a major role in ensuring tax efficient pension provision, life assurance and school fees planning.

Transferring assets, which qualify for full agricultural or business property relief, to a discretionary trust under which the transferor is excluded from all benefit will ensure that the assets in question no longer comprise part of the transferor's estate. The transfer to the trustees will be a disposal for the purposes of capital gains tax, but the availability of holdover relief will mean that any charge to tax can be deferred. The gift will be an immediately chargeable transfer for the purposes of inheritance tax, but the availability of agricultural or business property relief means that no inheritance tax charge will actually arise.

Much has been written about possible changes to the legislation to restrict the availability of holdover relief where the transfer in question does not in fact give rise to a charge to inheritance tax. Yet for now it remains possible to settle assets on discretionary trusts without crystallising an inheritance tax charge and, nevertheless, claim holdover relief – thereby avoiding a charge to capital gains tax. It follows that a transfer into a discretionary trust, which is restricted to relievable property or to the amount of the available nil-rate band (currently £250,000), neither gives rise to an inheritance tax charge nor a capital gains tax charge.

The creation of a discretionary trust during lifetime to receive the death benefits payable under personal pension policies or life assurance arrangements is another way of mitigating inheritance tax. Provided the transferor is in normal health at the time of the transfer, the transfer itself should not give rise to a charge to inheritance tax. The proceeds will not suffer inheritance tax on the death of the life assured and a further advantage is that the insurance company will usually pay out the proceeds on production of a death certificate alone, rather than a Grant of Probate.

Transfers between spouses also enjoy exemption from inheritance tax and, for the purposes of capital gains tax, are treated as giving rise to neither a loss nor a gain. Judicious inter-spouse transfers followed by gifts into trust can therefore allow a trust to be created at no tax cost. Once the assets are in trust, funds can be created and appointments made in favour of different classes of beneficiaries without capital gains tax becoming an issue, provided that care is taken not, inadvertently, to effect a resettlement. The opportunities for efficient tax planning once assets are held within a settlement are generally regarded as far greater than those which exist where assets are held in personal ownership.

The tax benefits of trusts speak for themselves. The public policy arguments for allowing property to be managed for the benefit of those ultimately entitled are also powerful and likely to ensure that trusts remain a key part of the English legal system for a long time to come.

Jane Dearle

Jane Dearle is a principle in the private client department at Withers^{LLP} and is a member of their specialist Landed Estates Group. Jane trained at Withers, becoming a partner in 1999. In addition to her landed estates practice, she co-edits International Trust Precedents *and regularly contributes to a number of specialist tax and trust journals.*

Wills

18

Robert Brodrick, Solicitor
(Private Client Department, Withers^{LLP})

- **Plan a Will effectively**
  Tax planning can be achieved through a well drafted Will. Intestacy must be avoided at all costs – land is a very valuable asset that must be protected.

- **Save around £100,000 in tax with careful planning**
  This chapter looks at specific examples of saving tax.

- **Take advantage of all available tax exemptions and reliefs**
  It is very important to make sure that advantage is taken of all the exemptions and reliefs that are available.

- **Avoid disputes**
  Historically, farming families have wasted unnecessary time and professional fees in disputes as a result of intestacy and badly drafted Wills.

- **Manage the client's affairs in the event of mental or physical incapacity**
  Few farmers retire and land always needs to be managed to protect against incapacity.

Note from the Editor

18.1   Many farmers and landowners die 'intestate' – without a Will – and this not only causes huge problems for the family, but also makes winding up the estate more complicated.

These are times of change for farmers and there is no better time than now to review asset ownership and the tax efficiency of current arrangements. A complete review has to incorporate the drafting of Wills for all the family. In this chapter Robert Brodrick, a solicitor in the private client department at leading city law firm Withers[LLP], and a member of their specialist Landed Estates group, sets out why a Will is not just an 'evil necessity' but is also a useful tax planning device. He covers areas such as how to hand assets on to the next generation tax-free, how to make the most of tax reliefs, as well how best to deal with personal possessions and funeral arrangements.

It is a practical approach to a subject that so many clients are loath to embrace. It ties into the theme that the affairs of the farming/landowning family have to be looked at 'in the round'. One aspect of tax planning is not enough and all good tax advice must incorporate a review of Wills.

Although the chapter is not exhaustive, it deals with the main points to consider when planning a Will.

Introduction

18.2   There are many reasons why people should make Wills, but the principal ones are tax and succession planning. Unlike most European countries where there are strict rules of succession (known as forced heirship) which restrict the way in which you can leave your estate, people in England and Wales have testamentary freedom which means that they are free to dispose of their assets as they wish on death. (Scotland has slightly different rules that favour spouses and close family members and give them a right to inherit movable assets, eg personal possessions and bank accounts.)

One of the most visible effects of testamentary freedom is that landowners have been able to protect the integrity of their properties, hence English farms and landed estates have largely been kept together where, in other countries, forced heirship would give rise to successive divisions of the property amongst siblings. This is why, for example, vineyards and farms in France are often so small and have such disparate ownership.

Intestacy rules

18.3 Without a Will, you have to rely on the intestacy rules, which set out how a person's estate is to be distributed in the absence of any other direction; sometimes a person can die partially intestate (for example, if they left a Will that made pecuniary legacies but did not deal with the residue) and the intestacy rules would govern the distribution of the part of the estate not dealt with by Will. Although this may not be a problem in the context of a simple, low-value estate where the deceased left no surviving spouse or children, for anyone with an estate that includes land (or any other illiquid asset) who is survived by a spouse, the intestacy rules are likely to be very unsatisfactory: they will almost certainly mean that the surviving spouse has to share the land with children or other relatives of the deceased, which may force the land to be sold in order to achieve a workable division of the deceased's estate.

Where a person dies intestate with a surviving spouse and children, the intestacy rules allow the surviving spouse to receive a 'statutory legacy' of £125,000 (assuming the estate is worth more than this amount) and any personal chattels, with a life interest in half of the remaining assets. The children inherit the remaining half share of the assets on statutory trusts (ie dividing the assets equally between them and giving them a right to inherit at 18). Where there are no lineal descendants, the surviving spouse's legacy is increased to £200,000 plus a half share of the rest of the estate outright – the remaining half share is divided between the deceased's closest surviving relatives.

EXAMPLE

Henry is married to Harriet. Henry owns a small farm (worth £600,000), and shares (worth £200,000). Harriet owns a flat in London (worth £200,000) and shares (worth £50,000). Henry dies intestate. They have no children, but Henry is survived by his brothers Hector and Humphrey (their parents both having pre-deceased him).

Under the intestacy rules, Harriet is entitled to:

- a statutory legacy of £200,000; plus
- a half share of the rest of the estate (ie £300,000).

As his closest surviving relatives, Hector and Humphrey are entitled to share the remaining half share of Henry's estate on the 'statutory trusts'. Their share is £300,000. However, the shares are not worth enough to satisfy their entitlement of £150,000 each, so part of their entitlement must come from the farm.

There is a further complication in that the share of the estate passing to Henry's brothers exceeds the 'nil-rate band' which means that, unless the farm qualifies for 100% relief, there will be tax to pay.

As Hector is in the process of setting up a new business he needs cash, and he is likely to push for a sale of the farm. If Harriet had sufficient funds of her own, she could buy out her brothers-in-law, but she doesn't.

If Henry had written a Will leaving his estate to Harriet, he could have avoided leaving his widow in a very difficult situation.

It is worth pointing out that when a person gets married, their Will is automatically revoked and unless they re-write their Will (or sign a codicil to 'republish' their earlier Will), they will be intestate. On the other hand, divorce does not cause automatic revocation – instead, the divorced spouse will simply be treated as having pre-deceased the testator.

What other matters need to be considered when preparing a Will?

Guardians

18.4   Where a couple have children it is important to decide who should take care of them in the event of both of the parents dying. In the absence of an express appointment of a guardian (eg in a Will), it will be left to the Court to appoint a guardian for any children under the age of 18.

Legacies

18.5   It goes without saying that the intestacy rules do not cater for people choosing to leave legacies, either pecuniary or 'specific' (eg a particular item), to friends or family, nor do they allow gifts to be made to charity. Where a person dies owning a farm, it is not only his family who are likely to be affected, but also his employees, and it is quite common to see these people remembered in a person's Will, often with the proviso that the gift is only to take place if the individual is still in the deceased's employment at the date of his death.

Gifts can be made either 'free of tax', in which case the tax (if any) will be borne by the residuary estate, or 'subject to tax', in which case the recipient of the gift will have to pay tax on it at the rate of 40% to the extent that the value of this and other gifts exceeds the nil-rate band (see **18.3**).

Funeral wishes

18.6 Many people want to leave specific directions dealing with their funeral, cremation or burial arrangements and, although a testator has no power to dispose of his own body, any request included in a Will is likely to be adhered to by the executors. If there are any religious or other reasons why burial would need to take place very shortly after death, it would be more sensible for these wishes to be stated elsewhere, as people generally store their Wills either at a bank or in a solicitor's strongroom and it can take several days (and the production of a death certificate) before the Will can be released to the executors, by which time it may be too late.

Funeral instructions can either be included in the Will, or, where the instructions are particularly detailed, they can be set out in a side letter (which would usually be left with the Will addressed to the executors). Funeral wishes can range from the simple request for the deceased's ashes to be scattered in a particular place, to the more esoteric. For instance, those who have a fear of being buried alive can include a clause requesting the executors to arrange for the deceased to be given a medical examination prior to burial to guard against 'premature burial'.

Personal possessions

18.7 The best way to deal with personal possessions is by way of a letter of wishes. The Will should direct that the deceased's personal possessions be left either to the surviving spouse or to the executors to be distributed in accordance with a letter of wishes, or in the absence of any letter of wishes or specific instruction, to be distributed at the discretion of the executors. This makes the Will extremely flexible and allows the executors to rectify any oversights (eg failure to include a godchild) by giving them an item that belonged to the deceased.

It is important to bear in mind that distributing personal possessions in this way may give rise to tax, so if there are particularly valuable items, it would be better to leave them to the surviving spouse (so that they qualify for spouse exemption) and leave it up to him or her whether to follow any letters of wishes – for inheritance tax (IHT) purposes, the surviving spouse would then be treated as inheriting all the personal possessions and to the extent that any are handed on (eg to godchildren) he or she would be treated as making a gift for IHT purposes, which would be a 'potentially exempt transfer'.

Exemptions and reliefs

18.8   There are several exemptions and reliefs that need to be considered.

For instance, as the rules currently stand the first £250,000 of a person's estate is taxed at 0% and can therefore be given away tax-free to a beneficiary who would otherwise be chargeable. This is usually referred to as the nil-rate band because, although it is subject to tax, the rate of tax is nil.

Gifts to spouses and charities are also exempt from IHT, although where the surviving spouse is non-UK domiciled, the spouse exemption is limited to £55,000.

Certain assets also qualify for relief from IHT: the most significant are agricultural property and business property (dealt with in Chapter **13** in more detail).

Tax-efficient Wills

18.9   It is very important to make sure that advantage is taken of all exemptions and reliefs that are available, and although there will be no tax to pay if a husband leaves his entire estate to his wife, on the wife's subsequent death there is likely to be more tax to pay if the husband has not made full use of his allowances.

Why waste the nil-rate band by giving it to the surviving spouse when it could be given directly to children, or ideally held on discretionary trust for the benefit of a class of beneficiaries including the surviving spouse and other members of the deceased's family? By using the nil-rate band a married couple can save £100,000 on the second death, yet a great many people fail to take advantage of it.

A point to watch is that where a married couple own property as joint tenants, it will pass automatically to the survivor by right of survivorship, and would therefore not be available to make up a nil-rate band legacy; it is very easy to sever a joint tenancy and this can be done simply by writing a letter of severance to the other joint tenant. Where a couple owns property as tenants in common, it is advisable to record the fact by registering a restriction against the title at HM Land Registry.

EXAMPLE

Tessa and Tom are married. They own a house as tenants in common worth £500,000 and each have £250,000 in stocks and shares. They have two children, Tina and Terry.

Tom dies leaving his estate to Tessa outright. There will be no tax to pay on Tom's death because the whole estate is spouse exempt.

When Tessa dies, leaving the estate to Tina and Terry in equal shares, the first £250,000 is taxed at 0%, and the balance (£750,000) is taxed at 40%. There will be a tax bill of £300,000 leaving £700,000 available for distribution.

Tina and Terry will inherit £350,000 each.

If Tom had been properly advised, he would have included a nil-rate band discretionary trust in his Will. This would work as follows:

Tom dies leaving the nil-rate band on discretionary trusts, with the rest of the estate passing to Tina outright. There would be no tax to pay. The first £250,000 (taxed at 0%) would be held on discretionary trusts for the benefit of Tessa, Tina and Terry (and other family members). The balance of the estate (ie the half share of the house) would pass to Tessa.

On Tessa's death, her estate would consist of her shares worth £250,000 and the house worth £500,000. The first £250,000 would be taxed at 0%, and the balance at 40% giving a tax bill of £200,000. After tax, Tessa's estate would be worth £550,000 leaving Tina and Terry to inherit £275,000 each. In addition, the discretionary trust established under Tom's Will still contains £250,000 which can also be divided between Tina and Terry (or other members of the family): by combining Tessa's estate and Tom's trust, Tina and Terry would stand to inherit £400,000 each (as opposed to £300,000 if Tom had not included a nil-rate band discretionary trust in his Will).

Another common pitfall is to overlook other reliefs. For instance, as mentioned in **Chapter 13**, agricultural property is usually capable of qualifying for relief from IHT on death (provided that it was owned and occupied by the deceased for two years prior to his death for the purposes of agriculture, or was owned by him for seven years prior to his death, but occupied by someone else for the purposes of agriculture). It would make much more sense for property that qualifies for relief to be left directly to 'taxable' beneficiaries (or a flexible trust), rather than left to the surviving spouse: the property may not qualify for relief on the death of the surviving spouse which would give rise to an unnecessary tax bill.

Likewise, certain shares and business interests are capable of qualifying for 'business property relief' (BPR), and these should ideally be left to a trust for the benefit of a class of beneficiaries, rather than simply given to the surviving spouse.

Residuary estate

18.10   Assuming they have already made full use of the nil-rate band, most people if they are married leave the rest of their estate (commonly known as the 'residuary estate') to their surviving spouse with the benefit of spouse exemption from IHT. The surviving spouse does not need to inherit the residuary estate outright. Spouse exemption will still be available where a spouse is given the right to receive income from the residuary estate. This is because the IHT rules treat a person with a right to receive income as owning the underlying property for IHT purposes.

Life interest trust

18.11   Where people have children from more than one marriage there are rival concerns to consider. For instance, a man with two children by his first wife and one child by his second wife will want to ensure that his second wife is provided for, but will also want to ensure that his first two children are not overlooked. If he leaves his estate to his second wife outright, he is relying on her to 'do the right thing' and leave a third to each of his children, when her main priority may be to provide for her only child.

By giving the second wife a life interest, the husband effectively retains control over the devolution of his estate. His trustees can be given power to pay capital to the second wife, and she would have the right to occupy any property that formed part of the residuary estate. However, she would be unable to prevent the children from inheriting the estate on her death. In such a situation it is important not to underestimate the potential for conflict and great care should be taken when choosing whom to appoint as executors and trustees.

How to hand assets on to the next generation tax-free

18.12   Obviously, there is scope for IHT planning where a person's residuary estate is given to the surviving spouse on life interest terms, because, depending on the terms of the Will, it should be possible for the trustees to take away the surviving spouse's interest in favour of other beneficiaries without an immediate tax charge. For IHT purposes, the surviving spouse would be treated as having made a potentially exempt transfer and, as the rules currently stand, would simply have to survive the transfer by seven years for the assets to fall out of account. The transfer of value in this situation will not constitute a gift. It therefore follows that the surviving spouse can continue to benefit from the assets without falling foul of the reservation of benefit rules.

For capital gains tax purposes, assuming there was an ongoing trust, there would be no 'disposal', so no immediate charge to capital gains tax.

Other ways of dealing with the residuary estate

18.13   Where there is no surviving spouse, the residuary estate is likely to be subject to tax at 40% to the extent that it exceeds the nil-rate band and does not qualify for exemptions or reliefs. The residuary estate can either be left to one or more individuals outright, or on trust for their benefit. A trust is probably the most convenient way of dealing with a residuary estate that consists of land (or any other illiquid assets that are not easily divisible) that is to be held for more than one person (eg the grandchildren of the deceased). This is because a trust distinguishes between the legal ownership and the underlying beneficial ownership. In other words, although the land would be registered in the names of the trustees as the legal owners, they would hold it upon trust for the beneficiaries (who could be numerous) in accordance with the terms of the Will. Typically, where a residuary estate is left for the benefit of a person's grandchildren, each grandchild will become entitled to receive the income from their share at a specified age (usually 18 or 25), and until that time, the trustees would have power to use any income for the maintenance of each grandchild or to accumulate it.

Inheritance tax mitigation

18.14   It is worth emphasising that IHT does not distinguish between liquid and illiquid assets and, unless the assets qualify for relief from IHT, or pass to an exempt beneficiary (eg spouse or charity), IHT at 40% will be payable. In a typical family situation this means that on the death of the surviving spouse, the whole estate (except for assets that qualify for relief) will be subject to 40% tax. Therefore, where a person's estate consists of high value, or illiquid assets that are unlikely to qualify for full relief, it would be worth taking specialist advice at the same time as preparing a Will to see whether there is any scope for lifetime planning that could help to avoid a large tax bill on death.

Agricultural Holdings Act tenancies

18.15   Where a person has an Agricultural Holdings Act tenancy, it is possible to include a nomination for a successor by Will. Although this nomination is not binding, it can be persuasive where there is more than one possible successor.

Farming partnerships

18.16 If a person is a partner in a farming partnership, it will be important to ensure that the terms of their Will are consistent with the terms of the partnership agreement, and that between them they set out what is to happen on death to the share in the partnership. Under normal principles of partnership law, a partnership will dissolve on the death of one of the partners. Most partnership agreements provide for continuation on a death, but care should be taken when deciding how to confer a right on the surviving partners to acquire the deceased's partnership share because this can give rise to tax consequences.

Carrying on the business of farming

18.17 Where a person owns a farm and the executors and trustees of his Will are expected to carry on the business of farming, it is important to ensure that they are given an express power to carry on a trade. The statutory powers are very limited and although the executors would generally be able to carry on the deceased's business until it was sold, it would be advisable for them to be given wider powers. This is another situation where the choice of executors is likely to be important as it would be wise to choose executors with experience of farming and/or running a business.

Non-testamentary documents — enduring power of attorney (EPA)

18.18 When someone writes their Will they should also consider whether they have appointed anyone to deal with their affairs in the event of their becoming unable to do so themselves. This could come about either as a result of old age or infirmity, or as a result of an accident or illness. In any of these circumstances an enduring power of attorney (often referred to as an 'EPA') is invaluable. An ordinary power of attorney is only effective for as long as the 'donor' of the power (ie the person granting the power) has mental capacity – as soon as the donor loses mental capacity, the power of attorney lapses. However, an EPA continues to work even if the donor loses mental capacity (which is just when it is most needed). At that point, the EPA needs to be registered at the Court of Protection, which involves notifying various close relatives (to ensure that the EPA is not abused). Once registered, the attorneys can continue to manage the donor's affairs without interference from the Court. In the absence of an EPA it is necessary to appoint a 'receiver' to deal with the affairs of a person who is no longer capable of doing so themselves and this is a time consuming and bureaucratic procedure.

Under an EPA the attorney stands in the donor's shoes and can do anything that the donor could have done himself. This extends to operating bank accounts. So, for instance, if the donor had been involved in an accident, the attorney could ensure that enough money was available in the right bank account to cover mortgage repayments and other bills which might otherwise not be paid.

Living Will

18.19   Increasingly, people also write a Living Will (or Advance Directive) which sets out what should happen if they become terminally ill. Although not legally binding, Living Wills are becoming more common, and do carry a certain amount of weight, particularly if they are properly drawn up in consultation with the individual's GP (who should always be given a copy of the Living Will so that they know of its existence). The aim of a Living Will is to communicate a person's desire not to receive medical treatment designed to prolong their life in circumstances where they are suffering from a terminal illness or other 'intolerable condition' (eg persistent vegetative state), and are no longer capable of communicating their wishes. The Living Will also sets out whom the individual would like to be consulted before any such decisions about their treatment are made. Obviously, this is very important for unmarried couples because an unmarried 'partner' would not automatically have the right to be consulted about medical treatment.

Insurance

18.20   If it is impossible to reduce the impact of IHT on death by making lifetime gifts, it is always worth considering insurance, provided that the benefit of the policy is assigned to a trust so that it does not form a party of the deceased's estate for IHT purposes and simply exacerbate the problem by creating more tax to pay. The topic of insurance is dealt with more fully at **5.20** and in CHAPTER **19**.

Robert John Lee Brodrick

Robert Brodrick is a solicitor in the private client department at Withers^{LLP} and is a member of their specialist Landed Estates group; as a firm, Withers^{LLP} acts for the largest number of landed estate owners in the UK. The firm has represented many of its landowning clients for several generations which means that it has a unique wealth of experience in relation to the diversity of issues that are faced by farmers and landowners.

Robert moved to Withers^{LLP} in 1999 and as well as acting for domestic landowning clients, he also has a large international tax and trust practice.

Robert is a regular contributor to the weekend Financial Times and has also written articles for professional journals and the national press.

Tax Planning Through Financial Services

19

Andrew Miles
(Thomson's Wealth Management Limited)

- **Inheritance tax (IHT)**
  A brief look at some of the ways in which financial services planning strategies may be used to mitigate IHT.

- **Pension schemes**
  A look at the flexible self-investment rules, which may provide a tax efficient way of holding property and other assets within a farm or diversification venture.

- **Income and capital gains tax (CGT) mitigation**
  A look at the various tax efficient investment schemes for the potential mitigation of income and CGT. These may be particularly relevant to those considering a rural life in retirement for the first time.

Note from the Editor

19.1 This chapter explains with great clarity how looking at tax planning in the round has to incorporate consideration for financial services into the forward planning. Currently, in most cases, farming cannot generate the required income stream, and diversification projects have not yet generated income requirement. It could be that some land or property sale will take place in the near future and these funds are not going to be rolled-over and the generous business asset taper relief (BATR) used so that liquid funds can support the large land asset. This is only one example and there are many others.

This chapter looks at some of the ways in which planning strategies using financial services may be utilised and, in terms of inheritance tax planning, links very closely to Chapter 18. The emphasis is then on gifts and gift protection, which ties into other sections of the book, now dealing with making gifts and concerns over reservation of benefit and capital gains.

The chapter moves to trusts with clear links to Chapter 17 and inter-action with the whole question of gifts. This then leads to a brief expla-nation of various areas of tax planning not touched on in other chapters such as Small Self-Administered Schemes (SSASs), Self-Invested Personal Pensions (SIPPs), leading to Enterprise Investment Schemes (EIS), Venture Capital trusts (VCTs), the tax advantages of film partnerships and Enterprise Zone Trusts (EZTs). It is hoped that these provide ideas and inspiration that link in with other areas of tax plan-ning and tax protection shown throughout the book.

Introduction

19.2   Financial services can provide practical, and often innovative, solutions to help mitigate potential tax liabilities. To the frustration of many professional advisers, these solutions are often overlooked by those employed in agriculture, many of whom feel that they are of only limited relevance to them. The objective of this chapter is to demon-strate some of the opportunities worthy of consideration and how they may be best employed.

Inheritance tax (IHT)

19.3   In an age of ever increasing property values, IHT is becoming more relevant to a larger proportion of the population. Almost without exception, it is a potential problem for all farmers and landowners.

Agricultural property relief (see Chapter 13) and woodlands relief (see Chapter 6) do help to mitigate the effects of IHT; however, it should be remembered that the threshold in respect of other assets, which may potentially include diversification projects, remains relatively low with IHT chargeable at 40% on the total value of worldwide assets in excess of the nil-rate band (see Chapter 13).

This section considers in greater detail how financial services may help alleviate this situation. It may also be useful to refer to Chapters 13, 17 and 18.

IHT and pension funds

19.4 Self-administered pension funds can provide a vehicle for holding shares for the next generation where they are involved in an executive capacity in the company. This also releases cash to the present owner, paid for out of the gross profits of the company.

There are restrictions on the proportion of the pension fund that the shares may represent, and further limits on schemes effected on or after 14 March 1989. This is primarily a deferral exercise and has limited tax saving potential.

Funded unapproved retirement benefit schemes (FURBS) are free of IHT. These can offer a method of transferring cash funds out of a family business but retaining the IHT exemption.

The uses of life policies

19.5 Life assurance provides one of the most effective methods of using the limited annual IHT exemptions to create an immediate tax-free capital fund on death to provide for the tax liability. The appropriate insurance is normally a 'whole of life' policy since the main tax liability arises on death but there are different types available. (See **5.20** and **18.20**.)

Full with profits scheme

19.6 An annual bonus is added to the policy each year and this is then guaranteed. In addition, a terminal bonus is paid at the time of a claim reflecting investment performance over the policy term. This means that there is always a guaranteed level of benefit and the premium is fixed at outset.

Low or minimum cost

19.7 This is a combination of 'with profits' and decreasing term cover providing extra life cover for a given premium while still allowing the potential for a long-term growth element. It is an ideal alternative to full with profits scheme for the older estate owner where assets are largely income producing and will not necessarily increase in value by a significant amount.

Unit-linked

19.8 This combines temporary cover with an investment into a range of funds. The cost of the life cover is normally debited to the investment fund each year and this cost rises with age. The level of cover can be chosen for a given premium. If investment performance is poor, or even if there is simply a period when values do not rise, the policy can actually run out of money if the 'maximum cover' basis has been selected. The premiums are reviewed automatically on a regular basis and there are no guarantees.

Loan trusts

19.9   The scheme has the effect of freezing assets and allowing growth and income to accumulate outside the estate. There is the facility to take 'income' each year and recover capital if required in the future. It is simple and straightforward and represents an ideal IHT planning scheme for those needing to retain income and capital flexibility.

A trust is set up for the nominated beneficiaries and the settlor then makes an interest-free loan to it. The state of health or age of the settlor is not relevant. The basic principle is to freeze the value of the assets for IHT purposes, while allowing 'income' to be retained in the form of loan repayments. The repayments reduce the assessable asset or loan on a year-by-year basis with all growth accruing to the beneficiaries free of IHT. (See **CHAPTER 17**.)

EXAMPLE

Estate value			£600,000
Loan trust set up for			£100,000
Trustees repay 5% p.a. as tax-free 'income'			£5,000

Assuming investment bond increasing in value by 7% p.a. net of charges, including reinvestment of income

IHT position after	5 years	10 years	15 years
Trust value	£111,500	£127,630	£150,250
Remaining loan	£75,000	£50,000	£25,000
Balance free of IHT (trust value less loan)	£36,500	£77,630	£125,250
Tax saved at 40%	£14,600	£31,052	£50,100

Income tax position

19.10   The capital is held in the form of an insurance bond. This is essential, as otherwise income has to be distributed to beneficiaries whereas with a bond there is no income for tax purposes. Withdrawals can then be made to produce the 'income' for the settlor. High rate taxpayers currently benefit from the '5% p.a. allowance', which is exempt from the higher rate income tax for 20 years.

The above example shows how the scheme operates using investment bonds. It is not necessary to link the scheme directly to investment markets. It can be effected on a guaranteed or a deposit basis, where the return is directly linked to interest rates, or on a 'with profit' basis.

Split interest insurance plans

19.11   There are now many schemes available that are based on the principle of different interests in the same property. This is clearly defined in old estate duty cases. The Association of British Insurers (ABI) has formally cleared the position with the Capital Taxes Office (CTO) on endowment policies where the life cover can be held in trust, although the maturity value reverts to the policy owner. These schemes have all been vetted by Tax Council but are likely to be looked at closely by the CTO who, at the time of writing, are known to be reviewing some of the more aggressive arrangements.

Basis of schemes

19.12   They take different forms but all involve single premium insurance bonds. They are also available in an offshore form.

Most involve fixed-term bonds where the death and surrender benefits are held in trust and the maturity value reverts to the settlor. In these cases there is the option to extend the maturity date. Others use a combination of a fixed-term bond and a whole life policy issued in trust.

All schemes allow 'income' to be retained, either via bonds maturing on a year-by-year basis or as withdrawals from the fixed-term bond.

Inheritance tax position

19.13   The effect of all of these schemes is to create a PET at outset. On this basis, the total capital invested will drop out of the estate after seven years, based on current legislation.

The scheme providers also claim that a 'discounted value' can be applied to the gift. This is based on the value of the rights retained. This assumes normal health and if death occurs shortly after making the gift (other than by accident) we would expect the CTO to challenge the position.

They create an immediate gift while still allowing income to be retained for the future. Some arrangements can be 'unscrambled' if circumstances change in the future.

Recent Budgets have not attacked these plans, even after specifically blocking property-based schemes in the past.

Income tax position

19.14   Bonds issued in the UK are exempt from both basic rate income tax and CGT as this is paid internally by the life office at basic rate. Higher rate taxpayers will face an additional 18% (2002 rate) income tax charge on withdrawals and other encashments. The offshore versions are fully assessable to tax.

The 'dead settlor' trust loophole no longer exists for trusts where the settlor was still alive on 17 March 1998.

Gifts of assets with large capital gains

19.15   A significant problem with IHT planning is the potential CGT charge arising on a gift. The CGT charge can negate a large part of any IHT saving.

There is one form of CGT holdover relief currently available for non-qualifying assets such as quoted investments or property. This is a transfer of assets which are subject to an immediate lifetime IHT charge, ie into a discretionary settlement.

Discretionary settlements

19.16   The CGT holdover relief applies as transfers to this type of trust are chargeable. No IHT will be payable on transfers up to the nil-rate band but thereafter tax is normally payable at 20% on the excess.

Gifts which avoid reservation of benefit

19.17   Gifts are only effective for IHT if there is no benefit retained either now or in the future by the donor. This can be an inhibiting factor for IHT planning as many potential donors are concerned about the funds they should retain to cover longevity and lifetime care costs. The following sets out a course of action which enables a gift to be made with the ability to recover capital in the future.

Life interest

19.18   If a gift is made to a trust where the spouse has the life interest, ie rights to income, it is an exempt transfer. Exempt transfers are not caught by the 'reservation of benefit' rules simply due to the fact that the transfer itself will not save IHT. The effect of this exemption allows the donor and spouse to be beneficiaries.

Termination of the life interest

19.19   The settlement can include powers for the trustees to terminate the life interest at any time to convert to a discretionary trust. If this action is taken it has the effect of creating a chargeable transfer by the spouse in whom the life interest is rested. As the spouse is not the settlor the reservation of benefit rules do not apply.

Ultimate effect

19.20   Following seven years from the date that the life interest is terminated, the trust's assets are free of IHT.

The original settlor and spouse are potential beneficiaries from outset and can, therefore, recover part or all of the capital albeit at the discretion of trustees.

Furniss v Dawson ('the Ramsay Principle')

19.21   The scheme is open to attack by the Inland Revenue on the premise that the extra step (creating a life interest for the spouse at a later stage) is only added for the sole purpose of avoiding tax. The cases *Furniss v Dawson [1984] STC 153* and *Ramsay (WT) v IRC [1981] STC 174* have established a judicial anti-avoidance doctrine whereby the courts can go beyond a pre-ordained series of transactions, ignoring the normal tax consequences of each step, and look at the end result as a whole. This is of particular relevance when assets are moved but control is ultimately more or less retained in their original location but with a tax advantage.

Domicile

Going abroad

19.22   The concept of domicile is peculiar to the UK, as in most countries it simply means residence. Domicile of origin starts at birth and it is normally acquired by reference to the domicile of a person's father. It is difficult to lose one's domicile of origin and, while UK domicile of origin is retained, IHT is payable on worldwide assets regardless of where a person is resident.

For anyone seeking to avoid IHT by moving overseas, losing one's domicile of origin is all-important. In order to lose it all links with the UK have to be severed and it must be absolutely clear that the person intends to remain in the country to which he has moved for life, or at least indefinitely. Acquiring a burial plot there is a useful sign of future intentions.

Even if this action is taken, a person will still be subject to IHT on worldwide assets for three years after shedding his UK domicile.

It is also important to remove all assets from the UK. Assets situated in UK, with the exception of exempt gilt-edged stocks, remain liable to IHT. This means that a UK share portfolio, property and other investments/deposits should be held by offshore companies, trusts or within offshore insurance bonds.

It is very difficult to obtain confirmation from the Inland Revenue that a person has acquired a new domicile of choice, as opposed to one of origin. Now that the majority of lifetime gifts are PETs, no tax is payable at the date of transfer so the Inland Revenue is no longer required to give a ruling.

Non-domiciled but resident in the UK

19.23   The UK is a favoured 'tax haven' for non-UK nationals. Provided that assets are held offshore no IHT is assessable until the person has been resident for tax purposes for 17 out of the last 20 years. After that point the person is 'deemed' to be domiciled in the UK. Anyone who is considering long-term residence, or who is nearing this period of residency, should set up a discretionary trust to hold their assets and can include themselves as a beneficiary. The trust remains 'excluded property' for IHT purposes even after the deemed domicile rules apply, and even if the trust is UK resident, to the extent that the trust assets are situated abroad.

Non-domiciled spouses

19.24   It should also be noted that the full exemption from IHT between spouses only applies when the beneficiary is domiciled in the UK. Where a UK-domiciled spouse leaves assets to a non-UK domiciled spouse the exemption is limited to the first £55,000 of assets. This is in addition to the IHT nil-rate band.

Property purchase via pension schemes

19.25   Many farmers and landowners do not take full advantage of pension planning provisions, choosing not to 'retire' in the traditional sense but to continue to work and draw an income. In the twenty-first century, as pension provision becomes ever more complex, those ignoring pension planning run the risk of missing out on some valuable and effective tax allowances and solutions.

Small self-administered schemes (SSASs)

19.26   A small self-administered scheme, or SSAS, is a type of occupational pension scheme aimed at shareholding directors of limited companies. These schemes offer a greater degree of control of investments and the opportunity to utilise the pension fund within the business itself.

Contributions to occupational pension schemes by both employers and members attract tax relief and funds within a scheme grow without liability to UK tax on either income or capital gains. Employer contributions on behalf of a member are not regarded as benefits in kind and there is no National Insurance liability.

A SSAS is defined as an occupational pension scheme that meets the following conditions:

- fewer than 12 members;
- at least one of the members must be connected with another member, a trustee or the employer;
- a proportion of the scheme's assets must be invested other than in insured products (eg unit trusts, stocks and shares, property);
- one of the trustees is a pensioneer trustee.

The pensioneer trustee is usually appointed by the company which is chosen to operate the scheme and must be a party to all scheme bank accounts and transactions. A scheme may be set up for one member but more usually is established for shareholding directors and their families.

SSAS investments

19.27   SSAS schemes may invest in a wide range of investments, such as:

- Quoted stocks and shares
- Unit trusts/Open-ended investment companies (OEICs)

- Insurance policies
- Deposits (bank or building society)
- Property
- Self-investment*

(* Self-investment is a general term used to describe a loan by the trustees to the employer participating in the scheme, or the purchase of the employer's premises by the trustees (the premises are then leased to the employer at a commercial rent).)

The main specific restrictions on investments are as follows.

- The scheme trustees cannot directly or indirectly buy, sell or lease investments to or from a member of the scheme including any individual, partnership or company that is connected with a scheme member.
- Investment in 'pride in possession' assets are not allowed, eg jewellery, classic cars, art.
- The scheme cannot purchase assets that have been owned by a scheme member or connected person within the previous three years. Employers that participate in a scheme are not connected parties for this purpose.

Loans to the employer are allowable and must be for a specific purpose, eg the purchase of additional stock. 'Cashflow' is not deemed an acceptable purchase. There is no set term for the loan, which must be constructed at a market rate, the rule being that the term should generally match the purpose of the loan. Thus, a one-year term may be suitable for the purchase of equipment whilst a loan to purchase land could be structured over five or ten years.

Property investments are restricted to commercial property, with a few exceptions such as a shop with a flat above. Investment in farmland or forestry land is acceptable; however, care must be taken as the restrictions on investing in residential property will usually disqualify property which includes a farmhouse. The Inland Revenue will usually expect there to be no amenity rights, such as hunting or fishing rights, attached to the land from which the scheme member could benefit.

In principle, the Inland Revenue will allow the purchase of premises (for example, for riding stables, a golf course, a corporate event site or a paintball centre) again providing there is no residential element in the purchase. The Inland Revenue is, however, concerned that members may benefit from these facilities and will judge each case on its merits.

The pension scheme may make purchases jointly with the employer, another pension scheme or a third party. The scheme trustees may borrow money, subject to a limit of three times the ordinary annual pension scheme contribution plus 45% of the scheme assets. More restrictive measures exist for schemes which have been in existence less than three years. The trustees usually borrow from a commercial source such as a bank or building society. Borrowing from other sources is permitted provided the borrowing is on commercial terms.

A pension scheme may also purchase shares in the employer's company, whether listed or not. In practice, the restriction on the purchase and sale of scheme assets to connected parties greatly restricts these investments.

Self-invested personal pensions (SIPPs)

19.28   Self-invested personal pensions (SIPPs) were introduced in 1989 to widen the flexibility and appeal of personal pension provision. SIPPs are written under personal pension legislation and are subject to most of the same limits and controls.

Contributions attract income tax relief at the marginal rate and accrue in a favourable tax environment. Under current legislation, benefits can be taken from age 50 and up to 25% of the fund may be paid out as a tax-free cash lump sum.

There are many ways in which benefits may be taken at retirement, indeed it is not even necessary to actually retire in order to take benefits.

SIPPs work in exactly the same way as normal personal pension plans (PPPs). Regular or single personal contributions can be made as well as employer contributions or pension transfers (including from retirement annuities). Contributions, excluding transfers, must not exceed the relevant percentage of net relevant earnings in any one tax year, as follows:

Age attained *(as at 6 April 2002)*	*Maximum contribution* *as a percentage* *of earnings*
35 or less	17.5%
36 to 45	20%
46 to 50	25%
51 to 55	30%
56 to 60	35%
61 to 75	40%

The pension funds themselves are invested in accordance with the member's specific instructions into allowable investments and not restricted to those provided by any single insurance company or investment house.

Under current legislation, the member can take the benefits at any age between 50 and 75. The SIPP offers the facilities of 'phased' retirement by means of multiple policies, and 'pension fund income withdrawal'.

SIPP investments

19.29 *Joint Office Memorandum* (JOM) 101, issued in October 1989, provided the basic rules for allowable investments. The list has since been kept under review and was updated by the Personal Pension Schemes (Restriction on discretion to approve) (Permitted Investments) Regulations 2001 (SI 2001/117). Allowable investments currently include:

- stocks and shares quoted on the UK Stock Exchange (including securities traded on the unlisted securities market);
- stocks and shares traded on a recognised overseas stock exchange;
- unit trusts and investment trusts;
- insurance company-managed funds and unit-linked funds;
- deposit accounts;
- property.

As with a SSAS, property investments are limited to freehold or leasehold commercial property where the interest is not acquired from a connected person. The SIPP may lease a property to the employer but it is important to note that unlike a SSAS, a SIPP may not purchase a property from the scheme member's business. Similarly, it is not possible for a SIPP to make loans to the employer.

The borrowing restrictions for a SIPP are more relaxed than that of a SSAS. Borrowings, in relation to the purchase of a freehold or leasehold commercial property or towards the development of such property, are limited to 75% of the purchase price and must be secured upon that property.

The installation of a SIPP is also simpler, lacking the individual approval from the Inland Revenue that is required for a SSAS; thus, scheme costs are usually less expensive.

In conclusion, property purchase via a pension scheme can release valuable cash into the balance sheet making development capital available for the business. In the case of a SSAS this may be made available directly. There is no loss of control over the property asset, which is simply transferred into the pension fund for the future benefit of the owner/managers. The pension fund benefits from both future capital appreciation on the value of the property and current rental income as well as being an acknowledged 'safe haven' investment strategy. By structuring the scheme in this way, the expenses to the tax-exempt pension scheme are reduced as the company can pay the management fees for the future pension administration.

Income and capital gains tax mitigation

19.30 Over time, successive governments have introduced a number of tax breaks to stimulate investment in certain sectors, such as the British film industry and smaller entrepreneurial companies. Many of these tax breaks allow income tax and CGT to be deferred or mitigated to make investment more attractive.

Advanced tax planning of this nature can be complex as there are many factors that require consideration, but these strategies are not necessarily speculative and can cater for a wide range of attitudes to risk.

This section considers the types of scheme that are available and the specific tax reliefs applicable.

Enterprise investment schemes (EISs)

19.31 Enterprise investment schemes (EISs) were introduced by Finance Act 1994 as the successor to the business expansion scheme. The rules were amended with effect from April 1998, to harmonise the EIS and reinvestment relief scheme rules.

There are four potential elements of EIS relief.

1 Qualifying individuals can invest up to £150,000 in qualifying EIS shares in any tax year and obtain up to £30,000 income tax relief (whilst the lower rate of tax is 20%).
2 Investors can defer unlimited amounts of capital gain (only £150,000 of investment in any tax year will attract income tax relief and CGT exemption on growth). Subscriptions must be made within one year before or three years after the date of the disposal that gives rise to the gain or the date when a previously deferred gain crystallises.
3 Unlimited exemption from IHT via business property relief (BPR) if shares are held for two years.
4 Provided the investor holds the shares for at least three years and the company continues to qualify, the capital growth on the first £150,000 of any investment will be free of CGT.

The maximum tax relief/deferral available for an investor who subscribes up to £150,000 for EIS shares is 60% of the cost of the investment (20% income tax relief and 40% CGT relief). A husband and wife are each entitled to a separate £150,000 annual limit for income tax purposes.

A choice of qualifying EIS companies is usually available for investment throughout the year. The reliefs only apply when the investor subscribes for newly issued shares in a qualifying company. To qualify the company must be unquoted (although listing on Alternative Investments Market (AIM) is acceptable) at outset, carrying on a trade in the UK which is not, in broad terms, a financial or professional activity. If the company becomes fully quoted, the two-year IHT exemption may be lost.

The maximum that a company can raise under the scheme is £15 million. 'Arranged exits' are precluded although the company may make a declaration of intent to seek a means of enabling shareholders to realise their investments after, say, five years. There is no restriction on the company owning land.

A provisional confirmation that the company will qualify is normally obtained in advance. The certificate confirming this can only be issued after the company has traded for four months.

Investors may not be 'connected with' the company, eg an employee, an owner of 30% or more of the shares or in a position to control it either directly or indirectly.

Discretionary portfolio services invest in a series of qualifying EIS investments as and when they become available. Tax relief is not provided at outset but on an investment by investment basis as subscribed by the portfolio manager.

The relief is effectively only given in situations where there is sufficient risk involved and evaluation of this against the commercial prospects of the business is both difficult and essential. There are, however, some situations where the level of risk is significantly moderated, perhaps where a large part of the company's capital is held in tangible realisable assets such as land. The prospective value of such assets in the future cannot be ascertained, of course, but their existence in the balance sheet is some comfort.

Unquoted company shares are difficult to value and difficult to sell so the possibility of being locked into the investment beyond the initial three-year period must be considered: a longer-term view needs to be taken. (See **20.28**.)

Venture capital trusts (VCTs)

19.32   Venture capital trusts (VCTs) are quoted investment trusts investing in small companies and business start-ups. They were introduced in the 1993 Budget as a means of boosting new investment in industry generally and small companies in particular.

The total investment on which individuals, aged 18 or over, can claim tax relief is £100,000 in any one tax year.

New shares subscriptions benefit from:

- 20% income tax relief;
- tax-free dividends;
- tax-free capital distributions;
- 'reinvestment relief' is available for any capital gain reinvested. Only the taxable profit need be invested in the VCT; the base cost is free to be invested elsewhere.

VCT shares benefit from tax-free dividends and capital gains irrespective of the period of ownership and are CGT-free on disposal although they do not qualify for IHT relief.

At least 70% of the trust must be invested in 'qualifying' companies, which must not have gross assets in excess of £15 million each at the time of the investment. The investment must be made within three years. The maximum investment is £1 million p.a. in any one company, and the manager may invest an overall maximum of 15% of the VCT in any one company. 30% of the VCT must be invested in ordinary shares of the company.

The balance of the trust (up to 30% of total assets) can be invested at the discretion of the managers in ordinary quoted shares, gilt-edged stocks, deposits, unit trusts etc.

VCTs are quoted from outset on the London Stock Exchange so can be bought and sold at any time. It is unlikely that there will be many private sellers in the first three years (five years for shares issued prior to 6 April 2000) due to the loss of the tax relief on sale within that period.

Unlike most other tax shelters VCTs offer some benefits to subsequent investors, both private and institutional, due to continuing tax exemptions on dividends and gains but without the tax advantages at the time of investment.

These schemes should be considered by investors with realised taxable capital gains. An investor might also be one who is looking to diversify an existing investment portfolio and in particular to reduce a substantial holding in one stock where there is a large in-built capital gain, perhaps to assist in estate planning. Investors should be prepared to accept a capital risk, though this is balanced by the quoted equity/fixed-interest exposure.

Alternative Investment Market VCTs

19.33 By their nature, VCTs invest in smaller developing companies. The investment objective of some VCTs is to invest largely in the shares of companies quoted on the Alternative Investment Market (AIM) of the London Stock Exchange.

From an investor's viewpoint, this can have some advantages.

- There will usually have been 'due diligence' carried out on the company.
- Investors and managers can follow the value of AIM companies on a day-to-day basis as prices are quoted in the press.
- The fact that shares are traded on AIM provides increased liquidity when compared to private companies.

As VCTs are a relatively recent initiative there is only a limited amount of information available regarding past performance. In the main, performance has been encouraging, particularly for generalist and AIM VCTs.

VCT/EIS COMPARISON

Tax reliefs	VCT	EIS
20% income tax relief up to	£100,000	£150,000
Capital gains deferral limit	£100,000	Unlimited
Taper relief	n/a	Investments over £150,000
Capital gains exemption	Yes	3 years for EIS proportion to £150,000 limit
Dividends	Tax-free	Taxable (if any)
Offset of capital losses	No	Yes
Time limit (CGT deferral)	1 year before and 1 year after crystallising gain	1 year before and 3 years after crystallising gain
IHT benefits	None	100% BPR after 2 years
Minimum holding period for income tax and CGT reliefs	3 years	3 years

INVESTMENTS

Maximum holding	49%	100%
Maximum investment	£1 million	n/a
Maximum gross assets (pre/post) investment	£15 million/ £16 million	£15 million/ £16 million
Minimum holding period	n/a	3 years
Overriding test	70% qualifying after 3 years	none

Film partnerships

19.34   The larger proportion of film investment opportunities utilise the film 'sale and leaseback' structure, typically arranged over 15 years. These schemes are designed to take advantage of the 100% write off for UK film production or acquisition cost announced in the 1997 Budget. The schemes are constructed so that the principal return to investors is unaffected even if the film fails completely.

Due to the generous tax reliefs available, this market is extremely competitive and accessibility is restricted as there are only a finite number of UK-certified films made available each year, as defined in the Films Act 1985.

The mechanics are that the partnership purchases a number of qualifying films, creating a trading loss which enables the tax relief to be reclaimed by the partners.

Immediately after the partnership has acquired a film, it is leased back to the original vendor for a term of at least 15 years. A financial institution, normally the vendor's own bank, must provide security for the amount of the minimum rentals for the term of the lease.

Each partner makes an initial cash contribution, with the balance of the investment funded by a loan from the partnerships bank. The cash contribution required from investors on partnerships that are currently available is in the region of 18%, with the balance of 82% provided by way of a loan.

The interest on the loan is met from the rentals paid by the original vendors, with the loan repaid over a 15-year period. The rental income will exceed the amount of interest due on the loan, which results in taxable income for the investor. It is important to note that the investor will have a tax liability even though he will not be receiving any surplus income, as the income is used to repay the original loan. Effectively, the tax relief that the investor has had at outset is repaid over a 15-year period as a result of the rental income exceeding the loan interest.

The attraction of the scheme is the income tax offset in the first year, and as the rental income is secured by the original vendor's bank, the commercial success or failure of the film is irrelevant.

The Inland Revenue is in effect providing the investor with a loan for the amount of the tax relief at a competitive, fixed-rate of interest.

The investor needs to earn a rate of return on the tax relief that has been obtained in order to make the exercise worthwhile. This breakeven rate of return is known as the 'hurdle rate', and on currently available partnerships is in the region of 4.4% p.a.

Approximately 95% of the capital contribution should qualify for immediate UK tax relief whereby any trading loss arising in the tax year of acquisition may be:

- offset against total income in the current or previous tax year;
- offset against total income going back up to three years (taking the earlier year first);
- offset against capital gains both in the current and previous tax years if all taxable income in the year of investment has been sheltered.

These schemes impact 'net relevant earnings' and may affect tax reliefs obtained on other investment contracts such as personal pension plans, venture capital trusts and enterprise investment schemes.

The use of different partnerships to target discreet amounts of income in separate tax years should be considered.

It is important to note that these plans are tax deferral schemes, and that the tax relief obtained at outset will gradually be repaid over the 15-year period.

Extra caution is needed where venture capital trust, enterprise investment scheme or personal pension contributions have been made. In these circumstances, these schemes may only be appropriate for individuals whose capital gain is so large in relation to these items that the loss of relief on them is minimal.

Enterprise zone trusts (EZTs)

19.35 Enterprise zones are specially designated areas of the UK which have been granted special status for a period of ten years during which they may qualify from government and local authority aid. The last enterprise zone was created in October 1996. The key concession amongst these is tax relief on the cost of constructing any building erected in these areas.

EZTs are the generic name given to property investments within an enterprise zone. Enterprise zone property unit trusts themselves are now rare, if available at all, however, the acronym EZT is still used to describe enterprise zone investments which may be made either individually or as a member of a syndicate.

Investors may offset 100% of their investment against income tax at their highest rate as new enterprise zone properties benefit from industrial buildings allowances. There is no upper limit on the amount which may be invested.

Tax relief is not granted against the cost of land and other purchase expenses and typically between 15% and 25% of EZT investments are not allowable to income tax relief.

Once let, rental income from the property may be offset against interest from bank loans and schemes therefore utilise bank borrowings to fund the majority of the investment. With tax relief and bank borrowings to fund property development and rental income offset against bank interest, the investment should not necessitate any further capital outlay and may produce a small surplus for the investor.

EXAMPLE

Total gross investment	£100,000
Funded by:	
Bank loan	£65,000
Cash investment	£35,000
Tax relief (assuming 85% allowable)	£34,000
Net investment	£66,000
	£100,000
Rental income (7% net yield)	£7,000 p.a.
Bank interest (8.50% interest rate)	£5,525 p.a.
Surplus taxable income	£1,475 p.a.

The above figures are shown for illustrative purposes only, bank charges and other sundry expenses are not taken into account.

Tax relief may be 'clawed back' on disposal by way of a balancing payment. However, if the property is held for more than seven years and a lesser interest is granted, for example, a 998-year leasehold from a freehold, no balancing charge is made. Any gain is chargeable to CGT on the gross investment.

Properties are usually either pre-let or rental guarantees are provided by the developer.

The income stream, and to a certain extent the success of the scheme itself, is therefore reliant on the financial strength of the tenant or developer or the financial guarantees arranged by the developer.

These schemes must be regarded as long-term property investments where ultimately the success of the investment depends upon the sponsor attracting a tenant of acceptable quality and the ability to sell the property to another institution in order to secure an exit route for the investor. Property values may fluctuate and the location, quality of building and general prospects for the area are important considerations.

EZT property values are subject to price distortions in recognition of the tax breaks available to new enterprise zone properties as opposed to properties that do not carry similar benefits.

Important notes

It should be stressed that it is necessary to obtain specific advice with full background information. Levels, bases of and reliefs from taxation are subject to change.

Andrew Miles

Andrew Miles has over 12 years' experience in financial services and is a holder of the Chartered Insurance Institute's Advanced Financial Planning Certificate. Andrew is Head of Research for Thomson's Wealth Management Limited – a leading Independent Financial Adviser with over 20 offices in the UK. Thomson's is regulated by the Financial Services Authority and is a member of the AWD Group, one of Europe's foremost financial services organisations.

Independence is central to the philosophy of Thomson's and AWD, whose business is not a matter of placing products with individuals, but of developing tailored financial concepts on their behalf. For further information visit www.thomsons.com.

Miscellaneous — Sundry Tax Planning Points

20

Julie Butler

- **Tax benefits**
  The tax benefits available for farming and alternative land usage are extensive. This chapter aims to highlight different areas such as stud farms, land drainage, orchards, reclaimed scrubland etc, and hopes to point the tax practitioner in the right direction.

- **Land complexity**
  The traditional and alternative usage of land can present complex tax alternatives. This is set out in the complexities of mineral royalties, gravel extraction and contaminated land together with the 'hidden taxes' of aggregates levy and landfill tax.

- **Reluctant farmer — specialist advice**
  There are a large number of potential reluctant farmers and practitioners who are being forced into having to understand the complexity of the tax reliefs. If in doubt, contact a specialist.

- **Enterprise Investment Scheme (EIS)**
  The need to redefine farming.

Farmers' averaging

20.1 This book does not have the scope to deal with the full detail of averaging – these can be found in the Inspector's Manual (at

IM2321a–IM2332d). Averaging is also dealt with in great detail in Stanley's *Taxation of Farmers and Landowners* (LexisNexis Butterworths Tolley).

In simple terms, the position is set out in the Inspector's Manual at IM2325 and IM2322b as follows:

> 'Where the difference between the profits of two consecutive years of assessment is 30% more than the higher of the two figures of profit (and regardless of whether the difference is a rise or a fall), the profits of the two years may be averaged. The sum of the two profit figures is simply divided by two and the resulting figure becomes the chargeable profits for each of the two years of assessment.'

An averaging claim can cover any two consecutive years of assessment during which the claimant was carrying on a trade of farming or market gardening, except:

- a year of assessment that precedes a year which has already been included in an averaging claim;
- the year of assessment in which the trade commenced;
- the year of assessment in which the trade ceased;
- a year of assessment in which the trade is treated as having been discontinued and recommenced under Income and Corporation Taxes Act 1988 (ICTA 1988) s 113(1).

The key points for the tax planner are the effective use of this advantage for maximum utilisation of personal allowances and lower bands for tax together with the careful use of losses. CHAPTER **12** looks at losses, averaging and the need to check the tax computation.

Losses

20.2 A trading loss is treated as a nil profit for averaging purposes. This enables the loss relief to be claimed under the normal rules without the measure of the loss available for relief being affected by averaging.

Stud farms

20.3 It would be impossible to look at diversification without considering the tax planning angles of stud farms and racing. The position concerning stock valuation and losses has already been considered (see **8.7** and **12.8**).

The Inspector's Manual at IM2350b sets the overview as follows:

'Stud farming, which in these paragraphs is taken to mean the occupation of land for the purpose of breeding thoroughbred horses, is a very expensive and high-risk activity. In some cases it may be carried on by wealthy individuals essentially as an adjunct to their racing activities. Nevertheless, for tax purposes it is treated as farming and thus – by virtue of ICTA 1988 s 53(1) – as the carrying on of a trade regardless of its commercial viability.'

Horseracing, however, is not a taxable activity. Where, as is often the case, a stud farmer also races horses, considerable care may therefore be needed to ensure that the division between the two activities has been correctly made. In particular, attention should be given to any transfers of animals from the stud farm to training (that is, being kept for the purpose of racing) or vice versa. For the VAT position for racehorse owners see **9.9**.

If a breeder transfers an animal to training and it is then returned to stud at a higher value after a successful racing career then the uplift in the market value whilst it was in training is tax-free. Furthermore, the value at which the animal is returned to stud is relieved over the rest of its life. The valuations of animals at the dates of transfer to or from training are, therefore, significant.

It is essential to see the difference between racing and stud farms. The racing adjustment is fairly complex from the angle of accounting and tax treatment. The tax planning point that a racehorse returning to stud with an uplifted value is tax-free is of importance. The other side of the tax angle is that the drop in value does not attract tax relief. The Inspector's Manual at IM2350e sets out the tax treatment.

If the occupier of a stud farm races animals bred by him:

- the stud farm accounts should be credited when animals are transferred to training with the then market value of the transferred animals, as if they had been sold at that value (*Sharkey v Wernher (1955) 36 TC 275*);
- when animals return to the stud farm after racing, the stud farm accounts should be debited with their market value, at the time of return, as if they had then been purchased at that value;
- if an animal purchased and not bred on the stud farm is brought into the stud after racing by the occupier, the stud farm accounts should similarly be debited with the then market value of the animal as if it had then been purchased at that value.

The same tax treatment should be applied to a person who is assessable under Schedule D on the profits of dealing in thoroughbred animals but which business is carried out on a stud farm occupied by some other person.

A form of income can be stallion syndicates. The tax position on the sale of the share in a stallion together with the sales of nominations must be considered. Since the cost of buying a successful stallion outright is prohibitive for some bloodstock breeders, ownership may be shared in a syndicate. The usual form of syndication is into forty equal shares, representing the number of mares which, traditionally, was regarded as the standard for a stallion to cover in one season. Each syndicate member contributes towards the costs of keeping the stallion and is entitled to one 'nomination' each season per share owned. The member may use the nomination to cover one of his or her own mares, or it may be sold on the open market. The shareholders appoint a committee who deal with the day-to-day management of the stallion.

Where the occupier of a stud farm owns a share in a stallion for the purpose of obtaining services for his or her own mares, the tax treatment will depend on whether he or she has made an election for the herd basis. The proceeds of any sales of nominations are treated as trading receipts. Any contribution by the stud farmer towards syndicate expenses will be an allowable trading expense.

However, in the following situations the sales of nomination are assessable under Schedule D Case VI:

- the owner of the stallion share is not carrying on a trade of stud farming or horse breeding; or
- the owner is carrying on such a trade but does not use the stallion share for the purpose of obtaining service for his own mares.

The situation on losses in stud farming is dealt with in **12.8**.

Land drainage expenditure

20.4 With the move towards diversification the consideration on the tax planning angles on land drainage is important. There are clear opportunities to claim the expenditure as revenue but there are parts where it should be treated as capital. This can be used to careful tax planning advantage.

Inspector's Manual at IM2280b sets out the position:

> 'Land which in the past was reasonably well drained but subsequently becomes wholly or partly waterlogged because the maintenance of efficient drainage was uneconomic is sometimes made available for cultivation by the restoration of drainage or by re-draining. In such cases so much of the net expenditure incurred (after crediting any grants receivable) as restores the

drainage to its effective state may be admitted as revenue expenditure in farm accounts. This excludes:

- any substantial element of improvement – for example, the substitution of tile drainage for mole drainage; and
- the capital element in cases in which the present owner is known to have acquired the land at a depressed price because of its swampy condition.'

Orchards

20.5 The move towards fruit farming cannot be overlooked. Therefore, the tax planning position on orchards should be considered. This is set out in the Inspector's Manual at IM2281 as follows:

'The initial expenditure incurred by a fruit farmer on the planting, staking etc of a new orchard is disallowable as representing capital expenditure (see *IRC v Pilcher (1949), 31 TC 314*). After the trees have been planted, all subsequent expenditure on cultivations etc is allowable in full as a revenue charge (see *Vallambrosa Rubber Co Ltd v Farmer (1910) 5 TC 529*).'

The expenditure incurred by a fruit farmer on the grubbing up of an old orchard and the subsequent planting of new fruit trees (whether or not of the same kind) is normally allowable as a revenue deduction on a 'renewals' basis, provided that the replanting takes place within a reasonable time after the old orchard is grubbed.

Again, care in the identification (and justification) of revenue as opposed to capital expense is important.

Cost of reclaiming scrubland formerly under cultivation

20.6 The focus on diversification and maximising the utilisation of the land will make some entrepreneurs look to the possibility of buying scrubland and converting it into cultivation.

The Inspector's Manual at IM2280a sets this out as follows:

'Where land, which was under cultivation within a reasonable period in the past has been allowed to relapse into a wild state, the net expenditure incurred on cleaning it for cultivation may normally be treated as revenue expenditure in computing profits for taxation purposes. However, where the present owner is known to have acquired land at a depressed price because of its uncultivated condition, the capital element of the expenditure should be disallowed.'

The entrepreneur landowner must be careful to see how the expenditure can be used most tax efficiently.

Mineral royalties

The royalties generally

20.7 Mineral royalties receivable by persons resident or ordinarily resident in the UK are divided in equal capital and income parts under ICTA 1988 s 122. Previously they were taxed as to 100% income. The income half is taxed to income tax and corporation tax whilst the capital part is subject to CGT (or as a chargeable gain for corporation tax.) It is considered that the gain does not qualify for BATR. Management expenses are only allowed against the income half. Generally, the whole of the mineral royalty (ie the income half and the capital half) is received with deduction of tax.

To qualify for the treatment mentioned above, the royalties must relate to the 'winning' and 'working' of minerals. 'Winning' means to get at the minerals. 'Working' means getting them out of the ground. The mineral royalties must also be received under an agreement under which minerals are being, or are to be, worked in the UK.

The repayment of income tax can be calculated after calculating both the income tax liability (after deducting half the total management expenses) and the CGT liability. The income tax deducted is first set against the income tax liability and then the CGT liability.

Yet again, this shows the harsh and complex tax treatment of alternative land usage.

The next section shows tax planning alternatives. Where mineral royalties relate to other matters than winning and working minerals there can be apportionment provisions. Examples of these matters are exploration as opposed to exploitation, rent and outright sale.

Where 90% or more of the royalties qualify no apportionment needs to be made. Generally, the Inland Revenue will accept a reasonable apportionment suggested by the taxpayer.

Gravel extraction tax planning

20.8 Not everyone may be aware of the taxation of mineral royalties which is still half income tax and half capital gains tax (CGT). Mineral royalties are not eligible for taper relief, which is significant from 6 April 2002 when full taper relief became available. The review of the taxation of mineral royalties has become even more relevant with the introduction of aggregates levy from 1 April 2002.

One of the most common commercial minerals is gravel, and there are a number of ways of trying to have the extraction taxed as efficiently as possible. The article 'Mineral Royalties' published in *Taxation* (9 May 2002) discusses the merits of gravel extraction planning.

Outright sale

20.9   One could sell the land containing the pit. It is to be hoped that this has the advantage of CGT classification with all the business relief associated therewith, such as rollover relief, business asset taper and indexation up to 5 April 1998. This assumes that business status can be shown, ie farmed in hand. The disadvantage is that many landowners do not want to lose ownership, and this leads to the next point.

Buyback option

20.10   One could sell the land containing the pit with an option to buy back the land afterwards. The sale of a gravel pit with the option to buy it back after exhaustion means that the extracted proceeds will be liable to income tax [ICTA 1988 s 36]. This forgoes any advantage of CGT relief.

Sale of gravel

20.11   Capital tranches of gravel may be sold without selling the land itself. The problem is that the Inland Revenue claims that unless the surface is sold, the tranche of gravel will not be a business asset for taper relief purposes.

The Treasury route

20.12   The Treasury route is a well-tried method where the landowner sells a capital tranche of gravel with a licence for the aggregates company to enter the land for purposes of extraction. The key is to establish a capital gain in-house; for instance, put the land into settlement or gift it to a member of the family. This should result in 10% CGT (assuming full taper relief is available), which is funded out of the first tranche sale to the aggregates company. If the calculation is correct, there should be no further tax. It is a good idea to put a restrictive covenant on the number of cubic metres. The downside is that for the aggregates company, under Capital Allowances Act 2001 (CAA 2001) s 418 capital tranches are subject to capital allowances at only 10% a year. However, when the tranche is exhausted, the company is entitled to claim a balancing allowance for the balance amount spent (s 428), ie the aggregates company will not receive 100% relief until the end of the tranche.

Contaminated land — the tax relief

20.13   It would be impossible for a book that attempts to cover tax planning for land put to an alternative use not to look at the tax planning for the remediation of contaminated land.

Contaminated land features in Tony Jenkinson's article in *Taxation* (21 February 2002) and follows on from Allison Plager's article 'Where there's muck there's brass' in an earlier edition of the journal (11 October 2001). The question has to be gaining maximum available tax relief for expenditure incurred on or after 11 May 2001.

In Callum Macfarlane's letter to *Taxation* on 7 March 2002 he confirmed that the relief is not confined to capital expenditure, it also covers revenue expenditure. This will be great news for dealers and developers acquiring the land with a view to sell. The important point is that the relief only applies to *companies*. Purchase through a company may have to be considered by landowners and tax planners alike for maximum tax efficiency.

Land is contaminated if it has substance in, on or under it which causes or might cause harm, or if there is a danger of pollution in controlled waters. Nuclear sites are not included. Substance is defined as 'any natural or artificial substance, whether in solid or liquid form or in the form of a gas or vapour'. Harm is defined as 'harm to the health of living organisms, interference with the ecological systems of which any living organisms form part, offence to the sense of human beings, or damage to property'. Finally, 'pollution in controlled waters' means 'the entry into controlled waters of any poisonous, noxious or polluting matter and/or solid waste matter.

The definitions of 'substance' and 'harm' in para 31 seem generously wide, and encompass the great majority of situations which common sense would describe as 'contaminated land'. Nonetheless, it remains necessary to identify the substance (which may be natural or artificial, solid, liquid, gas or vapour) which causes the harm. There are some grey areas. For example, would harmful plants such as knotweed, or animal life such as termites, count as substances? Some Inland Revenue clarification on such matters would be helpful.

Before any relief is given, the claimant must also satisfy the Inland Revenue authorities that the expenditure must have been incurred on employee and material costs, or on a qualified contractor.

Simple planning points are that the relief is not available to anyone who contributed to the contamination and that a company must be found to buy it. It will be important to identify the harmful substance and quantify the expenditure immediately.

There is great scope for farmers and landowners to buy and sell contaminated land now as the tax relief might be reflected in the sale price. However, the contract for sale must be carefully reviewed; if the vendor provides a warranty or indemnity concerning the land and has to meet remediation costs, then this will disqualify the eligibility of the tax relief.

A company can elect for capital expenditure incurred on remediation of contaminated land, acquired for use in its trade or Schedule A business, to be allowed as a deduction in computing the profits of that trade. So, even if all the relevant costs represent capital expenditure, they will be allowed against profits. Land remediation relief of 150% of qualifying revenue expenditure on remediation of contaminated land acquired for a Schedule A business or trade has been introduced.

Capital expenditure will, therefore, qualify for 150% relief immediately. Revenue expenditure by a dealer/developer will, however, probably form part of the company's trading stock. It only becomes (wholly or partly) deductible when the land in question is either sold or, if a loss is anticipated, written down to net realisable value: in either case, this will often be in a later period. The extra 50% relief is therefore deferred.

Companies are entitled to the relief if the following conditions are satisfied:

- the land must be in the UK, and have been acquired for the purposes of a trade or Schedule A business carried on by a company;
- at the time of the acquisition, all or part of the land must have been contaminated; and
- the expenditure incurred by the company must be capital expenditure on qualifying land remediation.

The deduction will be allowed in the accounting period in which the expenditure was made, and is available for expenditure incurred from 11 May 2001. It is not retrospective, nor can it be given on expenditure subject to a capital allowance claim.

'Unrelieved' losses arising from land remediation relief are permitted to be turned into cash payment by the Inland Revenue. It is assumed that losses will be offset against profits of the same company for the same year for this purpose, but broadly there remains a choice for existing losses between, on the one hand, claims to carry these back to the preceding year, surrender them as a group relief, or carry them forward, and on the other hand, taking the money. The cash option should not be taken without careful consideration. The cash payment is 16% of the unrelieved loss, that is (with the 50% 'bonus') 24% of the qualifying remediation expenditure. If, however, the losses are carried back, group relieved, or carried forward, then the effective relief (again the 50% bonus) will be 45% of the expenditure assuming the current full corporation tax rate, or 30% at small companies rate. In many cases, it will be better to wait for taxable profits rather than cashing in the losses.

In order to obtain the deduction, an election must be made in writing to the Inland Revenue within two years following the end of the relevant accounting period.

The legislation prevents the deduction where expenditure is 'wholly or partly as a result of anything done or omitted to be done at any time by the company or a person with a relevant connection to the company'. So, in effect, a company cannot get a reduction for clearing up its own mess.

Some property companies may have the in-house expertise to undertake remediation work, and there may be strong commercial reasons for retaining such work. The advantages of using an unconnected subcontractor should not, however, be overlooked.

Where the work is undertaken by the company itself, relief is restricted to the costs of employees and materials (which excludes items qualifying for capital allowances). It is therefore necessary to track how much of each director's and employee's working time is devoted to such work, and to apportion the wage costs. Support staff costs cannot be included. It is similarly necessary to track materials used. There is therefore a considerable record-keeping headache. Using a connected subcontractor involves similar restrictions, but may reduce the tracking problem if a group company is dedicated to remediation work.

On the other hand, if an unconnected subcontractor is used, the whole payment for qualifying remediation work is allowed. In effect, all the subcontractor's employee and material costs, plus, for example, its support and administrative overheads, plant and transport costs, will qualify, as will its profit margin. This broader base for 150% tax relief for the owner will often make contracting out more cost effective, and save a mountain of paperwork.

Property development groups should consider whether land requiring remediation work should be acquired by a property investment company within the group rather than a dealer. It is a matter of fact and case law whether an acquisition is on revenue or capital account but, in marginal situations, perhaps where no firm decision has been made on whether the land will be retained, the use of an investment company is likely to accelerate the relief. The remediated land can be transferred to a trading company later if appropriate.

Since the relief is not available to anyone who has contributed to the contamination, either by action or inaction, the vendor may well not qualify. In some cases purchasers will not take the commercial risk of acquiring contaminated land. Where possible, however, the purchaser should undertake the remediation, presumably with the additional cost reflected in the price for the land. (No doubt the vendor will wish the price also to reflect some of the additional tax relief that the purchaser will receive.)

Care is needed when wording the contract. Relief for expenditure which is 'met directly or indirectly by any person other than the company' is precluded. This could presumably apply if the purchase price is shown to be specifically discounted for remediation costs. It is preferable simply to state the price for the land (which inevitably reflects its contaminated state). Similarly, if the vendor provides a warranty or indemnity concerning the land, and subsequently has to meet remediation costs, this will fall foul of the rule in para 8.

The relief applies when a company acquires contaminated land. It does not apply if a group acquires the shares of the company holding the contaminated land, assuming that company was wholly or partly responsible for the contamination. It will not help to transfer the land to another group company before the remediation work is undertaken in view of the definition of 'relevant connection'. This is based on the normal connected persons rule, and connection between the claimant and the 'polluter' at any one of three possible times will be enough to deny relief. The three times are:

1   at the time of any action or omission, which has wholly or partly resulted in contamination;
2   when the land was acquired by the claimant; or
3   when the remediation is undertaken.

The label of 150% relief on qualifying expenditure is very attractive but any areas of associated tax planning should be thoroughly researched.

Aggregates levy

20.14   Aggregates levy cannot be ignored by the landowner, the farmer or the tax planner – any extraction of an aggregate (which includes gravel) must be considered.

Anyone who is responsible for commercially exploiting aggregate in the UK will need to be registered for tax. Customs & Excise have issued their *General Guide to Aggregates Levy* following the publication of the relevant legislation in FA 2001 ss 16–49, Schs 4–10. The tax point is when a quantity of aggregate is first subject to commercial exploitation. This is the earliest of the following, ie when:

- it is removed from its originating site or a site under the same registration as the originating site or a site where it had been intended to apply an exempt process to it but this process was not applied;
- it becomes subject to an agreement to supply it to another person;
- it is used for construction purposes; or
- it is mixed, otherwise than in permitted circumstances, with any material or substance other than water.

The person who has to be registered for the levy is the legal person, as with VAT, who is exploiting or intends to exploit aggregate commercially in the UK. Unlike VAT, however, there is no registration threshold. A quantity of aggregate may be relieved from the levy, by way of credit or repayment, after a liability to levy has occurred, under the following circumstances:

- It is exported from the UK in the form of aggregate.
- It is used in an exempt process after the levy has been brought to account.
- It is used in a prescribed industrial or agricultural process.
- It is waste aggregate disposed of by dumping or otherwise, eg sent to a landfill or returned to the originating site.

Certain aggregates are deemed to be non-taxable where the aggregate is not commercially exploited in the course or furtherance of a business because it:

- is moved between sites under the same aggregates levy registration;
- is removed to a registered site to have an exempt process applied to it;
- is removed to any premises where china clay or ball clay will be extracted from the aggregate;
- has previously been used for construction services;
- was removed from its originating site before the commencement of the levy;
- is being returned from the land from which it was won; or
- is being used for an agricultural or forestry business for the purpose of that business on the site or land held or occupied with that land.

Anything that consists wholly or mainly of the following is exempt from the levy:

- clay, soil ,vegetable or other organic matter;

- coal, slate and shale;
- china clay waste and ball clay waste.

The registered person must be able to demonstrate from the records kept, that the amount declared on the aggregates levy return is the correct tax liability. As well as commercial documentation for aggregate that has been commercially exploited, records have to be maintained relating to levy paid aggregate purchased, and non-taxable materials brought on to a site. Mixing records and other records demanded as a condition of approval must also be retained.

The rules for accounting for the levy are very similar to landfill tax and VAT, in that returns are submitted on a quarterly basis and must be accompanied by the payment due within one month of the period end. With the aggregates levy, Customs offer a direct debit facility when the payment will be taken from the nominated bank account seven days after the due date for manual payment.

There is no legal requirement to show aggregates levy on the sales invoice, but a statement that levy has been accounted for at £1.60 per tonne is acceptable. If the registered person wishes to show the amount of levy paid, it can be shown on a separate line on the invoice.

An aggregates levy account must be maintained showing the levy due each quarter and any credits to which the registered person is entitled, and errors adjusted.

If a customer becomes formally insolvent owing money in respect of levy, bad debt relief may be claimed provided that the customer is not a connected person, aggregates levy has already been accounted for and paid, and the debt is written off in the financial accounts and transferred to a bad debt relief account.

Aggregate is defined as being commercially exploited if it is exploited in the course or furtherance of a business by the person carrying out the exploitation. A quantity of aggregate is subjected to exploitation if any one of the following applies:

- it is removed from the originating site; a connected site that is registered under the same name as the originating site; or a site where it had been intended to apply an exempt process to it, but this process was not applied;
- it becomes subject to an agreement to supply to any person, eg when a contract is made;
- it is used for construction purposes; or
- it is mixed with any material or substance other than water, except in permitted circumstances.

'Used for construction purposes' is defined as being used as material or support in the construction or improvement of any structure, or it is mixed with anything as part of a process of producing mortar, concrete, tarmacadam, coated road stone or similar construction material. This is reasonably straightforward, but problems may arise when a contract is entered into. Consider an agreement between a quarry owner and a motorway construction company to extract one million tonnes of granite road stone. This immediately leads to the tax point question.

Section 11 of the Customs & Excise' publication, *General Guide to Aggregates Levy,* deals with calculations necessary to determine the levy payable when taxable aggregate, tax paid aggregate, recycled material, and other non-taxable material are mixed. Provided that a weighbridge is available on site, the calculations are straightforward. Like landfill tax, if there is no weighbridge, agreement has to be reached with the local aggregates levy officer on an alternative method. Essentially, levy is due on the weight of taxable material included in the mix at £1.60 per tonne. As with landfill tax, VAT is payable on the levy inclusive amount charged for the supply.

The review procedure is available to anyone who is, or who will be affected by, one or more of the 12 decisions listed in the guide. These generally cover the same areas as VAT, eg amount of levy due, liability, penalties and interest, registration, security payments, and entitlement to credit of levy.

The system for resolving disputes involves a two-stage process. The first is a mandatory review by Customs carried out by a nominated reviewing officer, independent of the officer who made the decision under review. If the decision of the reviewing officer is not acceptable, or no decision is given within 45 days, an appeal can be lodged with VAT and Duties Tribunal.

The land-owning community have never been faced with more complex times and situations which require dedicated specialist help.

The Finance Act 2002 (FA 2002) did make some adjustments. Aggregates levy will be extended to cover all rock (as opposed to crushed rock) and subject to specific exception, overburden from china clay and ball clay extraction. Aggregates arising as a waste material from the processing of certain industrial minerals once extracted will be relieved from the levy. The existing exemptions for aggregates extracted from forestry and agricultural land and drill cuttings will be extended.

There are certain other technical changes to the scope of the levy arising from the Finance Act 2002. One main feature is that from 1 May 2002 a civil penalty will apply to customers who provide incorrect evidence of intended or actual use of aggregate to their supplier. This penalty will be 105% of the levy involved. There is a current civil evasion penalty, which is twice the amount of levy involved and will be extended to unregistered persons where their conduct involved dishonesty. Included in this will be cases where customers provide false evidence of intended or actual use of aggregate to their supplier.

Tenant farmers and diversification

20.15 Most tenant farmers will be faced with the prospect that the land they occupy must be farmed in compliance with the terms of their tenancy. This can mean the land must be used for agricultural purposes only. The landlord could have serious concerns over the loss of APR. It might be that with 'let land', BPR might not apply. Clauses of the agreement must be looked at carefully by both sides.

So how does a tenant farmer try and legitimise non-agricultural use of the land if the landlord does not approve? The tenant can apply for declaration from the Court that the tenant is entitled to carry out that activity. There is little case law on this so it will be very interesting to see what reaction the Court will have. As it is generally accepted that it has become increasingly difficult to make a living from traditional farming the Courts might want to help worthy schemes which retain the general fabric of farming.

An answer could be for the Government to reconsider the definition of agriculture. Whilst this might be of great help in various legal and commercial matters, consider the impact for taxation. This could provide lots of complications. Would a broadening of definition affect agricultural property relief (APR) for IHT? It could be argued that it would simplify the interaction of APR and business property relief (BPR) and problems over identification for the tax computation. Watch this space - interesting times ahead?

Land within conservation schemes and sale of turf

20.16 Farmland and related buildings which have been dedicated to wildlife habitats on or after 26 November 1996 qualify for 100% APR where the normal ownership tests have been satisfied. Land used in such a scheme must be managed in accordance with the scheme. Whether or not this type of diversification arises from genuine concerns over conservation or the attraction of the grant it is encouraging to know that it does attract full 100% inheritance tax relief through APR.

Receipts from sales of turf should be treated as part of the farming receipts assessable under Schedule D Case 1. However, these can be treated as receipts arising from a right over land (that is the right to take turf from the land) assessable under Schedule A [ICTA 1988 s 15(1)(c)]. Also see *Lowe v J W Ashmore Ltd (1970) 46 TC 597*.

Landfill tax

20.17 The recent Select Committee Report dated 2 July 2002 found that the agency overseeing the landfill tax lacks 'accountability, transparency and bite'. The tax was devised to encourage waste producers to recycle. DEFRA currently controls waste management strategy. The landfill tax scheme is regulated by Entrust, a private sector company.

The standard rate of landfill tax was increased to £13 per tonne (from £12 per tonne) from 1 April 2002. Indications are that it is anticipated that the rate of landfill tax will need to increase significantly in the medium term as part of the mix of future policy measures on waste. This tax was the UK's first specific environment tax.

This book does not have the scope to go into detail. This can be found in a whole chapter of Robert Maas' book on *Property Taxes* (LexisNexis Butterworths Tolley). It also forms a whole book *The PricewaterhouseCoopers Guide to Landfill Tax* (LexisNexis Butterworths Tolley). A brief synopsis is that the tax was introduced from 1 October 1996 and applies to all waste disposal operations at landfill sites in the UK. It is imposed on the site operator. Customs & Excise oversees the Scheme's regulation. It applies to all forms of landfill disposal which involve the deposit of waste in or on land. There is no de minimus exemption.

The landfill tax will qualify as a deductible expense in calculating profit for income or corporation tax purposes provided that the other costs of disposing of the waste are deductible as well, ie wholly and exclusively for the purpose of the trade.

The informed tax planner should be aware of the exemptions. A brief synopsis is as follows.

- Material removed from contaminated land subject to Customs' certificate being in force at the time the waste is removed.
- Temporary disposals pending the material being incinerated or recycled, removed for use elsewhere and being sorted pending permanent removal for disposal elsewhere.
- Material removed from water such as dredging.
- Site restoration after 30 September 1999 – notification in writing must be made prior to the disposal.
- Mining, quarrying and quarries – there is an exemption for the disposal of naturally occurring material extracted from the earth in the course of either commercial mining operations or commercial quarrying operations. From 30 September 1999 a quarry that has a planning consent which includes a requirement that it was wholly or partly refilled would qualify subject to certain conditions.

In the report dated 2 July 2002, the Public Accounts Committee said that there were no arrangements for evaluating either the success of the landfill tax credit scheme or the projects it funded. It considered that these 'green taxes' face an uncertain future.

The need for a land tax specialist

20.18   One of the aims of this chapter is to focus on some different and complex areas of the tax planning associated with land usage. This helps to highlight the great need for specialist experience.

Ironically, the article on 'The Reluctant Farmer' (see **10.1** and **A.2**) that was included in *TAXline* (April 2002) was reprinted in Kestrian's *Small Practitioner* (May 2002). The advice given in this publication was:

> 'Farming has become a complex and specialist area with matters such as herd basis, profits averaging and the interaction of CGT and IHT amongst other complications. If you find that you have reluctant farmers amongst your clients you should consider taking specialist advice.'

The author in the *Small Practitioner* could not have summed up the position better. It is hoped that this book highlights the basic areas of tax planning whilst showing those areas where the general practitioner might benefit from specialist advice.

Farming outside the UK

20.19   So the landowner/farmer is fed up with the UK? When considering all farming tax planning it should be noted that activities of husbandry conducted on land outside the UK are not within the definition of farming ICTA 1988 s 832(1). Whether or not activities constitute trading is subject to the normal principles.

Expenditure incurred by a UK farmer for the purposes of farming outside the UK is not deductible in arriving at UK farm profits. This should be taken into consideration when deciding the structure or looking at the structure in overseas ventures.

This book does not cover in detail overseas farming ventures and UK farming operations for those who are not resident in the UK.

1% increase in employers' NIC for 'workers in the field'

20.20   The National Farmers' Union (NFU) have been in correspondence with the Inland Revenue about workers at field level. The increase in NIC will presumably only serve to increase investigations by the Agricultural Compliance Unit into status for employers and self-employed. The big problem for farmers, especially growers, is the casual worker element.

Casual workers may be 'irregular' for National Insurance purposes if they work in large gangs and are paid daily for piecework – but the employer must find it impossible to identify them for deduction purposes.

Let us look at extracts from the Inland Revenue letter:

'... to be able to confirm the impracticality of making deductions, there first has to be a system in place that would in all normal circumstances make the recovery of deductions possible. This system has to be every bit as tight and robust as that of other employers ....'

'... where farmers put such systems in place they are almost always able to account for Class 1 NIC ....'

The response from the NFU is interesting.

'... simple identification for tax purposes is not sufficient to remove the concession ... in many cases there will remain a substantial difficulty in dealing with large numbers of people waiting to be paid off at field level in cash at the end of the day ....'

'... whether or not members of your department have encouraged growers to use methods which are not strictly legal in order to meet your requirements, the grower's willingness to do so indicates clearly that a substantial practical difficulty does exist even for those who seek to comply ....'

Growers have enough problems without further burdens and it will be important to try to protect their cause.

The Countryside Agency — suggestions for Rural Taxation

20.21 Rural Taxation is currently being considered by the Countryside Agency as a means of trying to solve various countryside issues. Whilst these are only possible suggestions they can provide food for thought for the tax planner and an opportunity to lodge protest or support at an early stage. They are:

1 *APR subject to management and access provisions*
  APR to be made conditional upon sustainable land management and public access provision. (Note: the NFU and the Country Land and Business Association (CLA) oppose this suggestion.)

2   *Farming and diversification all one*
All income from farming and farm diversification (including lettings) to be assessed under Schedule D, Case 1 so that losses can be offset.

3   *Affordable housing*
While 'affordable' housing needs to be clearly defined, the proposal under consideration is to give 100% relief from capital gains tax to gains on land sold for the provision of 'affordable' housing.

4   *Farm buildings – increased allowances*
5% annual allowances on investment in all buildings used by farmers for farm diversification and 20% initial allowances for such buildings.

5   *Tax relief for environmental and access improvement*
Includes costs of specific habitat/environmental and access improvements as allowable expenses for the calculation of income and corporation tax.

6   *Rural rates relief for small businesses*
Business rate relief – a mandatory 50% relief (discretionary 100% – to retain current reliefs) to all rural businesses with a ratable value of less than £12,000.

The Curry Commission Report — farming and food

20.22   The report by Dr Curry did not in fact make many tax recommendations, but some of these are worth considering.

1   *Retirement tax advice*
No retirement fund for agriculture but a possible package of financial advice including taxation advice.

2   *Improved capital allowances on pollution control*
Enhanced capital allowances for specified new environmental pollution control and monitoring equipment in agricultural use. (Similar thinking to the Chancellor. The NFU seeks such allowances for all environmental water pollution and animal welfare capital expenditure.)

3   *Pesticides tax*
The Report recommends that the introduction of pesticides tax be kept under constant review. The Chancellor mentioned pesticides tax in his speech. There are clear indications that these taxes and others of their type are prominent in Government thinking.

4   *Landfill tax*
The Report recommends that the rate of landfill tax be kept under constant review. Again, clear indications that the Government are focusing on these issues.

5 *Farm business tenancies (FBTs) – defer CGT for landlords*
   A new form of capital gains tax re-investment relief to allow landlords to defer capital gains re-invested in improvements to let land
   under the 1995 Act during the term of the tenancy.
6 *CGT relief for FBT assets*
   Land and buildings subject to a FBT, which is used for the purpose
   of trade by an unincorporated tenant, should qualify as a business
   asset for the purposes of capital gains tax taper relief. (Note: the
   NFU position is that whatever the possibility of these measures
   becoming law, any relief should be restructured to tenancies of 10
   years or more.)
7 *Biofuel*
   There should be a reduced rate of duty on biofuel. (Note: also that
   there is a proposed EC Directive concerning the blending of biofuel
   with other fuel to a maximum of 50% – and setting targets for its
   use by 2005.)
8 *Rates relief for stores*
   Stores that handed over part of the store to growers to sell local produce should receive business rate relief.

To quote Valerie Elliott, Countryside Editor of *The Times*, from an
article on 28 June about the Curry Commission Report:

> '... the blue print for food and farming by Sir Don Curry and his
> team. His vision depended on a 20% switch from wasteful hand-
> outs for food production towards more environmentally friendly
> farm practices by 2007, and is being hailed by all leading green
> campaign groups.'

This switch, known as 'modulation', has to question not how the environment will survive but how the dying breed of land manager (formerly known as a farmer) will survive.

Farming grants and subsidies

20.23   There is a wide range of grants and subsidies which farmers
may be eligible to receive from both governmental and non-govern-
mental bodies. This is dealt with in great depth in Stanley's *Taxation of
Farmers and Landowners* (LexisNexis Butterworths Tolley).

In the period after the Second World War, grants were given to
improve efficiency and encourage agricultural production (including,
for example, grants to grub up hedges). In recent years there have been
surpluses and the emphasis has changed to limiting production (for
example, by set-aside) and improving the environment (including, for
example, planting of hedges).

The range of available grants, and the rules relating to any particular grant, are subject to frequent change. These paragraphs do not therefore set out to provide details of the rules or the tax treatment of particular grants (except for a small number of grants, which have been found to cause doubt or difficulty – see IM2266d). Instead, pointers are provided towards the general principles by which you should be able to determine the correct treatment of any particular grant.

The principles governing the tax treatment of grants and subsidies, together with examples from case law, are set out at IM419, to which reference should be made in any case of doubt or difficulty. The main general principle is the distinction between capital and revenue and the main determining factor is the purpose for which the grant is paid. Usually, there is little doubt in the case of farming grants (but see IM2266d). In cases of doubt you will need to examine the formal documentation.

Decided cases on farming grants include:

- *Higgs v Wrightson (1944) 26 TC 73* (ploughing grant held to be a trading receipt).
- *Watson v Samson Bros (1959) 38 TC 346* (payments for rehabilitation of flood-damaged land held to be capital receipts).
- *White v G & M Davies (1979) 52 TC 597* and *IRC v Biggar (1982) 56 TC 254* (premiums payable under scheme for conversion of dairy herds to beef production held to be trading receipts).

The time at which income should be recognised for tax purposes can be a complex area. Detailed guidance is provided at IM542 onwards, to which reference should be made in any case of doubt or difficulty. Some general principles applying to the recognition of a grant that is revenue in character were set out in an article on Arable Area Payments published in *Tax Bulletin* No 10 (February 1994) on page 108 (see **8.2**).

General principles

20.24 A valid basis for determining timing issues is one which is arrived at from the correct application of generally accepted accountancy principles to the particular facts provided it does not offend the taxing statutes as interpreted by the Courts. In some cases there may be more than one acceptable basis; but a valid basis, once adopted, should be used consistently unless there is good reason for a change. Where an acceptable basis has been adopted in the accounts, attempts to use some other acceptable basis by means of adjustments in the tax computations are usually resisted by the Revenue.

Revenue interpretations on farming grants

20.25 The Revenue's views on acceptable bases for recognising certain farming grants have been published in an article in *Tax Bulletin* No 10 (February 1994) on page 182:

- Suckler Cow Premium Scheme
- Beef Special Premium Scheme
- Sheep Annual Premium Scheme
- Hill Livestock Compensatory Allowances
- Extensification Payments

See Business Economic Note 19 (see Appendix **B**) regarding the effect of certain grants on stock valuations.

Timing issues can be complex and hard to resolve. Unless, in a particular case, a substantial deferment of tax is potentially involved, the Inland Revenue will not normally challenge the basis used for recognising grants and subsidies in farming accounts so long as:

- it is consistently adopted, and
- the whole of the payments are brought into the computation of profit at some time.

Farm Woodland Premium Scheme

20.26 Under the Farm Woodland Premium Scheme and its predecessor, the Farm Woodland Scheme, farmers receive annual payments to compensate for lost farming profits. Unlike most woodland grants, and despite the fact that the woodlands themselves are likely to be commercial woodlands and thus outside the scope of income tax, these payments are taxable as part of the farming profits (see IM3277).

Apple Orchard Grubbing Up Scheme

20.27 Under this scheme apple growers may receive grants in respect of any trees they 'grub up' (that is, dig up). Such grants are not, in contrast to payments under the Set-Aside Scheme, treated as income in the growers' hands. They may, however, attract capital gains tax liability (see CG78110 onwards in the Revenue Capital Gains Manual).

Management agreements

20.28 There are various provisions (for example, the Wildlife and Countryside Act 1981) under which farmers may receive payments for managing their land in a particular way. Where the payments under such agreements are made annually there is no doubt that the sums are income.

Sometimes, however, farmers receive a lump sum for managing their land in a particular way for a period of years. In this situation it can be argued that the payment is capital because it represents compensation for some sort of sterilisation of the land.

However, under these agreements the farmer is not prevented from using the land for the trade of farming. The management undertaken by the farmer comprises acts of husbandry and, whilst his scope may be restricted by the agreement, there is no doubt that he remains the occupier of the land for the purposes of husbandry and therefore a farmer as defined by ICTA 1988 s 832 (see IM2253). The Revenue will therefore argue that this is income and not of a capital nature.

The concept of partial sterilisation was rejected by Browne-Wilkinson J in *White v G and M Davies (1979) 52 TC 597* and the argument that the Revenue will use is by reference to his judgment.

Farmers may also receive contributions towards specific capital expenditure under such agreements. Such sums are capital receipts.

Sadly, the commercial viability of many farming units can rest with the ability to claim the maximum amount of grants and subsidies. The tax treatment can, as set out, be in some cases marginal and will depend upon the wording of agreements and the facts behind the monies received. The tax planner should work with the client on looking at what grants have been claimed, checking the timing, the accounting and the tax treatment to include the marginal areas of capital versus income.

Ideally, a schedule of all grants and compensations should be kept on the permanent section of the client's file, reviewed and checked. Although it is the client's responsibility to ensure maximum advantage is made of claims, it is more the responsibility of the land agent to help with this and if there is clearly some omission year-on-year or client-on-client then this should be highlighted. This permanent record should obviously be regularly updated and would be a very useful document for the accounts department when looking at the correct timing and cut-off treatment for all such compensations.

The Set-Aside Scheme and incorporation

Set-Aside

20.29   The fact that land has been set-aside will not affect the basis of computation of any gains arising when some, or all, of the land is disposed of. In particular, rebasing, TCGA 1992 s 35, will only apply to such a disposal if the taxpayer owned, or is deemed to have owned, that land as at 31 March 1982. This rule is not affected by the introduction of the Set-Aside Scheme in 1988.

Where the set-aside land is left fallow, the Revenue take the view that farming nevertheless continues on the land and that the set-aside receipts are income of the farming trade. This is so where the whole of the arable land on a farm is set aside. The farmer remains in occupation of the land and is obliged under the rules of the scheme to maintain the land in good agricultural condition by performing certain acts of husbandry – sowing and cutting a clover crop, maintaining drainage, hedges, fences, etc. This is sufficient to constitute the continuation of 'farming' for the purposes of ICTA 1988 ss 53(1) and 832(1).

Set-aside land which is left fallow will still be a chargeable business asset (see CG63260+) for retirement relief purposes. It may therefore qualify for retirement relief under:

- TCGA 1992 s 163 (2)(a) – if the disposal of it was comprised in the disposal of the whole or part of the farming business, see CG63530+.
- TCGA 1992 s 163 (2)(b) – if the disposal of the land was within the permitted period following the cessation of the whole farming business, see CG63570+.
- TCGA 1992 s 164(6) and (7) – if the disposal meets the qualifying conditions for being an 'associated disposal', see CG63720+.

Incorporation

20.29A   Historically, the farming industry has not embraced incorporation and there are many sections throughout this book that point out the disadvantages of incorporation. In the recent CLA document 'Reform to Perform', the point is made that recent budgets have favoured incorporated entities but not the sole practitioner and the partnership. There are ways that certain elements of farming units can trade through an incorporated body and use all the current advantages thereof.

In summary, incorporation and the ownership of land should be looked at very carefully. However, incorporation and moving into a diversifying risk operation with possibly the land not being owned within the limited company should not be dismissed. It should be important for farming tax practitioners to report back on what diversified activities have qualified for EIS and what activities have not qualified and the reasons given. Help can be obtained from the CLA and the Farming Group of the Institute of Chartered Accountants. There are a number of arguments to say that the Government should be lobbied to change the rules.

Farm shops

20.30 It was set out in Chapter **1** that farm shops that sell produce from the farm count as farming and farm shops that sell bought-in items count as non-farming. This instantly shows a need for very careful bookkeeping as a lot of farm shops would have a combination of own produce and bought-in produce. The question will then be raised on the share of overheads such as wages, heat and light and, once again, this makes for complicated accounting and gives a clear example of why many accounts staff find the preparation of accounts and the associated tax computation of diversifying farms very complicated.

Essentially, the bought-in produce element of the farm shop should be shown as a separate trade and should qualify as a business within the provisions of the capital gains tax and inheritance tax reliefs. The advantage of a farm shop not qualifying for farming status is that it could qualify as an EIS activity (see **20.33–20.35**). Within the rules it should qualify as a non-prohibited activity because under the section dealing in goods, other than in the ordinary trade of retail or wholesale distribution, it should qualify as the trade of retail.

From a practical accounting point of view it is likely that the accounting requirements of a farm shop are far different from that of a farming unit and they should operate separate clear records, even a separate bank account.

Treasure seekers

20.31 The potential money that can be received from treasure seekers can be firstly in the form of a licence given to seekers to search.

Receipts from licences given to treasure seekers to search on farmland are, in strictness, chargeable under Schedule A by virtue of 1(c) of ICTA 1988 s 15(1). Where, however, such receipts are comparatively small in amount no objection is usually raised by the Revenue, in practice, to treating them as farming receipts within Case 1 of Schedule D.

Secondly, there could be the actual finding of treasure itself and the farmer, landowner, land agent and tax planner should be aware of how the current position stands.

Treasure trove belongs to the Crown unless the true owner claims it.

Treasure trove is money or coin, gold, silver, plate, or bullion found hidden in the earth or in any other private place, where the true owner of it is unknown or unfound.

The local Coroners Court has jurisdiction to hold an inquest under Coroners Act 1887 s 36 to decide if an object is treasure trove.

If the finding of the object is promptly reported the Crown will repay the full value of the treasure trove to the finder as a reward if it wishes to retain the object. Alternatively, it will return the object to the finder and he or she is then free to dispose of it as they wish. The landowner does not have any rights as regards an object that is treasure trove.

If a found object is not treasure trove the person with the best title to it is its original owner. The owner may pay a reward to the finder but this is an ex gratia payment and is not taxable.

By way of contrast the following were found to belong to the finder.

- Some bank notes found on the floor of a shop, *Bridges v Hawksworth (1851) 15 Jur 1079.*
- A bracelet found in an airport departure lounge, *Parker v British Airways Board (1982) 1 QB 1004.*

One other area that is of interest is the payment for protection of field monuments. Token payments received from the Department of the Environment by an occupier of land used for arable farming or tree planting who undertakes to protect an ancient field monument on that land are to be treated as tax free and ignored for the purposes of income tax, corporation tax and capital gains tax.

Council tax — business rates

20.32   The move to diversification will mean that activities carried out on the land, or the alternative use of land, are no longer classified as farming and will have a different category for rates. This can be an added expense, which should be allowed for by the planners when looking at diversification projects. The council tax situation is set out below:

Nature of activity	Liability
Studs and stables	Uniform business rate
Farm shops	Uniform business rate
Caravans (sole or main residence)	Occupier's personal charge
Caravans (not sole or main residence)	Owner's standard charge
Holiday caravans let	Uniform business rate
Other holiday accommodation	Uniform business rate
Grass drying plant	Exempt
Charities	80% relief
Non-profit making bodies	Discretionary relief
Beekeeping	Exempt (LGFA 1988 Sch 5 para 6)

Fish farm ('the breeding or rearing of fish, or the cultivation of shellfish for the purpose of … transferring them to other waters or producing food for human consumption')	Exempt
Sporting right ('any right of fowling, of shooting or taking or killing game or rabbits or of fishing')	Uniform business rate ('when severed from the occupation of the land on which the right is exercised')

The Enterprise Investment Scheme (EIS)

20.33   Currently farming does not count as a qualifying trade for EIS and there are those that argue that the rules need to be changed.

EIS has already been looked at in **14.61–14.65**. The IHT position of the limited company is set out briefly at **13.14–13.16**. Chapter **14** covers business asset taper relief (BATR) problems.

There is not the scope in this book to go through the full position concerning EIS, however, this section tries to set out the tax reliefs that are available, what trades qualify and how diversifying businesses can try and attain tax relief. The purpose of EIS is to help certain types of small higher risk unquoted trading companies to raise capital. It does so by providing a range of tax reliefs for investors and qualifying shares in those companies. However, one of the trades excluded from the rules is that of farming. In addition, market gardening, holding, managing or occupying woodlands or other forest activities or timber production and property development, managing hotels, leasing or letting assets on hire together with dealing in land are also excluded from EIS.

A larger list of those trades which do not qualify is set out below (see **20.35**). In principle, this means that the farmer cannot benefit from EIS as farming is an excluded trade, however, some of the forms of diversification that are mentioned in this chapter could qualify and it is important to take strong professional advice to see whether a diversified trade does fall within the qualifications. There are many reasons against farms trading through a limited company. One of the disadvantages of the limited company is that assets do not qualify for BATR when they are held in the company, although shareholdings qualify companies eligible for BATR. However, with the industry taking complete review of the business structure with the availability of EIS and the move towards diversification there are possibilities to trade through the limited company. It is not necessary to have the asset of the land owned within the limited company.

There are also those who argue that the rules for EIS should change. Farming is in crisis and it does need help from the Government; to make farming an 'included trade' in the EIS rules could be a good move. It is assumed that farming is not allowed because the trade is not considered to have a high enough risk. However, all those currently involved in farming and in diversification will appreciate that at the moment there are some very high risks and tax reliefs should be of assistance.

In summary, it could be that the new diversified trade seeks the protection of limited liability, seeks the separate legal identity of a limited company and tries to attract outside investors through EIS. If the investors are to be attracted into the investment it is important to understand briefly what the tax reliefs are. These are set out as follows.

The tax reliefs

20.34 An individual who subscribes for shares in a company that qualifies under the scheme may be able to get an income tax reduction based on the amount invested. (This is called income tax relief in this document.)

Individuals and trustees of certain trusts who subscribe for shares in qualifying companies may be able to postpone the charge to capital gains tax on gains arising on the disposal of other assets around the time that they make their investments. (This is called deferral relief in this document.)

If you obtain income tax relief you may also be eligible for one of the following reliefs when you dispose of the shares in question.

- If the disposal takes place after five years and gives rise to a gain, you may not have to pay capital gains tax on it. (This is called capital gains tax exemption in this document.)
- If the disposal gives rise to a loss (irrespective of when the disposal takes place), you may be entitled to deduct the loss (less income tax relief attributable to the shares) from your income for tax purposes. (This is called loss relief in this document.) You may, of course, set the loss (less income tax relief attributable to the shares) against chargeable gains in the usual way instead of claiming loss relief.

You may also be eligible for loss relief if you make a loss on disposing of shares to which deferral relief, but not income tax relief, is attributable.

Do all trades qualify?

20.35 In order to qualify, throughout the company's 'relevant period' the trade must be conducted on a commercial basis with a view to making profits.

A trade will not qualify, however, if, at any time in the relevant period, one or more excluded activities together amount to a substantial part of the trade. The main excluded activities are as follows:

- Dealing in land, in commodities or futures in shares, securities or other financial instruments.
- Financial activities such as banking, money lending, insurance, debt factoring and hire purchase financing.
- Dealing in goods other than in ordinary trade of retail or wholesale distribution.
- Leasing or letting assets on hire, except in the case of certain ship-chartering activities.
- Oil extraction activities, except where the qualifying business activity for which money is raised through the scheme is oil exploration leading to oil extraction.
- Receiving royalties or licence fees, other than, in certain cases, such payments arising from film production or from research and development.
- Providing legal or accountancy services.
- Property development (see **Chapter 14**).
- Farming or market gardening.
- Holding, managing, or occupying woodlands, any other forestry activities or timber production.
- Operating or managing hotels, guest houses or hostels in which the company carrying on the trade has an interest or which it occupies under licence or any other form of agreement.
- Operating or managing nursing homes or residential care homes in which the company carrying on the trade has an interest or which it occupies under licence or any other form of agreement.
- Providing services to another company in certain circumstances where the other company's trade consists, to a substantial extent, in excluded activities.

Whether excluded activities amount to a substantial part of a company's trade is a question which can be decided in any particular case only by reference to the relevant facts and circumstances. The Inland Revenue will generally consider that they do where they amount to more than 20% of the trade.

It is hoped that the Government will help the farming community, who are having to diversify, to take advantage of the generous EIS tax relief, hopefully encouraging more outside investors and generally more interest from the outside.

Foot and mouth

20.36 In the midst of the foot and mouth crisis in late May 2001, the Inland Revenue issued a special edition *Tax Bulletin* on the whole subject of foot and mouth. This set out information about the tax, National Insurance and VAT issues surrounding foot and mouth.

The tax situation surrounding the crisis has been extremely well documented and did attract a large amount of coverage in the technical press. Some of the provisions have already been mentioned in CHAPTER 15 on furnished holiday letting. One of the main areas of impact is that on herds basis where herds were destroyed.

Some of the detail of that *Tax Bulletin* is now relatively out of date, such as applying for time to pay, interest on payments for tax, appeal funds, stock taking valuations, DEFRA aid package etc. It is also likely that the compensation for the slaughter of the animals has already been dealt with in tax computations and that the tax planning angles surrounding this were looked at at the time.

The focus of the tax planning angles of this book must therefore rest with those farmers and landowners who suffered in the crisis, received compensation, possibly had to cease trading and are looking at ways of utilising the compensation monies to either get out of farming, stay in farming or diversify into other projects.

A brief synopsis of these points would be as follows.

1   *Foot and mouth victim ceases farming, stays in farmhouse and lets out farmland.*
    The problem here is that inheritance tax reliefs on the farmhouse could be at risk (see CHAPTER 4) and capital gains tax relief on any subsequent disposal of land or buildings that are let could be at risk as well (see CHAPTER 14).
2   *Foot and mouth victim takes compensation, lives off the money and ceases to farm in complete disillusionment and takes several years to decide to what to do.*
    Effectively, the farm loses business status and the inheritance tax reliefs and capital gains tax reliefs, which are set out in CHAPTER 5 and again in CHAPTER 14, are put at risk. The key point for the tax planner (and this could apply to a non-foot and mouth victim who is just very disillusioned with the farming crisis, ceases to farm and takes some time to work out just what to do) is that business trading activity has to continue to preserve the very valuable tax reliefs.

    In this instance the foot and mouth victim would be advised to have the land contract farmed whilst decisions were being made so as to preserve business status (see CHAPTER 11). Other alternatives are share farming and an FBT, although with the latter there are again the problems over the farmhouse and the capital gains tax reliefs.
3   *Foot and mouth victim decides to hand over the farm to his son, to retire completely from farming but to retain the farmhouse.*
    This could have the advantage of gifting to the family now, so that the ownership is put in the hands of the next generation so that, if

the current favourable inheritance tax reliefs for businesses were to be changed, a generation had been 'skipped'. There would have to be capital gains tax considerations as effectively it would be a disposal of the property (see CHAPTER **14**) and there could be some disadvantages. If the son should change the trade or cease to farm there could be problems with a failed PET as set out in CHAPTER **13**, ie the gift should escape inheritance tax due to APR and BPR. However, should the gift be 'tampered with' in the seven years from the date of transfer or upon the death of the transferor, whichever is the sooner, there could be problems and the suggested solutions are again set out in CHAPTER **13**. Again there could be problems with the farmhouse (see CHAPTER **14**).

4   *Foot and mouth victim gives up farming and uses the whole of the land for a diversification project.*
Whilst such a project would qualify for business property relief and the business reliefs for capital gains tax, there could be some question as to whether it is a farming unit and therefore the inheritance tax and other reliefs on the farmhouse could be at risk. Again this is covered in CHAPTER **4**.

These are only a small selection of the permutations and combinations of alternatives available to both foot and mouth victims and everyday victims of the farming crisis who are having to think about ceasing, restructuring, diversifying, gifting and just plain trying to cope in this crisis somehow.

In the same way that all agreements should be reviewed by a tax planner before they are entered into, all decisions about changes to the farm unit should be planned ahead.

Articles   **A**

In the lead up to the publication of this book there has been a large number of articles on diversification and farming issues. It is hoped that they have asked some challenging questions whilst highlighting practical tax planning points.

It is considered relevant to produce some of the articles here and cross-reference to the text.

A fair time for agriculture?

Accountancy (July 2001), Julie Butler (see **8.1***)*

A.1   IAS 41, *Agriculture,* requires biological assets to be measured at their fair value less estimated point-of-sale costs, except where fair value cannot be measured reliably. Its main provisions were described in Rieko Yanou's article in the April [2001] issue of *Accountancy* (pp 102–103). It does not deal with the processing of agricultural produce after harvest.

IAS 41 was published in December 2000 and applies for accounting periods beginning on or after 1 January 2003. In the absence of a relevant UK standard, IAS 41's provisions are not mandatory in the UK, but earlier adoption is 'encouraged' by the IASC – and, technically, even appears to to be allowed by the provisions of existing UK company law.

However, the ICAEW has recommended that, for reasons of comparability, UK companies should not be allowed to comply with IASs before they are fully incorporated into UK requirements. Before a relevant standard is introduced in the UK there will have to be the usual processes of consultation and exposure. At the time of writing, there has been no official response to IAS 41 form the UK Accounting Standards Board.

IAS 41 raises a number of interesting questions for the agricultural industry. It has been in such crisis recently that the introduction of what could be a very major change for agriculture has to date received little publicity in the farming press. The key issues include taxation. IAS 41 appears to be in direct contravention of the UK's tax guidance on farming stock valuation, BEN 19 Inspectors Manual IM2292, which states that the Inspector of Taxes is looking for a figure (commonly referred to as a valuation) that represents the stock's cost or, if lower, the net realisable value.

When looking at IAS 41's full impact on UK accounting procedures, it must be borne in mind that under current accounting principles it is normal to use the historical cost convention. So the current UK basis for valuing growing and harvested crops is the actual cost of production. It can prove difficult, however, to calculate actual costs, particularly feed costs for livestock, and in this instance 'deemed cost' is acceptable. Deemed cost should be used when it is not possible to obtain actual costs from the records. It is the use of deemed cost that prepares the industry for fair value, because it involves arriving at a reasonable estimate of cost by taking on a specific percentage of open market value. BEN 19 gives the following rules for arriving at deemed cost:

	% of open market value
Cattle	65%
Sheep and pigs	75%
Harvested crops	75%

If an agricultural enterprise is using a significant amount of deemed cost calculations, it is easy to see the impact of change to fair value and accounting for unrealised profit. So it could be arranged that large parts of the industry are already prepared for IAS 41.

The 'herd basis', as we now understand it, would apparently have to go, at least for accounting purposes. The herd basis treats animals kept for production (or reproduction) as fixed capital. But IAS 41 applies to fixed capital as much as to stocks, so herds would have to be revalued regularly. As the use of current values for 'fixed assets' is allowed by FRS 15, *Tangible Fixed Assets,* there should be no need to amend existing standards in order to accommodate this. However, perhaps some adjustment to the accounting figures through the tax computation, which will effectively preserve the herd basis for tax purposes, will be allowed?

It is unclear how the new standard will impact on tax computations. Taxable profits are increasingly reflecting accounting profits under UK GAAP. Revenue practice is to accept any method the accountancy profession recognises, as long as it doesn't violate the taxing statutes as interpreted by the courts. If the ASB were to adopt IAS 41, then it is assumed that it would supersede BEN 19, unless a rule of law supervened. This would have the disadvantage to the industry of increasing taxable profits and reducing taxable losses. Is the agricultural industry prepared for this?

There could also be concerns that fair value might give a misleading picture of the financial position in view of the UK weather and livestock problems – BSE and so on. Recent events demonstrate the problems of using fair values – soon after IAS 41 was published there were no UK markets for many biological assets, especially livestock, because of the foot-and-mouth crisis. This highlights the problems there could have been in recognising unrealised profits before the outbreak, or indeed during it.

As noted above, IAS 41 states that earlier application is encouraged, and existing UK standards already allow for 'fixed assets' to be shown as current values. But what about stocks? In theory, current values for stocks could be included in accounts, using alternative rules in the Companies Act. However, as we have already noted, the ICAEW has come out against early implementation of IASs, so businesses should await further direction. We assume that this will involve a lot of deliberation, debate and liaison, not least with the Inland Revenue.

These are certainly interesting times. Floods, plagues, pests and a change in the basis of measuring biological assets – look out, a rush for headache tablets!

Farming and business asset relief

TAXline (April 2002), Julie Butler (see **10.1** *and* **20.18***)*

A.2 A reader's question submitted to *Taxation* magazine on 22 November 2001 by a taxpayer entitled *Reluctant Farmer* raised the important question of how farmland should be held and the importance of business status.

The difference between a grazing agreement which is effectively rental income and therefore does not attract business status and the correct grazing agreement which meets the criteria for Schedule D income was established at some length in the answer submitted. This raised some important tax planning points setting out the advantages of business status with regard to the eligibility to capital gains tax business asset taper relief and the ability to roll over the gain.

The size of the land in question was only 20 acres. What the article shows is that with farm accounts generally being considered a specialist area carried out by dedicated farming and agricultural departments within accountancy firms, there are, however, many 'reluctant farmers' within the general client base of most firms of accountants. Historically land has been passed down from generation to generation and not necessarily to those interested in farming. Often when farms are disposed of, any element of farmland that was close to a village was often retained where any potential development was recognised and retained with an element of hope value.

There are, therefore, many little parcels of agricultural land held in trusts, non-farming companies and by individuals which might only really come to light with a small amount of rental income being shown on a Tax Return. With the current beneficial position concerning business asset taper relief and the continued shortage of houses for development it is a good planning opportunity for practitioners to ensure that the tax status of all reluctant farmers is dealt with correctly.

It is not just the capital gains tax reliefs that are beneficial under the current legislation but also the inheritance tax position must also not be overlooked with regard to the agricultural and business property relief.

The establishment of business status can be achieved through well-constructed contract farming agreements or correct grazing agreements. It is, however, essential that while reviewing the eligibility for relief, consideration is given to non-business use of the asset for taper relief.

In the same way that many landowners can fall into the group aptly named as reluctant farmer so could many tax practitioners fall into the category of reluctant farming practitioner! With the generous but complicated reliefs available to agricultural businesses and accounting and tax rules associated with this such as herd basis elections, averaging rules, hobby farming and extra statutory concessions on rent of farm buildings this can be quite a minefield even for a small reluctant farmer.

With many practitioners carrying out complete reviews of the eligibility or otherwise for business asset taper relief of all their clients' assets this reluctant farmer angle could be an extremely important consideration for future and current planning purposes.

Farming and the Enterprise Investment Scheme

TAXline (April 2002), Paul Aplin, AC Mole & Sons, Taunton (see 1.3)

A.3   In practical point 49 in March 2002 *TAXline*, Julie Butler highlighted the statutory definition of farming for tax purposes, as set out in

ICTA 1988 s 832(1). The full definition, which can be critical when considering whether a company carries on a qualifying trade for EIS purposes, is:

> '"Farm land" means land in the UK wholly or mainly occupied for the purposes of husbandry, but excluding any dwelling or domestic offices, and excluding market garden lad, and "farming" shall be construed accordingly.'

Some ventures, which appear at first sight to be farming, can in fact turn out to amount to qualifying trades. The Inland Revenue Inspectors Manual considers the definition at paragraph IM2253 *et seq.* Some key points emerge. Occupation under lease for less than 365 days normally confers farming status on the landowner rather than the tenant; occupation under a longer lease normally confers farming status on the tenant. In contract farming, the landowner rather than the contractor is treated as farming. Several paragraphs in the manual are devoted to share farming arrangements. Farming outside the UK is outside the definition (though to qualify for EIS the qualifying trade has to be carried on wholly or mainly in the UK). The definition of husbandry can also cause problems as the term is not defined in statute, but processing activities do not constitute husbandry (see *IRC v Cavan Central Co-Operative Society (1917) 12 TC 1*).

IM2260b says: an intensive enterprise, in which livestock are kept entirely separate from the land (for example entire indoors or, in the case of fish, in tanks) and not fed entirely on purchased feed is not farming. This can bring some further activities within the EIS qualifying trade definition. Interestingly, the averaging provisions are extended to include this type of enterprise, as is the definition for agricultural buildings allowance by virtue of section 133(1) CAA 1990. For IHT, paragraph L.234 of the CTO Advanced Instruction Manual sets out the Revenue's view of the agricultural property status of fish tanks and ponds.

In short, the material in the Revenue's manuals can be of considerable assistance in establishing whether or not an activity is a qualifying trade.

Furnished holiday letting

TAXline (March 2002), Julie Butler (see 13.47)

A.4 It is important that clients who own holiday cottages should try and ensure, as far as possible, that they qualify for inheritance tax (IHT) relief. With property prices appearing to be permanently on the increase, the need to shelter these assets from inheritance tax is greater than ever.

Case law suggests that in order to qualify for business property relief, it will be necessary to own a number of properties. However, it will also be necessary to be actively involved in running the properties. The CTO Advanced Instruction Manual (at paragraph L.99.3) states:

> 'The Inland Revenue Solicitor has advised the office that in some instances the distinction between a business of furnished holiday lettings and, say, a business running a hotel or a motel may be so minimal that the Courts would not regard such a business as one of 'wholly or mainly holding investments' for the purposes of s 105(3):
>
> You should therefore normally allow relief where:
>
> - the lettings are short term (for example, weekly or fortnightly); and
> - the owner – either himself or through an agent such as a relative or housekeeper – were substantially involved with the holidaymaker(s) in terms of their activities on and from the premises even if the lettings were for part of the year only.'

As usual, whether this test will be satisfied will depend upon the facts.

Milk quota and a 'fungible' asset

Taxation (28 February 2002), Julie Butler (see 8.6)

A.5 It is understood that the Revenue takes the not unreasonable view that milk quota is a fungible asset. It is worth considering what benefit this could have to the farmer.

The Capital Gains Manual (at paragraph CG77821) states that a producer primarily holds milk quota to produce and sell milk profitably and not run the risk of financial penalty. The manual states that such producers do not ordinarily buy and sell quota in the course of their day to day trade. Quota is an enduring capital asset of the business in the same way as buildings or farm machinery. Thus, where some of a producer's quota was allocated without cost in 1984 and some was subsequently purchased, the Revenue originally considered that the acquisition cost should be apportioned under Taxation of Chargeable Gains Act 1992 s 52(4) by reference to the total holding.

This could seem unreasonable to the producer who has had to buy and sell quota to reach production targets. The result could be a high sale price matched with a relatively low acquisition cost. The Capital

Gains Tax Manual now confirms that milk quotas are regarded as fungible assets, under s 104(3), Taxation of Chargeable Gains Act 1992, and the same identification rules will apply as for shares and securities. For milk quota disposals before 6 April 1998, it could be said that the share pooling rules may be analogous with the apportionment rule in s 52(4), but disposals on or after that date should be identified with acquisitions under the share identification rules.

It could be argued that the application of s 54(4) was unfair on those producers who, from time to time, had to purchase and dispose of quota and the disposal was matched against the much reduced cost due to the inclusion in the apportionment of the 1984 allocation with £nil base cost. In these cases the disposal proceeds largely represented the gain, which was produced by what could be said was transitional, and better matched with the purchased quota. It is hoped that applying the current 'fungible asset' rules will help to present a 'fairer' position and also a clearer representation of the correct position.

It could be argued that both methods could be used by the taxpayers. The earlier method could produce gains to offset against any unused annual exemption, whilst keeping the base cost higher for future disposals. However, the latter treatment could produce gains, which would not otherwise have been taxed.

The need for diversification

TAXline (March 2002), Julie Butler (see 1.11)

A.6   With the farming industry moving towards greater diversification there is a need to consider carefully how business tax computations are prepared and to plan for future reliefs.

Farming has always been a unique industry. There are tax reliefs that relate exclusively to the business of agriculture. Clear examples of this are farmers' averaging, the 'five-year rule' for losses (as extended 'temporarily' in December 2000), agricultural property relief (APR) for inheritance tax (IHT), reliefs available for farmhouses, and the fact that farming is treated as 'one trade'.

As the returns from agriculture may no longer be sufficient to generate sufficient income for the farmer to live on, many farmers are having to look at alternative types of farming or alternative use of land and building to generate an income. It is very important when looking at diversification to ensure that income is clearly split between farming activities and non-farming activities. The definition of farming is set out in section 832(1), ICTA 1988 as 'the occupation of land wholly or mainly for the purposes of husbandry'. So what activities are considered farming? These can include 'set aside', income from grazing, short rotation coppice together with farm shops selling farm produce. However, items which are not considered farming include land let for 365 days or more, crops that grow naturally, grazing for horses, income from industrial units, quota leasing and share farming agreement with minimum return.

When practitioners prepare the farm tax computation it is important to remove the above non-farming income items and also to match the expenses. In practice, many practitioners are just preparing a computation which arrives at a Schedule D Case 1 net profit or loss, with little regard for the allocation of expenses and income. It could be that income from items such as quota leasing and grazing by horses are inflating the profit for the purposes of the five-year rule.

As a practical planning point, it is important to review all clients who are associated with farming to ensure the correct treatment of income and expenses. It will also be essential to review what future reliefs the client may need to claim, eg considering the 'commerciality' of the farm or the business. It is also useful to ask such questions as does the client intend to claim APR for IHT purposes? If APR is lost will business property relief (BPR) still be available? Could the eligibility for retirement relief be utilised before it disappears?

While reviewing the tax computation it is essential to see that our clients are still eligible for tax reliefs that are dependent on 'business/commercial' status. Examples of reliefs which could be lost are business asset taper relief (BATR) and rollover relief for capital gains tax.

Inland Revenue Business Economic Note 19 (BEN 19)   **B**

BEN 19 explains the Revenue's views on the valuation of stock and is reproduced below in its entirety.

Introduction

This statement explains the basis of valuation of farm stock at the end of periods of account which is acceptable to Inspectors of Taxes. It has been prepared to assist farmers and their professional advisers. It has been prepared after consultation between the Inland Revenue, the Central Association of Agricultural Valuers, the Institute of Chartered Accountants in England and Wales, the Institute of Taxation, the Royal Institution of Chartered Surveyors, the Country Landowners Association and the NFU. It supersedes all previous arrangements made by the Inland Revenue and the NFU. It does not affect rights of appeal in individual cases. Other methods of valuation may also be acceptable to Inspectors of Taxes in particular cases provided they are recognised by the accountancy profession as a whole as giving a true and fair view of the results for the period concerned and do not violate the taxing statutes as interpreted by the Courts. A valuation which, although in form made on a recognised basis, pays insufficient attention to the facts will not be acceptable.

General principles

The reason for valuing stock at the end of an accounting period is to identify and carry forward those costs which were incurred before that date but will not give rise to income until a later period. By carrying forward those costs they can be matched with the income when it arises. Profit will be understated if stock is not brought in. However, if there is no reasonable expectation that the proceeds from the sale of the stock in a future period will be enough to cover the costs, then relief for the expected loss may be obtained in the period for which the accounts are being prepared by valuing the stock at what it is expected to realise when sold in the normal course of trade.

For tax purposes we are looking for a figure (commonly referred to as a valuation) which represents the cost, or, if lower, the net realisable value of the stock. In some circumstances there may be more than one acceptable method of computing the value of stock but the basis of valuation in a particular case should be consistent. If it is decided to change the basis of valuation the Inspector of Taxes should be advised when the accounts are submitted. The Revenue's practice on changes of basis in valuation is set out in Statement of Practice SP3/90.

Occasionally Inspectors discover that the stock figure in the accounts is net of a provision (reserve), for example, for dilapidations. If the creation of such a provision is considered appropriate the Inspector should be made fully aware of it. Provisions are only allowable for tax purposes if profits would not be properly stated in their absence and the amount referable to the year can be quantified with reasonable accuracy. Even if these conditions are met tax law provides that some provisions are not allowable for tax purposes (for example, for repairs to premises which are not allowable unless expended).

The value of stock is primarily a matter of fact which is ultimately to be decided by the Commissioners in the absence of agreement. Valuation problems can be complex, and farmers normally seek the assistance of accountants and agricultural valuers and surveyors. But this is not compulsory and some farmers prepare their own valuations. Although strictly livestock should be valued on an animal by animal basis, it is acceptable for farmers to value animals of a similar type and quality together on a global or average basis classified according to age. If deemed cost is used (see below) homebred animals should be distinguished from animals which have been bought in. If tax is lost or delayed as a result of incorrect valuation of stock then interest and penalties may be due in addition to the tax.

Livestock, growing and harvested crops

Production costs

Production cost is the actual cost of getting the stock into its condition and location at the balance sheet date. Farm stock valuations should include the costs directly attributable to producing or rearing the stock in question. From an accountancy point of view it is preferable but not mandatory, except in the case of certain limited companies, also to include a reasonable proportion of the costs which are only indirectly attributable to the production of the stock to the extent that those costs relate to the period of production as this will result in a more accurate matching of costs with related sales income. Either method, if applied consistently, is acceptable to Inspectors of Taxes.

Direct costs

Costs which are directly attributable to buying, producing and growing the livestock or crops should be included. Such costs will consist not only of the expenses of acquiring the 'raw materials' for example, seeds, but also of any expenses which directly relate to producing or rearing the stock in question. There can be no definitive list, but the following are examples of direct costs:

Livestock

- Purchase costs; or
- Insemination costs plus additional maternal feed costs in excess of maintenance.

PLUS costs of rearing to the valuation date or maturity if earlier including:

- feed costs including forage;
- vets' fees including drugs;
- drenches and other medicines;
- ringing, cutting and dehorning;
- supervisory employee or contract labour costs.

Growing and harvested crops

- Seeds;
- fertilisers;
- beneficial sprays (the term beneficial sprays includes preventative sprays and means any sprays which are not applied to remedy a particular infestation or crop deficiency);
- seasonal licence payments (for example, short-term hire of land to grow a particular crop) but not normal farm rents;
- drying;
- storage;

- employee (including director) or contract labour and direct machinery costs (for example, fuel, servicing, rental, spares and the reduction in value due to wear and tear caused by actual usage for the activity concerned) incurred on;
- cultivations;
- crop working;
- harvesting.

Indirect costs

Once again there can be no definitive list of indirect items, but examples of such costs are:

- depreciation and maintenance of farm buildings;
- rent and rates (excluding licence payments above);
- general employee (including director) or contract labour and machinery costs.

Cost to be based on expenditure incurred

Except where the deemed cost method is used cost must represent the actual costs incurred by the particular farmer on producing the stock as established from his own records. Larger and specialised businesses, such as intensive pig rearing units, will usually have adequate records to compute cost. The current Guide to Costings as issued by the Central Association of Agricultural Valuers and figures produced by other independent institutions provide useful models to help farmers establish their own costs.

Labour costs should not include anything for the notional cost of own labour for sole proprietors or partners.

Deemed cost acceptable in some circumstances

If it is not possible to ascertain actual costs from the farmer's records, Inspectors will accept deemed cost valuations (see paragraph below).

Net realisable value

If there is no reasonable expectation that the net realisable value of stock will cover costs incurred then the stock should be stated at net realisable value.

Net realisable value consists of:

- The sale proceeds that it is anticipated will be received from the eventual disposal of the stock in the condition in which the farmer intended at his balance sheet date subsequently to market it. It is important to note that the valuation should be made on a normal commercial basis, for instance, it is not acceptable to value stock on the basis that it would have been sold in a forced sale on the balance sheet date in its then possibly immature state.

PLUS

- Grants and subsidies intended to augment the sale prices of stocks.
- For breeding/production animals the ancillary stream of income from the sale of their progeny and produce.

LESS

- The further costs to be incurred in getting the stock into marketable condition and then marketing, selling and distributing that stock. Where the proceeds from the sale of progeny/produce are brought in then the costs relating to their production and marketing should also be deducted.

It is not acceptable to treat cull value as the only future revenue from production animals as this does not recognise the value of the future income stream from the produce and/or progeny.

The Revenue recognises, however, that farmers may not have the extensive records necessary to calculate net realisable value with reasonable accuracy, therefore:

- For production animals such as laying hens and breeding sows which are not usually sold except for slaughter at the end of their productive lives, the Revenue will accept that a reasonable approximation of the net realisable value is the value at the balance sheet date arrived at by consistently writing off the cost, down to anticipated cull value, on a straight line or other appropriate basis over the animal's expected productive life.
- For other production animals the Revenue will accept the use of the open market value of animals of the same kind, quality and condition based on the assumption that there is a willing buyer and a willing seller of the particular animal as a production animal at the balance sheet date.

Where net realisable value is used as being less than cost the Inspector may want to establish the basis of valuation.

Co-operatives

In the same way as any other stock held by a farmer, stock marketed through co-operatives acting as agent for the farmer must be included in the valuation unless it has been sold.

Stock held off the farm which is identifiable as belonging to the farmer must also be included.

Where stock held off the farm has been pooled and cannot be identified as belonging to a particular farmer the unsold proportion must be included. This may be computed by taking A x B/C where A is the amount in the pool which came from the farmer, B is the amount in the pool not sold at the valuation date and C is the amount in the pool not sold at the valuation date plus the amount sold from it up to that date.

Where a co-operative acts as agent for the farmer but the relevant stock can be identified as not being part of a pool, no apportionment is necessary. It should be included in the valuation.

Stock which has been sold to a co-operative which does not act as agent should not be included in the valuation.

Grants and subsidies — effect on stock valuations

Grants and subsidies towards specific expenses should be regarded as reducing those expenses. If those expenses are included in the cost for stock valuation then the figure used should be the net cost after deducting the related grants.

Grants and subsidies intended to augment the sale prices of stocks should be taken into account in calculating their net realisable values.

Consumables

Consumables include spares for plant and equipment, oil, diesel, sprays, fertilisers, feedstuffs and bags. For any stock of unused, but usable consumables held at the balance sheet date, normally the valuation should be made at cost.

If, however, the consumables have deteriorated or become obsolete then their net realisable value should be used if it is lower than cost.

Deemed cost valuation

When deemed cost is acceptable

Valuations should only be based on deemed cost where it is not possible to ascertain actual costs from the farmer's records. Deemed cost should not be used for purchased animals if it is less than the original purchase price plus, if the animal was immature when purchased, the costs of rearing from the date of purchase to the valuation date or, if earlier, to maturity.

In such situations Inspectors will accept that a reasonable estimate of cost, 'deemed cost', is given by a specific percentage of open market value. It may be necessary, from time to time, to review the percentages if the relationship between costs and market value changes. Current percentages are set out in paragraphs below.

For production animals open market value should be based on the assumption that there is a willing buyer and a willing seller of the animal as a production animal free from, for example, movement restrictions. It is not acceptable to treat cull value as the open market value of production animals as this does not recognise the value of the future income stream from produce and/or progeny.

Livestock

The percentages in the case of livestock are:

- cattle – 60% of open market value;
- sheep and pigs – 75% of open market value.

The following points should be noted:

Deemed cost valuations are only valid for homebred or home-reared stock or stock acquired some time before maturity and matured on the farm. (See above in the case of stock other than homebred stock.)

It is preferable for deemed cost to be fixed at maturity but Inspectors will accept valuations at deemed costs based on open market value at the balance sheet date if that method has been used consistently. Farmers should be aware that using deemed cost at each balance sheet date may result in profits coming into tax earlier.

The valuation of immature and unweaned animals using deemed cost methods based on the open market value of animals of a similar age and type is acceptable to the Inland Revenue except in the situation described in the paragraph below. If it is appropriate to value mother and progeny together because that is the market unit, this should be done.

The method set out above is not appropriate where the mother is on the herd basis and where there is no market or a very limited market in unweaned progeny (for example unweaned lambs at foot). In this situation failure to recognise the young stock at all in the valuation is not acceptable. The costs of producing the progeny should be carried forward to be set against the eventual sale price.

Deadstock (that is, harvested crops)

Deemed cost based on 75% (85% for valuations as at dates before 31 March 1993) of open market value at the balance sheet date will be accepted by Inspectors.

Useful Internet Sites   C

www.architecture.com

Royal Institute of British Architects (RIBA)

An extensive website outlining the work undertaken by members of the Association and their current policy on architecture in general.

www.butler-co.co.uk

Butler & Co.

An introduction to the firm and the services that are available.

www.cla.org.uk

The Country Land and Business Association (CLA)

Another website which gives a further viewpoint on the rural economy and looks at ways to diversify. Model form of agreements, such as share farming and grazing agreements.

www.cpre.org.uk

The Council for the Protection of Rural England (CPRE)

This website looks at the rural economy as a whole and includes sections on the latest planning thinking, as well as campaigns. CPRE exists to promote the beauty, tranquillity and diversity of rural England by encouraging the sustainable use of land and other natural resources in town and country.

www.defra.gov.uk

Department of the Environment, Food and Rural Affairs (DEFRA)

This website includes the current thinking of the Government on the farming industry and the rural economy. It contains sections on sustainable farming and food and rural development. It can be used to ensure that any diversification fits in with current thinking, which will enable it to be accepted quicker.

www.hmce.gov.uk

Customs and Excise

Similar to the Inland Revenue website, but not as clear.

www.inlandrevenue.gov.uk

Inland Revenue

The latest Revenue interpretations can be found on this website together with copies of all the Revenue's manuals, some of which are quoted in this book. Fairly easy to use.

www.nfu.org.uk

National Farmers' Union (NFU)

This website gives the farmers' point of view of the rural economy.

www.planning.odpm.gov.uk

The Office of the Deputy Prime Minister

This website includes details of all the current planning policies of the Government, including copies of all the PPG statements.

www.pvprojects.com

Pro Vision Planning and Design

An emerging website with a practice outline, introduction to the company and contact details.

www.rics.org.uk

Royal Institute of Chartered Surveyors (RICS)

An introduction into the work undertaken by members and the policy and views of the Institute.

www.smmt.co.uk

The Society of Motor Manufacturers and Traders Ltd (SMMT)

Useful for CO_2 emission details.

www.thevatconsultancy.com

The VAT Consultancy

www.thomsons.com	**Thomson's Wealth Management Limited**
	An introduction to the firm and its breadth of private and corporate client financial planning services.
www.ukonline.gov.uk	**Open Government** with links to all national and local government department websites.
www.vcacarfueldata.org.uk	**Vehicle Certification Agency (VCA)**
	Details of CO_2 emissions are available on this site.
www.withers.co.uk	**Withers**[LLP]
	A comprehensive guide to the services that are provided by the firm.

Sources **D**

Country Land and Business Association (CLA) document 'A Tax Framework for Jobs and Enterprise in the Rural Economy'

Wildblood and Eaton *Encyclopaedia of Financial Provision in Family Matters* (Sweet and Maxwell)

Customs & Excise *General Guide to Aggregates Levy*

The PricewaterhouseCoopers Guide to Landfill Tax (LexisNexis Butterworths Tolley)

Allison Plager 'Where there's muck there's brass' *Taxation* (11 October 2001)

Matthew Hutton 'Meeting Points' *Taxation* (13 December 2001)

Tony Jenkinson 'Base Metal into Gold' *Taxation* (21 February 2002)

Julie Butler 'Casual Lettings' *Taxation* (11 April 2002)

Julie Butler 'Mineral Royalties' *Taxation* (9 May 2002)

'Battle lines are drawn for EU farm reforms' *The Times* (28 June 2002)

Toby Harris *Tolley's Business and Agricultural Property Relief* (LexisNexis Butterworths Tolley)

Robert W Maas *Tolley's Property Taxes* (LexisNexis Butterworths Tolley)

K R Tingley *Tolley's Roll-over, Hold-over and Retirement Relief* (LexisNexis Butterworths Tolley)

F Michael Cochrane *Tolley's Taper Relief* (LexisNexis Butterworths Tolley)

Oliver Stanley *Stanley: Taxation of Farmers and Landowners* (LexisNexis Butterworths Tolley)

Index

bed and breakfast, position of
13.48
business property relief *see*
Business property relief
business, determining content of
capital employed 13.42
employees, time spent by
13.43
overall context 13.41
principles 13.40
profit 13.45
turnover 13.44
capital gains tax charge, saving
negated by 19.15
capital gains tax, interaction with
13.8
contract farming, planning for
11.12
debt rescheduling 5.14
divorce, impact of 16.32
exemptions and reliefs 18.8
farm business tenancy, planning
for 11.17-11.22
farm's assets, protection of 5.1
Farmer, case of
activities of business, tests of
13.35
authority of 13.39
business accounts, contents of
13.33
business, factors surrounding
definition of 13.38
decisions, reasons behind
13.37
evidence 13.29
executors, arguments of 13.35
facts of 13.27, 13.28
furnished lets, impact on 15.2
history of farm 13.31
importance of 13.26
Inland Revenue, arguments of
13.36
lettings, facts and history of
13.32
probate values 13.34
structure of farm 13.30
tenancies 13.32
unified management, theme of
13.46
way forward from 13.46
financial services, alleviation of
liability by 19.3

furnished holiday lettings, position
of 13.47
gifting assets, effect of 5.8
heritage property *see* Heritage
property
insurance against 18.20
life policies, uses of
exemptions, using 19.5
full with profits scheme 19.6
low or minimum cost 19.7
unit-linked 19.8
lifetime gifts, making 18.20
loan trusts, use of 19.9, 19.10
mitigation 18.14
money deposits, managing 5.14
nil-rate band, utilisation of 5.6
non-domiciled spouses, position
of 19.24
overall picture, consideration of
13.39
plant and machinery for purposes
of 7.8
potentially exempt transfer *see*
Potentially exempt transfer
quotas, treatment of 8.5
related property
meaning 5.13
rules, application of 5.11
valuation 5.12
reliefs, emphasis on 1.14
reservation of benefit, gift with
5.10
reservation of benefit, gifts
avoiding 19.17
residuary estate, planning for 18.12
retirement, tax consequences of
5.18
self-administered pension funds,
use of 19.4
share farming, planning for 11.7
single unit, valuation of
agricultural land as 5.9
split interest insurance plans,
position of 19.13
spouses, position of 16.32
surviving spouse exemption 5.6
trusts, occasions of charge 17.7
valuation rules 5.12
woodlands
deferral relief 6.6
sale of timber 6.7
short rotation coppice 6.7

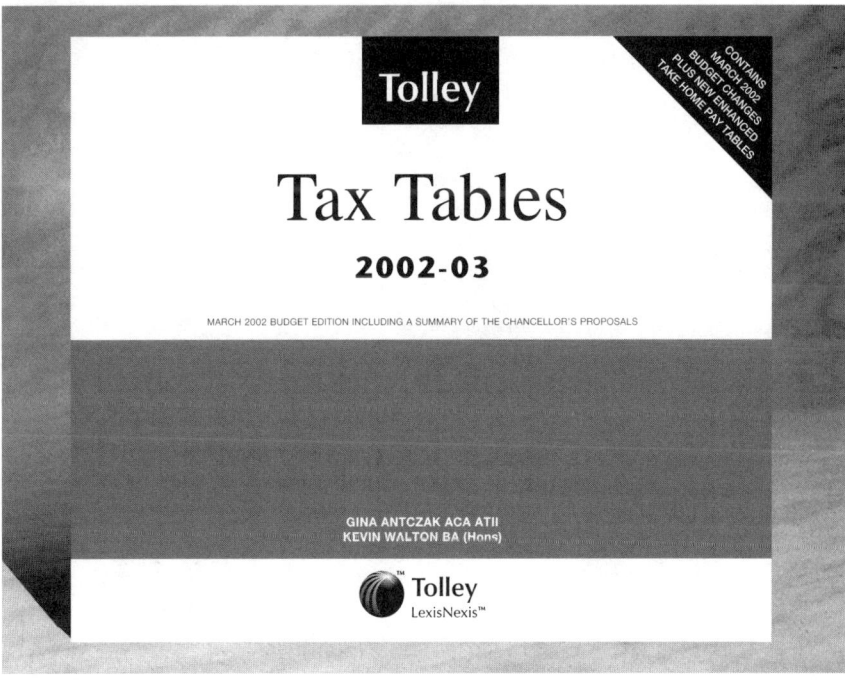

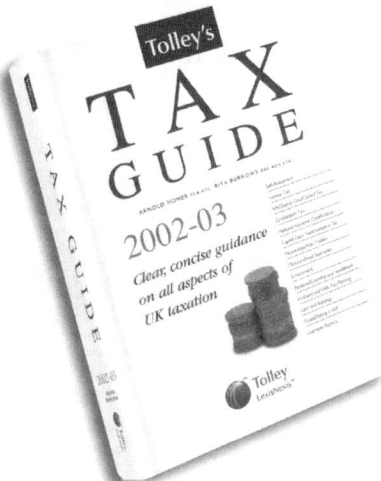